INTO THE MAELSTROM: MUSIC, IMPROVISATION AND THE DREAM OF FREEDOM

INTO THE MAELSTROM: MUSIC, IMPROVISATION AND THE DREAM OF FREEDOM

Before 1970

David Toop

Bloomsbury Academic
An imprint of Bloomsbury Publishing Inc

B L O O M S B U R Y
NEW YORK • LONDON • OXFORD • NEW DELHI • SYDNEY

Bloomsbury Academic
An imprint of Bloomsbury Publishing Inc

1385 Broadway	50 Bedford Square
New York	London
NY 10018	WC1B 3DP
USA	UK

www.bloomsbury.com

**BLOOMSBURY and the Diana logo are trademarks of
Bloomsbury Publishing Plc**

First published 2016

© David Toop, 2016

All rights reserved. No part of this publication may be reproduced or transmitted in any form or by any means, electronic or mechanical, including photocopying, recording, or any information storage or retrieval system, without prior permission in writing from the publishers.

No responsibility for loss caused to any individual or organization acting on or refraining from action as a result of the material in this publication can be accepted by Bloomsbury or the author.

Library of Congress Cataloging-in-Publication Data
Names: Toop, David, author.
Title: Into the maelstrom : music, improvisation and the dream of freedom / David Toop.
Description: New York, NY : Bloomsbury Academic, 2015. | Includes bibliographical references and index.
Identifiers: LCCN 2015039498| ISBN 9781501314513 (hardback : alk. paper) | ISBN 9781628927696 (pbk. : alk. paper)
Subjects: LCSH: Music–Philosophy and aesthetics. | Improvisation (Music)–History and criticism.
Classification: LCC ML3877 .T62 2015 | DDC 781.3/6–dc23
LC record available at http://lccn.loc.gov/2015039498

ISBN: HB: 978-1-5013-1451-3
PB: 978-1-6289-2769-6
ePDF: 978-1-4411-0277-5
ePub: 978-1-4411-8370-5

Typeset by Deanta Global Publishing Services, Chennai, India
Printed and bound in the United States of America

CONTENTS

1 (only begin) A descent 1
2 Free bodies 33
3 Collective subjectivities 1 69
4 Overture to dawn 81
5 Collective subjectivities 2 129
6 Into the hot 139
7 Solitary subjectivities 171
8 Troubled sea of noises and hoarse disputes 183
9 Collective objectivities 225
10 Imaginary birds said to live in paradise 229
11 Postscript: The ballad of John and Yoko 287
12 Rain falling down on old Gods 293

Notes 301
Discography 318
Index 321

1 (only begin) A DESCENT

thinking before acting
acting before thinking
acting in darkness

Humming in the background of all life – and familiar and alien as breathing – is improvisation. Even the most regulated life has its perpetual micro-incidents of improvisation, periodically spiked by volcanic eruptions of haphazard behaviour that release pressure. Settled situations are continually disrupted by crises both grave and petty; life, like improvised music, is a disturbing conflict between predictability and contingency. In this sense, composition may be the more utopian strategy, since one of its intentions is to counter our fear of catastrophe with orderly outcomes.

Sit, do nothing: this is improvisation. Allow stray thoughts, inner tremors, sensory impressions to pass through the body. To listen is to improvise: sifting, filtering, prioritizing, placing, resisting, comparing, evaluating, rejecting and taking pleasure in sounds and absences of sounds; making immediate and predictive assessments of multilayered signals, both specific and amorphous; balancing these against the internal static of thought. From moment to moment, improvisation determines the outcomes of events, complex trajectories, the course of life. Humans must learn to improvise, to cope with random events, failure, chaos, disaster and accident in order to survive. Yet as an antithesis to this improvisational necessity, we find an insidious culture of management strategy, militaristic thought, planning and structured goals expanding through all social institutions, a desperate grasping at simplistic political antidotes to global and economic instability. In this context, the central role of improvisation in human behaviour is consistently devalued.

A music exists that embodies the strange dream or nightmare of a life almost entirely improvised, a life that is given a setting in which to unfold, an instrument through which to articulate its unfolding, a time of beginning and a time of ending. Companions exist to share in this experiment – skilful, responsible, committed but also impossible individuals, if only because the dream of freedom is so implausible, its practice so difficult, its nature so slippery and its reception within broader society so hostile and uncomprehending.

Yet improvisation stripped of the structuring principles that make jazz or Indian ragas so instantly recognisable is not exclusively chaotic and anarchic, any more than music tied to those principles is necessarily formulaic. Some years ago I was invited to perform with a Los Angeles group called Extended Organ. I was deputizing for artist Mike Kelley, unavailable for a trip to London at that time. All but one member of the group were old friends from the days when I first came across the Los Angeles Free Music Society – Tom Recchion, Fredrik Nilsen and Joe Potts. Paul McCarthy I had never met before but I knew his work. As we were setting up and sound checking, never once discussing what we might do or making any plans for the concert, I watched McCarthy organizing his small collection of lo-fi electronic devices. He looked like a person encountering the world for the first time, struggling to make sense of the intractable behaviour of earthly phenomena. I had to remind myself: this is one of the most successful artists of our times, a man who creates works on an industrial scale, directing huge teams of technicians to craft extraordinarily ambitious installations and sculptures. The results may be messy, scatological, grotesque and shocking, yet he is capable of withstanding the constant pressure of negotiations, finance, deadlines and organisational logistics. On stage he looked like a man who couldn't open a box without help. It was as if this group allowed a glimpse into the generative aspect of his character, the inchoate imagination out of which these works grow.

Speaking personally, improvisation allows me openness, allows me the range of my character – to be quiet, to be receptive, to be brutish, to be analytical, to be stupid, to stop and be still and so on. In communality with others who are also experiencing that self-allowance I can go beyond the edges of my character (to find that character is an edgeless construction). I also forego the option of telling others what to do or entraining them to my purpose. That I believe to be a good thing. I am forced to find contingent settlements that are not compromises, forced into acceptance of what is not mine, obliged – in public and in the unfolding of an event – to find meaning in an aesthetic that may not be my own. Perhaps 'forced' is too strong a word because improvisers choose to be in their situation but improvisation without some degree of obligatory self-examination can become very content with itself and subsequently less vital.

In certain respects improvisers have something in common with surgeons, chemists, biological researchers or quantum physicists – a fascination and total absorption in phenomena that are relatively unattached to conventions of beauty, ugliness, boredom, even moral judgement or logic. I wonder what happens if I listen closely, push in the direction of my listening, follow and lead at the same time, maybe find myself in a world which is like an alien landscape even though I know it to be of this world. Of course a surgeon must be mindful of the patient, not kill the body, but then that is also true of the improviser.

What does it mean, I ask myself, if I can walk on stage to play in a group, sit next to one member – Paul McCarthy, say – who I have never met before, sit next to another member who I have known for forty years but rarely get to see, and then we play with great intensity and closeness, shadowing each other without imitation, enabling each other, exploring violence or absence, tenderness or impermeability, without censure? Many limitations are hidden within this formulation. This is something I try to draw out with students. What is going on under the surface with this activity that has been described as free? What are the hidden rules, the unspoken constraints?

If I work at instruments, at materials, then I find something within myself that is otherwise dormant and that quality has a social component. It is communicable and has the strength to move outward to others who may wish to engage with it in their own way. That may be simplistic but its constructive aspect, both on a personal and social level, is almost miraculous by comparison with current ideas of democracy in which participation is promised yet hollow. Improvised music has survived in this way since the early 1960s and it continues to attract new generations. That suggests that it embodies a way of living that is necessary, even if only for a minority, and so it persists as anomaly, as conscience, as critique and as refuge.

Music is happening all the time

This is a book about beginnings: not only the beginnings of scenes, musical histories and significant historical moments but also a state of beginning to play without knowing what will be played, how it will develop, how long it will be played, what form it will take, how it will end and how it will be resumed.

First a word about my approach. I am not so interested in overarching theories or dogmas of improvisation. My original intention was to scrutinize and contextualize a music that has been misunderstood and disparaged since its inception. As the writing progressed I found myself increasingly fascinated by its elusive origins and the way in which fundamental questions about the nature and limits of freedom, control and self-organization have been addressed by musicians and non-musicians of sharply contrasting backgrounds and philosophies. At a certain point it became evident there was too much material. Rather than trying to condense this into one volume I decided to expand into two. This first volume is largely devoted to events prior to 1968–9; the second will begin with overlapping material from the second half of the 1960s, particularly developments in Germany, the Netherlands and Japan, followed by the so-called second generation and continuing to the present, though there is no clear divide. As an inhalation of breath throughout both volumes I enfold contemporary practice and more general themes – audiences, solos, voice, the subjectivities of group playing – into a convoluted and no doubt contentious arc of historical development. Many musicians who began playing in the 1960s continue into the present. The timeline is fluid and reversible.

The writing of the book has been on my mind for many years. Its gestation began with my first 'live' exposure to the music in 1966, not that I knew it at the time, and continued through many years of fluctuating involvement as a player, organizer, critic, listener and teacher. There are easier, less contentious and far more popular subjects on which to write. I am perturbed to admit that none of them seem so compelling a challenge at this point. Additionally, there is the prospect of doing a lot of work for little reward other than being shot down somewhere over the uncharted ocean of hubris. But that is the lot of improvisers. How deluded to think that human beings can organize themselves into musical coherence without a leader, one who takes all the money and credit leaving the rest to die in penury. I have avoided the worst of that fate by diversifying from improvisation into other forms of music, by writing books and criticism and working within academia and the art world, yet I recognize this moment of necessity. For some, free improvisation is a lifetime commitment to a single way of working with sound, for others a process out of which profound insights into human potential can emerge.

Improvisers are a stoic, stubborn bunch. Despite factionalism and feuds they build enduring if precarious communities and support each other's efforts even when those efforts are not to their taste. What they discover and nurture through playing and the insistence of their own community is tough enough to sustain most of them through difficult lives. Partly this is because they dedicate these lives to finding an exchange balance between competition and cooperation. By its nature the music lacks obvious external structure; hierarchies are more or less absent. Consequently, what they do is so out of step with prevailing ideas of value or media excitement that it fails to register on any known scale of attention. Public and critical responses have always been polarized and presumably will remain so until human society becomes the opposite of what it is now. Writing a review in 1971 of two records – *Nipples* and *Balls* – by Peter Brötzmann, Han Bennink, Fred Van Hove, Derek Bailey and Buschi Niebergall, Richard Williams wrote: 'The music on these records will inspire nothing less than violent reaction, pro and con, and as far as I'm concerned it's the former. There's a wild, feverish excitement about these players that makes the limbs twitch, the mind race, the heart beat faster. Others it will repulse entirely.'

Audiences come and go, grow and diminish, flicker back into vibrant life again over generations. In May 1966 a group called AMM were featured in *Vogue*. Momentarily the fashionistas buzzed, a sound easily mistaken for the allure attached to Mary Quant, Pink Floyd, David Hockney and *Blow Up*. 'The music exists,' guitarist Keith Rowe told Polly Devlin. 'All the time we manifest it. It's part of the fact that music is happening all the time and everything has music in it.' As I write this the group still exists (albeit with only one of the original personnel) but you would struggle to find news of their activities outside the specialist press. Instead, Eddie Prévost, the last remaining member of that original line-up still working under the name of AMM, self-publishes books and recordings, performs on percussion in the same concert venues as any newcomer and runs an improvisation workshop that consistently introduces highly sharpened musicians onto the scene. Though not notably glamorous or conducive to the acquisition of property portfolios, this, it seems to me, is not a bad way to conduct your life. Despite being what Prévost himself describes as a '(perhaps) microscopic arena' it remains connected to a living practice, to what he calls the 'minute particulars' of its participants and their materials, and to civil society.

In 2013, Takuro Mizuta Lippit, better known as DJ Sniff, sent me an email:

> For my tour in Europe last month, I did the old 'free improv' circuit where it barely survives in Switzerland and rural areas of Germany. Particularly in Germany, these shows were organized by old free jazz fans that gather every year at the festivals in Ulrichsberg, Nikolsdorf, and Weil. They are still passionate about the music, but are growing old with their audiences. It felt quite weird for me to play in a room where I was the youngest one by at least fifteen years. It really feels like to me the genre of free improv is dying, and improvisation means something else to younger musicians. In Basel a young organizer told me that he could only take so much of old men scratching their guitars and making fart sounds. Ouch. Next month in Tokyo, I am playing with a whole new group of musicians coming from different genres (not experimental nor free improv) which makes me very excited and curious.

Pessimistic? I don't think so. For one thing, Taku is one of the most positive musicians, organizers and teachers you could hope to meet, an impressive turntable improviser who has used improvised music records, particularly solo albums by Evan Parker, to interrogate the paradox of a contingent music that marks its transience with durable documents. He also highlights the glaring contradiction of a music that celebrates the 'eternal now' by gradually succumbing to the fate of Roderick Usher, the ageing hyperaesthesic whose response to change was to bury it alive.

But as Taku suggests, beyond this venerable and in its own way admirable improvisation circuit an even less defined foment of activity is taking place, one with looser ties to the ethics, methodology and materials established for free improvisation in a time when revolution seemed just around the corner and home computers were a sci-fi fantasy. There is also a renewed taste for music that refuses every opportunity to capitulate to whatever temptation is on offer. Some of that taste is acquisitive and nostalgic, closely linked to the fetish value of high-priced old vinyl traded online; some of it is more productively linked to bigger questions of how artists can work with any integrity within the conditions of hypercapitalism to maintain belief in a cooperative, non-hierarchical music practice. Inward-looking and paradoxically conservative it may be but this refusal to go away offers an intriguing model of difference, a long-view variant on the notion of cultural capital.

Musical genres rise and fall but as ways of life and complexes of musical functioning they endure through other forms, just as a dye soaks into fabric. Nobody would argue that the blues today is as vital as it was between, say, 1915 to 1985, yet to imagine contemporary music without some trace of the blues is unimaginable. When I was writing my first book – *Rap Attack* – in 1984 I was repeatedly told that hip-hop was finished. I was wasting my time – in a few years nobody would even remember breakdancing, graffiti, rapping, electro and turntable scratching. Not being in possession of a crystal ball I wrote in the knowledge that these detractors could be right but with the conviction that I wasn't wrong. In a sense it didn't matter because that break point of change is the best vantage point for understanding the significance of what has occurred and what may transpire in the future. This is why I am writing about improvised music now.

The question then is how: as a practitioner how to be within and outside the text; how to give voice to multiple perspectives; how to honour a convoluted, largely undocumented history; how to write as an individual author about group music and collective organization; how to avoid falling into linearity and the straight line of bad history; how to speak with conviction about the many scenes that emerged in different countries in the post-war period when my own experience was so tied to events in Britain; how to convey in words a music largely wordless, without structures such as verse/chorus or theme/variation? Like improvisation itself, impossible. Like improvisation itself, we can only begin.

I am here; just it

Sachiko M sits on a theatre stage alone. Her instrument looks more like a compact device for telepathic communication than a musical tool. She begins in silence, a silence intermittently pin-pricked by high tones, small clicks, some abrasive electronic bursts. The theatre is full (free entry with the expectation of hearing radical experimental electronic music) but after a while an ugly reaction starts to build in the auditorium. Soon there are sections of the crowd given over to shouting, booing and whistling. Sachiko continues, seemingly unperturbed. The sounds she produces are not loud or disturbing in themselves yet they seem to propose something too unsettling for this crowd, something about form, the way sounds can articulate time in order to penetrate the body, connect the body more closely with its environment, most of all force the body to listen without ears or memory.

She survives the ordeal. Later in the evening the same audience is quite happy, ecstatic even, to see breeze blocks demolished onstage by F. M. Einheit in an explosion of noise and dust. I had been sitting next to turntable composer/improviser Philip Jeck during Sachiko M's performance. We turned to each other afterwards and one of us said, 'Hardcore.' Asking him for his impressions five years after the event was a little unfair. 'I have like you a sketchy memory of that show,' he replied.

> In fact it took me sometime to even remember it at all, it's only the audience's reaction that conjured it up. I think there was some sympathetic applause at the end but I may have confused this with another show – a product of my wishful thinking. I don't think there was constant shouting all the way through after it had started but the undercurrent was always there. It's terrible I can't really dredge up anymore even the nature of the show other than the audience.

Naturally, I asked Sachiko M if she remembered anything. Her response to my enquiry seemed cryptic at first: 'I don't remember exactly about it – anyway it is not first time, I already know it – I keep my sounds because sounds are there – just it.' Read past the clipped English, however, and there is a philosophy of action encapsulated: the player exists within the sounds, is sustained and protected by the persistence and physical actuality of those sounds, their presence as materials 'belonging' to their creator. People (philosophers) can say what they want or (audiences) react as they wish but the playing remains as incontrovertible fact in that moment. What do we learn? That if you take people to the edge of a void in which nothing is familiar and the outcome is uncertain then they will kick and scream. That even in the most dramatic concerts of improvised music, details of the music itself slip out of the memory. Only the human drama remains. That improvising musicians have something so powerful in their grasp that they can survive no matter what the reaction. At its basic level, to play is both sign and symptom of existence. I am here – just it.

A descent

Edgar Allan Poe's short story, *A Descent Into the Maelström*, was first published in 1841; not until 1919, when the cultivated morbidity of fin-de-siècle decadence and the Gothic had been overshadowed by a war of horrors beyond common imagination did the story find an illustrator worthy of Poe's macabre visions. A contemporary of Aubrey Beardsley who shared his fate of early death by tuberculosis, Irish artist Harry Clarke created a set of black-and-white drawings that visualized Poe's imagination as a world of haunted landscapes, thin crooked bodies, sunken eyes, corpses and cadavers.

Only one body survives in Clarke's illustration for *A Descent Into the Maelström*. The world has become an intestinal vortex, a pit reaching down into the earth's unknowable heart. Flotsam and jetsam spin around this wall of death; a man screams, hanging on for his life to the metal hoops of a barrel.

Poe's story is set in Norway, in a place where the sea forms itself into one voracious whirlpool, the transformation audible as a crescendo of sound 'like the moaning of a vast herd of buffaloes upon an American prairie'. This Maelström or Moskoe-ström was known to drag down boats, yachts and ships, trees, even whales, into its immeasurable depths, their 'howlings and bellowings' an anguished symptom of the vortical implacability of this phenomenon. 'A bear once, attempting to swim from Lofoden to Moskoe, was caught by the stream and borne down, while he roared terribly, so as to be heard on shore.'

An old man recounts his experience of being drawn into the whirlpool. At the edge of the abyss, 'the roaring noise of the water was completely drowned in a kind of shrill shriek – such a sound as you might imagine given out by the water-pipes of many thousand steam-vessels letting off their steam altogether'. The boat in which he sails careers round and round the belt of the surf encircling its 'horrible inner edge' until finally plunging down into the black walls of a spinning funnel. The description of this descent bring to mind the mechanics of a gigantic vertical record player: 'Round and round we swept – not with any uniform movement – but in dizzying swings and jerks, that sent us sometimes only a few hundred yards - sometimes nearly the complete circuit of the whirl. Our progress downward, at each revolution, was slow, but very perceptible.'

The narrator recalls an onset of delirium in which he seeks amusement in trying to gauge the velocities of each passing object – to his surprise, for example a Dutch merchant ship descends faster than a fir tree. Finally he lashes himself to a water cask and throws himself from the boat into the sea. This rash act saves his life; the barrel sinks only a little further before the whirlpool subsides with the setting of the full moon. Carried into fishing grounds by the violent after-effects of the hurricane he is picked out of the sea by another boat: 'Those who drew me on board were my old mates and daily companions – but they knew me no more than they would have known a traveller from the spirit-land.'

Smashed blocked

London, May 2014, Cafe Oto.

In the grey time of the gig, the drift away time, smell of room time, the time when magical implements and instruments are compressed into their road-sick cases, I watched from an eye corner as the tall man persuaded Christian Marclay to hand over a shard of plastic, placed the black dagger in his bag, then headed home. This savage triangle I recognized as debris from a moment of reflective violence, one of many during a duo with cellist Okkyung Lee in which their streams of interpenetrated sounds felt as volatile as live power cables, lightning strikes, snake bites, roaring bears, the finessed husbandry of potentially catastrophic rock falls. Something about the implacability of Okkyung Lee, the steel edge of her cello, not in its sound so much as its unmoveable force, something about the need to react to her presence as grit, as grinding, enforced a move away from the turntables out of which Marclay had been unleashing sound up until that point. Close in to a microphone, he was scratching a record with his fingernails, as if the evolutionary function of nails was as a polystylus designed to scrape music out of any surface: rocks, tree bark, elephant skin, the mist surrounding a waterfall, the bald head of an old person. Scraping two records together, maybe overcome by the realization that the only music left in them as objects was the crack of their own destruction, he suddenly snapped one into pieces. One minute the constrained body is practising calligraphy with sharp objects on black surfaces; the next second it smashes down a wall. Somebody in the audience gasped at that point, maybe from shock in response to the sudden violence, maybe in reaction to vinyl's recently regained status as a fetish object. The smashing of a sacred relic (a James Last record, perhaps?) had been witnessed.

I imagined the tall man arriving home, cataloguing his remnant – *Christian Marclay (Okkyung Lee), Cafe Oto, 25.04.14, LP fragment (artist unknown)* – photographing it, then placing it with reverence into a sealed vitrine filled with similar ephemera. Well why not? When I was a teenager I took away fragments of books strewn on the floor after seeing John Latham cut them up with a circular saw, later transforming their sundered narratives into poems and songs. I also stole a page of music hand-notated by Frank Zappa. This was after the first Mothers of Invention concert at the Royal Albert Hall in 1967 (a short extract of this concert can be heard on *Uncle Meat*). Maybe I shouldn't have stolen the music but my seat was on the stage behind the band and the three members of the Royal Philharmonic Orchestra invited to play with the group had behaved like fools so opportunism aligned with the righteousness of theft-as-protest.

During the night after the Marclay/Lee concert I dreamt I was giving a lecture for which I was inadequately prepared. Such a banal anxiety, not uncommon either in sleep or during an actual lecture, but this scenario was a little different. I was lecturing to an evening class in American literature, discussing William Faulkner's novel, *The Sound and the Fury*. As always in dreams there is no language or conscious logic, but part of my ramshackle theme was that Faulkner's big influence at this point in his life was the boxing of Louis Jordan. Jumpin' jive and boxing fans will immediately spot both the anachronism and the conflation of names here. As I spoke to the students I played them footage of a Joe Louis fight; how sense was made of these connections in the lecture, I cannot say. As Louis Jordan might have said by way of comment: 'What's the use of getting sober (when you're gonna get drunk again)?' What the dream reveals is a strange link between the idea of improvisation as pugilism, no doubt stimulated by a duo as demanding and ruthless in its way as the legendary first round between Thomas 'Hit Man' Hearns and Marvellous Marvin Hagler, and then the so-called stream-of-consciousness of Faulkner's opening chapter to *The Sound and the Fury*, a spectacular if initially mystifying passage, a loosening of the tongue that shares some characteristics with improvised music, notably its confusion and polyphony of voices contrasted with an intensely personal perspective, its shifting of registers and manipulation of time, its dwelling in voices in the head, a speaking in tongues of the vernacular, the elusive, the micro-audial, the turbulent and conflicted: '*What is the matter with you, Luster said. Can't you get done with that moaning and play in the branch like folks. ... And folks don't like to look at a loony. Tain't no luck in it.*'

After the gig I had stood still on a spot that seemed to confer invisibility, observing, waiting, listening. Somebody new to the whole business said to me, why doesn't everybody know about this music, why isn't it celebrated and presented in big concert halls to huge audiences? She was alight with excitement, the shock of the new. Somebody else said, but it's not always as good as this. I said, well isn't that true of all music, whether it's composition, improvisation, popular, esoteric, critically acclaimed, classic, old, new, whatever? Some is great; the rest is mediocre or otherwise unforgiveable. Improvised music presents many difficulties, not least its unreliability, its unwillingness or inability to locate itself in a place from where consistent judgements and steady support can be fashioned. In practice it may be a case of routines repeated in a blank daze but whether blankness or a rage of concentrated energy the hope is identical: that music without precedent will emerge new-born. Faint hope, yet it happens.

With the means available

Two things came to mind out of the boxing and the tensions of a music that aims to leave no trace. One, whimsical yet truthful, represented this arena of frenetically cooperative conflict – a record cover designed by the late Mal Dean for an album released on Incus Records: *Derek Bailey & Han Bennink: selections from live performances at Verity's Place 16&17 June 1972*. Dean's drawing depicts two figures, probably male since his inspiration came from a predominantly masculine phase of improvisation, but it could serve as a response to Lee and Marclay. Tied together by opposite ankles with the other feet tethered to stakes in the ground, they are locked in combat, battling over a narrow but deep crevasse, perhaps the abyss over which a cradle rocks in Vladimir Nabakov's memoir, *Speak, Memory*: 'Our existence is but a brief crack of light between two eternities of darkness.'

One, tin can man in pantaloons, turnip-head, wields a lusty swordfish; the other, encased in a box, face protected by a fencing mask pointed to the sky, has raised a heron over his head and is poised to strike. A sentence from Joseph Conrad's *The Duel* comes to mind: 'To the surprise and admiration of their fellows, two officers, like insane artists trying to gild refined gold or paint the lily, pursued a private contest through the years of universal carnage.' But in the waste land of absurdity they are also fighting for life, or a meaningful version of it.

A second thought recalled my conversation with Christian Marclay in 2007, commissioned by John Zorn for his *Arcana* series of books. My opening gambit was this:

> Could we talk about composition, improvisation and recording and their relation? I think it's a very interesting area at the moment. Particularly at the moment because people used to be quite fundamentalist about what area they felt they belonged to: so, if you were a composer, you were a composer; if you were an improviser, you were an improviser; if you were a video artist, you were a video artist, and so on. And now, I think, there's much less clarity. Certainly in that area of composition versus improvisation, there's a younger generation which feels much less pressure to define clearly where, if there is a fence at all, which side they're on. And, personally, I find that quite healthy. I don't know about you?
>
> Christian Marclay: Well, I'm in that weird position of not being a composer in a traditional sense, being more of a live performer and mostly improvising. I never really worried about it being composition or not. I mean, when a performance ends up being recorded, does it become a composition? Or when working on a recording in the studio, then it's not really a document, but a composition. These days there are countless recordings of people improvising, because it's much easier to record, it's so easy to put things out now, there's maybe too much of it, I think, of stuff that should have existed live only. This sort of recording has its interest and its value as document but when you go into a recording studio and you work towards a piece of music – which will then only exist in that recording format– is it composition if it cannot be played again, you know, in the sense of writing the music? What makes something a composition? I don't know. I don't know how to 'write' music because I'm not trained to do that. And if I had been trained to do that, I probably would have never played with records. For me it's a way to make music with the means available.

Loosening the tongue

So we are speaking of music that works with available means, resistant to a settled position, nomenclature, preservation, pedagogy, writing, hence respectability, in order to conduct life-and-death battles over the deep fault lines of culture. 'Music is not made to be spoken of, but for one to *do*,' wrote Vladimir Jankélévitch in *Music and the Ineffable*. 'It is not made to be said, but to be "played". No. Music was not invented to be talked about.' Naturally, he chose to ignore his own dictum by talking eloquently about and around this supposed ineffability. His eloquent, interrogative text slides around music as if a complex water flow endlessly diverted by unseen rocks below the surface. What he seems to be saying is that music should not be confused with language; music has undeniable power but whatever meaning or moral purpose it may or may not possess can only be approached by stealth, by degrees, by questions without hope of resolution.

And if this were true of music by Debussy, Ravel, Fauré and Liszt, music whose structure and detail can be read at a glance from the writing of notation on a page or known by heart from previous performances, how much more is it the case with improvisation, a music that lacks writing other than incomplete records – audio and film, oral and scribed - of its transience, the sounding that takes place in a moment between here and gone? Throughout its history – a period of sporadic, largely clandestine activity from the 1930s, a slow acceleration from the late 1950s, a sudden eruption from around 1965, then a continuation to the present that enjoys brief feasts of attention and endures longer trials of cultural and economic starvation – so-called free improvisation has resisted analysis or critical discourse, lacks a decent account of its history, misses out on the supposed glamour of media attention and curatorial cachet (not a bad thing), instead chooses the *doing* recognized by Jankélévitch, more particularly the 'playing' which he mysteriously parenthesized, further than that a 'playing' that he would have found unimaginable.

The practitioners themselves are ambivalent, pleased to be noted, even feted for their contribution to an austere life dedicated to an ideal but reluctant to be fixed within the simplifications of an overview. Most resign themselves to poor treatment and so settle for scepticism. At some point in the late 1990s guitarist Derek Bailey responded to my first murmurs of an improvisation book with a letter that was simultaneously encouraging and scornful: 'A book about the British imp. music scene would be a brave venture. Do you know any two people who agree about anything?' A few years later I raised the topic during an interview session in which I was asked to talk about drummer John Stevens, one of the early pioneers, advocates and teachers of what he called 'free music'. The convener of this interview was Steve Beresford, a musician gifted enough to have had a far more easy and lucrative career than the one he chose (or chose him) back in the early 1970s. 'Career suicide' was his reaction, even more succinct than Bailey, arguably closer to the truth from a music writer's perspective (though this largely undisturbed subterranean lake has rich potential in the oilfields of academia).

Disagreements and lack of popular acclaim are not good reasons for avoiding the task of writing a book; the difficulty of writing about improvisation is cautionary, however, if only because all music is problematic for writers, particularly music that foreswears the narrative of sung texts. How to describe a sound, the effects of a sound, the meaning of a sound or formalized techniques of structuring sound except in relation to the expectations of a genre and its disciples?

The type of improvisation that concerns me here exacerbates the problem through its basic aims: to make a music without score, notation, image or text, composer, director or conductor; a music spurning reliance on tradition, established forms or hierarchies of labour; lacking in plans, rules or protocols of any kind other than the act of playing through listening. The reality has been more complex, differentiated and variable than that, of course, but utopian aims separate this type of improvisation – once known as free improvisation, free music, open music or, simply, free; now skewered by the infantilizing abbreviation of improv – from more or less codified, often very ancient styles of idiomatic improvisation that hold varying degrees of importance in jazz, blues, Indian Hindustani raga, Arabic maqam, Korean sanjo, street musics of the world, celebratory, shamanistic and folk musics of many kinds, along with rock, R&B, African American gospel or any other music not wholly tied to the strict instructions of a composer.

Classing these rich forms together with free improvisation is seductive and to some degree comforting for the free improvisers, if discomfiting for traditionalists. The question is whether this assumption of shared family values obscures fundamental discrepancies of social position and purpose. For improvisers working both from within and outside specific cultural traditions – komungo player Jin Hi Kim, pipa player Min Xiao-Fen, koto players Michiyo Yagi and Miya Masaoka, sho player Ishikawa Ko, percussionist Thebe Lipere and Tuvan singer Sainkho Namchylak – free improvisation offers the potential to crack open musical forms that are otherwise sealed. At their most conservative they may have become closed to radical change, in some cases to the point of being national treasures regarded as sacred to racial identity. The profound rupture implicit in breaking such rules may be a means of establishing a modern, global identity for the individual yet at the same time retaining some connection to local traditions and their techniques. For Sainkho Namchylak, for example, free improvisation offered a way out of the limitations of Soviet cultural policy. As lead singer for Sayani, the Tuvan State Folk Ensemble, she grew bored with pop arrangements whose purpose was ideological – a disguise to conceal the shamanistic and ritual origins of religious songs. 'Improvised music is a lot more challenging,' she has said. Certainties disappear; rhythms buried deep in muscle memory have to undergo a blurring of memory; the note that comes next is no longer fixed.

A territory of vertiginous ambiguity opens out here. Can any music be imagined in which the composer's instructions form an unassailable law, a pure line between intent and consequence? Even in electronic music, the behaviour of sound has its own wilful life both within the studio and its reception chambers, the places in which such works are heard. Words such as interpretation and extemporization indicate an unmarked zone where there is latitude for performers to reclaim autonomy, to insist on their humanity, to make decisions, to reflect the temper of the times, the qualities of an instrument, the potentialities latent within any script or score. Even for the most scientific of composers there are listeners who also 'play' through the act of selective hearing. Variously schooled in musicology, philosophy and ideas of how best to live a life, these silent players listen according to unpredictable agendas in order to make their own music. They draw their own conclusions from within a field of sensations aligned to their own beliefs, their existence in the world.

If the practice of listening is an improvisation, which I believe to be the case, then how can these various categories of improvisation, not to mention interpretation and extemporization, be differentiated? Living itself is an improvisation, or an oscillation between involuntary behaviour, habits, formulaic variation, determined actions and responsibilities and a bewildering range of improvisational responses from within the flux of events. I flex some stiffness from my shoulders, then decide to extend the movement as I become aware of its effect; in that break in the continuity of work another possibility arises, to pause and listen to birdsong outside my studio, to sit back and gaze at the shimmering of water in the bottle on my desk, the quiet friction creak of plants moving imperceptibly in the breeze reflected as heard and seen image in its silver surface. This flow of perceptions is not exactly unprecedented. It exists within cumulative memory, a tradition, perhaps aligned with what de Certeau calls 'a tradition of the body', yet it offers small freedoms from the narrow determinism of efficiency and productivity.

Improvisation is often celebrated as a life-enhancing model of creative engagement, whether with sound, materials, time, the movement of the body, a free flow of ideas or communication with other people in an atmosphere of shared communality. In *Free Play: Improvisation In Life and Art*, Stephen Nachmanovitch locates improvisation within a history of the edges, a history whereby all art emerges out of improvisation only to become fixed products that overshadow their origins. He quotes Arnold Schoenberg, writing in 1933: 'Composing is a slowed-down improvisation; often one cannot write fast enough to keep up with the stream of ideas.' A lineage of hearsay is sketched out: Leonardo da Vinci's improvisations on the viola da braccio; Baroque improvisations against a figured bass; the renowned improvisations of Bach, Mozart and Beethoven; the emergence of jazz; automatism as a tradition, as he puts it, in the visual arts, and Wassily Kandinsky's breakthrough series of paintings called *Improvisations*. 'There is in all these forms of expression,' he writes, 'an intuitive experience that is the essence of the creative mystery. The heart of improvisation is the free play of consciousness as it draws, writes, paints, and plays the raw material emanating from the unconscious. Such play entails a certain amount of risk.'

If this legitimizes improvisation in the realm of high cultural arbitration, which is doubtful, it does so only through a fragile history of speculation and deference, of vague formulations and capitulations. Unlike Jankélévitch who by stealth and virtuosity voices the unsayable, the conclusion here is that improvisation is born out of mystery, exists in wonder, returns to mystery. As a practitioner, this is not my experience. Expression, creativity, intuition, free play, raw material, risk; these are terms applicable as easily to gardening, cooking or sport as they are to improvised music. Perhaps, for the composers and artists who have bestowed some use value on improvisation, there is little difference. Ideas emerge out of distraction; an industry of self-realization through creativity exists to support that truism. But musical improvisation as an end in itself, though dependant on all these life-affirming qualities, is also an experimental public struggle with the limits of the self, profoundly fulfilling and yet painful for what is revealed about the abjection of being human and embodied, as autonomous individual, social being, political animal.

Talking improvisation blues

Critics of improvisation repeatedly challenge those aspirations – freedom, spontaneity, transience, tabula rasa, the eradication of habit or routine – which are by now implicit, unwittingly carried along as historical baggage from an era when musicians dared to express utopian ideas for a different kind of society. They are orthodoxies from a different time, to be interrogated by each new generation. To some degree, improvisation is a dirty word signifying, at its mildest, a tactic of making do when conditions are unpropitious; at its worst it signifies something nefarious, as in IED, the military term for an improvised explosive device. This latter meaning invokes the anti-social implications of improvisation as a form of wilful destructiveness undermining classical ideals of perfection, planning, craft, established knowledge and order.

Speaking at the beginning of the 1980s, Luciano Berio delivered a far more precise critique. Withering may be the word and maybe even effective, since it could have reinforced an existent feeling that improvisation was neither intellectually nor sentimentally worthy of funding or media support. For him, improvisers (with the qualified exception of some special pleading for his friends in the New Phonic Art ensemble) were dilettantes, fraudulent and without a genuine history, their practice only worthwhile as a therapy for eradicating complexes and gaining self-knowledge, their technical innovations only useful as additions to an increasingly formalized repertoire of so-called extended techniques. 'Which is not to say,' he conceded, 'that you can't sometimes get some fairly astonishing things happening on the level of time, technique and instrumental anecdote: it's just that nothing interesting ever happens, even by chance, on the level of musical thought. And by musical thought I mean above all the discovery of a coherent discourse that unfolds and develops simultaneously on different levels.'

For Berio, improvisation was not a method that could be taught. Founded in schooling and a respect for tradition, the methodology that would take even the most radical composer from a point of origination to the rational resolution of a fully structured piece whose existence as a score allowed analysis after the fact, seemed to be absent. Listening for recognisable structuralist procedures – origination and transformation – Berio failed to hear them. There is a trace of lofty disapproval at this break with tradition but also the implication that improvisers are irrational primitives by comparison with composers, fatally compromised in their political ideals by inciting revolt courtesy of the people who pay to see them revolt, ultimately incapable of articulating anything lasting. Unhappily for the politically astute Berio, these arguments seem very much of their time (in our time they appear almost outlandishly remote or insoluble). But this was a moment when libertarianism was almost imperceptibly shifting from the left to the neo-liberal right. Sharing a concurrent disdain among right-wing ideologues and Marxist apostates for all things sixty-eight, Berio's critiques would carry more weight were it not for the lifeless corpse of so much academic composing in the twenty-first century, his legacy ground into bones by studiously joyless applications of an exhausted language.

Could this be a discourse about masters, then? If John Cage was absent from a Cage concert then Berio was bored, his lack of interest arising from the idea that music lacking in intellectual rigour is dependant on personality and should remain private, even stay out of the concert halls where proper music takes place. What he demands instead is the geological complexity of strata that can only be brought into being gradually, over time, by a single mind in control of a self-conscious, reasoned arc to be realized by willing, capable musicians who accept their role as servants to the master (my intention is not to be either gender specific or disparaging here, least of all to Berio). Since improvisation is fundamentally cooperative, closer to group mind than singularity, it will exhibit entirely different characteristics, many of which will be out of step with the hierarchical, logocentric traditions of European pedagogy and its critical canons of genius.

Philosopher Simon Critchley has written of collaboration in art and its relational aesthetics as an almost mystical conception of the group, close to what Jean-Paul Sartre called the 'group-in-fusion':

> We still expect the artist to be that titanic figure who is divinely inspired and who satisfies our yearning for meaning. Again, why I'm interested in things such as collaboration and collective praxis is because it's a way of disappointing that expectation. It's a way of saying there won't be an artist, there'll be a plurality of people working in related ways.

Many of Berio's arguments have been overtaken by events, not least the ubiquity of life online and its consequences for the arts, but what intrigues me about his condescending dismissal of improvisation is the question of how much improvisation was involved during the early stages of pieces such as *Visage*, created for and with the extraordinary voice of Cathy Berberian (his wife at the time, which is not to place her in a diminished relation to the 'great man' but to suggest a more intimate and accommodating kind of working relationship than in normal employer/employee relations, particularly in a case where the body is in extremis). As Linda Hirst and David Wright wrote in the *Cambridge Companion to Singing*: 'A striking example of new music traditions being generated within the boundaries of convention as part of a living, creative process is evident with the recorded legacy of Cathy Berberian, particularly with the music of Berio written expressly for her.' Hirst is a leading practitioner and authority in the field of contemporary vocal techniques and their notation. When I ask for her opinion the response is inconclusive: 'I think it's unlikely that much improvisation passed Luciano's testing ears – and he mostly didn't like it, but I'm just not sure about how *Visage* was put together, or *Epifanie*.' Composer Bruce Christian Bennett is more forthright: 'To obtain the sound material for *Visage* Berio had Cathy Berberian improvise a series of monologues, where each one is based on a collection of phonetic materials and a repertoire of vocal gestures as defined by a given linguistic model.' Composers can act as colonizers of innovation and improvisation, he adds, exploiting these qualities for their use value, then claiming sole and final authorship of work that should be treated as collaborative: 'The voice that is Cathy Berberian is truly amazing. I believe she deserves nearly as much credit for *Thema*, and in particular, *Visage*, as Berio himself.'

Who is improvised here?

Two of the most trenchant criticisms of improvisation have been voiced by supporters. In a prescient essay from 1964, Eric Hobsbawm addressed the problem of art in an industrial age, celebrating live arts as a resistance to mechanized mass production exactly because of their resistance to perfection and consistent productivity: 'For on the stage, as in the jazz session, the creator cannot be reduced to the cog, because no effect can be precisely repeated, nor the relation between artist and public deprived of its dangerous, exciting and unpredictable immediacy.' But Hobsbawm also identified such qualities as fatal flaws: 'And yet, improvisation can provide no solution, but only a palliative. Its relation to industrialised culture is that of leisure to industrialised life, an enclave of (sometimes factitious) freedom in the vast territory of compulsion and routine.'

For Jacques Derrida, speaking in an unpublished interview from 1982, the problem lies deeper than improvisation's divergence from the endgame of capitalism:

> It's not easy to improvise, it's the most difficult thing to do. Even when one improvises in front of a camera or microphone one ventriloquizes or leaves others to speak in one's place the schemas and languages that are already there. There are already a great number of prescriptions that are prescribed in our memory and in our culture. All the names are already pre-programmed. It's already the names that inhibit our ability to ever really improvise. One can't say whatever one wants, one is obliged more or less to reproduce the stereotypical discourse. And so I believe in improvisation and I fight for improvisation. But always with the belief that it's impossible.

The improviser's strategy to counter such fatalism is to improvise, thinking of improvising not as a holiday but as a potential dynamic for change. In his liner notes to *Karyobin* by the Spontaneous Music Ensemble, Victor Schonfield, an early promoter of both improvised and experimental music in Britain, found John Stevens speaking of improvisation as 'another little life', not a diminished life but its opposite, a tangential life in which ideals could be pursued as a vision of potentiality:

> Music is a chance for self-development. It's another little life, in which it's easier to develop the art of giving, an art which makes you more joyous the more you practice it. The thing that matters most in group music is the relationship between those taking part. The closer the relationship the greater the spiritual warmth it generates, and if the musicians manage to give wholly to each other and to the situation they're in then the sound of the music takes care of itself. Good and bad become simply a question of how much the musicians are giving – that's the music's form.

This was 1968, a year of impassioned ideals; easy to dismiss, though perhaps less so now, in a time when dominant ideas about music or politics are largely impoverished, worn out, nostalgic, in few senses new. Of the five musicians assembled under the auspices of Stevens at Olympic

Sound Studios in February 1968 to be recorded by Jimi Hendrix engineer Eddie Kramer, four progressed to become what we call 'internationally celebrated': bassist Dave Holland with Miles Davis, trumpeter Kenny Wheeler with many jazz groups, Evan Parker and Derek Bailey through technical innovations on their instruments, saxophone and guitar respectively, and through prolific work as solo and group improvisers. The joy did not increase with any consistency for Stevens, though his formidable ability as musician, organizer and educator sustained him until his premature death in 1994. Nor did he achieve that elusive international celebrity, for reasons I will examine later. As for spiritual warmth, two of these musicians – Parker and Bailey – grew to abhor each other, all of which is a long way from free play. A stark example of Nachmanovitch's element of risk? Perhaps not exactly what he had in mind.

I often ask students how we might distinguish a good improvisation from a bad one. After more than ten years of teaching improvisation I have yet to hear 'giving' as the answer. Yet in their playing and the collective analysis of what is played they identify commitment, engagement, connectivity, listening and concentration as indicators of, if not a definitive assessment of quality, a music that is tensile, compelling, detailed, diverse, decisive, unpredictable, replete with life. Stevens spoke for the musicians only; at that time the audience for improvisation was tiny. Musicians were working out this new non-hierarchical, ostensibly rule-free group music almost as monks, albeit in 'monasteries' reeking of beer or with the stage set up for a theatre production. Now we consider the role of the audience more closely; the act of giving, in the sense of a mode of attentive, fluent and educated listening shared by all parties present, is critical to the music's success or failure. Listening begets listening.

In the 1940s, Louis Jordan became hugely popular by breaking away from a milieu of jazz musicians who he believed were playing just for themselves. With humorous catch-phrases, strong musicianship and addictively danceable beats he addressed himself directly to 'the people', enjoying a string of big hits and playing a vital, if underrated part in the evolution of rock 'n' roll. Without him, popular music would not be as it is now, yet his popularity waned soon enough, his reputation eclipsed by progressive players – Charlie Parker, Miles Davis, Thelonious Monk, Charles Mingus, Dizzy Gillespie – who were, according to him, indulging in a self-absorbed music that made no concessions to the audience, its tastes, its knowledge and its needs.

Improvisation is acutely vulnerable to such criticisms: a music in which players turn inward in search of time not yet passed; a music without detailed memory of itself, without established formulae to which strict adherence could be judged as slavish or mistakes damned as failures; a music seemingly of secret codes that follows its own volition rather than responding to the desires of a general audience. Suddenly a leaderless music rose up whose practice addressed questions simultaneously current within politics, anthropology and feminism. In 1972, for example, anthropologist Peter Rivière delivered a lecture for BBC radio in a series entitled *Are hierarchies necessary?* In *Tribes Without Chiefs* he described political organisation among the Trio Indians of Surinam and Brazil, tropical forest cultivators whose lives unfolded within flexible organizations lacking any formal institutions. Leading could only be accomplished by example and by the ability to organize, to make good choices, to settle disputes. If a village leader was incompetent or excessively dominant then other members of the village would simply leave, migrating either to another village or to set up a new village independently. 'Given this type of political leadership, if it could be called that,' wrote Rivière, 'and the lack of any more inclusive political unit, it isn't surprising to find a complete absence of any hierarchical structure – of offices, roles and positions; and yet there is no sense in which it can be said that Trio society is anarchical, despite the fact that there is no one who can tell anyone what to do.'

These ideas were persuasive at the time. Although the pattern of life in small rainforest communities could hardly be extrapolated to the complexities of a heavily populated and stratified industrial society, the notion of improvisation as a laboratory of social experimentation was strengthened by evidence of non-hierarchical organization that actually worked, even though the implications were disturbing. If communities such as these could only be self-regulated by violence and flight, might the same be true for improvisation? Mal Dean's illustration – two creatures armed with ad-hoc weaponry battling to the death over a ravine – could indeed be interpreted as a serious analysis of conflict and relational dynamics within improvisation groups, a legacy of the brutal cutting contests and dues-paying central to jazz. As for flight, few of these groups could be described as permanent, their constant flux an indicator of both the pursuit of novelty and a thermostatic control of personal relationships exposed to an excess of hyperacusis.

Even less comfortable was an influential essay – *The Tyranny of Structurelessness* by feminist scholar Jo Freeman, aka Joreen – written in response to the emergence of clandestine power in the leaderless, structureless groups that typified organizational forms of consciousness raising in the early days of the women's liberation movement. Initially given as a conference paper in Mississippi in 1970, the essay spread around the world, largely through pamphlets, acting as a corrective to utopian aspirations of limitless freedom in areas beyond its original intended audience. 'Contrary to what we would like to believe, there is no such thing as a "structureless" group,' she wrote. 'Any group of whatever nature coming together for any length of time, for any purpose, will inevitably structure itself in some fashion. … Only if we refused to relate or interact on any basis whatsoever could we approximate "structurelessness" and that is not the nature of a human group.'

In defiance of the warmer-hearted zone of improvisation ethics there exists a long history of improvisers who have developed player strategies from this latter point, sometimes to the point of destruction (the duo of Han Bennink and Derek Bailey, to which I shall return in the second volume of this book, is a perfect example). Rich in moral instruction, a music of refusals, smothering, wilful ignorance and unlistening explodes out of this knowing perversity. Bullying to a threshold (to see what happens), passive-aggressive unresponsiveness and deliberate solipsism are lifted out of highly charged contexts – the workplace, sexual relations or authoritarian institutions – to acquire potential as laboratory experiments in collective human behaviour. They are heard as music but a music that aspires to the precarious unfinished business that is bound to issue from such anti-social behaviour. At the gentler extreme, any group believing itself to be within a milieu (intimate or extended) that is entirely democratic and free, an instrument of pure giving, is naively unconscious of clandestine power and its pervasive manipulative force. Freeman listed some of the negative attributes that might count against acceptance in 'all the informal elites of the [women's] movement', including not being 'hip', being too old, working full-time, lacking any kind of college background and not being 'nice'. Inevitably, improvised music has its own versions of such hapless impedimenta.

As with many political and cultural movements of the 1960s–70s founded in collectivism and the rejection of a prevailing order of power, improvisation struggled to break down inherited models of authority and then struggled to survive without them. Freeman's essay was valuable for being a constructive critique of this fragile situation from an insider, rather than a reactionary attack or ideological hijack.

'The more unstructured a group it is,' Freeman wrote, 'the more lacking it is in informal structures; the more it adheres to an ideology of "structurelessness", the more vulnerable it is to be taken over by a group of political comrades.' Improvisation has been afflicted by this syndrome and yet much of its energy is generated by the public nature of these conflicts, audibly embodied within performance as sound and gesture.

Richard Sennett has written about cooperation as a skill rehearsed, explored in its many forms and gradually learnt in the early stages of life, then divided into two main strategies in adult life. In *Together: The Rituals, Pleasures and Politics of Cooperation*, he contrasts the two models of conversation: dialogics and dialectics. One – dialogic – is based on literary theorist Mikhail Bakhtin's concept of an unresolved discourse, a type of communication that explores ideas without bringing them to a commonly shared settlement. Requiring attention and responsiveness to others, the skills of dialogics are not the declarative assertions of dialectics – a belief that synthesis can be reached through the logic of argument. 'Though no shared agreements may be reached [through dialogics],' Sennett writes, 'through the process of exchange people may become more aware of their own views and expand their understanding of one another.' In this mode, a sensitivity to assumptions, doubts, misunderstandings, implications and the unsaid is in operation. But for all this sensitivity and close listening there needs to be a recognition of core ideas. As Sennett writes:

> The heart of all listening skills, though, lies in picking up on concrete details, on specifics, to drive a conversation forward. Bad listeners bounce back in generalisations when they respond; they're not attending to those small phrases, facial gestures or silences which open up a discussion. In verbal conversations, as in musical rehearsal, exchanging is built from the ground up.

Sennett's coda concerns Montaigne's cat:

> At the end of his life, the philosopher Michel de Montaigne (1533–92) inserted a question into an essay written many years before: 'When I am playing with my cat, how do I know she is not playing with me?' The question summed up Montaigne's long-held conviction that we can never plumb the inner lives of others, be they cats or other human beings.

To go deeper, there is the mystery of how a thought arises, who initiates an action, who is follower and who is leader. Anybody who has read the chair's notes of a meeting in which they participated will know the feeling that this written account of a discussion often misses the generative points, settling instead on summations of their final effects. In improvised music, Montaigne's question – its ambiguity of action – is central to the dynamics of exchange. Nobody can agree about anything and yet they give themselves up to a propulsive energy based on the acceptance of ambiguity, almost to a loss of the self. I didn't know who was doing what, improvisers often say. I didn't always know who was making the sounds, listeners often say. The generative points in any performance may be so slight as to be inaudible – a pause, a shift in atmosphere, an unintended noise, an unvoiced thought picked up through implication or body language, a feint – often followed by a strong assertion that conceals its 'follower' nature by sheer bluff.

In *Haunted Weather* I wrote about such moments in a CD called *Dark Rags*, recorded live in concert by guitarist Keith Rowe and saxophonist Evan Parker: 'This is a mischievous dialogue too. Aware of Parker's natural tendency to build upon what he hears, Rowe feeds him "Strangers In the Night" from short wave. When Rowe pulls back from an intense assault, leaving only a shivering metallic micro-dance in motion, Parker sidles out of hushed ruminations into the barest hint of "Fascinating Rhythm".' This begins with breathing. Is the exhalation more important than the inhalation? Who can know what goes through the mind of the other? They respond in mysterious or obvious ways, and if the obvious becomes too prevalent, threatening predictability, then the answer is to withdraw, lay false trails, surrender to the subservient role of unheard originator. To compound its difficulties, improvisation is a dialogic conversation of unvoiced and half-voiced thoughts, actions often unresolved or disregarded, spurned overtures and fierce arguments of uncomfortable passion. Notes written by Paul Haines for *Dark Rags* offer another perspective:

> Evan Parker has a way of easing phrases into causes so unplanned that their effects extend into further causes, the wakes of which themselves become sources to Rowe, and vice versa. You will notice that not all effects are immediate effects, and that the calling up here of long-ago echoes of sounds in slow streaming is far from wearying – it's riveting. And as timeless and as weightless as bugs on water.

In its way this is as esoteric for non-specialists as Formula One drivers negotiating clean air, dirty air and slipstream at high speed to give themselves a microsecond of advantage. The in-breath may require closer attention than the out-breath. Time is not only right now, but before or later. Am I playing you or are you playing me?

Unsure even to yourself

If one problem of improvisation is how to speak it, another is how to speak of it. Yet another is *who* should speak of it. Improvisation articulates collectivism, a sounding out of group listening and responding. Its ethos is at odds with the principles of single authorship embodied by the majority of books. Improvisation develops not through a singular argument; its form emerges, as John Stevens once claimed, from the mutual engagement of all participants. Improvisation might have the external appearance of a utopian community or cult, may even share some characteristics of both, but distinct from those two models, it is not a coven of seekers dominated by masters, nor is it an exercise in hidden control so much as an unspoken contract. Musicians choose to take part on the basis that nobody will tell them what to do (unless they agree to accept some degree of direction beforehand). The territory they claim must be open to highly developed individual voices – players who have developed unprecedented techniques or work with self-made instruments – yet that territory must also be made open and kept open by acts which are simultaneously self-serving and collectively motivated. Though a single player of extravagant gifts or selfish intentions can dominate and manipulate this vulnerable space, there is no way to determine its individual elements or control its outcome.

Recognition must be given to the various histories in which collective improvisation is rooted. Writing of the meeting of African American musicians on 8 May 1965, that led to the formation of the Association for the Advancement of Creative Musicians (AACM) in Chicago, George Lewis has this to say: 'Indeed, it is entirely understandable that a people who were silenced by slavery would develop a music, jazz, in which everyone would have their say, and the ring shout-like, performative nature of the May 8 meeting was evident from the first moments.' Lewis also acknowledges artist Alan Kaprow's term 'participation performance', an example of the convulsive mood of post-war arts worldwide, art and life bleeding into each other, fault lines of race, class and gender traversed, divisions between performer and audience breaking down, boundaries and authoritarian structures of all kinds under assault. As Kaprow said of his eleven rules for a happening, self-narrated on *How To Make a Happening*, a record released by Mass Art Inc. in 1966:

> The point is to make something new, something that doesn't even remotely remind you of culture. You've got to be pretty ruthless about this – wiping out of your plans every echo of this or that story or jazz piece or painting that I can promise you will keep on coming up unconsciously. Two, you can steer clear of art by mixing up your happening with life situations. Make it unsure even to yourself if the happening is life or art. … If you get stuck for ideas an exception to the slice-of-life idea is the greatest source book of our time: the yellow pages of the telephone directory.

Ways of life

Above all, improvisation turned its back on the final authority of the composer, turning inward to body, feeling, thought; outward to group and place. This is not to say that improvisation has lacked compositional sensibilities or refused composition entirely; only that it hands over responsibility to the undirected group. 'Improvisation is relational, then,' wrote Tim Ingold and Elizabeth Hallam,

> because it goes along 'ways of life' that are as entangled and mutually responsive as are the paths of pedestrians in the street. And by the same token, the creativity it manifests is not distributed among all the individuals of a society as an agency that each is supposed to possess a priori – an internal capacity of mind to come up with intentions and act upon them, causing effects in the vicinity – but rather lies in the dynamic potential of an entire field of relationships to bring forth the persons situated in it.

If audio recording, with its fixed stereo listening point, is one betrayal of this 'field of relationships', then the single-individual, authorial voice of a book amounts to multiple murder: its linear form and fixity in time, the failure of words to fully convey an experience founded in presence, the singular voice that arbitrates, selects, assumes a Solomonic role within disputed events, dismisses all divergent opinions, most of all speaks for itself rather than speaking in multiple tongues. 'Do you know any two people who agree about anything?' Derek Bailey's question resonates at its loudest when opposing subjectivities undergo the flattenings and reconciliations of the Gutenberg parenthesis. Bailey's book, *Improvisation: Its Nature and Practice in Music* went some way to addressing this problem by allowing practitioners to speak for themselves. 'I couldn't imagine a meaningful consideration of improvisation from anything other than a practical and personal point of view,' he wrote in 1980. 'For there is no general or widely held theory of improvisation and I would have thought it self-evident that improvisation has no existence outside its practice. Among improvising musicians there is endless speculation about its nature but only an academic would have the temerity to mount a theory of improvisation.'

Given its polymorphous nature, is a definition of improvisation anything other than the illusory, momentary freezing of perpetual movement, that descent into the maelstrom in which recognisable objects spin round in a slow fall to oblivion? Previous attempts, whether from musicians or academics, suggest that such a definition is as unwise as the theory factory now humming itself into existence through university conferences and scholarly papers, particularly those in which neuroscientists play jazz piano clichés of the early 1960s in MRI scanners to demonstrate something vague about improvisation and brain activity. All of these activities are easily, even wilfully, unmoored from practice; practitioners (particularly improvising musicians) 'don't know' what they are doing; improvisation can only take place in the maelstrom that connects unknowing with hyperconsciousness. So who would presume to step into this maelstrom without previous experience? Alarm bells need to ring periodically, reminders from Bailey, perhaps Berio also (both of them long gone), that improvisation is both personal and social, a practice-based group activity whose lack of coherence between action and dialectic is catastrophic for credibility but vital to adaptation.

And what of history, if that is possible, given the unrecorded origins of free improvisation, the fragmented documentation of its trajectory since 1960 and its transient form: performances that disappear into thin air or recordings that become highly prized, expensive rarities? Existing attempts at a history are cursory and partial at best; at their worst they are fictions, though consistent in following the orthodox narrative: in the late

1950s jazz shed itself of popular song's harmonic structures – a leap into the hot, the free jazz period shaped by Cecil Taylor, Ornette Coleman, Milford Graves, Sunny Murray, Albert Ayler, John Coltrane and many others. At approximately the same time, composers such as John Cage rejected existing compositional systems, instead structuring their music according to chance procedures. At a middle point in the 1960s these two strategies of the avant-garde converged to make a third stream (though not Third Stream), hence free improvisation. As a convenient tale this is not without a grain of truth; it is also a lineage of which I am highly suspicious.

Roger Sutherland, for example, in his *New Perspectives In Music*, prefaced a chapter on improvisation with an open admission that his principal concern was 'those forms of improvisation which evolved within the post-war classical tradition and which were a logical extension of compositional practices in the work of such composers as Cardew, Stockhausen, Rzewski and Evangelisti'. He excused himself from the impossibility of extracting this highbrow strain from the jazz milieu with the admission that 'an entirely different account of improvised music could be written with an emphasis on jazz and ethnic influences'. Mike Heffley's *Northern Sun, Southern Moon: Europe's Reinvention of Jazz*, fills in the gaps left open by Sutherland but adds the emotive image of improvisation moving 'so far away from its parent idioms – Western art music, including the American experimentalists from Charles Ives to John Cage, and American jazz – that its initial free-jazz handle has given away to the more wide open, less jazz-specific descriptor "new and improvised music"'. Roger Dean, in *New Structures In Jazz and Improvised Music Since 1960* is far more inclusive; he is also sceptical of American bias from jazz writers unable to see beyond their own borders and he is willing to go deeper into the history than other writers, acknowledging a context that includes Percy Grainger, Pauline Oliveros, Alan Davie and Jack Kerouac: 'Could the developments in improvisation which we have discussed been influences on the development of other arts, such as painting or verbal art? Was there influence in the opposite sense?'

Although this has more potential as an approach, it also seeks some form of lineage, a pedigree of 'influences' as fixed in its way as the Book of Genesis. But what is apparent from my own experience as a listener since 1966, a practitioner since 1969 and an insider/outsider who has heard many musicians over that time talking freely about the evolution of their music, is that improvisation can have as many forms as there are participants, each of them working from within their own field of references and progenitors, their way of living, their relationship to instrument, body, space and listener. Improvisers are rootless, to some degree, though they share some characteristics with traditional workers in crafts. Not a job description or technocratic extension, the instrument is part of the same body that travels, shares anecdotes and stages, connects tenuously to a community without fixed abode. Ancestry is both important as something to build upon or react against, but dispensable, in that the music aims to begin each time from nothing other than the conditions of place, self and group (quite a substantial nothing).

'The artisan's understanding of society was rooted in direct, concrete experience of other people,' Richard Sennett writes, 'rather than in rhetoric, or floating abstractions, or temporary passions.' Describing the philosophy of Robert Owen, who founded craft communities in nineteenth-century Scotland and America, he wrote: 'Cooperative skills were meant to be built up in the worker's self, transferable from place. This is an itinerant-musician sort of cooperation in which performers become able to work with a shifting cast of characters in different venues.' The comparison is at its most apt with improvising musicians, who may be strangers, lovers or may actively dislike each other, who may have radically divergent views on the ideals of their practice and vast discrepancies in technical ability or experience, yet they come together with listeners in a public setting to make dialogical music that could be a car crash, violently enthralling, nothing much in particular, or, to quote Paul Haines, 'as timeless and as weightless as bugs on water'.

More interesting then to consider the broadest possible context of transferable ideas and actions – liberation movements; abject, absurdist and satirical comedy; surrealist automatism; stream-of-consciousness writing and speaking; the body as instrument; music as sound rather than system; strange anomalies of experimental improvisation within popular and folk musics; violent protest; mysticism or after-hours jamming – as originary sparks that ignited the possibility of group improvisation and, misguided or not, the elusive dream of complete freedom. What, then, were the conditions out of which this impossible dream of freedom became embodied as conscious action?

2 FREE BODIES

she speaks to me a language so soft that at first I do not understand …

                              AIMÉ CÉSAIRE, *Son of Thunder,* 1948

Magnetic fields

23 March 1941: Anthropologist Claude Lévi-Strauss and André Breton, founder of the French surrealist movement, boarded the SS *Capitaine Paul-Lemerle*, a steamer sailing from Marseille to Martinique. Both of them hoped to reach New York. Lévi-Strauss, Jewish, and Breton, banned writer, Marxist and surrealist, chose exile rather than risk persecution and internment under Nazi occupation and the collaborationist Vichy government. Appropriately, they met by chance on board, subsequently passing the time by discussing theoretical texts both were producing during the voyage. According to biographer Patrick Wilcken, Lévi-Strauss

> wrote a detailed commentary on Breton's doctrine of spontaneous creativity, trying to resolve the contradictions between surrealist 'automatic' art (in which the artist simply writes, draws or paints with no pre-planned ideas, guided by chance and random events) on the one hand, and the idea of artistic technique or expertise on the other. How could artistic creativity express itself through what was merely a reflex of the subconscious? He concluded with the notion of 'irrational awareness' (*'prise de conscience irrationelle'*) – a kind of creative inspiration that the true artist smuggles into a spontaneous work of art. In reply, Breton wrote of the 'para-erotic' aesthetic pleasure derived from art, which distinguished it from impulsive doodles, and concluded that Lévi-Strauss's idea of 'irrational awareness' might itself be produced at a subconscious or 'pre-conscious' level.

At Martinique, Breton came across another recently arrived refugee from France, André Masson, painter-explorer of automatism, chance and altered states. Despite efforts by secret police to keep Breton away from the 'coloured elements' of the island, a discovery of *Tropiques*, a literary journal found while browsing in one of Fort-de-France's shops, led him to a meeting with the poet of Negritude, Aimé Césaire. Seven years later, *Solar Throat Slashed* (*Soleil cou coupé*), Césaire's incandescent collection of surrealist–automatist poems published in 1948 wrenched automatism, along with the streams-of-consciousness of James Joyce, Virginia Woolf and William Faulkner, away from their attachment to the European and American psychology of Sigmund Freud, Pierre Janet and William James into the colonial realities of the tropics.

'… the air pauses I hear the grating of poles on their axles the air drones …' Aimé Césaire, 'Permit', 1948.

> howl strike the rock and the earth I people it with fish
> let flags loom over the factories
> and sound your cohort sound your renewal in flames
> sound your silver dais
> sound your array and disarray
> sound your lightning-rod spoons
> sound your onyx clogs
> sound your arachnoid horizon
> sound your cassolettes
> sound your little glasses twisted by disaster
> sound your groanings
> sound your grenade shrapnel
>
> Aimé Césaire, extract from 'Permit'
> *Solar Throat Slashed*, 1948.

Anticipating by more than ten years a glossolalic surge, a volcanic shout for freedom that finally found its true voice in breakthrough jazz recordings by Cecil Taylor, Ornette Coleman, Sun Ra, John Coltrane and Albert Ayler, Césaire's poem was a form of automatic writing. 'Free associative metaphor', his translators call it in the restored unexpurgated edition, a technique drawing on surrealist techniques but projected onto a more specifically political and magico–religious screen: his conception of negritude. A notion of freedom that predated the surrealist movement, *écriture automatique* had been enshrined by André Breton in the *Manifesto of Surrealism* of 1924 as a method for accessing 'the superior reality of certain forms of previously neglected associations, in the omnipotence of dreams, in the disinterested play of thought'. Breton went so far as to suggest that this was the 'true function of thought' and that all other psychic mechanisms would be permanently destroyed. Replacing reason, aesthetics and morals with pure psychic automatism, would lead, he claimed, to 'the solution of the principal problems of life'.

This intoxicating, flawed prescription implied a broader history of automatism, encompassing outsider art, spiritualism, occultism, divination, somnambulism, post-Freud and Breuer 'hysteria', isolated literary experiments, the utterances of trance mediums, spontaneous performative actions and other forms of apparently subconscious expression. 'Automatism should be differentiated from various so-called spontaneous literary techniques, such as the well-known "stream of consciousness" writing and the similar method popularised by Céline and later used by several "Beat" writers,' wrote Franklin Rosemont in his breathless hagiography of Breton, *André Breton and the First Principles of Surrealism*. 'Surrealist automatism has affinities with shamanistic and other trance states. Its aim is to escape the dust storms of all immediate frames of reference; to release the mind's wildest beasts and set them roaming far and wide; to permit the innermost dawn to embrace and conquer the outermost obscurity.'

Rosemont articulates this quest for freedom in crude terms of nature versus culture. As Breton suggested, this was a search for the real, yet versions of the real differ. Was there such a difference between automatic writing and stream of consciousness? Both sought to circumvent rationality, to liberate the mind from every censoring intercession of orthodoxy, from strictures of thought, habits of perception and the grammatical structure of speech. One is more literary than the other, perhaps, but as Jacques Derrida suggested in his conversation with Ornette Coleman:

> JD: Perhaps you will agree with me on the fact that the very concept of improvisation verges upon reading, since what we often understand by improvisation is the creation of something new, yet something which doesn't exclude the pre-written framework that makes it possible.
> OC: That's true.

Many forms of automatism existed before surrealism, ancient forms of divine communication accessing otherness through chance procedures – Tibetan drum divination and late Sung Dynasty *fu chi* automatic writing, or symptomatic manifestations of shamanistic crisis. Deguchi Nao, founder of the Omoto sect, one of the new religious sects of nineteenth-century Japan, underwent the classic pattern of extreme hardship followed by visions, strange behaviour and sickness, eventually assuming a healing role with shamanistic characteristics. According to Carmen Blacker in *The Catalpa Bow: A Study of Shamanistic Practices* in Japan, Nao was placed under house arrest at the height of her crisis: 'During this period she became quieter, and began to scratch with a nail on the pillars of her room rough hiragana characters. These words were the beginning of the immense *Ofudesaki*, the transmission of her revelations in automatic writing which continued for the next twenty-seven years of her life and which eventually ran to more than 10,000 fascicules.'

Other manifestations of spontaneous automatism emerged from interstices between art, occultism, psychoanalysis and literature. Brixton-based occult artist Austin Osman Spare, for example, privately published *The Book Of Pleasure (Self-Love): the psychology of ecstasy*, in 1913. 'Automatic drawing', he wrote, 'is a vital means of expressing what is at the back of your mind (the dream-man) and is a quick and easy means to begin being courageously original – eventually it evolves itself into the coveted spontaneous expression and the safe omniscience is assured.' In recent years such exercises in self-experimentation have been re-evaluated for their similarities to modernist art practice. In *The Place of Enchantment*, Alex Owen describes occultism of the early twentieth century as 'a crucial enactment of the ambiguities of the modern. Committed to a rationalized understanding of the irrational, involved with the elaboration of a worldview that claimed allegiance to much older religious and magical traditions, and caught up in some of the most avant-garde preoccupations of the day, fin-de-siècle occultism exemplified the spiritualized investments of modern disenchanted subjectivity.' In their catalogue introduction to *The Dark Monarch*, an exhibition devoted to magic and modernity in British art, Martin Clark and Mark Osterfield argue that occultism was just one aspect of modernity's fascination with the esoteric and arcane in ethnography and the underworld: fetishism, totem and taboo: 'Often thought of as antithetical to modernism, these products of illusion and delusion that were thought to disappear through secularisation are here seen to belong to modernity.'

Interior monologue

At the same time, I will not positively answer for my never having dropt a hint, because I know I do sometimes pop out a thing before I am aware. I am a talker, you know; I am rather a talker; and now and then I have let a thing escape me which I should not.

JANE AUSTEN, *Emma*

Implicit within music predicated on spontaneity of utterance and response is the unlearning of language at each moment of hearing. Routines and habits adapt to perpetual changes in relationship between individual players, the dynamics of a group and conditions of performance. As Gary Peters writes in *The Philosophy of Improvisation*: 'To be logically consistent, the artwork (and particularly the freely improvised work) should rehearse the intense interpenetration of singularity and universality that constantly opens the work up to another beginning, and another, thus protecting the homelessness of the productive imagination from the conceptual structures that would limit its play.'

Destabilizing the self risks dangerous consequences – psychic disintegration and functional incapacity. The vocalists of improvisation are the most revealing of what it means to improvise: their burden of words; their immediate and intimate relationship to the gendered body and its suppressed sounds, inside the mouth, thought-flooded, observably in a state of over-hearing within the environment if only because they have no technically distracting instrument, 'only' their own talking noise-box mouth instrument and the respiratory body. To an outsider they are derangement itself, arms waving, face contorted, exhibiting similar symptoms to the tragic homeless person who shouts back at and shouts out of those voices described in clinical terms as 'verbal auditory hallucinations'.

As a public experiment, vocal improvisers sound out lines into a deep pool, fishing for creatures that will speak, yet unlike voice-hearers they have the skills and self-knowledge to control each creature that comes thrashing to the surface. The singer may seem out of control, close to madness but will be exerting, close to unintendedness and through technical expertise (Derrida's pre-written framework), force of will. For Daniel B. Smith, the loss of control, a split in the conscious world, is what troubles the voice-hearer. 'But it is worthwhile to consider that when the illusion of control is lost,' he writes, when the brain whirrs in such a way that it seems as though someone who is not there has spoken aloud, when it seems that there is no will in our thoughts or our experiences or our perceptions – perhaps it is not the encroachment of unreality that we are witnessing but the arrival of reality, of the horrible truth: the absence of true will.

He concludes by cautioning against confusing these two very different states of inspiration and suffering, the inspired William Blake declaiming visionary poetry as he passes a suffering lost soul shouting violent obscenities:

This is not to say we should glorify the voice-hearer. To do so would be to glorify what is often a disturbing aberration in consciousness. Those voice-hearers who jealously uphold their originality and their insight are to be envied by those voice-hearers who don't, but they are not in the majority.

Is improvisation the audible play of voices in the head, or, to borrow de Certeau's description, is it those bodily sounds, the sound that things make, pleasurable sounds, rhymes, counting jingles, or noises that become words that he calls 'sounds waiting for a language'?
'On the modern stage the oral trajectories are as individual as the bodies,' he writes,

and as opaque to meaning, which is always general. Thus one cannot 'evoke' them (like the 'spirits' and voices of earlier ages) except in the way Maguerite Duras has presented 'the film of voices': 'Voices of women … they come from a nocturnal elevated space, from a balcony overhanging the void, the totality. They are linked by desire. Desire each other. … Do not know we exist. Do not know that people hear them.' *Destroy, she said*: 'Writing has ended.'

A dictionary of charm and shame

Vocalist Ami Yoshida has written:

When I first started performing, what I used was really just the sounds from my lips and mouth, which I heard with my ears. But when I started using mikes and mixers more skilfully, after a while I started to be able to pick up sounds that hadn't been audible before, and also to pick up the subtle expressiveness and special quality of sounds. That increased the variety of my techniques, or of my materials. I think the solo album I'm going to make will be like a pictorial dictionary, arranged by category, of the sounds I'm currently able to produce.

And so her record – *Tiger Thrush* (2003) – is a mouth wide open, hearing as an explorer inside the mouth (journey to the centre of the earth). Sounds that a baby makes, a small child, sounding spit, compression, forcible propulsion of air, high constricted tones shaped by the nasal passages and oral cavity, quiet screams held back, squeals, choking, gagging, the sound that might be heard on a tape recording of torture, yet no drama. A dictionary within a library, and yet a deeply disturbing dictionary, a dictionary of charm and shame in which each entry connects us to the acoustic leakages, accidents and edges of intimate mouth sound: quite unbearable yet no more unbearable than a late Rembrandt self-portrait in which the body is ruthlessly exposed; in its humble way, a kind of beauty distantly linked to Rembrandt's forensic gaze. She seems to ask: can we live with ourselves?

A room of one's own

Sounds float in available space, latent within the flow of living, waiting to be heard. Listen to Fats Waller sing 'Spring Cleaning (Getting Ready for Love)' in 1936, ancient vacuum cleaner thrown aside by more urgent desires: 'Brrrrrrrbbbrrrthat ain't the cleaner … brrrrrbrrrbyeah, that's the real cleaner, back up.'

The improviser begins with the possibility of spontaneity, a pursuit of automatic writing and what William James described in 1892 as 'the stream of thought, of consciousness, of subjective life', the flowing of thought, speech and sensation found in Marcel Proust's *Remembrance of Things Past*, Jane Austen's *Emma*, James Joyce's *Ulysses* or Virginia Woolf's *The Waves*. This intimate relationship to the everyday, to rumination and daydream, to Alan Kaprow's turn to the Yellow Pages and the talking cure of psychoanalysis illuminates those improvising vocalists such as Maggie Nicols, Shelley Hirsch and Phil Minton who sing-speak, drawing on the body, its spaces and the commonplace objects and events of life.

In *Haunted Weather* I wrote about a performance in Austria in 2000 by Shelley Hirsch and DJ Olive. Over dinner before the concert Hirsch was wracked with period pains and seemed in no fit state to play. As it turned out the duo was magnificent. DJ Olive cued up a succession of beautifully chosen records on two decks, over which Hirsch free-associated, babbled, sang in a bewildering confusion of styles, whispered asides as if in a Shakespeare play, acted out little mini-dramas, used two microphones to shift spatial illusions and personae around the room, generally bouncing off any available stimulus that struck her. She even weaved in a little of our dinner conversation. A newcomer might hear it as chaotic randomness but its foundations lie in allowing the body to move through layers of time, clustering paralanguage along with speech and song, grounding the supposedly non-idiomatic practice of improvisation within the quotidian.

Fourteen years later I asked her, what is the relationship between 'voices in the head' and the way audible vocalization is formed during an improvisation; could she be more specific about her description of the body as a work space, both in not-performing and performing (if there is a big difference between the two)? 'I am always aware of the sounds/sites around me,' she replied,

> from the drones of appliances in the kitchen to the sound of steps in the hallway, to chatter in a cafe, the movement of someone walking or trees brushing against the sky – so many different tempos, melodies, rhythms in the everyday. In performance I respond as well to the people in the audience – listening, weaving what there is in the room into the music we are making.

Maybe it's a shadowing, I suggested, like Breton's Mouth of Shadows? 'Connections … memory,' she responded,

> the music reminds me of … so and so. … I put it back in to the music – a word stretches – its meaning slanted with the music formed. I wish I could capture the voices in my head when I lay down at night to sleep and a rushing stream of consciousness is set off. I can't always transfer it. But the walking and interacting and sitting by a canal or listening – stepping through different acoustic spaces and listening to sound transformed – then my body is working, capturing, recording. My body – moving through space finding shapes compositions. … It is working – it is a place I can call my own.

Signs from the body

Dorothy Miller Richardson was the quiet pioneer of stream-of-consciousness writing. Her *Pilgrimage* series of thirteen novels, the first published in 1915, was a meticulous, if highly selective recording of a life, each instalment given an enticing title: *The Tunnel, Pointed Roofs, Honeycomb, Deadlock, Revolving Lights, The Trap, Dawn's Left Hand*. The protagonist – Miriam – lives a modest, unspectacular life. In *The Tunnel* (1919) she is ecstatic to be renting a dingy room that gives her some measure of independence. Time barely seems to move, yet the cycles of life, day and night, work and free time, drudgery and tea, the tasks to be performed at a given time within the patterns of her job, her walks through a London that feels both hostile and magical, the surging and ebbing of feelings, convictions, confidence and often silenced opinion open out, fold upon fold, light and dark as she learns how to live and finally to write. The reader is caught in the stream of this interior monologue (as Richardson liked to call it), absorbed in the particles of life:

> As she began on her solid slice of bread and butter St. Pancras bells stopped again. In the stillness she could hear the sound of her own munching. She stared at the surface of the table that held her plate and cup. It was like sitting up to the nursery table. 'How frightfully happy I am,' she thought with bent head. Happiness streamed along her arms and from her head. St. Pancras bells began playing a hymn tune in single firm beats with intervals between that left each note standing for a moment gently in the air.

An ordinary life; a dull life even, yet the polyphony of emotions and sensations is hallucinatory in its precision and accumulation: 'The lecturing voice was far away, irrelevant and unintelligible. Peace flooded her.' Why do we have to spatialize time, sound and thought, reducing all three to a manageable linearity and locus that has nothing to do with the way we think or hear? Because they are elusive, everywhere and nowhere. The pouring of thoughts may take place in a dark room as if a kind of ectoplasm gushing out of some hidden spring and dispersing into nothingness, into the blood or becoming a sound recognizable as audible words, the marks of writing or some other signs on or from the body.

Dead of night

A fox screams as it moves, mapping acoustic territory, making contact, spiking silence. Some elusive quality in its voice seems to speak of disgust and dismay, yet the sleeper who is pulled so abruptly back to consciousness by this uncanny effect is sufficiently awake to identify an anthropomorphic untruth closer to human dreaming than the social life of an urban fox.

Just as the fox maps out an auditory terrain for itself, so the sleeper maps a response to its eerie screams by using analogy, perhaps poetic, perhaps banal. Without coming any closer to a full understanding of these sounds, a bioacoustician's analysis would deal in terms such as energy, frequency bands, natural harmonics, simple and complex components. To describe our perceptions of an experience essentially alien, we must overlay an interpretative map that communicates by means of unrelated images. Joining with the trope of horror is some vestige of textural thinking, as if a haptic perception of physical surface could act as translator for the thinking out of sound's apparent ineffability.

As I write this I am conscious that the 'words' I wish to pour out are blocked, as if (to use analogy) held in behind a tap that frequent usage and a corrosive proliferation of philosophical difficulties have stiffened. The fox experiences no inhibitions of this kind, no sense of nocturnal quiet and its inappropriate soundings, no concept of the scream as blue murder, no binaries of pleasure/disgust or joy/dismay.

As an improvising musician I know a little of this state. The question is how to be, not through the romance of becoming natural but through adjusting the balance of being and thinking about being. An audience waits: for a moment there is a putative 'nothing' (filled up with all the precursors of a familiar situation, the many and varied preparations for such nothingness, not to mention the abject conditions of somethingness). I can tap a surface – simple – and the field of potentiality opens up, whereas with writing, at which I am practiced, I can write a single sentence which may close down the field of potentiality for hours, days, even years. In music, the tap, to conflate these analogies of water and surfaces, is unscrewed by act – a gesture leading to a sound; from this point, an analogical process unfolds, one sound and its elusive qualities leading to others, working laterally or in flat time rather than in clock time, or, least of all, to pick up a vulgar expression with tweezers, 'moving forward'. The branching verbal chatter of the mind is to some degree stilled, but can it be assumed that this is less the case for the improvising listener we call audience?

After years of conflict, some sort of accommodation has been reached. I can play without overthinking and during the same evening listen in reasonable balance between absorption, engagement and analysis. In March 2013 I performed at Cafe Oto with Sharon Gal, Elaine Mitchener, Steve Beresford and Phil Minton. To be alone is part of this experience, not to be caught up in social encounters, not to be stuck in one place. I sheltered in a dark corner to hear Minton solo, wanting to see the side of his face, then for a vocal trio centred myself among other listeners, two hemispheres of the brain working both with and against each other's versions of the world, language and intuition, organization and civilization.

Of course there is no way to remember all or even a millisecond of the singing. To write observations in a notebook is merely to compile analogies. There was a moment, startling, almost supernatural; his mouth open like a trumpet bell, a pure whistle exuding from the back of his throat, querulous, fragile but clear in the concentrated hush. Many singers develop these secret weapons into street magic tricks posing as superpowers. With Minton, they penetrate the wracked body from within, slithering into the social air as if voices of dissociated personalities exorcised by a fission of 'internal' pressure and 'external' politics.

Later, he laughed when I asked how the whistle is executed, demonstrating how easy it is (for him). A technique tells us nothing much; like sportspeople, musicians can expend vast amounts of energy on developing knowledge and mastery of their own bodies. Spend any time working with Phil Minton or listening to him and you will hear him yodel. In conversation he tells me about his grandmother:

> Where I lived, Torquay, was heavily bombed around D-Day period and I was evacuated up to South Wales where my grandparents lived. They were miners, or had been. I was staying with my grandparents and aunties and I heard the word 'yodel'. I must have been only about three and a half and it intrigued me, this word yodel. Grandmother goes into the parlour on Saturday morning and yodels all on her own. I went in and she yodelled. It's one of the first audio memories I have of a grown up being quite surreal. What on earth is it? It was an absolutely beautiful, lovely sound and I was always trying to emulate

it as a boy, trying to find the break which I couldn't do. Just physically I couldn't make the jump, the oscillate. I kept trying for it until I was about thirteen. Then I could do it when my voice broke.

You still do it, I say. A superfluous comment; his anecdote is punctuated by yodels – oyeeoyeeoyee – so conversation has the texture of interspecies communication.

'All the time. I use it as like a voice bowl. Any time I go into any extreme voice placings I do a little yodel afterwards as an antidote to it. It gets the blood running in the right place again. Push-ups for the voice.'

What communicates as an energetically emotional state may be dispassionately technical in its shaping of materials without being predictive of the way they develop in a cooperative setting; conversely, that which seems detached from words – abstract, some would say – may be a mixing of gut acids, bile, bloody foam from the lungs. Minton appears along with singer Joan La Barbara in Matthew Barney's operatic cinema epic, *River of Fundament*, both producing 'tones of growling, farting death' as Ross Simonini wrote in *Frieze*. But this concentration on possible associations stimulated by sounds may also be misleading. 'If I perceive the sound it's there,' he says, 'I'm hearing them as abstract sounds, not associated with any emotions. I try not to do pain. I don't think I have any pain sounds in my repertoire. I also don't like the sounds of illness.' He pants, shallow and desperate. 'You might be able to get a nice rhythm but it sounds like you're dying of emphysema.'

We talk about the way that stray and inadvertent mouth sounds are suppressed. To spit during a conversation is disgusting, to belch is rude, to yawn is ungracious, to open the mouth very wide is disconcerting. 'Some people find it surprising,' he laughs. 'I should be behind a screen. I would always have been happier with that.' Is there a factor of disturbance, to witness such sounds being produced? 'I think for some people singing is a fear thing.' Sounds to confront the unruly body exist in jazz already: Rex Stewart playing 'Menelik the Lion of Judah', for example, the trumpet breaking up into the most remarkable low flatulent growls, or trombonist Joe 'Tricky Sam' Nanton's plunger mute solo on Duke Ellington's 'Blue Serge', uncanny in its simulation of speech in an unknown language.

Listening at Cafe Oto to the vocal trio of Sharon Gal, Elaine Mitchener and Phil Minton I witnessed his body's pulling back and leaning to the side, the voice a mutter stream of dissociated almost language, a virtuoso repression of sense. Improvising vocalists work in this way at the edge of words or within words, resistant to words. Sound metamorphosis scatters discarded word-form cocoons to float at the edge of cognition. Categories, difference, the particular, all blur into possibilities of non-verbal polyphony; writing has no words to describe a withholding of words.

This sounded voice is prolix, an endless variation, yet its silence is in the realm of the coherent voice, the voice of words articulating meaning stripped of the meaning of the sounding voice, its paralanguage. There are beautiful precedents for this in comedy – the motif of standing on the precipice of playing, seen in the comic art of Max Wall, Les Dawson and Jack Benny, more recently the broken microphone routine of Yorkshire comedian Norman Collier. Listening to Phil Minton makes me think of Jonathan Miller's BBC television production of the MR James ghost story, *Whistle and I'll Come To You* (1968). Actor Michael Hordern plays an academic philosopher taking a solitary reading break on the spectral Norfolk coast. A man whose cloistered masculinity and learning has detached him from sociality, his interactions with others are channelled obliquely through distracted fragments of speech, tics, grimaces, gestural idiosyncrasies, eccentric outbreaks of oral noise, humming, whistling, misplaced laughs, rhetorical questions where there should be answers, most of all unspoken absences in the flow of sense. In one scene, the Professor arrives at his hotel, waits in the monastic silent of the entrance hall for signs of life. Finally the hotelier appears. In a very English dance of discomfort at the proximity of other bodies, they negotiate the signing of the register, luggage, the showing of the room and all its facilities with murmurs, truncated questions, singing, sighs, heavy breathing, unformed words, most of all the desire to be alone, even when in company.

Such encounters with the abject unsayable bring to mind the Formless of Georges Bataille. First published in the critical dictionary of *Documents* in 1929, Bataille's short entry – *Formless* (*Informe*) – proposed the Formless as an active agency designed to bring things down in the world, a counter to the academic drive to describe, systematize and categorize all phenomena. 'On the other hand,' Bataille wrote, 'affirming that the universe resembles nothing and is only formless amounts to saying that the universe is something like a spider or spit.'

In the case of improvising singers it is literally spit. No argument leading to a rational conclusion: simply spit, gesticulations of the mouth, sounds from the lower depths. As Michel Leiris wrote (*Spittle: Mouth* in *Documents*): 'Given the identical source of language and spittle, any philosophical discourse can legitimately be figured by the incongruous image of a spluttering orator.'

In search of free bodies

Despite early twentieth-century plunges into the maelstrom of the Freudian unconscious – André Masson's drawings, the frottages of Max Ernst, Dora Maar's eerie photographs, the decalcomania of Oscar Dominguez, transcriptions of borderline psychotic trance utterances delivered under hypnosis by Robert Desnos, André Breton's collaborative literary experiment with Philippe Soupault, *The Magnetic Fields* – music from the same milieu was strangely immune to the concept of unfettered spontaneity. The limits of pure automatism became quickly apparent – Césaire later made politically directed revisions and cuts to *Solar Throat Slashed*, while Masson's work had shifted away from automatic drawing by the late 1920s. Music, facing the audience but unlike dada, encumbered by its administrative baggage of scores and technique, may simply have been too timid, too slow to catch the moment. With its greater emphasis on group performance (in which automatism becomes a far more complex process) and the need to please both proprietors and audiences, public music of the early twentieth century dissuaded those who might have gone further in that direction – Sidney Bechet or Charles Ives, for example – from taking such a fateful leap.

The technical demands of musical instruments, acquired over many years of repetitious practice that embed technique within muscle memory and involuntary brain functioning, discouraged abandonment (a paradox identified by Lévi-Strauss during his flight from the Nazis in 1941). Then there was the difficulty of listening within a declamatory context. As André Breton wrote (paraphrasing Victor Hugo) after the aural hallucinations that preceded his espousal of automatic writing: 'I still think it's incomparably less difficult to satisfy the demands of reflection than it is to put one's mind in the state of total receptivity, to have ears only for "what the mouth of shadows says".' They may be recuperated for avant-garde nostalgia in our time but assaults on textual logic pioneered by the futurist free words of F. T. Marinetti were entirely consistent with the fascist project of eliminating history to build a new empire. Marinetti was not an advocate of listening or receptivity. As John Gray has argued, fascism was the dark side of modernism: 'In Germany and Italy, the far right recruited supporters from avant-garde cultural movements such as expressionism and futurism.' This unsavoury pre-history of noise as the audible violence of futurity links uneasily with the relentless pursuit of new sounds to expand the instrumental and structural constraints of the concert tradition. Dadaist chaos at the Cabaret Voltaire in 1916 expressed disgust with the advent of global war. For Romanian Jewish artist Marcel Janco, 'Everything had to be demolished. We would begin again after the tabula rasa', but under the growing shadow of Fascism there is little evidence of any musician – whether in the context of orchestra, jazz band or avant-garde performance – throwing away the rules with the abandon of a Masson or Kurt Schwitters.

A partial explanation may lie with the available means of documentation. During the period of acoustic recording, from the last years of the nineteenth century up until 1925, the music industry was dominated by commercially viable recordings that suited the limitations of the medium at that time. Subtlety, sibilants and small instruments all presented difficulties. 'Large numbers of performing musicians could not be recorded at all,' wrote Timothy Day in *A Century of Recorded Music: Listening to Musical History*. Compositions reliant on detail and complex harmony such as Scriabin's *Poem of Ecstasy*, Schoenberg's *Pierrot Lunaire* and Debussy's *L'après-midi d'un faune* were not attempted. He asks the question why the record catalogues were filled with 'a succession of operatic potboilers and popular salon pieces and hackneyed ballads' during 'an epoch of intense musical creativity, one of the richest periods in the history of western music'. The answer lay with economics and technicalities. Markets had to be created, records were expensive to produce; sonically, the recording process was not yet capable of capturing anything beyond the obvious.

With a few exceptions, extreme experiments in spontaneous sound vanished into the aether, preserved only in excitable written accounts. Noise of smashing glass and struck metal accompanied Nikolai Foregger's *Mechanical Dances*, performed in Russia in 1923; in the previous year a state-sponsored jazz orchestra presented music and jazz poetry alongside Foregger's noise orchestra. Jazz and the art avant-garde were closely entwined. Jed Rasula, a specialist in the literary avant-garde, identifies noise as the common link: 'Berlin dadaist Walter Mehring called for an international lingual work of art, the language – ragtime. Dadaist sound poems do in fact bear a striking resemblance to scat singing.' Listen, for example, to 'King of the Bungaloos' (1911) or 'From Here to Shanghai'

(1917) by Gene Greene, a comic singer from the ragtime era. Greene's version of scat conforms to this vision of an 'international lingual work of art' though surely not in the way that Mehring – an anarchist campaigner against anti-Semitism who became a victim of nazi book-burning – would have envisaged. Greene's scatting gave voice to racial stereotypes, faux languages derived from cryptolects sung in both his natural voice and a deep rasping growl. This rasp was far from innocent, particularly in the context of blackface minstrelsy and Greene's depiction of a jungle kingdom. 'In an African tradition, the rasp could be heard as a sophisticated stylization of tone,' wrote Jacob Smith in *Vocal Tracks*, 'but white critics and audiences immersed in the turn-of-the-century musical culture dominated by bel canto would tend to hear it as "noise," interfering with the pure signal of the round tone.'

There is nonsense and noise in scat, also much evidence that Europeans were in thrall to the noise of jazz percussion, but during the same period, a small group of African American musicians suffered exposure to the noise of European war and used their own 'noise' to convey these traumatic experiences to audiences back home. 'A Chicago concert by James Reese Europe's band in 1919,' writes Rasula, 'concluded with a sonic rendition of trench warfare called "In No Man's Land", during which the house lights were completely extinguished.' Born in Alabama in 1881, James Reese Europe led large ragtime ensembles in New York from 1910 onwards, not quite jazz but entirely written by black composers despite external pressure to include works from the European canon. The first African American officer to lead troops into combat in the First World War, Reese Europe experienced the horrors of poison gas and artillery bombardment as a lieutenant in the 369th Infantry, otherwise known as the Harlem Hellfighters: 'You see, some of the shells would burst prematurely in the air and oh, how they would scream – and shrapnel was hizzing hither and thither.' As director of the regimental band he performed throughout France in 1918 and was said to have launched the craze for European 'ragtimitis'. Noise carried a double significance, the traumatic onslaught of modern war experienced at first hand, running in parallel with an instrumental 'noise' so unfamiliar to white audiences that it necessitated explanation as an invention and defining trait of African American musicians. 'With the brass instruments we put in mutes and make a whirling motion with the tongue,' he told a journalist. 'With wind instruments we pinch the mouthpiece and blow hard. This produces the peculiar sound which you all know. To us it is not discordant, as we play the music as it is written, only that we accent strongly in this manner the notes which originally would be without accent. It is natural for us to do this; it is indeed a racial characteristic.'

'Hear them go over the top of the musical trenches,' an American poster blared. 'Hear the bombardment of the percussion twins.' But James Reese Europe's post-war celebrity was brief. After an altercation at the Mechanics Hall in Boston, May 1919, James Reese Europe was stabbed to death by one of the percussion twins. Just a few months earlier he had recorded a version of 'On Patrol In No Man's Land' for the Pathé Frères Phonograph Company. Noble Sissle's vocals describe the scene – 'There's a Minenwerfer coming – look out. Hear that roar. There's one more. Stand fast – there's a Very light. Don't gasp or they'll find you all right. Don't start to bombing with those hand grenades. There's a machine gun, holy spades! Alert, gas! Put on your mask. Adjust it correctly and hurry up fast. Drop, there's a rocket from the Boche barrage' – with every incident punctuated by drum explosions, rattling metal and sirens. At the end the music stops as the whole band enacts an attack with shouts, yells and Sissle's encouragements of 'Get 'em, stick 'em with the bayonets'.

Semi-improvised *bruitism* played a part in performances at the Cabaret Voltaire in Zurich in 1916. Important as they were, solo recitations by Hugo Ball or the simultaneous poems of Richard Huelsenbeck, Marcel Janco and Tristan Tzara all began and ended with transformations of literature – exploded, interrupted, rendered into nonsense – yet still tied to human vocal utterance. In an atmosphere of chaos, Mary Hennings sang her songs, Huelsenbeck banged relentlessly on a big drum, Janco bowed an invisible violin, Ball played the piano; there was so-called Negro music and when Ball recited his sound poem, *Karawane*, in 1916, he added mystique and power by imitating the chanting of the Catholic mass.

In 1919, artist Hannah Hoch took part in a Berlin dada soirée led by Richard Huelsenbeck and Yefim Golyshev, drily recalling in a later account: 'Only one single time did I stand on the Mount Olympus of DADA.' 'On the occasion described,' writes Deborah Lewer, 'as one of a "choir" of around ten performers, she briefly joined an improvised "simultaneous chorale" at "maximum decibels" with "infernal-bruitistic orchestra". She was armed (as she put it) with distinctly domestic weapons of cacophony: "a saucepan lid and a toy gun".' The impression left from written accounts suggests that these moments of sonic anarchy were almost an afterthought, a dive into infantilism that flooded the proceedings with extra mayhem.

Poets or visual artists raised an undisciplined racket without having to confront problems of embouchure, intonation and fingering or the absence of a score. From what we can gather, no individual musician was deconstructing performance with the same demonic verve as the poets, though new instrumental techniques, compositional forms and sonic technologies were undergoing constant reinvention. This view may change as the history of sonic art matures sufficiently to move beyond its current emphasis on European and American trends and embrace research into avant-garde art movements elsewhere.

In other countries, the synthesis of local initiatives and a mixture of foreign influences ranging from anarchism to constructivism produced a different balance. The charismatic central figure in the Japanese Mavo artists group, Murayama Tomoyoshi, absorbed the influence of German expressionist dance in early 1920s Berlin, seeing Mary Wigman dance her Heroic Parade to Beethoven's Fifth Symphony. 'While attending the Dusseldorf Congress of Progressive Artists,' writes Gennifer Weisenfeld in *Mavo: Japanese Artists and the Japanese Avant-Garde 1905-1931*, 'he witnessed an impromptu dadaist performance by the Dutch couple Theo and Nelly Van Doesberg, who sang and yelled while dancing half-naked on tables and chairs. The combination of expression and provocation fundamental to expressionist and dadaist performance pervaded Muruyama's, and later Mavo's approach to drama.'

In 1924, Mavo's self-identification was apocalyptic: 'Lazily, like pigs, like weeds, like the trembling emotions of sexual desire, we are the last bombs that rain down on all the intellectual criminals (including the bourgeois cliques) who swim in this world.' In the same year Murayama and Okada Tatsuo performed *The Dance That Cannot Be Named* at the Tokyo Imperial University Christian Youth Hall. A newspaper photograph of this event shows them dressed in women's clothes, contorted into expressive poses of ambiguous sexuality that clearly indicate a connection with the Butoh dance imagery developed by Tatsumi Hijikata and Kazuo Ohno more than four decades later. 'The news article accompanying this photograph', Weisenfeld writes, 'describes their writhing movements and identifies Takamizawa Michinao as providing the music, playing unusual instruments constructed out of tin cans, a spinning wheel, oil cans and logs.' Takamizawa (an anarchist provocateur who later became a highly influential manga artist) rubbed these various objects together to produce sounds, calling them 'sound constructors', presumably a reference to the instruments of the same name used by the futurist Luigi Russolo in Italy but possibly inspired by Russian futurists who exhibited work in Tokyo, Kyoto and Osaka in 1920.

There were two types of sound constructor, 'wind sound constructors' and 'broken instrument constructors'. As with the majority of comparable contemporary events, the totality of the performance has to be imaginatively constructed from anecdotal description and a grainy photograph. Despite that limitation, *The Dance That Cannot Be Named* implies a more consistently avant-garde fusion with sound than Mary Wigman's use of Beethoven and a more considered approach than the Doesbergs or any other dadaists (excepting Kurt Schwitters). There was a precedent, in dance at least, for uninhibited performance in the 1920s. Negotiating a difficult path between classicism and expressionism, dancers such as Niddy Impokoven, Josephine Baker and particularly the doomed and scandalous duo of Anita Berber and Sebastien Droste were part of a richly experimental dance scene, home to Margaret Morris, Isadora Duncan, her noncomformist brother Raymond and their famously enthusiastic pupil, Lucia Joyce, who, some say, was the inspiration behind her father's final work, *Finnegans Wake*.

The demanding relationship between technology and musician – the craft worker who learns through dedicated repetition – would account for a relative lack of abandon, compounded by the embedded hierarchical system of composers, music publishers, conductors and musicians, a structure that perpetuated both deference and economic dependence. The focus turned instead to a slow, painstaking task – liberating techniques and systems – rather than the more radical dream of total freedom. By the twentieth century, most of the musical instruments commonly used in European and American musics conformed to the tempered system of tuning and standardized pitch. Despite the glissandi and microtones available to string players and trombonists, instruments were accepted by classical musicians as tools that forcibly imprinted the rules of the system they represented through the necessary process of learning their mechanics, repeatedly playing scales and developing a 'good' orthodox tone. Implicit in virtuosity was an acceptance of the matrix – the ability to play in tune within the tempered system, to understand the rules of harmony and the language of notation, to articulate the machine of sound.

There were exceptions. Within this cultural context, African American jazz and blues musicians were developing a progressive approach to instrumental virtuosity that challenged these rules without discarding them entirely. For this reason, Edgard Varèse praised the jazz band as a tiger; to his ears the symphony orchestra had degenerated into a dropsical elephant. These attitudes were reflected in workshops sessions held in 1957 at Greenwich House Music School, New York, in which Varèse, Charles Mingus, Teo Macero, Art Farmer, Teddy Charles (possibly) and other players experimented with a new musical approach embracing both directed and free improvisation, Varèse verbally guiding the musicians through graphic scores of sinuous lines marked with sparse conventional dynamic indications – f, sf, p subito, portamento – a grid of bar lines and some specific pitches. To some degree the results (heard on poor-quality tapes) extended existing trajectories – Mingus and Macero with the Jazz Composers Workshop and Teddy Charles's New Directions groups from earlier in the 1950s – but Varèse's contribution was a multi-directionality of wild expressivity, lines flying and swooping, lunging and growling as if tearing at the edges of all restraint.

Density 21.5, the solo for flute Varèse composed in 1936, anticipated the advanced (or extended) techniques catalogued and published in the mid-1960s by John C. Heiss and Bruno Bartolozzi. Though the piece implies an unfamiliar freedom, a continuation of the potentiality unlocked by Debussy's flute solo of 1913, *Syrinx*, the differences of emphasis are greater than the twenty-three years that separate them. Originally called *Flûte de Pan*, *Syrinx* was languorously symbolic, an evocation of the randomness of reeds sounded by wind (Toru Takemitsu touched on similar ground in his 1971 essay, *A Single Sound*: 'Now we can see how the master *shakuhachi* player, striving in performance to re-create the sound of wind in a decaying bamboo grove, reveals the Japanese sound ideal: sound in its ultimate expressiveness, being constantly refined, approaches the nothingness of that wind in the bamboo grove.'); *Density 21.5*, on the other hand, is named after the density of platinum, the metal of George Barrère's valuable flute. Between reed and platinum lay a cavern of horrors: the brutality of the First World War, with fascist and Nazi activity of the 1930s signalling the imminence of a second. Varèse's solo, composed during a protracted personal crisis, is full of tension and uncertainty, sudden stops and abrupt leaps, shrill high pitches and labyrinthine structure. After composing this piece, he devoted ten years to unrealized projects, searching for further advances in sonic production that would voice any sound at the speed of thought.

The epitome of a musical instrument embodying a utopian vision of freedom, Leon Theremin's etherphone was patented and first demonstrated in Russia in 1921. Capable of emitting sweeping parabolas of sound, the theremin, as it came to be known, was operated by the musician's hand movements. Since the operator never actually touched the instrument, only gesturing close enough to interrupt an electro magnetic field, there was a suggestion of detachment from corporeality – the flesh of the trapeze artist floating on air currents. Theremin envisaged possibilities that would be realized by others later in the century: spontaneous music generated by the movements of dancers' bodies and a synaesthetic performance art that drew together all the senses.

Paradoxically, the absence of physical contact with the theremin's surface demanded even more control and concentration than a conventional instrument. Accurate intonation, articulation and particularly speed were so difficult to achieve that the theremin turned out to be a poor conduit for spontaneity. One or two genuinely progressive composers tried to use it. From 1932 to 1934, Varèse worked on *Ecuatorial*, originally scored for two custom-built theremins, an ensemble of acoustic instruments that included six percussionists and a bass voice, though the published score and later recordings have used Maurice Martenot's invention, the ondes martenot, in place of the theremins. 'Varèse used the theremins for their timbre and the glissandi and long sustained notes he couldn't find on any other instrument,' wrote Albert Glinsky in *Theremin: Ether Music and Espionage*.

Free lines

Varèse was frustrated by what he described in a letter to Leon Theremin as 'the old Man-Power instruments'. His use of electronic prototypes mirrored the visions of Antonin Artaud, writing his first manifesto for The Theatre of Cruelty in 1932. 'Musical Instruments,' wrote Artaud,

> These will be used as objects, as part of the set. Moreover they need to act deeply and directly on our sensitivity through the senses, and from the point of view of sound they invite research into utterly unusual sound properties and vibrations which present-day musical

instruments do not possess, urging us to use ancient or forgotten instruments or to invent new ones. Apart from music, research is also needed into instruments and appliances based on special refining and new alloys which can reach a new scale in the octave and produce an unbearably piercing sound or noise.

This was exactly the case in *Ecuatorial*, in which the electronic instruments soar to stratospheric pitches that reach beyond the highest reaches of even the piccolo. A sense of otherness drew Varèse to electronics. Until the rebirth of the theremin as aetherial voice of aliens, alcoholics and mad magicians in 1950s cinema, Theremin's futuristic ideas about his revolutionary instrument were hardly borne out by its repertoire: recitals of Chopin, Rachmaninoff, Tchaikovsky, Mozart and Handel. Varèse and Olivier Messiaen, who composed the eerie, weightless *Oraison* for an ensemble of ondes martenots in 1937, were exceptions. Both composed through a mystical glass: Varèse invoking an awe-inspiring future-past of pagan magic, alchemy, beast cries in the urban night; Messiaen synthesizing Catholicism, platonic love and the complex manifestations of nature into a music that was 'more than a work of art, it was a way of existing, an inextinguishable fire'.

Percy Grainger, the most improbable of composers, devised the clearest articulation of this convergence of weightlessness, ecstasy and free lines. Perhaps the first composer to use the expression 'free music', Grainger believed (along with his teacher Busoni, Henry Cowell and Harry Partch) that sound was trapped in the grid of twelve-tone equal temperament. Cowell's composition of 1923, *The Banshee*, delved into the bowels of the piano, reenvisioning the rigid frame as a well full of spirits; Partch embarked on the monumental work of theorizing a new approach to tonality, notation and musical function, then built the musical instruments to play it. 'Grainger thought that music was unique among the arts by its woeful dependence on the type of segmentation inherent in temperament,' wrote Douglas Kahn. Grainger had been thinking about '… nonharmony, gliding tones, total independence of voices, and what he called "beatless music" as early as 1899, when he was seventeen years old,' says Kahn.

Despite enjoying the 'lovely and touching "free" (non-harmonic) combinations of tones in nature,' Grainger marvelled, 'we are unable to take up these beauties and expressiveness into the art of music because of our archaic notions of harmony.' Prior to the Second World War, the theremin was one of the few devices that allowed him to realize these dreams. In 1935, using a graphic notation method of curving horizontal lines drawn on graph paper in coloured pen, Grainger wrote a visually notated arrangement of his string quartet, *Free Music No. 1*, for four theremins. Corresponding with American critic Olin Downes in 1942, Grainger described his vision of the new freedom: 'In this music [Free Music], a melody is as free to roam through space as a painter is free to draw and paint free lines, free curves, create free shapes (Current music is like trying to do a picture of a landscape, a portrait of a person, in small squares – like a mosaic – or in preordained shapes: straight lines or steps.).' Unfortunately for Grainger, his *Beatless Music* for six theremins and *Free Music No. 1* for four theremins have lost their purity, now attractively reminiscent of altered states and otherness conjured up by theremins in films such as *Lost Weekend*, *Spellbound* and *The Day the Earth Stood Still*. Tones glide in fluid counterpoint, swooping through extreme intervals, hovering in the air like birds sailing on thermals. They aim for total abstraction yet conjure images of alien creatures, spectral forms, ghosts.

In his rejection of segmentation, Grainger came close to imagining the digital future of zeros and ones, the curves that reveal themselves as stepped straight lines under high magnification. His own inspiration came from reflections of the sun on the movement of waves – a familiar sight when he was a young boy growing up in Melbourne. Waves in the ocean contain within themselves a model of complexity, of infinity, of temporal division, endless variety and disintegrating curves, an infinite horizon of content to which music can only aspire. Paradoxically, Grainger's idea of free music was inorganic. He put his faith in the construction of machines, believing that humans would never be able to rise to the potential of a superior machine (perhaps inventing the computer in his imagination, though building his own machines from a bizarre collection of utilitarian flotsam collected from rubbish left on the streets). In an article called *Free Music*, written in 1938, he contrasted the age of flying with the goose-step, music's future suppressed by militaristic formality. Here was another paradox: Grainger was a practicing sado-masochist with unsavoury convictions: Aryan masculinity, eugenics and anti-Semitism. As with the Italian futurist free words of Marinetti, dreams of freedom could be tainted by association with nightmares.

Tongues like flames of fire

'There are a thousand ways of probing the future,' said Olivier Messiaen in a 1958 lecture in Brussels. 'I only wish that composers would not forget that music is a part of time, a fraction of time, as is our own life, and that nature – an inexhaustible treasure house of sounds, colours, forms and rhythms, and the unequalled model for total development and perpetual variations – that nature is the supreme resource.' Messiaen turned to bird song, which also displayed an infinitude of parabolas, pitch relationships, rhythmic sequences, tonal variations, alien melodies and unpredictable juxtapositions. Finding inspiration in natural phenomena may be as old as music itself – a wealth of documentation over centuries shows that animals and meteorological phenomena have always represented otherness, the mystery of communication that holds its meaning at a tantalizing remove from human understanding. The distinction between nature and culture, never entirely clear or stable in any society, could be dissolved in shamanistic communications with animal familiars, or in possession by spirits or demons in animal form.

Some artists courted this danger, or found their artistic visions of otherness and the extra-human liable to unravel into uncontrollable states of disturbance and disorder. Olivier Messiaen and Antonin Artaud were thrown together in collaboration in 1932, when Artaud was commissioned to devise sound effects for Alfred Savoir's play, *La Patissière de Village*, at the Théâtre Pigalle. Messiaen's role was to interpret these sound effects on the theatre organ but Artaud insisted on the integrity of real sounds, rejecting the musicality of Messiaen's mimetic approach. The collaboration, an unhappy one, added to a long series of frustrations and disappointments, small steps leading to the crisis that lasted from the late 1930s until Artaud's painful death from rectal cancer in 1948.

'Artaud was so entrenched in his own world,' wrote Bettina L. Knapp in *Antonin Artaud: Man of Vision*, 'so overcome by his "other preoccupations" that the rapport with the "normal" "outer" world ceased. He would begin telescoping his syllables, indulge in verbal gyrations, make strange noises, change his intonation and the vocal range of which he was the master: speak first in a sonorous, then monotonous, and finally in an insipid register; whereupon he would break out in mellow and full tones.' In this deteriorating condition, experienced in 1943, he would get down on his hands and knees, spit, belch in rhythm, psalmodise, draw magic circles and make strange noises. 'Hours were spent in articulating the words forcibly,' wrote Knapp, 'injecting each syllable with a kind of metallic ringing sound; treating words as something concrete, actual beings possessing potential magic forces.'

Artaud is particularly germane to any interrogation of the limits of improvisation, its relationship to otherness and freedom. Knapp describes his behaviour during this period of madness, shortly before his incarceration in the asylum at Rodez, as a form of glossolalia, yet glossolalia, or speaking in tongues, is characteristically stereotypical and repetitious. In its Christian form, glossolalia represents baptism by the Holy Spirit. This phenomenon, an acquired babbling expelled involuntarily during trance, replays the Feast of Pentecost after Christ's death, imprecisely described in the New English Bible as a moment of 'tongues like flames of fire, dispersed among them and resting on each one. And they were all filled with the Holy Spirit and began to talk in other tongues, as the Spirit gave them power of utterance.'

Artaud's behaviour was a more convoluted entwinement of poetics, theory and psychosis; he consciously sought new forms of theatrical language, yet was also the victim of psychic disintegration. 'The theatre of cruelty necessitates a new form of language,' writes Alan S. Weiss in *Breathless: Sound Recording, Disembodiment and The Transformation of Lyrical Nostalgia*,

> the archetype of which is glossolalia: a performative, dramatic, enthusiastic expression of the body; language reduced to the realm of incantatory sound at the threshold of nonsense; speech as pure gesture. Such instances of glossolalia are not mere symptoms, as Artaud explained to Dr. Ferdière at Rodez: 'Half of the chants in the Catholic church were exorcisms at the beginning of the Christian era, and they have now passed into the liturgy of the faithful.' ... Originating as a private speaking in tongues within Artaud's religious delirium, this glossolalia was first transmogrified into an apotropaic incantatory technique, a veritable curative magic, to protect him from the gods and demons that tormented him; ultimately, it was raised, through textual performance and production, to the level of poetry.

In her analysis of glossolalia based on fieldwork conducted among an Apostolic movement in Mexico, anthropologist and linguist Felicitas

D. Goodman concluded that glossolalia of this type 'mirrors that of the person who guided the glossolalist into the behaviour'. Contextualizing this discovery within a general contemporary ambivalence towards dissociative states, a fear of sinking into 'chaos beyond the threshold of awareness ... an uncontrollable realm, into the uncharted depths of chaos' she maintains that the opposite is true, that 'beyond the threshold of the conscious there is not disorder but structure'. According to Goodman, in many cases: 'what looks like a spontaneous occurrence is not really that. A powerful conditioning factor is present, often out of awareness but still decisively affective.' This factor was cultural expectation.

In *The History of Surrealist Painting*, Marcel Jean compared automatism to the photographer-seaweed of Raymond Roussel's *Impressions d'Afrique*: 'an aquatic plant which is a kind of living magic lantern and whose functioning might symbolise the return to consciousness of first memories.' 'In Roussel's novel,' wrote Jean,

> the spectators are fascinated at the beginning by the performance of the screen plant, but in the end their attention wanders: the same cycle of images repeats itself indefinitely. Habit tends to make a conscious action nothing less than automatic and monotonous; inversely, it introduces a factor of monotony, of real stereotype, into any too long prolonged or too often repeated unconscious experience.

As Jean points out, even the surrealists wearied eventually of Desnos, his 'sleeps' and his endless monologues dredged up from the depths of reverie: 'the eighth day's obedient sun illumined their corpses, presided over their decomposition and saw the majestically pacific waves throng to bring their tribute of spume to the tyrant barometer ...' and so on ad infinitum.

This objection to spontaneous expression was more or less John Cage's point of view whenever the subject of improvisation was raised. 'I've always been opposed to improvisation,' he told Joan Retallack, during the conversations collected as *Musicage*, 'because you do only what you remember.' During the same conversation, less than a month before he died, Cage admitted a change of heart: 'I became interested because I had not been interested. And the reason I had not been interested was because one just goes back to one's habits. But how can we find ways of improvising that *release* us from our habits?' Retallack responds with the thought that performers are occupied by their habits, repeating what they've already done. 'What they already know,' Cage replies. 'Then you might as well not continue. If you already know something, you might as well stop. Other people think that's when they should start – is when they start repeating themselves. *(laughs)* When they *know* how to do something.'

Cage's strategy for confronting this problem was to present himself with a forbidding performance task. In a score for improvisation called *One* (1992), he vocalized the letters of the alphabet from a score of 640 numbers between one and twelve but spoke words of different types or sung pitches according to the numbers. The obstacle was to find the words and pitches without preparing them beforehand: 'So I was obliged to, by myself, to think in the performance situation of a full word, of an empty word, and to vocalize. … And I had to practice and practice until I wouldn't be afraid, you know, to perform, in a situation where there would be people who know my work very well. I didn't want to do badly for them.' After persistent questioning by Joan Retallack, Cage's reasoning, which only emerges as incomplete speculations through a convoluted, interrupted series of anecdotes, is that the structure of a musical instrument, its technical demands and its intimate relationship with the player's sense of self, develops and determines a performer's world view, their motivational force and their idea of what music should be. Once you have put in the hours is it ever possible to become free of that conditioning?

Cage's piece was reminiscent of Marina Abramović's *Freeing the Memory*, performed for ninety minutes in Tubingen in 1975: 'I sit on a chair with my head tilted backwards. Performance: Without stopping, I continuously speak the words that come to mind. When words no longer come to mind the performance ends.' What becomes apparent from the film of this event is that her mind is working through association, strings of words linked by categories such as the body, a part of the body or the kitchen; then a random word implants itself within this sequence, a moment of spontaneity, and within a few steps has triggered a new category. More explicitly ritualistic than Cage, Abramović's strategy was to work towards a purification of the self through an ordeal in which the body was emptied of its habits, freed into a state of nothingness, silence or collapse.

'Unless we go to extremes, we won't get anywhere,' Cage told interviewers Cole Gage and Tracy Caras, failing to recognize the relative nature of freedom for those outside his immediate social and artistic circle, let alone the varying interpretations and consequences of what is taken to be extreme within different communities. 'If Cage changed his attitude toward improvisation in the 1970s,' wrote Sabine Feisst,

> what was his view of jazz, which had undergone many changes and become freer since the 1950s? His opinion on jazz does not seem to have changed at all. Cage commented on free jazz as follows: 'Everyone tells me that jazz is free today. But when I listen to it, it always seems to me to be confined within a world of ideas and musical relationships. ... And what is called free jazz probably tries to free itself from time and rhythmic periodicity. The bass doesn't play like a metronome any more. But even then, you still get the feeling of a beat'.

Setting aside the illogicality of Cage, of all people, critiquing music for being 'confined within a world of ideas', one thing is clear – Cage had far more knowledge of ancient Chinese bronzes than he did of the musicians playing jazz and mambo in night clubs not so far from his apartment on the Lower East Side in New York City – yet his fastidious rejection of improvisation can now be seen as a key, one of many, that unlocked the possibility for total improvisation in the 1960s. Alvin Curran, a founder member of the pioneering improvisation group MEV, saw it as a paradox rooted in Cage's refusal to break with the lineage of notated composition:

> It seemed to me that with all the discussions about utopia, anarchy, etc., the interesting thing is that we (MEV) were clearly making a new kind of chance music – not made from known or invented systems, but based on the risk (in every sense) of bringing people together to make music anytime anywhere without a score. This is something that Cage could not consider nor likely ever approve of. And in view of his voracious imagination and rigorous radicalism, it is curious to imagine that this one small step toward liberating the music from the composer and ultimately from itself, is one Cage never took. That is, for all his dedicated commitment to freedom, liberation of the spirit, mind, and body, he remained a modernist composer true to his time – fully horrified at the thought of taking one's own music and throwing it away.

For Cage, indeterminacy and chance methods were strategies for asking questions without the necessities of also providing answers. Discussing a

Mark Tobey painting with Joan Retallack, Cage says: 'What's so beautiful is that there's no gesture in it. The hand is not operating in any way.' In *Writings Through John Cage's Music, Poetry, + Art*, Alvin Curran talks about the formation of MEV in a similar way:

> We found ourselves busily soldering cables, contact mikes, and talking about 'circuitry' as if it were a new religion. By amplifying the sounds of glass, wood, metal, water, air, and fire, we were convinced that we had tapped into the sources of the natural musics of 'everything.' We were in fact making a spontaneous music which could be said to be coming from 'nowhere' and made out of 'nothing' – all somewhat a wonder and a collective epiphany. And learning that Cage had done these things even ten years earlier was no shock, but a confirmation of a 'mutual' discovery.

The possibility of amplifying sounds inherent within inanimate material, a kind of aural microscopy, was made possible through the rapid advances of electronic music. The intense struggle of Varèse to liberate sound from the custody of acoustic instrument technology, heard so clearly on *Density 21.5*, was answered by tape music and live electronics, both of which consigned Percy Grainger's experiments in freedom to footnotes in the history of music's search for freedom. As a partial answer to harmonic limitations in so-called Western music, percussion had become increasingly important in twentieth-century music, whether through jazz, the influence of musical practice from regions outside European/American hegemony (the vastness, diversity, sonic richness and structural complexity of African and Asian music, in particular), or the rejection of equal temperament. Any hopes that electronic music would achieve the total control proposed by serialism were usurped – electronically generated and manipulated sound allowed greater freedom to abandon control, particularly in collective settings.

In 1946, John Cage began composing his *Sonatas and Interludes*, an extended cycle for prepared piano (which, incidentally, utilized both musical relationships and 'the feeling of a beat'). As with other works he had been composing since the late 1930s, this was a further development of Henry Cowell's innovatory placement of objects within the piano interior to radically alter sonority and tuning, in essence to transform the piano into a tuned drum. In the same year, the New Orleans drummer Baby Dodds hauled his drum kit into a studio to record a set of solos for Folkways Records. Intended as an unpretentious document of the skills that lay behind a glittering career, working with King Oliver, Louis Armstrong, Jelly Roll Morton, Sidney Bechet, Bunk Johnson and Merce Cunningham, *Baby Dodds: Talking and Drum Solos* went beyond any other percussion showcase of the time. Dodd's control of dynamics, sound and swing made this ten-inch album the spiritual ancestor of many solo percussion records made by improvisers, from the Milford Graves Percussion Ensemble with Sunny Morgan, released on ESP-Disk in 1965, to Han Bennink's *Solo*, released on the Dutch ICP label in 1972 and containing, in homage to the Baby Dodds recordings, two tracks entitled 'Spooky Drums'. The major difference, from Milford Graves onwards, was that rhythm was explored microscopically as pure sound, freed from linearity.

The post-war generation was shaped by cold war paranoia, race politics, anti-colonial struggles and the global theatre of mass media. A strong undercurrent of resistance to technology – in the military sphere, the weapons of total annihilation that stood armed and ready; in the cultural sphere, the amplified instruments of popular music – contributed to an overwhelmingly acoustic feel in early free jazz and free improvisation. Inside the studio, sound recording was beginning its experiments with physical and audio separation; beyond that, the sense of alienation in an increasingly mediated, commodified landscape intensified. 'To feel is perhaps the most terrifying thing in this society,' Cecil Taylor has said. 'This is one of the reasons I'm not too interested in electronic music: it divorces itself from human energy, it substitutes another kind of force as the determinant agent for its continuance.'

Sun Ra's use of electronic keyboards was prophetic of a less technophobic future. His enthusiastic embrace of Moog, Clavioline and tape effects confirmed his place as a lone pioneer in jazz, but even within the highly structured and theorized (or mytheorized) trajectory of the rest of his work his use of these instruments and techniques allowed passages of total freedom. If hearing Sun Ra's Arkestra was an audio hallucination of the ballrooms of Chicago transplanted into the midst of verdant rainforest on a lonely planet where chaos was beauty, the effect of hearing Albert and Donald Ayler for the first time was like hearing the drum and fife music of Napolean Strickland and Othar Turner, the gospel saxophone of Vernard Johnson, the slide guitar moans of Blind Willie Johnson, the R&B tenor shriek and roar of Big Jay McNeely, the androgynous whooping and screaming of Little Richard, the New

Orleans marches of George Lewis and the Eureka Brass Band, all refracted through the turmoil of civil rights, America's assassination epidemic, race riots, the media futurism of the space race, the escalating war in Vietnam.

In his dream of freedom Albert Ayler rose up from this chaos to commingle with the ghosts of jazz – New Orleans and its marching bands and street bands, spirituals and the tightly interlocked group playing of King Oliver's Creole Jazz Band. As James Lincoln Collier has said of the first Oliver band recordings, made in 1923:

> It is, first and foremost, an ensemble music. On a number of cuts there are no solos at all, aside from a few short breaks, and rarely is more than a quarter of a cut given over to solos. All seven or eight musicians play at the same time, and it is the wonder of this kind of music that there is no chaos; everything goes in an orderly fashion.

This absence of chaos was largely due to the heavy hand of Oliver himself, dictating who did what, how and when; it was also due to the lack of improvisation. 'Once they had worked out a satisfactory way of playing a tune,' Collier writes, 'they saw no reason to change it.'

These revenants from the early history of jazz – unisons, repeated melodic cells and ragged counterpoint, what Collier described as lines meshing and unmeshing 'in a fashion suggesting the principles of African music' – typified the way free jazz musicians expressed unity within turbulence, inner calm contrasting with outer passion but with the addition of improvised solos and expressive ensembles inspired by high-energy players from a later period. The potency of emotionally charged solos flying on the collective energy generated by strong bass riffs, explosive drumming and band unisons was already a proven formula in jazz, physical generators of excitement for dancers that pushed soloists to the limits of their inventiveness and technique. For a startling example from the Count Basie Band, listen to Eddie 'Lockjaw' Davis solo over 'Whirlybird', like a powerful creature given chase by furies whose shouts whip up a chaos barely contained by the conduction of Basie.

Listen also to Ornette Coleman's 'Ramblin' (the opening track of *Change of the Century*, released in 1960), to the way Coleman takes the final note of a phrase as if chastising a straggler, bends it and burrs it around the joyful bounce of the drums and bass; then listen to Coleman and Don Cherry conversing in the ensemble passages that conclude the song, the dynamics of Cherry's pocket trumpet dropping to a soft murmur,

Coleman's alto saxophone dipping likewise so they whisper across the room, two shy young men exchanging secrets of life. The performance is so cute, so tight; unsurprising that it fed back into the stream of popular music when Ian Dury repurposed eight bars of Charlie Haden's bass duet (itself a version of an old-time fiddle and banjo breakdown called 'Old Joe Clark') with drummer Ed Blackwell for 'Sex and Drugs and Rock and Roll', released eleven years later.

There are no linear chains of influence in this web. St. Clair Pinkney's squealing tenor saxophone solos with James Brown's band, for example: were they inspired by what was happening with the new thing in jazz or were they extensions of the R&B showmanship traditions from which many free jazz players had graduated? In their teenage years, many free jazz saxophonists apprenticed in blues, R&B and the commercial big bands. John Coltrane, for example, worked with Eddie 'Cleanhead' Vinson and Earl Bostic; as a young saxophone player in Philadelphia he reluctantly walked the bar (literally walking along the bar in a club, booting out foghorn honks and shrill screeches for the drinkers). Giuseppi Logan also played with Earl Bostic, Albert Ayler with Little Walter and Lloyd Price, Pharoah Sanders with Kool and the Gang, Ornette Coleman with Pee Wee Crayton, and Frank Wright with Bobby 'Blue' Bland (whose so-called 'love throat' singing, a cross between a roar, a scream, and a gargle, can be heard as a precursor to Pharoah's guttural overblowing on tenor). Invisible lines connected all of them to the tenor saxophone tradition of Illinois Jacquet, Johnny Griffin and Eddie 'Lockjaw' Davis, the razor tones of R&B players like Big Jay McNeely, Willis 'Gator Tail' Jackson and Jack McVea screaming over R&B riffs, and the repeated riffing, call-and-response testifying of gospel vocal quartets such as the Sensational Nightingales, the Soul Stirrers, Five Blind Boys of Mississippi and Swan Silvertones, their fluid collective harmonies moving between the extremes of the voice in support of the raw, exalted soloing of soloists who, like Julius Cheeks, sang themselves beyond language, close to death.

Of the secular and the sacred, watch and listen as Miami-born tenor saxophonist Willis 'Gatortail' Jackson (one of the key influences on Jamaican ska) performs for 120 eyeball bursting seconds on the Ed Sullivan Show in 1955, all pretence at musicality jettisoned after two choruses, Jackson shredding and blasting notes as if trying to ignite the air of the television studio. Listen, also, to the radical formlessness of the

Five Blind Boys – 'Sermonette: Father I Stretched My Hands To Thee' – tension held by a pedal note from the organ, the chord changes of the song almost imperceptible in their slowness, the lines, the syllables of each word prolonged, stretched out as an auditory enactment of the sermon, Archie Brownlee hoarse, urgent ('the beautiful scream', as Bobby Womack put it), 'One more thing I wanna say, one more thing I wanna say', the voice an improvising instrument repeating and exchanging between other voices, listening and responding.

All things are possible

A black-and-white film, blurred and aged, perhaps from the 1950s, the Swan Silvertones on stage, a sparse backing of bass and guitar, five men in light suits, four grouped around a microphone on a stand; to their left, standing alone, Claude Jeter, tall, angular, his glasses and eerie body language – head and body inclined forward, knees bending pressed together, torso twisting, arms raising slowly as if wings preparing to strike, as if guiding the long sustains of his falsetto as they glide through the air, his voice bird-light over the thick syrup harmonies of the quartet, tones entwined in movement like Percy Grainger's 'Free Music' for theremins, all slow, calm; one of the other singers drifting away from the group, a shouter, sings away from either microphone as if in some other place, comes close to Jeter who as if unconscious of his presence, as if picking up stray voices from the aether, tilts the microphone to one side to pick up the voice of this new companion to his solitude; now they converse, the rough voice and the smooth, microphone passing between the two – 'Did you ever meet him?' – 'I met him one morning' – 'Ohhh' – 'Listen' – 'My soul' – 'My soul …' – 'was feeling bad' – 'feeling so bad' – 'Let me tell you about my heart' – 'my heart'; they drop to their knees, the shouter laying his hand on Jeter's shoulder in consolation – 'it was heavy laden' – 'He lifted my burden' – 'not tomorrow but …' – and the instruments stop – 'right now' – 'right now Lord' – 'my soul is glad' – Jeter's six-note melisma on 'glad' the most exquisite faint line rising up to an almost inaudible 'Yes it is' hovering close to the top of his range – 'That's why I can stand here tonight and tell you that …' – 'all things' – 'things' – the words separated out from their sense into fragments as the group becomes one-voice speaker of five mouths – 'are possible with God' – 'if you will only believe.'

Sounding the warning

One morning I was awakened by all the kids upstairs running to the window because of a sound outside that was so piercing it was paralysing. It was revealed to me a few weeks later that it was Gabriel sounding the warning. This was the angel of Jesus standing on his right side, and that Gabriel is the spirit of sound and strength. The sound lasted for five minutes. Everything will happen fast so be ready.
    ALBERT AYLER, To Mr. Jones – I Had a Vision, The Cricket: Black Music in Evolution, 1969

The titles given by Albert Ayler to compositions he recorded between 1964 and 1965 – *Spirits, Spiritual Unity, Holy Holy, Spirits Rejoice, Witches and Devils, Ghosts, Angels, Prophet, Bells* – envision music as mediumistic, incantatory, a channel of communication through to the unearthly. As Ayler told Valerie Wilmer: 'We can get a divine harmony or a divine rhythm that would be beyond what they used to call harmony.' In the velocity and depth of his tone and his capacity to move away in sudden flights of freedom from the orthodoxies of musical rules there was an atmosphere of possession yet also the ecstasies and sadness of the African American church, its message of deliverance from cruelties of life on earth. 'The real, breathtaking power of gospel singing cannot be understood as anything less than the ecstatic shout of a soul set free at last,' Viv Broughton has written. 'It's not necessarily a pleasurable experience for the uninitiated. Even a childhood steeped in the rites of the gospel church won't always prepare you for the upset created by a certain song or a certain singer at an uncertain moment. For an outsider coming upon the dramatic fervour of gospel unprepared, the disturbance can be utterly overwhelming.'

  In 1964, Ayler recorded a selection of spirituals with pianist Call Cobbs, bass player Henry Grimes and drummer Sunny Murray. Gospel was the well-kept secret of African American music at that time, the voices of Archie Brownlee, Delois Barrett Campbell, R. H. Harris, Julius Cheeks, Claude Jeter and Inez Andrews little known beyond the sanctified circuit, despite being the foundation of the soul. These were voices that inhabited the body to a point beyond its corporeal limits, screaming to the spirit, rising to exaltation. Ayler inhabited the saxophone in the same way, bursting through its mechanics and materiality to otherness.

It was as if all the individual acts of instrumental subversion in jazz – from Bubber Miley, Joe 'Tricky Sam' Nanton, Rex Stewart and Cootie Williams of the Duke Ellington Orchestra onwards – had now found a form through which their true meaning was understood.

3 COLLECTIVE SUBJECTIVITIES 1

FIGURE 3.1 Drawing by Ross Lambert.

'We, all of us, wish to rescue, via memory, each fragment of life that suddenly comes back to us, however unworthy, however painful it may be. And the only way to do this is to set it down in writing.' These words, the beliefs of a barely sketched central character in Enrique Vila-Matas's novel, *Bartleby & Co*, are contentious enough for me to consider them as a truth (even though they raise insoluble questions, particularly on the point of writing). Vila-Matas's narrator is engaged in a pursuit of the No, a literature of not writing, of books that were never written by writers who became immobilized by theory, or waiting for the right conditions, or any number of other obstructions that prevented successive books from following a promising debut.

Improvised music is also a version of the No. Fragments of life are given licence to escape without trace, even though they may be among the most affecting moments of beauty or the most complete communication within a group that the player will ever experience. Their transience infuses them with meaning. Can they then be written, as recollection, a Proustian recovery of lost time? My experience as an improviser and writer is not conclusive but there seems to me a point to engaging in collective, or at least shared, writing about the experiencing of improvisation.

This is because improvised music is a collective experience, a making event that can only devolve into a single viewpoint by losing the provisional character of its origination. The problem is that most players don't actually want to write about playing and if they do, they tend to be flattering or maybe just disarmingly polite and positive. Evan Parker has made the point that most musicians are diplomats. Unlike solitary artists, they have to 'live' with each other. But revelations only unfold when thoughts of the personal are put aside in order to discuss feelings from within the maelstrom. These might include reactions to problems perceived to be either inside or outside, or moments of opening up, fracture, indecision, points of unpleasantness or pleasure, feeling lost, feeling completely absorbed, technical incompatibilities, ethical questions and so on. I have tried this exercise before, with mixed results, and yet I believe it has potential as a way of uncovering the drift of thought and action, particularly the oscillation between conscious awareness of group activity, a highly concentrated sense of self and the repercussions of external forces and other time frames, all of which contribute to the generation of a music.

Asked to take part in a series called Necessary Praxis by Matthew Waters I thought of nothing other than playing, even though the organizer, the venue and the musicians were unknown to me. The concert took place on 29 May 2012 at Servant Jazz Quarters, Dalston, London, a street-level bar with a basement room just big enough to accommodate a small group and audience. The members of the group invited by Waters were as follows: Jennifer Allum – violin; Adam Linson – double bass; Marjolaine Charbin – piano interior; myself – laptop, steel guitar, flute, percussion. Not all the members of the quartet had met (though Jennifer and Marjolaine had played together previously).

FIGURE 3.2 Drawing by Geoff Winstone, Servant Jazz Quarters, Collective subjectivities & Necessary Praxis, 31 May 2012.

What struck me after we played was the possibility of trying this experiment in dialogue. All members of the group were obviously thoughtful people dedicated to improvisation. The evening had been a success in that everybody – players and audience – listened intently and responded warmly. The music had thrown up some deeply affecting passages and yet left enough unresolved problems or questions to promise a revealing debate. I asked all the participants to contribute a short text, and also invited a member of the audience – Steve Beresford – to add his observations as an experienced (and honest) listener and practitioner. In addition I have added three drawings that were given to me afterwards, one by guitarist Ross Lambert, the others by designer Geoff Winston. Both of them attend concerts and draw. This is a reflection of the intimacy that typifies these small occasions but also indicative of a close relationship between listening intently and the act of drawing. The listening realm of the body responds along with the moving hand and its marks.

Jennifer Allum

Tuesday night was a challenge. I had been playing with the cellist Ute Kanngiesser since 9.00 am that day and I was perhaps a little 'talked out' when I arrived at Servant Jazz Quarters. Moving from playing with someone I do lots of playing with, directly to playing in a quartet of which two of the members I had not heard play before was an invigorating transition. My memory two days after the event was that in both sets we were creating layers of textures and that these were fairly static – perhaps even without much direction? This seemed to be a bit stylish, perhaps. When I did find myself contributing to this – *going along with it* – I was trying to stop myself because it didn't seem very constructive. David, I thought you were also contributing and disrupting in equal measure, and I sensed less resistance from Marjolaine and Adam. That might have been partly because of how we were seated and where the amplifiers were pointing. What was happening around me was leading me into some more known ways of playing, that is, not *really* improvising. Not doing this and trying to find another response I found a bit frustrating in this context as I wasn't sure where to go. After another session of playing, post Necessary Praxis, it also struck me that something is shifting in my playing right now, probably as a result of various things I've been thinking about. This is making most situations trickier than 'normal', but which I see as being the right situation for me as an improviser.

David Toop

At some deep level I believe I am still terrified of performing. There it sits as a background anxiety during the process of packing equipment or in the urge to prepare materials for playing, yet at the moment of sitting expectantly before an equally expectant audience there is no feeling of uncertainty or nervousness, only a calm desire to find out what can happen, even if there is humiliation on the way. Perhaps humiliation is invited, in that I notice a lack of preparation in myself, no longer taking necessary care of the devices I use, sometimes not packing the right cables, always looking for a set-up that can fail.

    I think this is an issue of control and what I noticed about our two sets was that control, the conflicting desire to apply it and shed it, rose up as a spectre repeatedly. Its influence lurked, an insidious presence that never really allowed us to release certain gestures or move too far from (or conversely, too far inside) each other's range. The range of pitch in which it's possible to operate is often very narrow in improvisation. You have to really know your instrument and have complete technical control in order not to play the wrong thing. What is the wrong thing? Maybe an embarrassingly obvious interval, a series of steps that is risibly familiar, a sound that lacks conviction or shoots into empty space with too much force, a motif repeated once too often.

I sensed an immediate closeness with Marjolaine's piano, some overlap or pleasurable confusion at times (which implies a relinquishment of control, so that 'my' sound may easily be absorbed by another or colonize another). When sounds become so similar that they can't be distinguished or identified as belonging to an 'owner', the convention is to marvel and there is a sensual release in giving up the responsibility of the self. But there must be conflict in this relinquishment, and struggle, as the boundaries of the self seem to lose definition. The vanity of 'doing well' in public is lost in the ambiguous source of a sound that has become nobody's property, nobody's child. Besides, this describes a kind of death, and there is not much vanity in death.

Variations of touch identify a source. In the beautiful cloudiness of the piano's interior voice, its subtle rising and mysterious (how is it done – I want to see?) emissions, there is exactly the right amount of restraint, a delicacy of touch that may seem like nothing but imposes a huge strain on the body, on touch and concentration. The smallest slip will unleash an earthquake.

But there was luxuriance in the piano as well, and a ghostliness, and so the danger of settling into roles – piano and electronics creating atmosphere, violin free to soliloquize within this field of potentiality, double bass given the familiar job of messenger supportively running between the underworld and the sibyl, the pit and the birds. One aspect of the quartet that I enjoyed was its understated refusal of those roles, not that they were refused all the time but a tension came up early on. There was some hint of a No and by the second set the tension generated by the No turned into an intensity that belied the quiet, respectful (too respectful?) nature of the music.

One agent of instability I was trying out was a combination of the Looper audio effect in Ableton Live software and a fairly complex distortion plugin, using a contact microphone fixed onto the steel guitar body. This was plugged directly into the laptop, with the normal guitar output plugged into the mixer. In theory, this would allow me to move between two different sounds from the same instrument. A malfunction somewhere in the chain made each link very volatile, and there is a lot to be said for volatility, the enemy of good taste and delicate restraint.

I was on the edge of feedback and pushing that without ever wanting it to be dominant or destructive. By its nature, feedback is always rising towards escalation and disorder so even the faintest signs of its presence are particularly disturbing, never quite safe or settled. There were long moments when I was happy for it to sit there, as a kind of background threat. Not a hostile threat but more a nagging reminder that the music could overbalance.

What is balance, anyway? In cinema, for example, I am drawn to films that suffer from imperfections, anomalies, ill-considered decisions that ruin a potential masterpiece. I believe we could have been a wonderfully balanced quartet and congratulated ourselves for that ability to locate perfection in unfamiliarity. But caution can be felt like a halo around every action and so the caution of balance is overpowered by the caution of withholding. I take this as a form of generosity, an understanding that perfect balance is a little bit precious and that it makes no sense for four people who have never played together or discussed music to immediately achieve balance in an instant romance.

I can sense early on in the first set, for example, that Jenny and I might differ on a number of issues. Whether I'm right or wrong doesn't matter because that thought influences my playing. As is often the case, the amplification situation is all wrong and so there's a sensation of presenting yourself in public wearing the clothes of another, so ill-fitting, in such bad taste that you want to protest, this isn't the real me! Years ago I might have been intimidated by that feeling. Now I enjoy it. Difference is vital to all dynamic relationships and I enjoy what I hear as the clarity and decisiveness of Jenny's playing, even though I suspect she is finding some difficulty in engaging with what I'm doing. The expectation is that improvisation should form itself quickly but there is too much complexity here to be resolved into unity without first being lost. Friction hovers as a presence, like sandpaper waiting for a smooth surface. The friction is a subjectivity but also rises up through the music and encourages other abrasive incidents. Looper is throwing out unpredictable bursts of garbage from my laptop, very loud, and these feel to me like explosions of Tourette's, obscenities breaking out through pressure, reactions to pent up energy. I can understand that they might feel like 'mistakes', incompetence, bouts of aggression, but they pierce a surface that is asking to remain calm.

At one point Adam plays fast arco bass in a high register and I go with him, on flute, playing for a moment a kind of free jazz that I've spent my life rejecting (and this way of playing, fast high register, sounds particularly bad on flute – hysterical hyperventilation). Jenny immediately stops playing, as if one door has opened and another slammed shut. I feel she is right to do so. So many interpretations were possible in that second (and here is why improvisation is so difficult – because it raises questions that have no definitive answer yet demand to be answered promptly despite the urgent need to focus on musical imperatives). The questions that may have run through my mind in that second: Is her withdrawal a personal slight against me; musical censure; a gesture of distaste or weariness; a dramatic intervention (of sudden absence) or decision of structuring? None of that matters. Whatever motivated her snap decision to stop, perhaps a mixture of some or all of those possibilities, the listening effect is structural: a sudden surge is mirrored by a sudden emptying.

In a slightly perverse way, this is exhilarating. Years ago, most players would tend to follow a consensus, so the music would rise and fall (or just rise and rise) as if held on strings by an invisible manipulator. Younger players can be wary of this internal simplicity, knowing from historical example its tendency to denial, its evasion of the difficulties of finding and keeping a wavelength. Sometimes the decision to stop acts as a turning point in much the same way that a tiny incident can act as a turning point in a sport like tennis. The same is true of the decision to start. There was a point in the first set when we all stopped. This is generally the cue for players to gradually look up, smile at each sheepishly and agree to finish. Pleasantly civilized as this is, it's also deeply irritating and predictable. Somehow our silence lingered as a necessary act of stepping away from all that we had found, an extended event of refusing utterance that crept into the audience as a question, and so the possibility of exchanging smiles of completion became intolerable because if we had indeed withdrawn from each other's sounding then we had to also test this withdrawal against a renewal of relations. That was why I began again and so we seemed to go deeper into something, with more confidence.

There is a style of improvisation that insists on silence within which lines can be marked, a process of impermanent drawing of many hands, the lines clear and relational, always sharp against an empty ground. It moves in an aura of purity and rectitude so invites purism. Although I can enjoy this kind of playing as a listener, it never interested me as a player (that could be because I'm not good enough as a player, but then improvisation should, I believe, allow different levels of aptitude).

I also believe that improvisation can only grow through impurity, even though the identity and continuity of improvisation depends on a degree of purism. It's also about linearity: does the music claim existence as interlocking lines moving in various directions with the same aim (again, like Percy Grainger's free, beatless music for theremins) or does it spread, falter, stop, thicken, disappear into a blurred shadowing of itself?

Somehow the first strategy seems closer to spoken language – as if, this is how we speak among each other – yet the resistance to language, the attempt to shed the specificities of language is always fighting with language. At its most polite, conversation is a waiting game, a counterpoint of speaking and listening, a sequence of solitary voices met with silences and not this simultaneity of speaker/listeners. In an improvisation like this one there are certain questions that might be cleared up just by asking: what's going on? But the questions are too huge – who are you, or why are we doing this? A sex therapist might recommend a conversation when something goes wrong during sex but that doesn't make it easy. Music tells us why we make music, even if that leaves an inexplicable certainty to deal with. I felt conscious that Adam's contributions were very expressive, sensitive and well-timed but also conscious that he had asked if he should use electronics. He seems to have a very gracious nature and so deferred quickly when Matthew suggested it might be too much. I wonder what might have happened if he had insisted. Maybe he felt a little bit frustrated as we played because all sorts of openings presented themselves for the kind of electronic extension of the bass that he uses in recordings. Certainly it would have overbalanced the group even further and then another dynamic would have come into play.

What I often feel during improvisation is the creeping grip of inhibition. Other players have very strong views on what is, and is not, legitimate. Although that slipped into my thoughts from time to time, mostly because I suspected (perhaps entirely without just cause) I was in the company of players who would only use electronic material generated by 'action in the moment', rather than pre-existing audio files, it didn't bother me too much. Holding back, excising, exercising good judgement, adapting to circumstances, daring to cause upset – these are all part of a necessary praxis in improvisation. I felt in good company, able to work around control and its loss, feeling the attention of discerning critical listeners in an atmosphere of intimacy. These are situations in which you learn the most. Sometimes after playing you feel too exhilarated to sleep. On this occasion I felt something more subtle, a growing satisfaction over the following days that we had approached a difficult situation with integrity and discovered the existence of a continuing unknown.

Adam Linson

Perhaps not uncommonly for a group of improvisers who meet and play for the first time, I think the first set primarily explored the social dynamics of the collective interaction; the second set took what we had established as the mode of collective interaction as a starting point from which to explore a wider set of sonic and musical concerns. In reality, I don't think those aspects of group improvisation can be effectively disentangled, but after the fact, different elements can be brought into focus through an analytical lens.

The range of timbres available to the group made for exciting combinations, but I think by the second set, the group was able to move beyond mere combinatorics and into the hazier regions of timbral and harmonic overlaps across instruments – not only from electronic (laptop) to electric (guitar) to electro-acoustic (processed acoustic sources, amplified objects, prepared piano) to acoustic (flute, percussion, violin, double bass), but also into harmonic territories shared in some cases across all the instruments, which at times led to an uncanny sense of sound seemingly coming from everywhere and nowhere.

In the second set, we were able to more effectively extend, support, or provide counterpoint to prevailing moments that in turn became a branching and merging series of developments. This translated into me not always knowing where we were headed, but at the same time giving me the feeling that wherever we were headed was emerging from the total unfolding improvisation and the richness of the immediate moment, as well as the interplay between the two temporal frames. (These may be general features of group improvisation, but it is always nice to experience them during a first encounter). And of course, the substantive material was itself emerging from the interwoven lines and textures being generated by us as individuals and subgroups, which I thought we took more advantage of during the second set, allowing for more subtle polyphony (perhaps some would have called it ambient?).

To get more concrete, a small handful of things I recall: pointillistic high frequencies from prepared piano and laptop, built upon by violin and bass harmonics; pitched percussive bowing by violin and bass

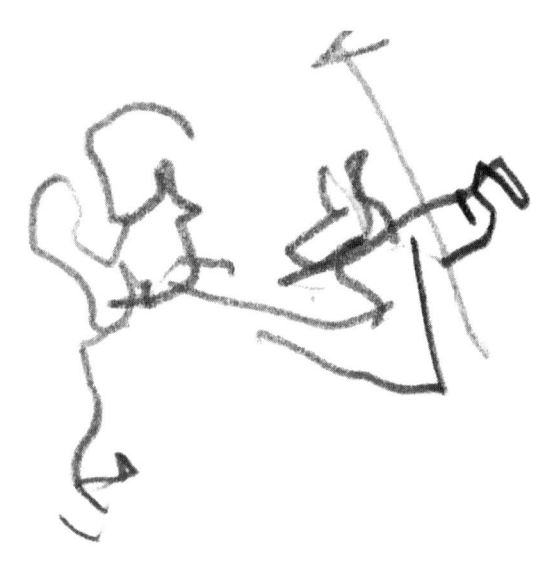

FIGURE 3.3 Drawing by Geoff Winston.

intermingling with the flute; unpitched laptop static with occasional percussive bursts being matched and developed in various ways by the other three instrumentalists; a beautiful contrasting moment with an acoustic gourd shaker. There was also a structurally interesting 'unstable' silence possibly around two-thirds into the first set; the second set closed by transitioning out of an absorbing hypnotic trance that left me unable to identify how long I (we?) had been in that state (and hence, even immediately thereafter, with no clear memory of what had been going on in sonic–musical terms during that time).

Marjolaine Charbin

I generally love talking about improvisation, sharing thoughts and feelings about a performance or a recording from an insider' and a listener's point of view. I am more used to do it spontaneously with my colleagues right after a performance than writing about it though. And on top of that I'm having a language crisis! As a native French speaker new in London I'm having trouble finding my personal voice in English. So please excuse my clumsiness.

The past week after the gig I wasn't available or in the mood for reflection on the performance. And now the details of its development are pretty much faded in my memory but here are the rest, facts and interpretation: I remember two sets, the second longer than I thought, which left me tired but charged with a feeling that something had been done, said, activated. It was the first time that I was using my contact mikes that way, daring to zoom in the piano to micro physical-sonic events, using them as a source in itself, in relation with the metals and woods of the piano. There was the pleasure of discovering the new sounds, as well as the struggle to cope with its limitations.

And the physical tension in my body implied by the sustain of very specific postures kept me awake! There were some accidents – sounds that I would have liked to sustain which transformed too quickly. And some magic with sounds that would appear just like that (or is it my fascination that appears?) that I would follow like a golden thread. I'm always balancing between whether or not to use techniques that are too unpredictable. At the end I just think, 'Let's understand and control the physics as much as I can, and when I can't, welcome the accidents!'

And there was the quartet. The constant negotiation of one's position in the acoustic picture with sometimes this question: What is going on now? Is this question important or not, a symptom of a disruption in my attention, or a way to maintain it? A lot of strings, textures from mild to harsh, bits of melodic activity, electricity, intimacy. Dry and wet sounds. Movement. Stillness. Parts. Stagnation. Explosion. Resonance.

And then it's over, claps, socialisation, feedback, so it really happened!

And the bigger picture, reality: everybody disappears to catch their train, the barmaid is kind enough to serve me a beer at ten past eleven, just after the end of licence time. I'm thinking: London. As the venue is empty, I'm still trying to fix something that is not right in the mechanics of this old upright piano that I just took away to access the strings, remembering the meeting with the instrument a few hours before.

That night I had come earlier to check the piano out, and I realize how lucky I was to have this excuse to be in the venue, on my own, making the space mine, opening myself to the space. In a way the performance started there for me, and at the soundcheck. Even our little stroll round the corner was part of the continuity: it was the meeting with the others. I guess that's what ties me so strongly to the practice of improvisation, it creates these situations where I have to connect deeply with people, places, the physicality of things, the time passing by. Shouldn't we live always like that?

Steve Beresford

I was wondering why I found the performance unsatisfying. It was a group of musicians I like a lot; that's why I was there. But, maybe dynamics were a problem: I'm not referring to David's small fortissimos, more about a general inflexibility – Louis Moholo is a moving drummer because his dynamics are always in flux. It felt like some people had made a big decision to play at a certain dynamic whatever was going on around them.

There were small moments of great beauty. But lots where things didn't seem to gel. Of course, it's possible to create music where 'not gelling' is an organizing principle. I think David and I both probably play stuff like that sometimes. But it wasn't non-gelling music either.

Maybe it was the sound of a band looking for a genre? But it felt as though the sounds were 'underpowered'. Not sure what that means.

A postscript from David Toop

Reading these observations some years after the event I am amused to note the guardedness with which I wrote about the relationship in the group between Jennifer Allum and myself. Since then we have performed together in a number of situations and I have become a great admirer of her playing. The initial wariness has developed into a productive working relationship. This seems to reinforce a general rule: some degree of friction stimulates curiosity and questioning, gently nudging towards further investigation.

4 OVERTURE TO DAWN

Free at last! Free at last!
                                          MARTIN LUTHER KING, 1963

Freedom is relative. 'Almost every moralist in history has praised freedom,' Isaiah Berlin said in the introduction to his celebrated lecture, *Two Concepts of Liberty*. 'Like happiness and goodness, like nature and reality, the meaning of this term is so porous that there is little interpretation that it seems able to resist.' Martin Luther King's famous speech of 1963, given at the steps of the Lincoln Memorial to more than 250,000 civil rights supporters, might be dismissed, a vague and hopeless dreaming destined to be frustrated in the world of humans. But King's speech (some of its most famous lines to some degree improvised after he put aside his script with the encouragement of gospel singer Mahalia Jackson) prophesied a freedom to dream any dream, even equality, following a long historical arc of striving for freedom from slavery and its poisonous consequences. At the beginning of the twentieth century W. E. B. Du Bois had written of the 'dawn of freedom', the work of the nineteenth-century Freedmen's Bureau that 'set up a system of free labour, established a beginning of peasant proprietorship, secured the recognition of black freedmen before courts of law, and founded the free common school in the South'. He also identified freedom's limits in having failed to give land to freed slaves and in failing to 'begin the establishment of good-will between ex-masters and freedmen, to guard its work wholly from paternalistic methods which discouraged self-reliance'.

The freedom of which Du Bois spoke has specific goals – the right of all human beings to sit anywhere in the bus, eat in the same restaurant, to form relationships without censure and to participate in political process – yet it also addresses less tractable areas of human potentiality, the moral dilemmas that open up with a gradual increase in personal and political freedoms, the loss of certitude as restrictive rules are overthrown and boundaries are transgressed, the reluctance or inability of people to change their feelings even though they adjust their outward behaviour. The dream of improvisation is to accomplish all of these goals, thus achieving not only the anarchist hope of equality in government without rulers but also the crafting of a new practice that enables solitary and highly individualistic behaviour within collective action.

A dictionary of shadows and eddies

In the buggining is the woid, in the muddle is the sounddance and thereinofter you're in the unbewised again.
JAMES JOYCE, *Finnegans Wake*

In 1881 the future King George V travelled to Kyoto with his brother Albert. On the first day of their visit they were introduced to the artist Kubota Beisen, a professor at the newly formed Kyoto Art School. After demonstrating various styles of painting on paper spread on the floor, Beisen asked Prince George to dot a sheet of paper with ink as a challenge for the artist to make something of it. In an action called sekiga – in Japan an impromptu painting performed for a guest, often at drinking parties – Beisen transformed the dots into fireflies.

A dictionary of spontaneous actions and gestures would be vast, unthinkable, unfathomable; a compendium of winks, obscene signs, doodles on paper, fragments of whistling, scratching and sighs, the smelling of a scented flower, murders, drunken graffiti, smiles at strangers, seductive movements of the body, acts of stopping and listening, actions endless and slight, some leaving a trace, others enfolded within the constant vanishings of human presence. Beisen's painting of 1881, conserved in the British Museum, is a field of nothingness crossed by the intermittent black flashes of a lightning bug, one trace within this vast, largely meaningless collation.

Such a compendium might also include the pomo style of Chinese painting, literally 'splashing and smearing ink', said to be invented by Wang Mo in the eighth century, 'noted for painting while drunk, by spilling ink onto a piece of silk and finishing the work with a few touches of the brush'. According to philosopher and sinologist François Jullien, Wang Mo would spatter ink onto silk by whipping about his hair. In *The Great Image Has No Form, or On the Nonobject through Painting*, Jullien describes eighth-century Chinese critics and theorists revelling in the Taoist eccentricities of painters such as Zhang Zao:

> Carried away by his natural bent, suddenly overwhelmed by an entire world of thoughts, he brusquely demanded silk from his hosts. He presented quite a spectacle to his entourage: seated, his legs spread, his clothes gaping open, breathing hard, his mind becoming unhinged. The sight of him was as terrifying as 'lightning shooting through the sky' or 'a whirlwind rising up.' The brush 'flies,' ink 'spatters,' as if the hand holding the brush 'will break in two' at any instant. Amid separations and reunions, in confusion and indetermination, strange configurations are suddenly born.

Collaborative spontaneity further complicates the picture. Like sekiga, a kind of game designed to impress a patron or peers, Japanese renga poetry (literally linked poem) constructed a work through collaborative exchange. Each poet would contribute alternate stanzas according to certain rules. Matsuo Bashō, the seventeenth-century poet famous for *The Narrow Road to the Deep North* and his celebrated haiku – 'an ancient pond/the frog jumps in/the splash of water' – was a prominent exponent of haika no renga. *The Kite's Feathers* was a thirty-six stanza renga shared between four poets – Bashō, Kyorai, Bonchō and Fumikuni:

    8. (Bonchō)   Comfortable to wear,
　　　　　　　　　　　His knitted socks.
    9. (Kyorai)   All things
　　　　　　　　　　　Silent:
　　　　　　　　　　　Peace and quiet.
   10. (Bashō)   They see their first village
　　　　　　　　　　　And blow the noon conch.

Similar techniques to sekiga and renga were used by European surrealists in twentieth-century explorations of the unconscious and manipulated chance: visual strategies such as frottage and decalcomania through which existing and accidental textures are given intentionality (extensively used by Max Ernst) and collaborative games, the best known of which is The Exquisite Corpse, in which each person writes part of a line or drawing on a sheet of paper, then folds the paper to conceal their contribution before passing it to the next person who continues the process.

All of these strategies designed to circumvent conscious thought have relevance to improvisation's emphasis on collective spontaneity, yet their illumination of improvisation in music is partial. Already a collective, performative art form in which improvisation and some degree of spontaneity of expression or inspiration are expected in even the most rigid score, music affords glimpses of freedom as a tantalizing, albeit private, subversive and clandestine potentiality. Think, for example, of the piano and its abject role in the barroom, the brothel, the rent party, playing for drinkers, diners, dancers, debauchers, playing through what James Joyce called 'sidereal and tankard time' for customers whose watches were set to the sporting life. The excessive temporal demands of this task and its distracted audience did not encourage qualities of focus or refinement. In his biography of Louis Armstrong, James Lincoln Collier describes the bands that played the early twentieth-century tonks of New Orleans as rough or ratty: a cornet player named Manuel Manette 'reported that at Segretta's the piano and the drums went round the clock'.

From within this fog of temporal oblivion some ruminative, digressive quality was bound to appear in the playing of instruments that could provide their own accompaniment, notably the piano and to a lesser extent the guitar. Think of the reflective atmosphere of pianist Jimmy Yancey's 'Melancholy Blues', recorded in 1951 shortly before his death, the fleeting discords and angular phrasing, the spaces which threaten to open out its calm simplicity into a softly humming resonance (easy to imagine the measured left hand walking its way off the keyboard, pressing against the body of the instrument to feel bass vibrations restless within the wood); then think of Art Tatum's solo performance of 'Moonglow', time out of joint, notes running in liquid torrents down a narrow ravine, their full flood cut off by chords smashed into tightly compressed zigzag patterns, no single thought allowed to rest unperturbed for more than a few seconds. The claustrophobic retreat of the after-hours club, its melancholy reversal of the working day, dark into light, and the obsessional battleground of the jam session are embedded within both extremes: Yancey's minimalism and Tatum's excess. 'Sometimes Art would go uptown to Harlem after a full night's and morning's work on the Street,' wrote Barry Ulanov,

> arriving at an after-hours place at, say, five or five-thirty A.M. He would look around the room eagerly, peering beneath the half-closed lid of his one good eye. He would find somebody to play with, somebody unusually courageous and similarly foolish. For Art played for keeps. These were battles of music, and their winner was always Art Tatum, who slaughtered his opponent with unmatchable keyboard demonstrations.

At his most flashy, Tatum clogged the outpouring of his music with quotations and interpolations; like a 1940s Keith Jarrett he harangued the drinkers whose chatter could be heard from the shadows. Common to both pianists, markedly different as they were, is the suspicion that left to their own devices away from the bear pits and booze chapels they would push the music beyond popular song and the blues into the unknown.

There is no question that some of the more adventurous musicians and player-composers were drawn to a music that was free from head arrangements, notation and leaders. In 1938 Charles Ives recorded a number of improvisations on the piano. They are very short – each less than a minute; if the sound quality were not so poor they could easily pass for a piano improvisation recorded three decades later. 'In his autobiographical *Memos*,' writes Frank R. Rossiter,

> Ives traced several of his innovative techniques back to 'boy's fooling' that he had done under his father's direction. For example, some of his dissonant chords (especially those used for their rhythmic, rather than their harmonic, effect) derived from his using the piano to practice the drum parts for his father's band and his discovery that certain dissonant chords – having 'little to do with the harmony of the piece' but 'used only as sound-combinations as such' – provided the best 'takeoff' of the drums.

Almost exactly one year before Ives recorded his improvisations at the Melotone Recording Company of New York, Django Reinhardt found himself being coerced into solo improvising by Gramophone/HMV as part of a licensing agreement with Swing label owner Charles Delauney. These tracks were demanded by the British wing of the company: fourteen specified songs and two guitar solos. Hughes Panassié, the pope of jazz as he styled himself, is quoted as saying:

> Django did not want to fulfil this demand. He had never made recordings like this and did not know what to play. Finally, Delaunay said to him: 'You only have to improvise something, it will surely go well.' Django abruptly decided what to play and nodded to the engineers he was prepared. He asked me to take out my watch and signal to him when he was approaching the third minute of the recording, so he could ready himself to finish his interpretation at the appropriate time. And thus was recorded this admirable solo, entitled, justifiably, 'Improvisation', which escaped from the frameworks of jazz and into the Andalusian Gitan spirit.

Afterwards, the people in the studio persuaded him not to listen back to what he had done since that would ruin the wax master for pressing.

Reinhardt may have been resistant to recording these two improvisations without prior warning, but in general he was notorious for his reluctance to conform to studio timetables or to make any preparations for a recording session. Coleridge Goode, bass player with the Joe Harriott Quintet (the first group to play free improvised music in Britain), recorded with Reinhardt at Abbey Road Studios in London in 1946. According to Reinhardt biographer Michael Dregni, Goode was amazed by Reinhardt's laissez faire attitude: 'It was very difficult – almost impossible – to organise Django. ... We didn't have any sort of pre-rehearsals; it was all just put together in the studio. ... It was all head arrangements and such. But the musicians were good musicians, and this is what good musicians can do.'

These improvisation by Ives and Reinhardt are not miraculously unidentifiable. They are of their time and place. Reinhardt is unmistakeably Reinhardt, playing what a virtuoso guitarist of French Romany origins might be expected to play if sitting among friends, even though it recalls the story of his refusal at the age of twelve to conclude a polka with its customary crescendo, playing 'with a drawn knife' as they said in the dance halls, according to Dregni, 'unreeling variations on the well-worn melody, pulling notes out of thin air, bending the song to his wishes'. Both of his improvisations from the Paris 1937 session are extended introductory cadenzas, comparable to the alap section of an Indian raga or the unaccompanied cadenzas with which jazz soloists sometimes conclude a piece. The extent to which these could become almost works in themselves, glimpses of less formalized music, can be heard in John Coltrane's lengthy cadenzas to various versions of Billy Eckstine's ballad, 'I Want To Talk About You'. The studio version heard on *Soultrane* (1958) passes in moments, gently indicative of different directions in which the song might be taken, whereas a live version released on *Live At Birdland* (1963) is famously protracted, over three minutes long, almost a complete solo improvisation in itself.

Sparrow music

Musicians often talk of 'hearing' a non-existent music, the music that would exist if human society became capable of rising to its better nature, if the transactional effects of commercial music were to disappear, if all the academic, proprietary and monetary classifications would evaporate. Evan Parker tells the story of Numar Lubin, the proprietor of Nimbus Records. Lubin lived in the same apartment block in 1930s Paris as Sidney Bechet. He could hear Bechet practice scales and arpeggios on his soprano saxophone, then finish up each session with strange animal noises. One day Lubin asked Bechet, why the strange noises? Bechet replied: 'You know, I sometimes wonder if what they call music is the real music.' In 2012, saxophonist Wayne Shorter told Larry Applebaum about a similar incident – Miles Davis had asked Shorter some searching questions as they stood together on the bandstand in the middle of a set. 'Some of the comments he would say to me while Herbie's soloing and all that. He'd ask me, "You ever feel like playing music that doesn't sound like music?" Then the other time, "Can you play as if you don't know how to play?".'

Until other evidence comes to light, these half-heard dreams of free improvisation are shadows: only second-hand accounts and momentary fragments of hard evidence. Nina Parish, a French studies scholar of text and image, makes a similar point about Belgian-born artist Henri Michaux. Since his death in 1984 many of his writings and drawings have been republished and exhibited, but his musical activities, most of which seem to have been untutored and intuitive improvisation, are lost:

> Michaux's passion for music is underscored in two articles included in *Passages: Premières Impressions*, parts of which were first published

in 1949, and *Un certain phénomène qu'on appele musique*, which was first published in 1958 as a preface to a music encyclopaedia. He owned a piano and apparently enjoyed composing and improvising for hours on end. Unfortunately, there exist no recordings of these compositions.

In 1949, Michaux wrote of making music as a strategy for confronting limits, a deeply private physical meditation capable of generating self-knowledge along with insights into the nature of materials, time and the senses:

> Playing, and my fingers playing with my ignorance … tired of pictures, I play to make smoke. … As the night progresses and my self goes further into the sounds … I used to think the skin of a drum was necessary. Now I see that's not true. Any old wood would do, as long as your fingers your hand can drum on it. Fast, faster, less fast, slowly, very slowly. Your whole life concentrated into this … not to decide really to make human music and especially not composer's music, and especially not Western music rather make sparrow music.'

As well as piano, he played an African drum, a broken sansa and perhaps, as the previous passage suggests, any material that came to hand. Why do I play my drum, he asked himself: 'To break through your dams/To cut through the rising wave of the new preventers/To auscultate myself/To take my pulse.' What he produced through these experiments in listening and repetition was a poor music without pretensions, a rough music (and rough music, a social noise of meat cleavers, pots and pans was, after all, an ancient vernacular tradition of streets and villages). 'It was not discourse. Nothing was joined. They were orphan sounds, musical rags,' he wrote of the 'cawing noises', broken sounds, refusals and the badly set tongue of the thumb piano that would 'hum and remain humming and doubtful'. His way of playing was to explore each part of the instrument, listening not only to each micro-particle but also to its embedded history of 'grieving and furious' slaves, hearing each sound unrelated to the other: 'I wandered among them.'

At the heart of Michaux's work was gesture, a liberating 'new language, spurning the verbal'; drawing, painting, poetry, music all fell into this living practice of imaginary alphabets, marks, signs and actions in search of a continuum: 'Later the signs, certain signs. Signs speak to me. I would gladly draw them, but a sign is also a stop sign. And at this juncture there is still something I desire above all else. A *continuum*. A murmur without end, like life itself, the thing that keeps us going. ... I want my markings [*mes tracés*] to be the very phrasing [*le phrase*] of life, but supple, deformable, sinuous.'

New World Two Worlds

Scene 1: black-and-white film, 1961, but redolent of an era long passed, a typically staged after-hours scene, an empty club on West 52nd Street, the cigarette girl with acting ambitions, the doorman, a 'for real jam session,' as the narrator confides, 'music that can never be duplicated because, well because it's pure improvisation'. Pianist Johnny Guarnieri, bassist Milt Hinton, guitarist Barry Galbraith and drummer Cozy Cole slip easily into a slow blues. In walks The Hawk, Coleman Hawkins, his indomitable tenor sound taking charge with a forthright cadenza leading into 'Lover Man'. The tempo quickens for 'Sunday', then a trumpet blasts from the doorway. 'Hey, look who just blew in,' says our tour guide, 'Little Jazz himself, my man, Roy Eldridge.'

This kind of informal small group swing is overlooked in the discourse of free jazz. Ornette Coleman was an exception. As explained in his liner note to *This Is Our Music* he conceived the music of the quartet with Charlie Haden, Don Cherry and Ed Blackwell as a synthesis of three periods that historians like to keep apart: collective interaction in early jazz, progressive harmony and melody in modern jazz and solos based on riffs in the swing era. To experience Eldridge's intensity is to hear not only a reminder of the way Louis Armstrong imposed his unabashed brilliance on the uneven musicianship of the 1920s but also pre-echoes of free trumpet players like Donald Ayler and Mongezi Feza. Reputedly a competitive man who even challenged his hero Rex Stewart to a cutting contest, Eldridge blew like a boxer – as sportswriter A. J. Liebling might have defined him, the type who would consider retreat a form of moral abdication. A fierce tone, body swagger and pugnacious colonization of the solo space in this clip illustrate the imperatives of small jazz clubs, their stages too small to accommodate expansive ensembles and all the formalities they carried with them (though such clubs made it easier for musicians of all races and ethnicities to share a bandstand without getting arrested or murdered). Small group swing was dependent on extrovert improvisation, yet it was a close-listening music, competitive yet cooperative, exuberant yet intimate. Though Eldridge was a master of chord changes, such niceties fade to a barely discernable schema at the back of his mind as the trumpet rasps and screams its effects over an unrelenting pulse.

Interviewing Roy Eldridge for *A History of Jazz in America*, published in 1959, jazz writer Barry Ulanov made a surprising discovery: 'He's interested in the possibility of free improvisation. "Clyde Hart and I made a record like that once. We decided in front that there'd be no regular chords, we'd announce no keys, stick to no progressions. Only once I fell into a minor key; the rest was free, just blowing. And man, it felt good"'. Eldridge recorded with pianist Clyde Hart from 1939 to 1945, the year of Hart's death from tuberculosis. No available recording seems to match this description so we can only surmise what it may have sounded like. In Paris, during an early 1950s European tour with the Benny Goodman Sextet, Eldridge recorded a piano solo called 'Improvisation'. The casual air of the piece suggests that this charming miniature of Harlem stride piano was named 'Improvisation' because nothing better came to mind, yet there are hints (the faintest touch of Thelonious Monk's solos perhaps), almost imperceptible breaks in the tempo, neoclassical flourishes and a witty cadenza, that reveal Eldridge's broad sensibilities.

All these tentative steps – Debussy's *Syrinx*, Hannah Hoch with her saucepan lid and toy gun, Percy Grainger's *Free Music*, Takamizawa Michinao's sound constructors, Sidney Bechet's practice routine, the scraps of improvisation recorded by Charles Ives and Django Reinhardt, the lost recording by Roy Eldridge – have been tracked as if following the faint trail of a fugitive – the paucity of signs a reminder that there were strong social, technical and professional reasons for holding back from Coleridge Goode's inference: musicians already know how to improvise without a score, an instruction, a leader; if they found the promise of liberation enticing – 'Man, it felt good,' said Eldridge – or even if they found a tiny opening into what Bechet imagined to be the hidden 'real' music – then what was stopping them? The gangsters who kept a hand in the clubs and record companies ('cockroach capitalism', as Frank Kofsky called it in *Black Nationalism and the Revolution In Music*)? Those audience members who preferred drinking to thinking, who wanted both genius and dependability twice nightly? Even the prospect of success, which brings with it the prospect of a downfall?

Sitting on the telephone

Scene 2: black-and-white film, 1964, the short man walks to a piano stool piled high with telephone directories. To his left, a bass player, to his right, a drummer. The short man sits down on the books and launches into a brisk passage of Harlem stride, leaving tantalizing moments of silence after four and eight bars as if inviting in his accompanists. Bassist Eddie Calhoun and drummer Kelly Martin ready themselves. At each entry point Errol Garner changes direction unpredictably, throwing in boogie-woogie, discords, back to stride, then florid escapades along the length of the piano keyboard. Calhoun leans on his bass, looks at the audience and raises his hand as if to say, who knows what this guy will do next? No doubt the routine was honed over years, yet it confirms the consistency of Garner's approach to improvisation from the beginning of his career to the end. Finally with a hammering of left-hand chords the trio jumps feet first and presto into Fats Waller's 'Honeysuckle Rose' as if all that wilfully erratic business at the beginning has been a hysteria show on the rooftop ended by a dive into the safety blanket. His face is shown in close-up, perpetually smiling mouth opening and closing as if speaking, at times actually voicing an audible 'yeah' (Garner was famous for singing along as he played), eyes opening and closing, turning upwards or towards the audience when open but looking down at the keyboard when they are shut. The expression is extraordinary, simultaneously a glaze of intense mental and physical concentration mixed with flickering puckish expressions that speak outwardly, to other listeners, of pleasure. Building on a hypothesis developed in the early 1950s, psychologist D. W. Winnicott asked the question: 'If play is neither inside nor outside, where is it?' He was speaking of play in the general sense – not musical, specifically of play in young children – but to hear Garner (and many other improvisers) is to feel drawn towards the same question. 'Playing is inherently exciting and precarious,' Winnicott wrote. 'This characteristic derives *not* from instinctual arousal but from the precariousness that belongs to the interplay in the child's mind of that which is subjective (near hallucination) and that which is objectively perceived (actual, or shared reality).' For Winnicott, this third area of play – a place which expands outwards into creative life and into the entire cultural life of humanity – was a potential space between the individual and the environment. Improvisation, similarly, is not simply joyful and instinctive, nor is it grounded entirely in the world of things. To play; where is it? Play's oscillation always lies between.

The apartment sessions

The first hard evidence of free improvisation comes from another after-hours session, again from that musically self-contained item of furniture, the piano. Born in Pittsburgh in 1921, Errol Garner was a musical prodigy with an instinctive grasp of piano technique. Mary Lou Williams, another pianist whose solo improvisations of the 1940s – stops, starts, digressions, tangents, deliberations, inferences, quickening, lingering, asides, cuts – were one small step from freedom, tried to teach him the rudiments of music but quickly gave up when she realized how uninterested he was and how little he needed them. As his career developed he worked in New York, listening to bebop in the clubs, eventually meeting a Danish jazz enthusiast, Timme Rosenkrantz, who loved American jazz but despised racial prejudice. Known informally as the jazz baron, Rosenkrantz was the son of a writer who speculated that the two Danish noblemen – Frederik Rosenkrantz and Knud Guildenstern (or Gyldenstieme) – who visited England in 1592 may have met William Shakespeare and so ended up as characters in *Hamlet*. Regular late-night and all-night sessions were convened in the apartment Rosenkrantz shared with singer Inez Cavanaugh on West 46th Street. Many musicians passed through – Lucky Thompson, Don Byas, Stuff Smith, Thelonious Monk, Duke Ellington, Willie 'The Lion' Smith, Slam Stewart – and Rosenkrantz would record these informal sessions onto sixteen-inch acetate discs.

In 1944 Garner was recorded playing either alone or for his peers, both situations releasing him from the pressure of pleasing an audience or club owner. These apartment sessions, released in 1953 by Blue Note on a series of ten-inch LPs entitled *Overture To Dawn*, eavesdrop on a musician of self-taught brilliance stretching out into reverie, channelling Fats Waller, then in a moment's turn braking tempo, falling quiet, loosening fingers to spill out florid arpeggios and chordal melodies. The direction of the music changes constantly, though without Art Tatum's oppressive need to impress. Tatum's presence is felt, of course, as is Claude Debussy's, yet the music feels relaxed, expansive, playful, its relation to popular songs always oblique as if operating under a repertoire of disguises. As Alun Morgan points out in his liner notes to the reissued

Apartment Sessions, Rosenkrantz's acetates gave playing times of over ten minutes to each piece, so Garner's improvising imagination was, for the period, relatively unrestricted by durational constraints, even less so by commercial imperatives. Each idea (rhythmic, harmonic, melodic, stylistic or sonic) contains within itself other ideas. The music is audible thought; as Garner imagines a possibility he changes course rather than suppressing it.

By the following year, Garner's 'Laura' began a highly successful sequence of releases, the best known of which is 'Misty', recorded in 1954. Solo records such as *Afternoon of An Elf* from 1955 (the sly reference in its title to *Prélude à l'Après Midi d'un Faun* making Garner's admiration for Debussy explicit) were little different in their approach to the acetates made in Rosenkrantz's apartment. To contemporary ears they may recall the background piano rarely heard these days in restaurants; from jazz writers they draw out a certain prose style: 'waterfall arabesques', 'impressionism', 'dreamy meanderings'. In the Free Improvisation series of his blog, *A Shot In the Dark*, Matt Endahl quotes Leonard Feather: 'Night after night [Garner] came back [to the Rosenkrantz apartment] playing long, rambling ad lib concertos. … Here is a man sitting down at a piano and, to all intents and purposes, playing to and for himself, quietly, contemplatively and with a serene beauty.' The problem for Garner as a historic marker in the evolution of free improvisation is that his music, no matter how innovative for its time, sounds personable, witty and accessible, vacillating between passages that are somewhat antique, others that expand from urgent rhythm into elaborate flights of exotic romance.

Another set of recordings made in 1944 by Timme Rosenkrantz on his precious acetates are closer to what we would now regard as 'experimental' free improvisation. Violinist Stuff Smith was a veteran of the swing band scene of West 52nd Street. Satirizing that fatal tendency of music critics to discuss musicians through exhaustive lists of comparisons and influences, Boris Vian wrote:

> We might ask ourselves if it is even possible to find one musician who has totally original ideas, sound, phrasing, attack, inflexion, or any of the attributes that would constitute the dream improviser. We could possibly cite Johnny Hodges, Stuff Smith, Harry Carney, Art Tatum. … I am sure that even this shortlist could be the subject of many arguments.

Smith was born in 1909, taught violin by his father who was also a boxer, and fell under the spell of Louis Armstrong. He was a heavy drinker, by all accounts a tricky man to get along with; his rhythmic fluency was a constant but the sentiment could be elegant or rough, dependant upon circumstances – trembling with pathos or slashing bow across string like a sword cut. There is a strange trio with Sun Ra, recorded in either 1948 or early 1949 in Ra's Chicago apartment. According to biographer John F. Szwed, Ra had recently acquired an Ampex tape recorder using paper-backed tape. Drummer Tommy 'Bugs' Hunter played brushes on a telephone book, Ra played piano with one hand, Hammond Solovox organ with the other, its monophonic theremin-like notes adding a queasy stratospheric counterpoint to Stuff Smith's violin.

A habitué of Rosenkrantz's apartment in New York, Stuff Smith recorded a series of duets there in 1944 with a pianist named Robert Crum. A piece called 'New World aka Two Worlds' exists in eight cuts, though some of these seem continuations. Perhaps it was a suite of some sort, moving through what might be considered neoclassical sections followed by episodes which are by turns rhapsodic, sentimental, whimsical, comic and violent. Some melodies are played in unison and clearly there is preparation involved; some sections swing like a barrelhouse band though nothing ever sounds quite as it should. The two seem well-matched: a wild swing section winds down into what might be an attractive closing cadenza but then they exchange percussive single notes, Smith plucking strings as if to say to Crum, we're not stopping there. Crum mimics him, then crashes the keyboards, they chase each other to arrive at a destination that could be the climax of a two-handkerchief weepie at the cinema. Despite the poor quality of the acetates from which the transcriptions have been made, their music gives the thrilling sense of eavesdropping on two musicians who are challenging each other, listening hard, following and leading, working with a freedom that would have been impossible anywhere other than this almost private space.

What's wrong with Mrs Upjohn? (nothing, in its most violent form)

Scene 3: black-and-white film, 1937, an exotic nightclub. Chico Marx is playing the piano, Harpo is conducting the orchestra, tuxedo shirt front poking out of his jacket at a crazy angle. With the bad guys' entry Chico makes a getaway using the piano as a springboard. Harpo realizes his only safe place is in front of an audience. He takes over the piano stool and starts in on Rachmaninov's C-sharp minor prelude. Certain notes in the lower register prove troublesome. Every time they throw up a discord he peers closely at the offending keys, hitting them repeatedly, playing harder and harder until chunks fall off the piano. He slams with both fists at either end of the keyboard, plays faster and faster, keys fly up into the air like jumping bugs. Finally there is a reverberant crash as the piano expires in final collapse, disgorging the inner frame onto the floor as if an elephant has given birth to a giant egg slicer. Harpo pulls out the frame, turns it on its edge and plays it like a harp. The mood becomes momentarily serene (*A Day At the Races*, 1937).

Scene 4: Corny-Gie Hall, a bald conductor in formal wear standing against a lurid sunburst backdrop:

> Gweetings music lovers, heheheh. First, we will hear a waltz, witten by Johann Stwauss [boink, dickey bow shirt front flips onto face, exposing bare stomach and bright yellow underwear]. Huhuhuh, and as we hear the wythmic stwains of the haunting wefwain, listen to the wippling whythm of the woodwinds as it wolls awound and awaound … and it comes out here [beough, shirt front flips up again, skreaagh]. Huhuhuh. (*Merrie Melodies: A Corny Concerto*, 1943)

Formal wear with white tennis shoes

Matt Endahl has written extensively about Robert Crum. Stuff Smith and Crum met in Chicago, 1943, playing together in Sunday afternoon jam sessions at the Hamilton Hotel. From Endahl's research it appears that Crum had played in this style before:

> During his Chicago years, Crum played regularly with Pete Pedersen, who would later become known as a member of Jerry Murad's Harmonicats. Pedersen remembered their collaborations fondly: 'We would make up songs together. We were never booked to do this … but we'd say, Give us a story, and we'd make a song to it. … He would play piano, I would play harmonica and we'd just improvise.'

Pedersen's description of the process illuminates this aspect of the duets between Smith and Crum. They are narratives without an evident storyline, episodic in the same way that organ or piano accompaniment would be in following the storyline of a silent film or orchestral compositions for cartoons. Carl Stalling's *A Corny Concerto*, for example, chases a sequence of improbable events only possible in the medium of animated film, the seriousness of the music punctured repeatedly by quacks, slaps, nail filing, sniffing, panting, kicks, a broken tree, a shotgun blast, blowing, splashes, spitting, bubbles popping, pepper shaking, fighter planes and an explosion.

Crum was born in 1915 in Pittsburgh (Errol Garner's city of birth). He studied classical piano at home and in Paris, then took lessons from Meade Lux Lewis, one of the leading boogie-woogie pianists of the 1920s and 1930s. The hybrid style of his playing disconcerted critics of the day. One complained of him running his thumb down the keys and playing with the backs of his hands (shades of Slim Gaillard), others grumbled about his lack of showmanship, his tendency to play with his head down (shades of Bill Evans). In December 1944 Barry Ulanov presented the duo of Crum and Stuff Smith to an audience at Times Hall in New York. 'The concert was arranged under the auspices of *View – The Modern Magazine*, a quarterly periodical, specialising in modern art, film and literature,' Endahl writes. Concert patrons included Alexander Calder, Aaron Copland and Marcel Duchamp. Endahl also quotes Ulanov's concert notes: 'Should [these] improvisations be confined to jazz? In a series of deliberations, first canonic, then less rigorously formal, the violinist with the jazz background, the pianist with a classical, offer a provocative answer, as they extend the resources of the improviser to those of all music.' Other critics were less impressed, drawing attention to Crum's nervous stage mannerisms. Endahl quotes Stuff Smith's widow on Crum's sartorial style: 'Formal wear with white tennis shoes which was pretty strange in those days.'

'Fugue In Swing (An Adventure In Feeling)', taken from the Times Hall concert, is the only record of Smith and Crum playing to a general public. It begins with applause, then an announcement of the title. In discographies the piece is called 'Fugue In Swing (Fuguish Feeling)' but whoever makes the announcement, presumably Crum, clearly says 'adventures'. Through the crackle and rumble of the acetate we can hear Smith making sure he's in tune. 'Robert,' he says. 'What?' Crum replies, nervously abrupt. The first chords, funereal as they are, lead the duo into a music that is dizzying in its suggestion of an unstable congruence of all musics – the serene formalism of Bach sliding sideways into Jewish and Gypsy music, jazz swing and a kind of neoclassical chase (apt, given that the term fugue is related to *fugere*, to flee, and *fugare*, to chase). Impossible to say how much of this is written (and under-rehearsed) or improvised on stage. Smith finds himself to be the pursuer in the mid-section, composure fading in some difficult passages as Crum powers on, then sounding completely lost in a fast and complex pizzicato section. The impression is that Crum is oblivious, actually seeming to play faster when Smith is at sea. They slow down again, Smith recovering himself with a startling cadenza that falls and slurs, bends and rises in a twisting line, cutting its way free from the neoclassical restraints that precede it.

Smith's final reassertion reminds me of Leroy Jenkins, a pioneer of improvising violin in the 1960s, but the somewhat mismatched duo of Crum and Smith in this case is more reminiscent of the piano and violin duets of Nigel Coombes and Steve Beresford. For their 1980 release on Bead – *White String's Attached* – Coombes wrote in his liner note:

> The combination of piano and violin might appear to be an obvious one, but this is not the case. In the early concerts it never occurred to us for Steve to use a piano instead of his objects, and when finally he did use the instrument we did not consider the fact that composers from Haydn onwards had immense difficulty with the medium. Beethoven went through such traumas at trying to make the instruments blend, marrying the percussive sounds of the piano with the singing qualities of the violin, that he gave up after only ten sonatas. Countless composers have tried since to contrive some kind of homogeneity out of the instruments only to prove that the combination is immitigable. This, I think, explains why the two instruments on this record sound as if they hate each other. For us to try and surmount Beethoven's problems, for example, in the heat of trying to make the music up as we go along is almost laughable.

Unissued piano solos by Crum were recorded by Rosenkrantz in 1944 and the first days of 1945, some with intriguing titles: 'Mighty Mellow Mood (part 2) (Garden of Allah)', 'The Wind Up and the Pitch', 'Champagne', 'Burgundy' and 'Sauterne'. A blurred and distant photograph shows Crum on stage at Chicago's Garrick Stage Bar with a seven-piece band. Crum is stage right at the piano, a white musician in a black band at a time when racial segregation was still violently enforced in many parts of America. Stuff Smith can be seen at extreme stage left, playing violin. What little evidence remains of Crum's life gives cause for speculation. He returned to Chicago in 1945 where his excessively intricate 'symphonic jazz interpretations' were dismissed by the critics. Nor did they enjoy his 'weird mannerisms and grimaces', the way he literally pounded the piano or his 'wild malange *[sic]* of introductions and arpeggios that don't mean much'. Errol Garner credited Crum with showing him what he wanted to do. The pounding, the symphonic jazz interpretations, the melange of introductions and arpeggios were all part of Garner's method yet he made an affable and charming style out of it, drawing in the audience as he toyed with their expectations, finally rewarding them with something romantic, something a little bit corny.

Crum either lacked or spurned such pragmatism. Judging from the few available recordings he would have fitted quite comfortably into the improvising world of the 1960s and 1970s alongside players such as Cecil Taylor, Irène Schweizer, Howard Riley, Keith Tippett, Alexander von Schlippenbach, Misha Mengelberg, Fred Van Hove and Steve Beresford. In 1947 Crum was reported to be in the hospital for observation. 'To the best of current knowledge,' Endahl writes, 'Crum seems to have made no further attempts at a public music career, living a private life and passing away in Joliet, Illinois, in May 1981.' Until further information comes to light we can only surmise that illness of one kind or another pushed him into premature retirement. These fragments of music and biography describe a personality too wayward or insufficiently robust to withstand the variable weather of a life in jazz. With hindsight we know that the Second World War was close to its end when these recordings were made. At the time, victory in Europe and the Pacific would not have been a forgone conclusion, nor would the eventual duration of the war or its overall outcome have been certain. Although cultural life was severely curtailed, there was a compensatory expansion of certain social freedoms. These recordings are clearly prophetic, not just because they anticipate free improvisation but because in their challenge to musical boundaries they reflect the consequences of a global war: violent clashes of cultural identities; heightened awareness of the thin membrane between order and chaos.

White jazz: Eavesdropping on *Jailhouse Rock*

Scene 5: black-and-white film, 1957, a 'real crazy pad'; we walk in on a party for the middle-aged.
Conversation: 'I think Stubby's gone overboard with those altered chords, don't you?'
'I agree. I think Brubeck and Desmond have gone just as far with dissonance as I care to go.'
'Oh nonsense. Have you heard Lennie Tristano's latest recording? He reached outer space.'
'Someday they'll make the cycle and get back to pure old Dixieland. I say atonality is just a passing phase in jazz music. What do you think Mr Everett?'

Like a dog driven stupid by heat, Vince Everett (better known to us as Elvis Presley) slouches on the couch, mouth hanging open and empty. Cool jazz by the fictitious Stubby Wrightmayer has been playing on the record player (a Shorty Rogers, Gerry Mulligan Quartet sort of sound though note the Jewish sounding name, as if the exiled Schoenberg were the secret hand behind this egghead turn in jazz); the cutting of its edge is viewed airily through cocktail glasses by those who stand confident in their age and sophistication. Vince comes back to life: 'Lady, I dunno what the hell you talking about.' Exit Elvis. Jazz audibly loses ground.

Out of the ruins – Into the maelstrom

Early 1948, Pierre Schaeffer begins a search for music without meaning, music rooted in the unresolved sounds of the everyday – whistling or snow – noises without text or context. His perspective was that of the craftsman bricoleur, scavenging, collecting and assembling. At organ makers Cavaillé-Coll and Pleyel he found parts of an organ destroyed by bombing during the war: 'My originality will be not to play them like an organist but to hit them with a mallet, detune them perhaps. The war had already taken this on.' On April 15 of that year he wrote, 'I'm giving up on music.' He interferes with sound, slowing the revolutions per minute of a recording from 78 to 33, separating the attack of a sound from its body. Schaeffer was a composer, theorist and broadcaster, an administrator at the Radiodiffusion-Télévision Française, but in those months he seemed more like a man in the grip of delirium, collecting the most worthless junk, an empty tin can, then making it sonically unrecognizable through one of the great musical discoveries of the twentieth century. On 30 May, Jean-Jacques Grunenwald agrees to play 'concrete' themes on the piano: 'He responds with great virtuosity to the "concrete" themes with a music that I would call abstract were it not so spontaneous. It is abstract insofar as it comes from his imagination, and it is expressed through his expert fingers and obedient keyboard.' Work on these recordings leads to disappointing results, of which Schaeffer noted: 'Gazelles die like this, behind bars.'

Some weeks later he returned to the piano recordings, transforming 'odd moments', fragments, varying speed and timbre, eradicating the musical ideas, radically adapting its physical form and purpose to transubstantiate the box of the piano into echoes, supernatural knocking, voices with no beginning, no end: 'a super-percussion section'. All notions of a symphony were abandoned; these were studies, near-scientific surgical operations on specific objects, 'incantations that had no reference to anything'. Pierre Boulez recorded a series of chords for Schaeffer in various styles – classical, romantic, impressionist, atonal – and so from these two experiments the piano etudes were born: *Etude violette* and *Etude noir*. *Noir* is cavernous, pounding, as if a piano is suffering torment, attacked by hammers, falling through deep water, smashing to the floor of a huge cave; *Noir* is obsessive, its rough surfaces circling wildly, spinning dangerously close to the listener then sucked into a vortex in which sound is nullified. On 5 October the first radio noise concert was broadcast. In a letter one listener described the profound emotions he felt: 'It was as if I were listening to superb Balinese music; the music that you could imagine coming from the centre of an atom: the ultrasonic music created maybe by the movement of the planets: the music that Poe and Lautréamont and Raymond Roussel would hear inwardly.'

Real weird

Not so long after Schaeffer's experiments created music for the hypersensitive mind of Edgar Allan Poe, Lennie Tristano recorded his own impression of Poe's short story, *A Descent Into the Maelstrom*. Born in Chicago in 1919, Tristano was a prodigiously gifted pianist. Blind from the age of nine or ten he showed early signs of mathematical brilliance and within the shambolic atmosphere of the Illinois School for the Blind in Jacksonville he learnt piano, saxophone, clarinet and cello. By 1946 he had written some arrangements for the Woody Herman band, rejected by Herman for being 'real weird'. Club dates were sporadic but Tristano was already assembling students, including his most famous pupil, Lee Konitz. In the same year he moved to New York, finding a steady job with a trio playing at a restaurant in Freeport: Tristano on piano, ex-Woody Herman guitarist Billy Bauer and bassist Arnold Fishkin.

'During the engagements at the restaurant Bauer observed something unusual about the pianist,' writes biographer Eunmi Shim. 'Tristano wanted to bypass the statement of the tune and rather start improvising right away on its harmonic progressions.' Tristano issued a number of directives: no rhythm guitar (too much like swing), no melody (too commercial); instead play counter harmonies and counter melodies. Initially, Fishkin and Bauer felt lost. Whenever Bauer picked up on an idea Tristano would move elsewhere, but whenever he fluffed notes Tristano would draw them into the harmonic structure. According to Fishkin: 'What Lennie said to me was … "Just don't have any fears about where you are going. Just keep your ears open." Just bearing that in mind it was quite free.'

Having befriended critic Barry Ulanov, a vocal supporter of modern jazz and co-editor of *Metronome* magazine, Tristano wrote two polemical essays for *Metronome*, both published in 1947. 'The boppers discarded collective improvisation,' he wrote, 'and placed all emphasis on the single line. This is not unfortunate, since the highest developments of both would probably not occur simultaneously. Perhaps the next step after bebop will be collective improvisation on a much higher plane because the individual lines will be more complex.' By 1949 Tristano had a sextet of new pupils in place, adding alto saxophonist Lee Konitz, tenor saxophonist Warne Marsh and drummer Denzil Best to his original trio with Bauer and Fishkin.

Conspiring in the creation of a legend, Barry Ulanov described life at home in the apartment Tristano shared with singer Judy Moore – an intensive nocturnal exploration of literature and music, Tristano wandering the rooms in pyjamas and slippers no matter what the hour, expounding on Dante, Freud or the orgone energy theories of Wilhelm

Reich. Reich was a disciple of Freud who moved from Vienna to Oslo, finally America in the turbulence of the 1930s when his work became a cause célèbre in the underground culture of the time. In the wake of McCarthyism, however, it provoked drastic reactions. He was imprisoned for fraud in 1956 and in a shameful episode his books were burned. This repressive atmosphere with its echoes of the Nazi Säuberung of 1933, the cleansing by fire of all things liberal or Jewish, was perceived by Tristano as neurotic and insecure. Reich, whatever the pseudo-scientific contentiousness of muscular armour, orgone accumulators and cloudbusters, gave voice to a growing disquiet about the entrenchment of a society founded on paranoia, conformism, materialism and sexual hypocrisy. Tristano saw this as one of the key reasons why his music was unpopular. If people were not free enough to experience intense erotic feeling they could never be receptive to music demanding total intellectual, emotional and sensual engagement.

Intuitions and digressions

Ulanov takes up the story of the sessions in which free improvisation was finally recorded:

> At eight o'clock on Friday evening, May 13, 1949, after two hours of fairly orthodox recording, Lennie and four other men – Billy Bauer, Arnold Fishkin, Lee Konitz and Warne Marsh – grouped themselves around two microphones and began to make permanent the most audacious experiment yet attempted in jazz. The experiment was to create out of skill and intuition a spontaneous music that would be at once atonal, contrapuntal, and improvised on a jazz base. The microphones were provided by Capitol Records. Logically enough, 'Intuition' was the name Lennie gave the first side of the four recorded between eight and nine that night. Not logically, but perhaps understandably, Capitol was bewildered by and uncertain about what it heard. As a result, two of the sides were erased from the recording tape, and, of the remaining two, those chosen as the best of the four, only one was released – and that two years after it was recorded. And yet these adventures in musical intuition are among the high points of jazz.

Of the two short tracks saved from Capitol's vandalism – 'Intuition' and 'Digression' – 'Digression' comes closer to a music released from forward drive into creative irregularity, Tristano's piano opening the piece, his customary harmonic ambiguity implying many possibilities, many digressions, never settling into what might become in other hands a conventional ballad; Konitz enters after the half minute, soft, exploratory, finding in Tristano's mathematical logic an M. C. Escher interior of stairs that climbs, circles, descends as it climbs; each player touches upon resolution, firm ground, yet the floated invisible structure turns in on itself again and again, the tempo fluctuating, slowing almost to stasis, picking up speed with a subtlety that might not have been so elastic with a drummer. Thirty seconds from the end all the players are in, shadowing each other's steps, suddenly close to climbing the same stair.

'Intuition' is shorter, quicker, arguably less successful. Again, Tristano leads the predetermined sequence of entrance, the flashing right hand a reminder that in his youth he claimed to play Art Tatum's 'Elegy' even faster than Tatum himself. Billy Bauer is more prominent on this track, struggling at times to play accurate fast runs in the absence of an exact destination. There are moments when the ensemble lapses into trite rhythms, scales flying in all directions like birds trapped in a windowless room. After two minutes Fishkin and Tristano halt the quick march with a shower of notes, Tristano calling in the full ensemble at 2' 12" by hammering at the keys. These were unrehearsed pieces without a known duration. The danger, then as now, is that a natural ending might be sabotaged by one member of the group deciding to launch a new idea. Despite the private ambitions of the musicians this was considered popular music, so they were still making ten-inch 78 rpm discs with an upper time limit of approximately three minutes. As Miles Davis has said: 'There wasn't any room for really free improvisation; you had to get in your solo real quick and then get out.'

Ulanov had agreed to give a signal to Lee Konitz from the control booth after two minutes though how this was communicated to Tristano is unknown. As with 'Digression', the concluding section sounds closest to the free jazz of the 1960s, though not unrelated to Miles Davis's work with Gil Evans in the same year, notably Gerry Mulligan's 'Jeru', recorded by Capitol in January 1949, later released on *Birth of the Cool*. There were other connections with the Miles Davis sessions. Lee Konitz played on all the *Birth of the Cool* recordings and arranger and Capitol

Records producer Pete Rugolo supervised both sessions. Both records were experiments with new voicings, new ways to frame improvisation, to think about individual lines and cooperative grouping; both were trialled in clubs before recording took place, with Tristano's group playing free improvised pieces of ten minutes duration every night at Birdland.

'If there is form in a good free improvisation it also is improvised,' Warne Marsh has said. 'It's not the standard thirty-two bars, it's not sonata form. It has unique form if it's a valid music. ... Finally form itself could be improvised.' Taking it further proved difficult. According to Marsh, the group had been improvising in this way for two years before the recording. By 1949 they were beginning to lose the spontaneity of it: 'But we stopped playing free music, the more we played, the more difficult it seemed to be – and today we don't take chances like that when we play.' Despite the setbacks, and despite Capitol treating the music as worker rebellion, initially refusing to pay for the sessions, wiping two historic tracks and then holding back the release of 'Digression' until 1954, Tristano was not quite finished with free music.

'Descent Into the Maelstrom' was recorded in his Manhattan studio in 1953. 'Employing multitracking and perhaps other recording techniques in an adventurous way,' writes Eunmi Shim, 'he succeeded in building a remarkable sound structure to portray the short story of the same title by Edgar Allen Poe. The liner notes for the recording, which was not issued until the 1970s, described it as "Improvised conception from Edgar Allen Poe's story," citing Tristano as the recording engineer.' Just under three and a half minutes long, the piece begins at the lowest end of the piano, dark notes repeated and echoed by mid-range and high eddies which rapidly gather in force and motion to evoke the tumultuously circling waves and static turbulence of Poe's intestinal vortex. The bass notes become dedifferentiated, a roar of noise and movement, while in higher registers the accumulation of hammered smashes, repeated phrases and sweeps across the keyboard thicken into an overwhelming sensation of unpredictable volition that only begins its subsidence when the thunder of the bass drops away at around 3' 19", the last few seconds given over to the maelstrom's fury expended with the setting of the full moon.

'I still feel that the notes are important and the rhythm is important and I feel that the harmony is important,' Tristano said in a recorded interview. 'It can't be accidental. Now, free form or free music as it stands today works on this kind of a premise: you can do anything you please. The important thing is to express the emotion. Well I can find that out if I go to any state hospital. We might call that musical psychodrama. I'm not interested in that.' For Warne Marsh this was 'a distinction between emotion and feeling which in English have essentially different meanings'.

'Descent Into the Maelstrom' is shocking for its time. Its closest contemporary relations are *Etude Noir* and *Etude Violette* by Pierre Schaeffer. Any likelihood of Tristano hearing these is slight, though he and Schaeffer were both manipulating sound through basic recording techniques of overdubbing and pitch variance. Both understood the potentiality of the piano frame as a resonant vibrating structure whose placid exterior conceals violent forces held in tension and darkness. Tristano also understood the piano as a convergence of mathematics and feeling. Perhaps the literary source that he found in Poe also led him on this occasion beyond the impasse of complex harmony for its own sake, into the deeper implications of chaos. In 1839 Poe even described a comparable style of improvising in *The Fall of the House of Usher*, performed by Roderick Usher:

> But the fervid facility of his impromptus could not be so accounted for. They must have been, and were, in the notes, as well as in the words of his wild fantasias (for he not unfrequently accompanied himself with rhymed verbal improvisations), the result of that intense mental collectedness and concentration to which I have previously alluded as observable only in particular moments of the highest artificial excitement.

The contradiction of Tristano's free music may be traced to the centripetal nature of his personality (his blindness cannot be discounted) and inner circle of collaborator disciples – inward-looking, hyper-critical, detached from the world – and so the experiments in collective free improvisation from 1949 are held back by the maelstrom created by Tristano himself, the musicians endlessly circling each other, noses pointed towards a central void. Despite its depiction of centripetal forces, 'Descent Into the Maelstrom' has more of a centrifugal feeling, a radial whirling outwards of energies too powerful to contain. Significantly, Tristano was only able to accomplish this in isolation, in conversation with himself and the tape recorder.

Duplexity

Scene 6: London, May 1987, Derek Bailey's Company Week. The sixty-year-old silver-haired saxophonist on stage is Lee Konitz, of all Tristano's disciples the one who sounded most inventive and confident on the free improvisation recordings of 1949, the survivor who escaped the guru to build a distinct identity of his own.

For the first night he takes a solo spot, in his Issey Miyake pyjamas and huge Glen check jacket looking like an American tourist in search of one of the local steak houses. It's a performance in the tradition of comedian Jack Benny. An air of hiatus hangs over the proceedings yet every second is absorbing. Pauses. Will he play or won't he? The atmosphere is so intimate that he suddenly seems alone in the room. You're reminded of the way he opened his liner notes to *Motion*, the great trio album he recorded in 1961 with Elvin Jones and Sonny Dallas: 'When asked on a radio show to comment on one of his records, Lester Young replied: "Sorry Pres, I never discuss my sex life in public". Bless his sweet soul!' he wrote.

At the end of Konitz's short but rich set, he switches on a tape of a tune recorded for the *Motion* sessions – 'Out Of Nowhere' – and threads a typically oblique counterpoint through his own twenty-six-year vintage alto lines. The following day I interviewed Konitz at his hotel. In person, he is not unlike his famous alto tone: plain speaking, charming but armed with a sharp edge. He was not slow to disabuse me of some fanciful notions about two George Russell compositions – 'Ezz-thetic' and 'Odjenar' – he recorded with Miles Davis in 1951. At that point in the 1980s, with jazz rapidly turning into a conservative copy of itself, it seemed to me that their application of Russell's method, complex and ambiguous as it was, had left unfinished business for younger musicians. Konitz felt otherwise, thinking those particular recordings nothing special and if there was unfinished business he was taking care of it.

I asked him first about his solo of the previous evening and its slightly awkward use of a tape. 'What I intended to do in that solo spot I couldn't pull off quite,' he says, adding that he meant

> to develop the music in as organic a way as I conceive of it personally, which is pre-instrumental. Somehow I got scared. I started to make some sounds with my voice and it sounded too personal. I didn't know

if it was to be shared and that got me a little upset. I never sweated so much in a performance in my life. I've been on some very hot bandstands and played with some very hot rhythm sections but just standing there alone trying to express that phenomenon, which was based on a jazz tune. I had one tune in mind – 'Out of Nowhere' – and I tried to give an impression of that and then at the end of the set playing along with my pre-recorded tape to play the harmonies very specifically.

For me, it recalled *The Lee Konitz Duets*, an album on which Konitz overdubbed his own playing using an electric alto saxophone. 'That, incidentally, is a very interesting phenomenon,' he says, 'to improvise along with yourself.' One of the most surprising choices for that record was violinist Ray Nance; most surprisingly they play a free improvised duet called 'Duplexity'. Born in 1913, Nance is celebrated for his twenty-three-year spell on trumpet, violin and voice with Duke Ellington. His first feature with the band in 1941 was a beautifully economic two-part trumpet solo on 'Take the "A" Train'; in the same year he recorded a sinuous violin solo on Juan Tizol's 'Bakiff', adding another layer of exoticism to a piece already promiscuous in its wanderings through a fantasy Afro-Cuban atlas.

The duet, recorded in 1967, was received at the time with some scepticism, the reaction being that there was too great a stylistic gap between the two musicians, resulting in a tentative, unresolved conversation. True enough, yet the incompatibility is strangely compelling. Critics, then as now, listen for accord, a shared purpose and happy endings, yet dialogic improvisation of this kind holds a less flattering mirror to human nature, giving insights into the ways cooperation can work through struggle and honesty in unpropitious circumstances. Konitz plays tenor, Nance plays violin; already they have a burden of uneven weights and textures to bear. Exacerbating that imbalance is the silence through which they move, a harsh light exposing every circumspect gesture of mimesis, every false step and indelible line. This note or that note? The infrastructure has gone – no piano or guitar to state the chords, no drummer's pulse, no bass to bridge the gap between those two functions. In one exquisite moment Konitz blows a soft sustained G, Nance countering with its antithesis – unsteady thin harmonics, scraping the string as if teetering on a high ledge. To misquote Marcel Duchamp, you *can* hear hearing, but the hearing of it is not an easy business. Ultimately, both players sound as if hesitancy is their purpose, know exactly how to make their paths run smoothly but instead take off their shoes to walk over sharp stones. The title, one of Konitz's collection of bad puns and word games (of which 'Subconscious-Lee' and 'Ice Cream Konitz' are probably the best), is worth consideration: a duplex, a building containing two apartments with separate entrances; duplicity, contradictory doubleness, deception; complexity, the state or quality of being intricate or complicated. Hence, 'Duplexity'.

'I was told,' Konitz recalls, 'don't mess around with Ray Nance cause he's a traditionalist who'd done the Duke Ellington thing. I went to Ray's house one afternoon and we played some tunes, "Melancholy Baby" and "Satin Doll" and whatever. The second time we got together I said, let's make one up. He said OK, and bam, into it, you couldn't stop him. It was beautiful.'

Of the time with Lennie Tristano and the free improvisation in 1949 he has mixed feelings: 'Lennie Tristano was playing with a Latin band across the street from where I was playing with a dance band,' he says, 'wearing brown suede shoes with a tuxedo, which I thought was very hip. I was totally taken in by what he was doing in that environment. I spoke with him and he immediately indicated that this was a good opportunity to get some good information and study with him. I'm deeply indebted to that part of his teaching. He wanted a band of students that he had trained. After some point I had to dissociate myself almost completely from that school. He had a tragic life because he wanted to perform and became a guru. He ended up being a very bitter man.

'We had rehearsals at his home, we tried some of that a couple of times, we'd have a little bit of a taste, you know' – he holds up his fingers as if he's smoking cannabis – 'just start playing and we'd hit it, right away. We did some of that at the concerts and it was thrilling. At the record date we did our tunes that we rehearsed and then we told the engineers we didn't know that he was going to try it, with the 78rpm three minute limitation. There was someone there who was going to give me a signal after two and a half minutes to wind it down. We made about three or four takes and each one wound down naturally and caught the three minute mark. The only dictate was that Lennie would set it up for a few seconds. I know that Ornette and Cecil Taylor used to acknowledge that music. Cecil used to be in the audience when we worked at Birdland and he studied with Lennie. For some reason, I think because Lennie was as critical as he was and trying to make a voice for the white musician in black jazz, the black musicians in turn were not so willing to acknowledge his contribution. That's what embittered him a little bit.'

This question of lineage, who owes what and who has legitimacy, is as acute in free improvisation as it is in musics which have more defined standards. For the two nights I attended Company Week (in fact from the first Company week of 1977 onwards, not least the 1981 Company week in which I played) I was struck by Derek Bailey's tendency, conscious or not, to bring together musicians from the earliest phases of free improvisation – in this case Konitz, synthesizer player Richard Teitelbaum and bassist Barre Philips – with younger players less committed to the same ethical sense of a tradition and its values. In his early life Bailey was employed in commercial music where technical standards were absolute and non-negotiable. This was the productive conflict of his own career – the maintenance and manipulation of such standards within a context in which pretty much anything goes. Could it be that his sometimes disastrous matchmaking was a projection, a way for him to observe from the outside the peculiarity of his position?

The first association between Konitz and Bailey was in 1966. A tour of English cities was arranged for Konitz with the Joseph Holbrooke Trio – Bailey on guitar, Gavin Bryars on bass and Tony Oxley on drums – as backing band playing tunes like 'I Remember You' and 'Out of Nowhere'. 'I had played with Derek many, many years ago, playing "All the Things You Are"', he says. According to Andrew Shone, the tour organizer, quoted in Ben Watson's book, *Derek Bailey and the Story of Free Improvisation*, 'He [Konitz] was surprisingly into free improvisation himself. He used to do strange things like carry a pocket radio in his inside pocket while he was playing on stage. He'd be listening to Radio 3 – or the Third Programme as it was called then – through an earplug, and picking up bits of music he liked and incorporating them in solos.'

From this perspective his attempt to use a tape of 'Out of Nowhere' during his solo forms a conscious link between the tour of 1966 and the exposed situation of Company Week, not only in the choice of that particular jazz standard and its archival trail (Coleman Hawkins, Don Byas, Charlie Parker, Paul Desmond, et al.) but also in reference to the way he used a radio on stage during the tour as random stimulus. In speaking self-consciously to himself, to Bailey, to tradition and to personal history he overloaded the situation, lost his poise, overheated. There are worse crimes in music.

'What surprises me is that I haven't participated any more in that activity myself,' says Konitz.

Left to my own devices I enjoy the discipline of playing in the tradition – trying to get spontaneous in the tradition with all the rules. Last night you had to shed all of the responsibilities to some extent, and then assume an even greater responsibility of trying to make it all make sense to someone else too without any of that structure.

Speaking of a duo played by Derek Bailey and Barre Phillips and its high level of interaction he says: 'It's fascinating. Philosophically it's been supporting a lot of fine art music. It's addressing the spirit very directly.'

The mediumship of the improviser

In 1909, the Russian composer Thomas de Hartmann wrote music for Wassily Kandinsky's 'colour tone drama', *The Yellow Sound* (Der Gelbe Klang). The original score survived only in incomplete form, later rearranged by Gunter Schuller for an American production of Kandinsky's experiment in bringing synesthetic colour theories to the theatre stage. Then in 1916, in a cafe in St Petersburg, he was introduced to the Greek Armenian charismatic guru, George Gurdjieff. The following year he and his wife fled the Russian Revolution. In Essentuki, in the Caucasus, they rejoined Gurdjieff and de Hartmann began a new life as composer/amanuensis to the court of the man he unfailingly called Mr Gurdjieff. At the beginning, de Hartmann played violin for the 'Sacred Gymnastics', a set of exercises based on movement from Turkey, Tibet, Afghanistan and other near and far Eastern traditions. The methods used for this compositional collaboration seem to have been dependent on de Hartmann's total compliance: 'Mr. Gurdjieff had said: "Write the music as you wish for the first act," and so, naturally, I did. Returning one evening after supper, he finally, on my insistent request, began to whistle the music for the second act, which I tried feverishly to write in shorthand on music paper.'

After a move to Paris, de Hartmann found himself mixing concrete, filling cracks in walls, running the kitchen for the whole community and composing music for the Sacred Gymnastics, always subject to what he perceived as the tests thrown at him by his autocratic teacher:

I had a very difficult and trying time with this music. Mr. Gurdjieff sometimes whistled or played on the piano with one finger a very complicated sort of melody – as are all Eastern melodies, although they seem at first to be monotonous. To grasp this melody, to write it in European notation, required a kind of tour de force and very often – probably to make the task more difficult for me – he would replay it a little differently.

From the 1920s, Gurdjieff had been improvising on a harmonium for his disciples. One of them, Georgette Leblanc, wrote about a session from 1936: 'After dinner he played. A unique sight – Gurdjieff playing on his little organ. One can see the music "pass" through him. He plays it, but it is not the player. He is the direct means of expression of an "impersonal thought" – the perfect vehicle of an idea.'

A number of recordings of Gurdjieff's solo improvisations were made by Donald Whitcomb between Christmas Day 1948 and 25 October 1949, a few days before his death. Whatever one thinks of Gurdjieff and his teachings, the music is strange for its time, a slow meander through some ancient Asian landscape pictured within Gurdjieff's imagination, the knocking and creaking of the bellows audible as if shoe leather on a mountain pass, its wheezing the breath of the footsore walker whose destination is uncertain but whose progress is inexorable. In Paris, Kenneth Walker was invited into Gurdjieff's inner sanctum, a private room that doubled as the food storeroom. 'If we have come here for music,' he wrote,

> Gurdjieff will have brought with him his special instrument, an unusual form of accordion. Balancing this on his knee, he presses backwards and forwards a hinged flap on the back of the accordion with his left hand and thereby obtains a rather spasmodic supply of air. His right hand rests on the keyboard and, sometimes improvising, and at other time remembering, he calls out of his instrument music of a kind I have never listened to before. It is in a minor key and at one moment it calls back to my memory the song that the Mohammedan dockers chanted when, many years ago, at Suez, our ship's coal bunkers were being replenished and at other times it is more reminiscent of the mournful music I listened to as a child as the sea surged backwards and forwards through the narrow entrance of a cave.

Most people agreed it was melancholy, some thought it unbearably sad. Gurdjieff called it 'objective music', music for people who have forgotten to listen to themselves, allowing themselves to be swamped by external sounds, the radio, phonograph, love songs, typewriter, eating, the jabber of talk. One branch of its ancestry could be traced back to the Swabian physician, Franz Anton Mesmer, theorist of animal magnetism and source of the word 'mesmerism'. Mesmer was a gifted player of the glass harmonica, using it alongside hypnosis and massage as a curative instrument for patients in his eighteenth-century group healing sessions. 'During the séance,' wrote Vincent Buranelli,

> Mesmer kept the doors and windows closed. ... Silence reigned except for whispers between patients and doctors (Mesmer or his assistants) in the give-and-take of diagnosis, treatment and prescription. One cardinal exception – the sound of a piano or glass harmonica came from a corner of the room. Mesmer had learned from his Viennese teachers about the healing properties of music; he had stated in Proposition 16 of his *Memoir* that animal magnetism 'can be communicated, propagated, and reinforced by sound,' and he combined the two ideas by placing instruments where his patients could hear and be moved by them.

Melody was unimportant to him; the aim was to generate and change moods, stirring up a crisis then calming it down, with Mesmer either playing the glass harmonica himself or using a form of conduction to indicate these changes to the musician. When Mesmer met Gluck in 1779, his improvisations on glass harmonica were so impressive that Gluck advised him to discard notated music entirely, to play only improvisations.

Wavering timeless microtonal

Alvin Curran, musically active and resident in Rome since 1965, speaks of Giacinto Scelsi:

> Scelsi, even to those who were close and knew him (well) as I thought I did, one simply could never get a full handle on this man or his music, elusive, intriguing and mysterious as both were. We all knew,

as he loved to recount, that when the mood struck him, he would sit at the piano (or ondioline keyboard) and improvise and record with one or two old Revox machines placed just to the left of his Bechstein piano (a crummy piano in my opinion, but presumably one he liked a lot). He then passed these recordings on to his faithful transcriber Vieri Tosatti (who in dramatic Italian exuberance after Scelsi's death claimed to be the 'real' Scelsi: 'Scelsi c'est moi'), having been a superb transcriber (and in some cases orchestrator) of his tapes. Tosatti's music, should you hear it, is so academically lacking any 'there, there' that one could not imagine him seriously claiming to be Scelsi the composer.

I find this far more interesting than anything else about Scelsi or his music. He was after all a proud aristocrat – we loved to call him 'count/conte' but as I got to know him he simply became Giacinto, and was a kind, generous, and good friend. On one occasion he gave me some Korean court music to transcribe. I did what I thought was a heroic job, to notate all the wavering timeless microtonal melodies. To my knowledge he never used it in any of his own music, but presumably that was his intention, unless this was a test of friendship. He was strange and definitely reserved about his ways and means … but he was a wonderful self-made center of 'otherness' which attracted and inspired everyone who knew him.

Scelsi's approach to composing was relatively conventional until the early 1950s, when he bought his first Revox tape machine and the electronic Ondiola, an Italian version of the Clavioline (the Clavioline is the keyboard instrument on which the lead melody of 'Telstar' by The Tornadoes was played). A rotary attachment on the Ondiola allowed him to produce microtones; these could be combined with other settings and controls for expression. A photograph of the interior of Scelsi's house shows the 'crummy' Bechstein, an Ondiola placed closely on each side by its pastel-coloured suitcase-style loudspeaker. Adjacent to the piano is a set of conga drums, a Japanese or Tibetan conch horn (or perhaps just a conch shell), a Tibetan telescopic rag dun trumpet and what may be a curved Tibetan ceremonial horn. A set of tuned bells set within a mahogany frame sits behind the rag dun; bowl gongs and other percussive instruments are visible on or behind the piano. Buddhist deities, an antique Tibetan thangka and what may be a small pellet drum are fixed to the facing wall.

To work with composers who could transcribe the recordings produced in this setting, clearly far removed from the conservatory, was one part of the process, but if the resultant work was performed with the timidity and formality of the conservatory – spellbound by the notes on the page with no feeling given to the sound of the music – then its difference would be squandered. 'Collaboration with specific performers became ever more vital,' wrote Andy Hamilton in *The Wire*. 'Scelsi was fortunate that improvisers of the stature of [Frances-Marie] Uitti, Joëlle Léandre and Curran entered his circle. Almost all his 1960s and 70s work involved collaborating with an improviser, the most successful improvisations being transcribed.'

Composer Giorgio Battistelli recalls playing Scelsi's *Ku-tha*, for guitar played horizontally as a percussion instrument:

> Scelsi invited me home to listen to my musical performance. I studied hard and my performance was technically perfect but, at first, his comment gave me pause. He asked me to imagine myself being part of a ritual during my performance; this imagery affected my performance; it brought freedom in my performance, a less faithful performance of the score with slight improvisation.

This was in accordance with Scelsi's concept, conveyed to Battistelli as a process of improvising through trance, 'developing a performative relation with both vocal and musical improvisation'.

As solo 'composers' of improvisation, Gurdjieff and Scelsi are somewhat peripheral to this story of free improvisation. Nor is this the place to explore Scelsi's improvisations in depth except to say that his perception of himself as a channel for music emanating from some unearthly higher plane is intimately connected both to the surrealist technique of automatism and to a less exalted understanding of spontaneity as a means of acting without recourse to habit, planning and all the other behavioural constrictions that come from within and without the self.

Decomposition

> Howdy, friends, we ask you please
> to pardon this intrusion. We just came out to tell you
> 'bout this musical confusion

Guns will pop, bells will ring,
but don't you be afraid.
There'll be an intermission
for refreshments and first aid.
You'll hear some funny noises
and some most unusual tones,
but whadya expect – Stokowski? –
when you came to hear Spike Jones.

> Introduction to *The Musical Depreciation Revue*,
> Spike Jones and the City Slickers, 1947

Bugged

'I've always been bugged by having to stay within certain boundaries,' wrote drummer Shelly Manne in his sleeve notes for Ornette Coleman's *Tomorrow Is the Question*, released in 1959.

> Here is a guy that came along that was able to free me – from my having played with him – of all those things I wanted to throw off. Metre structure, for example. Sometimes Ornette ignores it. He makes you listen so hard to what he's doing in order to *know* where he is in the tune and what he's trying to express. It's just a complete freedom from every way you might have been forced to play before. I don't feel I'm actually playing a song. I'm really playing *with* a person.

That approach – listening to others rather than working within the conventions of popular song – became evident in a Los Angeles session led by Shelly Manne in September 1954. The Three was a trio of West Coast musicians – Manne, trumpeter Shorty Rogers and Jimmy Giuffre on saxophones and clarinet. The trio had worked together in a variety of bands for five years, developing what Giuffre described as 'a mutual instinct which enables us to work together in volume, motion and sound'. For one track, 'Abstract No. 1', they improvised freely, slipping easily into an airy swing that drifts on snare drum press rolls, then drops away into a contemplative passage from Giuffre's clarinet earthed only by Manne's ritualistic bass drum. As Robert Gordon notes in *Jazz West Coast*,

> The trio sounds somewhat empty on first hearing; the lack of the jazz pulse usually supplied by the bass is especially disconcerting. …

The lack of a piano is an advantage here, as there is no implied tonal centre. The two horns listen closely to each other and respond quickly to changes in direction. Moreover, 'Abstract' breaks into swing, something the Tristano pieces never managed to do.

Giuffre, always searching, experimented with this kind of free and not-so-free counterpoint throughout much of his life, generating public affection with 'The Train and the River' in 1957 and total indifference with a free improvisation trio with Paul Bley and Steve Swallow in 1961.

Sufficiently brief to pass unnoticed by an orthodox jazz fan, 'Abstract No. 1' was symptomatic of a post-war mood for change. This need to establish new formats was exemplified by the music of vibraphonist Teddy Charles, Charles Mingus with the Jazz Composers Workshop, Chico Hamilton's groups and even the Sauter-Finegan Orchestra, a swing band whose heavily arranged music incorporated technical innovations (performing with a stereo sound system) and an aesthetic which negotiated the difficult path between experimentation, populism and the spectre of financial ruin. Television was persuading older Americans to stay at home; rock 'n' roll was seducing young Americans away from jazz. As a lure to lost audiences there was too much of everything in the arrangements concocted by Eddie Sauter and Bill Finegan – Bob Graettinger's modernist compositions for Stan Kenton's Orchestra, the influence of Stefan Wolpe (the German-Jewish composer who taught both Sauter and Finegan as well as George Russell, Tony Scott, Eric Dolphy, Morton Feldman, David Tudor and Gil Evans), Les Baxter's exoticism, Boyd Raeburn's highbrow swing, the mellow softness of Claude Thornhill's Orchestra and a hint of musical anarchy reminiscent of Spike Jones and His City Slickers.

This was the quintessential 1950s mood of equivocation, unable to quit the antique shop yet thrilled by the jet age, sunk in nostalgia for the ballrooms where swing bands hypnotized huge crowds yet dressing up as pipe-smoking college professors to affect sophistication. What sounded like chaos was often carefully scripted. 'The show looked improvised but it was all strictly routine,' wrote Jordan R. Young of the Spike Jones stage show. 'Spike's introductions would sound very ad-lib many times but they never were; they were always scripted.'

If the crazy antics and noises of Spike Jones could coexist with orchestration derived from the Second Viennese School, then free improvisation was as probable as bacterial growth in a Petri dish. Recorded in New York City in 1955, The Sauter-Finegan Orchestra's 'Two Bats In a Cave' featured the trumpets of Nick Travis and Billy Nichol. The first seven or eight bars of a grave opening theme were written out by Bill Finegan, the rest was improvised by the two musicians playing an unaccompanied fugue(ish) duet in an echo chamber. As in other examples of proto-free, the music resorts to mimesis, one trumpet shadowing the other's ideas with licks that might be expected of a professional jazz brass player of the 1950s – a quote from Kay Kyser's 'The Woody Woodpecker Song', a touch of the baroque, then a few rapid runs that anticipate 1960s free jazz.

Like the famous mirror scene in *Duck Soup*, in which Groucho Marx tests what appears to be his reflection in a mirror that is no longer there, one trumpet reflects and refracts whatever emerges as the dominant line; already an orthodoxy of free improvisation practice comes into being, a quasi-democratic relationship whereby any musician can be chief or subordinate (but does the strong lead the weak?). In practice workable – the musicians equal each other in their technical ability; they collude in which materials are shared references, which are taboo. The approach stored up problems for later, when melodic imitation and spontaneous counterpoint revealed its limitations. It would be interesting to know if the title was chosen beforehand as a programmatic guide or whether it was chosen after the recording, two instruments 'sounding like' interweaving bat flight in a dark enclosed space.

Shadows

Scene 7: The story – really a story, a single story? – ends with a statement: 'The film you have just seen was an improvisation.' Just that, telling you that *Shadows*, the first film made by John Cassavetes (there are two versions but let's date it at 1959), grew out of the improvisation exercises that were central to his acting workshop in New York. Figures are moving in a room, engulfed by wild music, colliding physically, sexually, violently, verbally, ricocheting off each other's incomprehension and confusion into new formations. 'We're just two strangers,' one says. Music is heard, primitive rock 'n' roll on the edge of chaos, flutes and percussion on the edge of order. 'I am what I am and nobody tells me what to do,' says the woman. Always movement, in streets, clubs, cafes, back alleys, parties. Movement in music always – solo saxophone by Shafi Hadi, solo double bass by Charles Mingus. Just small people, insignificant people, fuck-up people, late people, people caught up by race and by gender, on the edge of a big change. Conversations run over each other, foreground, background, commotion, crafted or scripted, just dumb, like life. Restless, dissatisfied, never finding resolution. Their stories, left adrift, still moving with the music.

Not weird

As if in fear of the implications of play without predetermination, free improvisation was coerced into naming itself as something other than itself: an abstract painting, animals flying around in the darkness, a literary narrative, psychological state or visitation from higher powers. Besides, how free could you be in a huge band booked to play seven nights a week in dance halls and summer resorts to keep itself afloat in a sea of agent's commissions, musicians salaries and bus company fees? In his biography of Charles Mingus, Brian Priestley highlights a general dissatisfaction with bandleaders during the period. Miles Davis, Lucky Thompson, Buddy Collette and others had formed a short-lived cooperative band called Stars of Swing in 1945. Priestley quotes Woodman: 'Each musician in it was leader conscious but at the same time maintained his feeling of individuality as a sideman. As a result, each idea that a musician put forward was treated with respect by the others and made use of.' Mingus claimed that Davis and Thompson came to his house in the mid-1940s with ideas for the kind of contrapuntal music and unusual instrumentation made famous by Gerry Mulligan and Gil Evans, long before either of them had met Davis.

Mingus returned to collective contrapuntalism and what later became known as instant composition with the Jazz Composers Workshop in 1954–5, notably with 'Gregarian Chant' and 'Getting Together'. For Mingus, they were fresh applications of strategies tried out in 1946 at the Down Beat Club, Los Angeles. 'Gregarian Chant', a group improvisation, begins with an arco introduction by Mingus, emotional and devotional, momentarily a lone voice calling out into darkness; John La Porta's clarinet joins, followed by Teo Macero and George Barrow on saxophones, Mal Waldron on piano, Rudy Nichols on drums. According to Priestley, Waldron recalled Mingus discussing his plan for the session: 'When we play this tune, we're not going to play any changes, we're just going to play moods. Just follow me and put your moods in, and we'll build something beautiful.'

Although Priestley derogates the group for being 'aridly experimental', they have a haunting sound founded in sensitivity and listening. Rudy Van Gelder's engineering skills add production touches that enhance the unique character – melancholy and ultramodern – of the sessions. In 'Gregarian Chant', for example, he uses reverb to situate the ensemble within an imaginary space in which the reeds can weave around each other's lines without confusion, not quite bats in a cave but beautifully suggestive of movement and depth. 'I feel that this style of playing is actually the sincerest method of musical expression,' Mingus wrote for his liner note to the original released on Savoy,

> but it is usually impossible to attempt such 'delicacies' with musicians who do not enjoy the usual freedom or understand the thought of the leading instrument. ... Since I don't believe that such music can be classified as 'atonal' or 'weird music' (as atonal is often classified), I would identify it as 'a little beyond the elementary'. If and when these present constructions are accepted, I will venture to delve a little more into the so-called dissonance of free form improvisation – which one may then label atonal. However, I wish to think of it as the way I feel, or rather, the way we feel – not weird, different, or atonal – just music I hear and would like an audience to hear.

Free form

Musicians were trying to make a living. Even Mingus, never much of a diplomat, was committed to an essentially social, outward facing scene in which the ultimate test for experiments took place in front of an audience whose tolerance could be quickly exhausted. There might be gunshots. As a bandleader, drummer Chico Hamilton specialized in maintaining a balance within this testing environment, picking up unusual ideas from what he heard around him and distilling them down into something immediate and accessible. A light, spacious drumming style, often using large mallets on tom toms, left plenty of space for the musicians – Eric Dolphy, Charles Lloyd, Paul Horn and Gabor Szabo among them – who passed through his bands on their way to individual recognition.

Hamilton's musical vision was 'cool' enough to be seen or heard in zeitgeist films such as *Sweet Smell of Success* (1957), Roman Polanski's *Repulsion* (1965) and *Jazz On a Summer's Day* (1960).

Chico Hamilton's first Quintet came together in 1955 through a series of happy accidents. Fred Katz, a classically trained cellist who had studied with a disciple of Pablo Casals, was playing piano in the backing band when Hamilton was called upon to back singer Jana Mason. A group started to form, first multi-reed player Buddy Collette, then Carson Smith on bass and Katz on piano. After a recommendation, guitarist Jim Hall was added. Club owner Harry Rubin gave them a two-week booking at the Strollers in Long Beach ('where the sailors and the hookers used to come,' according to Fred Katz) but with the success of a series of radio broadcasts on KFOX the residency extended to eight months. At first Fred Katz played improvised solo cello in the intermission. According to Buddy Collette:

> And Fred would always have the energy to play a lot of cello on the intermission. And the stand was very small, and we'd have to come back on the stand – because Fred wouldn't stop playing – not in a malicious way; he'd be playing with his eyes closed – so we'd sneak back on the stand, and once we'd do that he couldn't get back to his piano, it was just that tight. So he'd just stay there and play his lines on the cello.

On a Thursday evening, August 1955, tape equipment was set up to record a Chico Hamilton Quintet set in the Strollers. Of the five pieces later selected for release by Pacific Jazz, one was called 'Free Form', an exercise in free improvisation that had grown, according to Katz, out of his solo improvisations. 'No notes,' he has said, 'just the feeling of each other.' The liner note explanation – 'This mobile abstraction with interspersing excitement appeals to listeners of the third ear' – made it clear that this unfamiliar approach eluded satisfactory description. The piece opens promisingly with fast, loud mallet work by Hamilton, quickly pulled back for Katz's cello entry. Collette's flute picks up the brief hint of a theme, followed by Hall who shadows Collette closely. The most promising moments come from Hamilton and Katz, a robust call and response though not heated enough to unsettle the others. At the end there is applause, the audience is neither huge nor ecstatic but no gunshots are fired.

As with other experiments of this kind in the 1950s, the music enacted in its rather mannered, elegant way a broader political struggle in which radical views on race, suspicions of being a communist, an unusual appearance or any kind of difference risked violent repression. Hamilton's popularity quickly ensnared him in the commercial trap of pleasing agents, audiences, club owners and record companies yet his personal instincts attracted him to some of the destabilizing undercurrents that were becoming apparent from a nascent counterculture. The cover artwork of *Chico Hamilton Quintet In Hi-Fi*, released in 1956, shows one of the original Southern California freaks, Vito Paulekas, working on a sculpture. The Quintet, looking like typical 1950s American salary men in their matching suits, ties and white shirts, pose in the background. Vito and his partner Szou were later connected with many elements of the West Coast underground – Kenneth Anger, The Byrds, Arthur Lee and Love, hippie fashions and dancing, the Mothers of Invention.

Contested definitions of freedom were at stake here – on the one hand the social conservative's anti-collectivist notion of freedom based on tradition, Christianity, rule of law, family values, libertarian economics, technocracy and small government; on the other hand the unstoppable rise of cultural experimentation that ran in parallel with (sometimes at odds with) battles for social justice. Music was the laboratory, a means of exploring what was barely possible in wider society. Similar struggles were being played out in other art forms. In New York City there was Jackson Mac Low, a poet and actor associated with an anarchist group named Resistance. Mac Low worked with Dorothy Malina, co-founder of the Living Theatre with her husband, Julian Beck. Closely connected with pacifists and anarchists who demonstrated against nuclear testing and the escalating arms race, Malina and Beck built their own theatre in an old wooden building at Broadway and 100th Street. 'Before the building inspectors shut them down for code violations in 1955,' Lewis MacAdams wrote, 'the Living Theatre began to hit its stride with a production of *Tonight We Improvise*, Pirandello's "absurd" comedy in which actors take over the plot of a play. Its theme – the effort to obliterate the difference between life and art – would characterise most of the Living's Theatre's greatest work.'

For African American musicians in particular, the struggle to liberate themselves from commercial edicts, authoritarian bandleaders and musical orthodoxies signified a far deeper, more urgent need than cultural experimentation disconnected from both history and current political realities. Who owned the music? Who had the right to dictate the form of the music? Ultimately, who owned the musicians if not themselves?

There is an indication of this on the label of Chico Hamilton's recording of 'Free Form' – the composer credit noted as 'Improvisation'. Under the track listing on the cover of Jazz Composers Workshop No. 2 comes another small sign, conciliatory this time though still noteworthy: 'Although the majority of the compositions heard therein are credited to Mingus and Cirillo, they are actually collaborations of the groups used on the compositions. This is because the majority of the compositions herein are based on the improvisations of the men featured.' Free improvisation presented an ethical challenge to the legal framework of the record business, its hierarchical division of labour and its divisive, frequently exploitative application of copyright enforcement. These were small steps yet they tested alternative possibilities beyond the raw capitalism of the 1950s music industry. As such, they were judged harshly.

'The experiments … suffered the fate that happens to so many similar artistic searches,' wrote Robert Gordon in *Jazz West Coast*. 'At first they were lavishly praised as fresh and original; then a reaction set in and they were damned (often by the same critics!) as straying too far from their jazz heritage.' He quotes André Hodeir's judgement on Shelly Manne's experiments with free improvisation: 'They show us what mistakes can be made by estimable jazzmen working without any doctrine except, perhaps, the most detestable – eclecticism.' Hodeir could be an astute critic. Elsewhere he argued that jazz could never be a pure music but in this case could only hear 'a distressing lack of unity'. Like distant headlights seen intermittently through dense fog, these experiments with collective improvisation showed there was something out there in the unknown.

Behind bars

In New York in the late '50s, pianist Paul Bley has said:

> There were a lot of experiments being made on how to avoid playing popular standards and how to get improvising out of those constricting formats. I participated on several of them, the albums with Don Ellis in the early '60s were part of that problem/solution, some of Mingus' compositions, some of George Russell's compositions, these were

things that were handled by composers and therein lay the problem. It was an improvising problem, over and above a composition problem. So a composer could write something that wasn't thirty-two bars. But as soon as he let someone take a solo on it, it would become metrical, an eight bar system or what have you.

Latency

Scene 8: April 2011, Cork, Ireland. *Just Listen*, a sound event. An audience waiting for technical problems to be solved. Two musicians are in the room, one on a screen behind the stage, one to the side of the stage. The musician on screen is Pauline Oliveros, at that moment physically at home in America. The musician in Cork is guitarist John Godfrey. What separates them is not just the Atlantic Ocean but a secure Skype connection to the Deep Listening Institute. When the problem is solved their duo improvisation is time-lagged by a latency of two or three seconds. 'Yet it didn't seem to matter at all,' writes John Godfrey. 'Somehow the sense of instantaneous give-and-take was still there and there was no feeling of waiting for the other person.'

Play, playfulness, animals, gestures

'Were there factors in your childhood,' koto virtuoso, improviser and sound artist Miya Masaoka asked Pauline Oliveros, 'how you were brought up by your parents … that somehow cultivated and nurtured your ability to realise your personal voice?'
'Yes, straight from my mother,' Oliveros replied.

> She was a pianist and very creative. In the '40s she was playing for a modern dance class, and these women were doing modern dance and improvising, and my mother played little pieces that she remembered. At home we engaged in a lot of play, playfulness, animals, and gestures. It was fun. It continues to this day – having a sense of humour.

Born in Houston, Texas, in 1932, Pauline Oliveros is a composer, improviser and pioneer of electronic music. As the first director of The Tape Music Center at Mills College in Oakland, she used the Buchla Box

100 Series, a modular electronic music system, combined with her own tape delay system to create unearthly pieces such as *Alien Bog* (1967), inspired by the frogs that sang outside her studio window, and *Beautiful Soop* (1966), a dream field of modulating pulsation, high fading tones, male and female readings from Edward Lear and her own vocalizations, mixed with her spoken-aloud musings on the dynamics and workings of the piece. In 1985 she founded the Deep Listening Institute to promulgate her concept of sonic awareness through listening retreats. 'It implies listening below the surface and also listening inwardly,' she told me in 1995. 'So in these sessions with people I try and provide guidelines so that different forms of attention can be practiced. So that you can come away with a fuller sense of the variety of experiences that you can have by listening and not tuning out.'

From her explorations of free improvisation in 1957 she continues to improvise on acoustic and MIDI-retrofitted accordions in remarkable environments, whether the forty-five-second acoustical reverberations of the Dan Harpole cistern at Fort Worden, Washington State, or improvising with far distant collaborators in other countries via telematic media. Listening is at the core of her practice. 'I mean that improvisation is based in listening to all that I can perceive inside and outside of myself before I make a sound – or silence,' she told artist Cory Arcangel. 'Maintaining that level of listening is basic to my improvising.'

In 1957, Oliveros befriended fellow students Terry Riley and Loren Rush at San Francisco State College (in the 1960s a focal point of student unrest and campus protests against the war in Vietnam). Oliveros takes up the story:

> Terry, Loren and I hung out together a lot in those days as we attended San Francisco State College and were in a composer's workshop led by Dr. Wendell Otey. We each studied privately with composer Robert Erickson. He encouraged us to improvise. Terry got a small commission to write a five minute film score for a documentary on sculptor Claire Falkenstein. He did not have time to compose and write the score. Loren was a program associate at Radio KPFA and had access to recording equipment. So we went to the station and improvised some five minute tracks. Terry played piano, Loren played string bass and koto and I played French horn.

By the way we were not looking at the film when improvising nor had we seen it. All we had to go on was duration.

The film was *Polyester Moon*. 'The session occurred in summer 1958,' writes Robert Carl,

> even though the date on the film is 1957. … The music is probably more important for what it represents than what it actually is. Falkenstein's sculpture (a multicoloured globe, apparently the 'moon' of the title, made of what resembles fleshlike polymers, and slit in various places) is viewed as a montage from a variety of angles, both close-up and mid-range. Near the end, at 3' 40" it begins to rotate quickly as the music picks up tempo. The instrumentation sounds different from the way the musicians have described it, Riley's piano sounds mostly like a harpsichord (though he says this effect may be an artefact of the sound transfer to film). And Rush's contribution is clearly percussion – low drums, pieces of wood, and a cymbal (perhaps created partly by percussive knocks on the koto). For most of the piece the horn tends to be the lead, sustaining line, while the keyboard and percussion add ornamental flurries. Oliveros has observed that this may have been the first time 'classical' musicians undertook free improvisation publically, and if so it is a prophetic work.

Given the prevailing dominance of visual culture, film served as a Trojan horse for improvisation, electronic music and informal noise experiments: the barbarous chants and screams of Jean-Isidore Isou's 1951 film, *Venom and Eternity* (*Traité de Bave et d'Eternité*), Teiji Ito's soundtracks for Maya Deren's films in the 1950s, and in a similar style of culturally indeterminate global music, the soundtrack of gongs, piano interior, flutes and drums recorded by Philip Harland and Leona Wood for Curtis Harrington's 1956 profile of occultist Marjorie Cameron, *The Wormwood Star*. Harland and Wood are interesting as typical post-war polymaths, active in art, design, music, dance, anthropology and the occult. Wood was a dancer and designer who moved to California with her husband, physicist Philip Harland, in 1947. Both of them became active in the UCLA Department of Ethnomusicology, established by Mantle Hood in 1960. According to Bruno Nettl, it was Hood's belief that 'the scholar plays a musician's role, even to the extent of performing or possibly composing the music studied'.

La Monte Young has spoken about UCLA's impact on California-based musicians and composers during this period – suddenly they could hear Indian classical raga, Japanese gagaku and Javanese gamelan and the excitement of these previously unheard forms and timbres became gradually evident in their work. At the end of the 1950s Riley and Young recorded improvisations for films by dancer Anna Halprin, for example. Young has described these as 'wild sounds':

> natural sounds, abstract sounds, interesting material juxtapositions such as metal on glass, metal on metal – that I later worked with extensively in 1959–60 when Terry Riley and I were doing the music for Anna Halprin. Terry and I started making incredible sounds; they were very long and very live, and we'd really go inside of them, because they filled up the entire room of the studio. However, we were working with very irrational timbres.

Five recordings of the San Francisco State College improvisations can be heard online, said to be from 1957. The group is Oliveros, Riley and Rush with Laurel Johnson, Robert Erickson and Bill Butler. There is no unifying pulse, no tonal centre. The contemporary music language of the time is dominant – serialism, mobile form, Pierre Boulez's *Third Piano Sonata* and *Le Marteau Sans Maitre*, Karlheinz Stockhausen's *Klavierstücke XI* and Earle Brown's *December 1952* – albeit in a slow, episodic, wait-and-see succession of gestures within silence. Ethnomusicological influences broaden this palette somewhat and there is a notable respect for listening and silence, perhaps a consequence of the impact of John Cage's *4' 33"*.

'We liked doing it and the results worked so we decided to meet often to improvise more,' says Oliveros.

> We found out soon that it was best to just play, then listen to the tape, then discuss. If we tried to impose any structure before we played it just fell flat. When Terry and Loren left the Bay Area to go to New York and France respectively I met Ramon Sender-Barayon, a new student of Erickson's, and began to improvise with him. Morton Subotnick joined us and our venture continued as the San Francisco Tape Music Center was organized. We always included an improvisation on our concerts of tape music. One memorable improvisation included a long tape delay between two machines.

This tape delay became the basis of the long time development of my Expanded Instrument System (EIS).

The element of danger

Was Pauline Oliveros correct in her assumption that these sessions were the first time that 'classically' trained musicians had played free improvisation in public? Perhaps not quite. Lukas Foss was a musical prodigy from Germany. His family left Paris in the dangerous years leading up to the Second World War, ending up in Philadelphia where Foss studied at the Curtis Institute of Music (one of his classmates was Leonard Bernstein, who showed a passing interest in improvisation during the 1960s). In 1957 Foss formed the Improvisation Chamber Ensemble at UCLA. By 1961, when the group released a record on RCA Victor their methodology was well developed. Foss on piano, Richard Dufallo on clarinet, Charles Delancy on percussion and vibraphone and Howard Colf on cello followed graphic scores designating choices. Some themes were notated: for 'Fantasy and Fugue' the pianist used a form of conduction to indicate when chords should be played, how loud or soft, high or low, long or short they should be.

The notes written by Foss to accompany the record betray a curious ambivalence. 'To the classically trained musician,' he wrote, 'improvisation means something makeshift, random, haphazard.' He distinguishes between solo and ensemble playing, with the conclusion that a solo improviser is not limited by any preconceived structural principle, whereas in ensemble improvisation 'he must abide by melodic, harmonic and structural rules lest anarchy and chaos take over. Without order, direction and discipline, there can be no ensemble improvisation. In fact, ensemble improvisation is not possible unless specific ordering principles have been determined beforehand.'

The seven tracks recorded for *Studies In Improvisation* are more accomplished and confident than the pieces by the student group at San Francisco State College – inevitably, since Foss had been a professor of composition at UCLA since 1953 – yet they also close down the possibility of taking the experiment further. Foss's lack of faith in the musicians within an ensemble resulted in a polished but cautious music; despite its pretensions much of it could be the soundtrack to an animated cartoon (if Anton Webern had worked for Disney, perhaps). Even so, classical critics praised the Improvisation Chamber Ensemble for 'incredible delicacy, suggestive at times of the firefly imagery of Webern' and 'musical history in the making ... the beginning of an inspired concept in instrumental music', a sharp contrast to the scepticism of jazz critics.

The group was overpraised but Foss was prescient in foreseeing a time when ensemble improvisation would be taught in universities and conservatories and insightful about the listening process. 'This active listening', he wrote, 'is a combination of curiosity and excitement similar to that which we feel when we watch a game or contest (Peculiar to ensemble improvisation is the element of danger, of "hit-or-miss," which an audience is quick in grasping and enjoying).' As it transpired, other improvisation experiments of the 1940s and 1950s would persist and grow into unforeseeable forms. Think of the contrapuntalism of Miles Davis, the foundation of starkly contrasting periods in his later career, whether the great second Quintet of 1965–8, the free funk of *On the Corner*, the extraordinarily close, intense electric group that played the Isle of Wight Festival or the open improvisation of 'Ife', as played at Montreaux in 1973. Think also of Terry Riley's *In C*, La Monte Young's Sunday Morning Blues and its influence on the Velvet Underground, the Deep Listening Institute activities of Pauline Oliveros and all the music that has flowed just from those sources alone.

5 COLLECTIVE SUBJECTIVITIES 2

The power-logic was that control derives from formality, and formality entails theatricality of the sort separating celebrant and spectator.

RICHARD SENNETT, *Together*

February 2003. Immediately after the last of my recorded conversations with Derek Bailey, during which I tried to hold him to an account of what it is to play, not all the amusing, scurrilous and slanderous anecdotes interpenetrating the life of the player, but the actuality of improvising in its moment, I sent him a letter. In the previous year he had released *Ballads*, an album that acted as tacit acknowledgement of a hidden truth, that Bailey's singular method of improvising – the quick certainty of pitch relationships, clusters and implicit harmony – was inseparable from a certain tradition of jazz guitar of which the solo or trio ballad was a central core, a musician alone(ish) with melancholy and difficult sequences of closely voiced chords, glad to be unhappy.

Bailey had been offered a fee to play at a birthday party. In effect, he was the gift, which to him must have invoked the kind of scene in which a young woman in a bikini burst out of a cake. He took the job, but added a caveat that there would be no ballads, just in case the release of his album had precipitated a wave of nostalgia for American song book classics such as 'Laura' and 'You Go To My Head' among ageing improvised music fans around the world.

My letter ran as follows:

Transcribing the tape is very interesting (despite the drudgery of it). The evasions, diversions and moments of resonance are very telling. In fact, the loud and semi-conscious absence of our agreed subject –

to play – makes me think something I never thought before, never imagined I would contemplate and fills me with dread: that this would make a wonderful play. What we're trying to talk about in such a halting way has a significance that goes way beyond music, I think. It's kind of about the motion of living in such a way that makes living meaningful, all of which is then masked by music, pottery, cabinet making and the whole business of business. I remember we talked about that film, *The Fabulous Baker Boys*, which was quite alarmingly close to the truth of playing, at certain moments. … Your birthday party gig should probably not happen, because the imagined reality should be filmed by Lars von Trier as a kind of ghastly catastrophe.

To my knowledge, the party did not disintegrate into recriminations and beatings (I was muddling von Trier with Thomas Vinterberg's *Festen*); nor did the play come to pass. Bailey died before I could muster the confidence to embark on such a thing. But his reply was surprisingly enthusiastic. He thought of Beckett, naturally. As to the other idea, this vague thought about the 'motion of living', he was even more affirmative: 'YES. "It's kind of about the motion of living that makes living meaningful". You've either put your finger on it or pointed it in the right direction.'

Which was encouraging but what exactly was meant? Maybe that to play as an improviser opens up a life of potential. To think in terms of a continuum of playing – a practice not divided up into professional engagements, practice and the rest of life – is to generate momentum, to link up the most humble, abject experience with those fleeting moments with an audience.

By the way, *The Fabulous Baker Boys* was a film that Bailey found fascinating yet also astonishing in its focus on something so mundane, a story about musicians keeping on the move no matter what: wasted talent, dull lives, conflict, humiliation, flashes of what might have been, a parody of that feeling of completion as it dwindles to a bitter trace.

As Gary Peters writes: 'The peculiarity of free-improvisation is that it does not produce works.' Improvisers are continually refusing works, legacy, the archive (though recordings have complicated that position in the past, less so now with the collapse of recorded music as a commercial enterprise).

To follow the thought of Peters, they engage in incessant self-interruption, 'thus protecting the homelessness of the productive imagination from the conceptual structures that would limit its play'.

Every moment of an improvisation may be the last moment you will hear (until the next one). And if free improvisation could live up to those expectations of freedom that sit so heavily upon it and if audiences were still innocent in the age of ubiquitous information in which every kink niche is but a link to elsewhere, then according to Peters, improvisation might still have the fixity of wind-blown sand:

> Representing, along with the performers, the 'standpoint of the other' necessary for an improvisation to attain the intensity to begin, the audience is here denied the all-too-familiar pleasures of the known and forced instead to witness close up not only the contingency of the artwork's occurence but also the uncertainty of its continuance, the contestation of its identity, and its eventual destruction at the hands of the improvisers.

Though I believe this within the capsule of theory, experience tells me otherwise. It was true, perhaps, in the 1970s when an audience might react aggressively, impatiently, with disbelief or derision as if they had stumbled upon a Martian ritual.

Please respect our space

Alterations – Peter Cusack, Terry Day, Steve Beresford and myself – played at Amsterdam's Melkweg in the late 1970s. As if punk and disco had never happened, hippie culture was still alive within those dope-soaked walls, supine smokers littered about the floor like toppled statues in an abandoned museum. Woken abruptly from deep sleep they roused themselves in collective hatred of what we played, jeering and throwing missiles.

    The same group played at the Palais des Beaux-Arts in Brussels on a number of occasions, one of which is more memorable than the others. The venue has an open-plan stage area in its centre. As usual we spread instruments all over the floor. As I recall there was an exhibition of Magritte paintings elsewhere in the building. During our set a group of very wealthy Belgian art dealers walked to the edge of our performance area but instead of walking around us decided just to walk straight through our kit. The recording engineer, very mild up until that point, erupted and physically attacked them. Singer Maggie Nicols was in the audience and I distinctly remember her jumping up, shouting 'Oy, oy, oy' to stop the fight. I think we carried on playing and I also think the incident ended up on our second LP.

No doubt these incidents become conflated into a single all-encompassing memory, a lost Marx Brothers script or half-remembered Jacques Tati film. Mike Cooper was present at this concert. 'Steve Beresford was chased around the piano at one point', he says, 'by some crazed guy who seemed to object to Steve previously sellotaping himself to the piano.' In fact, Beresford had been using sellotape to block off the path that led straight through his instruments, raising a question about public space so reasonable (we are performing, please respect our space by taking the fractionally longer route to the coffee bar) and yet so inflammatory (a pipe that is not a pipe is important but your instruments that are not instruments are not) that it provoked violence.

Barging in

Inevitably, free improvisation invited trouble from the kind of anarcho–hippie libertarianism that aggressively imposed itself on any event deemed antipathetic to the 'free society' (free love, free entry to festivals, free food, free travel, imagine no possessions and so on).

Percussionist Andrea Centazzo writes below about the situation in Italy in the 1970s, when claims to possession of anything connected to public space – instruments, the performance stage, your name on a poster, even the duration of an event – was fair game for invasion.

I have memories of such invasions but they are incomplete. To organize a concert and raise an audience was difficult enough in those days; to have the concert sabotaged in this way was depressing; the frustration lingers but the good parts are forgotten.

In 1978, Steve Beresford wrote a think piece about the problem (specifically referring to a concert by myself and percussionist Paul Burwell) in *Musics* magazine. *Musics* was a London-based publication launched in April 1975 to address the problem of an almost total absence of public discourse around improvised music. Over five years and twenty-three issues the magazine was collectively edited and produced by improvising musicians and supporters of the music. Fractious, disputatious and occasionally excessive, it gave voice to the contestation of musical norms.

There is no information about the venue or date of the concert but it may have been the ICA in London.

> David Toop and Paul Burwell had been playing for quite a while; the French people behind me were giggling and making noises parodying the ones of the music. Eventually a woman from among them shuffled in to the performance area and tentatively lifted her hand to strike a gong. At this moment, Paul Burwell pulled the other end of rope suspending the gong, and it was hoisted out of her reach. She returned to her seat. The performance continued.
> A little later, a man entered the performance area and began playing a small drum of Paul's, repetitively, continuously. Paul went over to a bucket of water, played a small drum in it for a minute, and then emptied the water over the man. The man continued playing. Eventually he bored/irritated the musicians so much that they stopped playing. A conversation with him, still playing the drum, yielded the advice that Paul 'ought to read John Cage'. Nobody told the man that Cage dislikes people joining in or that Paul was well acquainted with Cage's writing. I went up to him, told him that his drumming was irritating and insensitive and asked him to stop. He said that it was good that I was irritated, and that I should not be a passive spectator. The question of passivity is an interesting one. Is a listener who doesn't take part in making music/dancing/heckling merely passive? I don't think so.

Beresford makes the point that this kind of invasion, a desire to enter and take over the loosely demarcated space of improvisation, is extremely rare in concerts where the space for music is marked with unambiguous signs of difference: a stage, conventional instruments, different lighting, special costumes, security guards and barriers and an attitude from the musicians which consciously distinguishes them from the audience. Informality in this case enables protest against excessive formality elsewhere.

On the next page of *MUSICS* was a feature on The People Band, one of the first free improvising groups of the 1960s. A photo caption listing the musicians shown – Terry Day, Barry Edgar Pilcher, Charlie Hart, Ian Jacobs, Davey Payne and one other – also comments: 'The bloke with bongos and mallet on marimba is a Jesus freak who joined in.' It was, to quote Prince, a sign o' the times, though not unrelated to online behaviour in our digital age.

Lines that cut across

Free improvisation, whatever else, is a site of anxiety, vulnerable to its own disintegration, to political lines of battle and their contradictions, to uncertainties from within and invasions from without. The anecdotes of musicians should not be taken lightly; in their oblique way, they address precarity and anxiety. For all musicians, particularly those who dedicate themselves to free improvisation, these stories give continuity, dark humour, a flimsy structure to lives that are more precarious than most. They accumulate as oral history, legends in which bathos is honoured alongside the more elevated moments of playing.

Life as an improviser is unstable by definition. Saxophonist John Butcher speaks about being engaged in a music performance, 'and not knowing where its going to lead and also, in the broader sense in your life, of who you're going to be playing with, what circumstances you're going to be playing what, what situations, who you're going to be collaborating with'.

I asked if that was true of other aspects of his life.

'It is,' he replied, adding:

> Years ago somebody in Sweden asked, do you improvise in your life as much as you improvise in music? Life is improvisation but I think I'd be inclined to say that in order to do it – to lead this kind of musical life – I try as much as possible to keep as ordered as I can be in the rest of my life, in my practical life. I need the stability of that. I mean there are players who can basically be on the road all the time, travelling, even not have a specific place they live and they just go where the spirit takes them. That aspect is not my temperament.

For improvisers there are questions about the lines that cut across sound. Listening recognizes few boundaries, has no sight lines, so the concert hall and club space establishes barriers, directionality, formality, not only for acoustic and visual enhancement but also to differentiate artist from listener. But improvisation demands an extra level of effort from its listeners, to follow its form as it emerges, to hear detailed interplay as the musicians hear it. To be within the invisible web of interconnecting sound is to hear the source of ideas, change, contingency; to be outside it is closer to receiving a work. Active listening (joining in without adding noise) is a skill learnt by audiences over the past fifty years. This has gone too far in the other direction, some might say, too reverential, too knowing, too resistant to being undone.

Some of these stories are prophetic in that they unwittingly rehearse for our current situation, life online, where experience, knowledge and skill can be trampled by self-absorbed, opinionated instant experts. Conscious of this link (ironic when improvisers have often been denigrated as amateurs) I used a social media site to ask the question: Improvising musicians and anybody who was ever a part of the audience for an improvised music concert – do you have stories of unusual audience reactions – funny, disturbing, bizarre, angry? Out of more than 140 responses I selected the following:

Fred Frith:

> Eugene Chadbourne at the Bimhuis in the 1980s. He's playing a really long and painfully loud feedback solo on The Rake [an amplified rake], and seems oblivious to anyone or anything. After about ten minutes a gentleman in a suit steps up on stage and pulls out the plug of the amp. They then have a rather surreal conversation (argument?) which ends after some time with Eugene proclaiming: 'It's alright for you, man, I have to do this every night.'

Raymond Salvatore Harmon:

> About ten years ago in Chicago I curated a series of shows and at one, a trio with a rather well known line-up of clarinet, vibes, and cello the crowd was almost non existent. Besides the wife of the vibes player and I there was only a couple with their child in a car seat carrier. The husband was sitting and watching intently and his reactions to solos was very over exaggerated. Ever time he cheered it was obviously painful to the cellist (who thought he was making fun of the group). At one point the cellist took a solo and then paused to do some prepared bit below the bridge and when he paused the guy cheered loudly and clapped, breaking the cellist's concentration. The cellist stood up and started shouting at the guy thinking he was trolling the musicians. After just a short outburst and an exchange of words it became clear that the cellist misunderstood and the fan was just not used to improvised music and the audience rules. The single most embarrassing thing I have ever seen at an improv show.

Daniel Pennie:

> The Michael Giles Mad Band on stage in Finland – a somewhat drunken Finn approached the stage rolling an oil drum. He hoisted it onto the stage exclaiming 'You're spontaneous musicians … play this!' We obliged with some drilling.

Fred Frith:

> There was a rock improv gig at Soundscape in New York in 1981 (I think) where Mark Miller had inevitably brought along a suitcase full of fireworks, and equally inevitably had managed to set light to the whole lot at once. As we musically wheeled and plunged he leapt up and down frantically on the case, each landing sending a sheet of flame sideways, and each leap up causing smoke to billow out vertically. This was both grimly entertaining and somewhat hair-raising and the music reached new heights until we were convinced we had done something quite extraordinary. Well, we had. The music ended when the last firework was extinguished. And we waited for the (we thought) inevitable ovation (there had been a full house). Alas at the first sight of smoke they had all left and were now standing on the street downstairs waiting for the fire brigade, a fact that said smoke had completely obscured from us.

Drew Daniel:

> At a Matmos show in the Nefertiti Jazz Club in Gothenberg, Sweden, we were improvising (er, or perhaps 'jamming' might be closer to the truth?) and a very flipped out woman holding a bouquet of flowers crawled up onstage and went over to our guitarist Nate and started inserting flowers into his pants, one at a time. She had the 'shining eyes' I associate with LSD but who knows? Also: once in Cleveland at DIY space Speak In Tongues were improvising and a cat emerged from a side room, leapt up onto my sampler, and fell asleep on my keyboard during the show. That was a blessing.

Andrea Centazzo:

> Playing crazy music you obviously step in crazy people. I remember a solo performance in Taranto at the beginning of my career probably

1972 or '73. I was doing my usual shit when a group of ultra leftists stormed in the venue. Note that the concert was a free concert organized by the Communist Party! They came on stage and said that the music belongs to all the people and everybody is capable of playing. Then they pushed me off the stage and they took all my instruments and started a cacophony adding chanting like 'free this, free that' … then they left with my instruments. At the last minute seeing that, I started yelling 'this is not a revolution, but a capitalistic stealing.' … Somehow the dumb audience since I was touching a 'political matter' started to react and the battle started. While they were punching each other in a total chaos, I recouped all I could and I exited the backstage, still some gongs and drums were missing but no physical damage whatsoever. Those were the years post '68 in Italy. Not to mention when in Padova in 1977 I was performing a duo concert with Evan Parker and somebody threw a barking dog at him on stage.

Sylvia Hallett:

Playing with ARC in Luton – after the gig a woman who had really enjoyed it said, 'But how do you manage to remember it all?' I tried to explain improvisation, but she just couldn't believe that you could start with no structure at all – 'So how do you know when to change what you're doing?'

Mike Cooper:

Lol Coxhill, myself and dancer Joanna Pyne at the London Musicians Collective. A woman in the audience protests that Lol and I are exploiting Joanna's body. Lol strips off to his underpants and exclaims, 'Who's exploiting what now?'

6 INTO THE HOT

This experience made me wonder about improvised music, specifically how it can work with its immediate environment, as an active part of it? Do we really need professional environments to make music in – black box, white box, stage or audience?
YAN JUN, The Wire, 2014

Gutai means something like 'concrete' or 'concreteness', the proof of a free spirit and mind, the desire to do something that nobody has done before. For one of the physical actions performed at the 1st Gutai Art Exhibition of 1955 in Tokyo, Saburō Murakami violently smashed his way, fists first, through three large paper screens. During the Gutai Art of the Stage exhibition, held in Osaka in 1957, Kazuo Shiraga's *Ultra-Modern Sanbasō* began with a lit stage empty except for a row of painted poles. 'The poles fell down one by one,' Ming Tiampo writes, 'producing a "painting" moving through time and space and incorporating the sound of the poles striking the ground.'

The Gutai group of artists was formed in 1956 in Ashiya, an affluent community of artistic celebrities and business people situated between Osaka and Kobe. For the leader of the group, Jirō Yoshihara, the process behind the paintings of Jackson Pollock not only collapsed illusionistic space and purified the elements of painting; they gave life to materials, even to the extent that their vitality could be felt through sound. According to Ming Tiampo: 'Yoshihara would develop this reading of the American artist even further in the Gutai Art Manifesto, writing that Pollock's work "reveals the scream of the material itself, cries of the paint and enamel".'

Tiampo argues convincingly for a decentred modernism that acknowledges movements like Gutai not as secondary shadowings and precursors of (usually) American innovation but as surges reactive to specific cultural and political situations. Post-war Japanese artists struggled to detach themselves from the past, whether the right-wing nationalists who pursued imperialism and war, orientalist stereotypes imposed on them from the occident or the weight of their own aesthetic traditions. After all, Murakami's burst through paper evoked paper walls and shōji dividers in traditional Japanese homes, while Shiraga's use of falling poles was a direct reference to the opening section of the Noh theatre. There were elements of traditional Japanese art that opened out new ways of thinking about music also. Toru Takemitsu's personal reconciliation with those Japanese traditional instruments – biwa and shakuhachi – tainted by nationalist conservatism is one example. Composer Matsudaira Yoritsune's incorporation of the indeterminate elements of gagaku court music is another. Citing the research of Judith Herd, Thomas R. H. Havens writes: 'Almost a decade before the chance operations of John Cage became known in Japan, Matsudaira was using an open-notation system based on the free-form structure of gagaku court music.'

By contrast, another Gutai artist – Atsuko Tanaka – created an unprecedented sound work (one that we might now describe as sound art) in 1955 with *Bell*. An installation of twenty connected electric fire bells set out on the floor, close to the walls of the gallery, *Bell* was activated by any visitor who pressed a button marked 'Please press the switch'. By encouraging this voluntary participation through a medium as intrusive and volatile as sound, Tanaka provoked questions of freedom and participatory creation also common to improvisation. 'The sound of the bells someone else pressed is very noisy,' Gutai artist Fujiko Shiraga wrote in 1956. 'If you press it yourself, you get just what you want. In other words, even though you did not make the work and are only a viewer, by pressing this switch, you are standing on the very edge of the act of creating. This means that you can immerse yourself in the joy of making something you would never have dreamed possible and, at the same time, you experience the terror of being responsible for yourself to the very limit.' Activators of *Bell* found themselves dramatically positioned in relation to space articulated by the ephemerality and intangibility of sound – hence Tanaka's description of her work as a painting. Many of these artists considered themselves painters yet they acquired a reputation among critics as anti-artists. In 1970, artist, composer and cultural commentator Yasunao Tone ventured a more positive interpretation: 'The work is always unfinished, fostering the idea that it is equivalent to the everyday, to real objects and daily activities. Thus it's not at all strange that every concrete object or ordinary action suffices as a painting.'

Falling/tearing

There is a sense of falling, of disintegration, of tearing the body apart; violent at times, yet also quiet to the very edge of insignificance.

In *Word Events*, a book of verbal scores, James Saunders quotes Takehisa Kosugi, an artist and musician who has been associated over a long career with Fluxus, John Cage, David Tudor, Peter Kowald, Akio Suzuki, Merce Cunningham, Steve Lacy, the 1960s improvising group Taj Mahal Travellers and many other collaborators: 'The sound object is not always music, but action, action. Sometimes no sound, just action. Opening a window is a beautiful action, even if there's no sound. It's part of the performance. For me that was very important, opening my eyes and ears to combining the non-musical part and the musical part of action. In my concerts, music became this totality, so even if there was no sound I said it was music. Confusing. This is how I opened my eyes to chaos.'

In 1958 Kosugi was improvising on violin with his fellow classmate at Tokyo National University of Fine Arts and Music, a cellist named Mizuno Shûko. 'After playing him a tape from these sessions,' writes William A. Marotti, 'Kosugi invited Tone to join them, unprejudiced and in fact utterly unmindful of Tone's degree of musical training – which was then nonexistent.' Tone bought a saxophone and a tape recorder and joined the group along with Mieko Shiomi, Tsuge Gen'ichi and Tojima Mikio, all students of the musicology course, and Tanno Yumiko, who was studying vocal music at the university.

Yasunao Tone recalls this first meeting:

Shûko Mizuno and Takehisa Kosugi had started when I joined them. They improvised without any score, but they might have [used] certain kinds of instruction or rather rules. I was a classmate of Mizuno's in Chiba University, where I had written a thesis on dada and surrealism. Probably I visited them at Geidai, Tokyo School of Arts, where they had been students of ethnomusicology. If my recollection is right, Mizuno and Kosugi invited me to watch and listen in the ethnomusicology study room, where there were many folk instruments. It could be that they wanted me to listen to their recorded performance. Kosugi suggested me to join them with other students. I had not had an instrument but Kosugi was going to buy a new alto saxophone so I decided to buy his old one. I had no formal music education.

Even before visiting Geidai, I had been listening to modern music on NHK educational radio. I went to a concert that performed Stockhausen's *Kontrapunkte* where I had seen Mizuno among the audience. Also, we listened to Indian music, which was one of the models for Kosugi and Mizuno's improvisation methods; the others were tango, which was the answer one of us proudly replied to Toru Takemitsu when he asked us if we were playing jazz like him. Others were Noh music and jazz. Listening to the duo I thought that wasn't enough and we needed radical change.

For Tone the barrier to achieving their ideal of improvisation was melody. He would play as many notes as possible on the saxophone or leave spaces in short passages, yet still not overcome the problem. His next step was to play many different instruments from the ethnomusicology department, all of them in quick succession. From the university the group shifted their sessions to Mizuno's home where they attempted collective improvisation of musique concrète by making sound on everyday objects.

As Tone wrote in his 1960 essay, *Improvisation As Automatism*, these objects included:

> an oil barrel, washtubs, water jugs, tuning forks, plates, hangers, metal and wood dolls, a vacuum cleaner, 'Go' stones, cups, radios, a voice reading a gardening reference book, a wall clock, a rubber ball, an alto saxophone's mouth piece, prepared piano, etc. that were readied as sound sources. Once we began recording, the innumerable sound materials arranged before us strangely and intensely impressed us with a sonic image. Our improvisational performance then began completely spontaneously. And so, these innumerable sounds that in everyday life go unnoticed, or are emitted according only to necessity, made us feel as if we had set our identities aside amid the movement and collision of the materials themselves, and been able to grasp their materialized unconscious breath.

Mieko Shiomi (also known at that time as Chieko) was born in Okayama in 1938 (the same year as Kosugi, three years after Tone). Through Yoko

Ono she came into contact with George Brecht and by 1963 she was creating what she called conceptual events.

I asked her if she used voice for the sessions at Mizuno's house, also whether they used any kind of score or instruction: 'Not only voice, I was using vacuum cleaner, egg beater or other kitchenware. In our weekly practices sometimes we made a rough regulation or order of the ensemble, but in the performance of "Automatism" we didn't.'

Where did the decision to play in this way come from?

> The motivation for me to start playing improvisation music was the experience of playing the piano part of Schoenberg's *Pierrot Lunaire* at a university festival. After that I had an interest in playing piano, not of other composers' works, but my own music. Then I started playing improvisation music with the members who played Schoenberg together, flutist and vocalist. When I found Kosugi and others already playing improvisation music with strings, I proposed we should do it together. It was the beginning of Group Ongaku. When I was a little girl, my hobby was to sing my own improvised song.

It was Tone who proposed the name Ongaku ('music', in Japanese). He was thinking of the sarcastic and antiphrastic title of *Littérature*, the magazine directed by André Breton and Louis Aragon, but there was an additional element: Ongaku could be written with different characters, as 'sound eats', or 'sound is pain'. Two recordings by the six members of Group Ongaku (their final choice of name) were made on 8 May 1960. One was titled 'Automatism', the other 'Object'. I asked Mieko Shiomi about 'Automatism', a clear link to surrealist automatic writing or painting.

> This performance was done in Mizuno's house, while we usually practiced in the school room. There were many objects in the house that we could use to make noise. This situation evoked our spontaneity. Tone had a lot of knowledge about surrealism. This title was put later. But I think this title described correctly the quality of our improvisation on that day.

Did you think of it as 'music' or was it closer to 'noise' or 'art'?

'At that time I was thinking of it as music.'

Tempest of immediacy

It may be that few other people thought of it as music. Very little exists from the same period that so comprehensively dismantles musical protocols, orthodox notions of form, the instrument, technique or 'legitimate' materials. The recording is primitive, suffering from distortion, a lack of clarity and strange depth perspectives, some sounds suddenly alarmingly close, some so remote that they could be from the house next door. Other sounds aggressively fill or flatten the spatial image, an effect closer to the abstract expressionist destruction of illusionistic space found in Pollock, Franz Kline, Arshile Gorky or the Gutai painters, Kanayama Akira, Yamazaki Tsuroko or Shiraga Kazuo. Voices whisper in the ear and in echoing distance, swamped by grotesque hums, untutored saxophone bleating, air blown directly into the microphone, nonsense language and cries, clock chimes, grinding and friction, radio signals, hammering, motors revving up then down again, fragments of prepared piano, deep gong sounds from the oil drum, squeaks, rattles, sounds of spit and mouth, water shaken in a jug, rustling and tapping audibly moving around the room. It is a chaos of action in which presence is palpable, as if bodies are colliding off bodies in claustrophobic space, each contact sparking a burst of noise.

Chaos is the spectre haunting free improvisation, the fear and revulsion implicit in its methodology, as if to create music with this intention is to invite social anarchy and the collapse of civilized society. In this case it was the opposite extreme – militarism and the repression of personal expression and social liberty led eventually to chaos, the aftermath of Hiroshima and Nagasaki, American occupation, poverty and abjection. This was the context out of which groups like Gutai and Group Ongaku emerged.

I asked Yasunao Tone, what do you feel about the concept of freedom in relation to what you did in Group Ongaku? Was this way of playing more 'free' than other ways of working with sound?

'Yes I was very much aware of both. I thought we were able to liberate ourselves from not only formal conventions but also our consciousness. Otherwise we would never materialize real freedom in improvisation.'

Simply to act in a disorderly way or play random sounds on an instrument (the stereotypical view of free improvisation in the 1960s and 1970s) would result only in quotidian sound, what he describes as the 'habitual corporeal reality of schematic actions'. To counteract that gravitational pull towards routine he felt it was essential to make sound with folk instruments and everyday objects, to work collectively and to draw on the historical example of the surrealists use of automatism. 'It was the surrealists use of automatism,' he says, 'including automatic writing, decalcomania, collage, exquisite corpse, coutage etc. [that were believed to access the] unconscious. I believe my thesis on dada and surrealism contributed to the theorisation of our group improvisation.' In his essay, Tone expressed the group's ambition to go beyond Pierre Schaeffer's conception of musique concrète as a compositional device; through collective, spontaneous improvisation they would reveal the 'true form of the *objet sonore* in which the degrees of transparency and opacity, dampness and hardness resound within a storm of immediacy'.

The group's sole public concert – *Sokkyo Ensou to Onkyou Objet (Improvisation and Objet Sonore)* – took place in Tokyo on 15 September 1961. The venue was Japan's avant garde centre, the Sōgetsu Āto Sentā founded by ikebana master Teshigahara Sōfū with programmes directed by his son, the filmmaker and close compatriot of Toru Takemitsu, Hiroshi Teshigahara. By this time their music was more reminiscent of free jazz, albeit a type of free jazz that barely existed at that time – certainly not Cecil Taylor's highly sophisticated 1958 recording, *Looking Ahead!* – which is alive with the presence of Fats Waller, Duke Ellington and Thelonious Monk, nor the Joe Harriott Quintet's 1960 *Free Form*, whose tight arrangements and quicksilver tempos were far beyond the capabilities or aspirations of the Tokyo students. With the presence of a public, the rough-grained image overload of 'automatism' was replaced by spasmodic surges of piano and drums, a saxophone apparently wandering through the auditorium, isolated amplified voices, bubbling water, a tape or record played in reverse. Pauses and outbursts in the music jolt audience members into spasmodic reactions, a lone person clapping, perhaps sardonically, some murmurs and laughter. As the group's activity subsides almost to inaudibility – strings plucked as if by accident – the audience applauds together.

For Yasunao Tone, this concert, their first, ended the collective activity known as Group Ongaku. Despite some recognition from composer Toshi Ichiyanagi, recently returned from New York and sufficiently impressed by the performance to invite them to attend his solo recital in the Sōgetsu contemporary music series, an internal contradiction had arisen which led the group to disband. In the previous year Group Ongaku had been invited as guests to a forum organized by young dance critics from the Association of 20th Century Dance. Tone describes the forum:

> One of the members of Hakudai Yamano asked a question, 'What do you think of *engagement*?' This French word for political participation was commonly used by students and intellectuals. The background of this question is: In the year 1960, there was a mass movement for Anti-US Japan Security Treaty (Revision of the US-JAPAN Security Treaty, 1960). We, too, participated in the demonstrations and protest marches. The circumstances fitted perfectly with our group activity so our group improvisation had not only an artistic but a political implication. We need the participation of audience in our work, I answered deliberately to the question, despite the fact that I knew his posited answer meant political participation. The reply to the question had changed my artistic direction. My answer to Yamano made me aware that our improvisation had been inadequate to revolutionize music as we had known it. I thought, we have to abolish the triadic hierarchy, namely composer, performer and audience.

Tone's answer to this realization was to create scores using graphic notation and written instructions: in essence, directed improvisation. Does this not signal the return of the composer, I asked. 'Yes, it is the reappearance of a composer but at least anybody is able to play the piece because it doesn't require musical training but an imagination.'

Takehisa Kosugi and Mieko Shiomi also followed this direction with succinct, poetic verbal scores:

Kosugi's *Theatre Music*:

Keep Walking Intently

and *Micro 1* (1964):

> Wrap a live microphone with a very large sheet of paper/Make a light bundle/Keep the microphone live for another 5 minutes;

Mieko Shiomi's *Boundary Music* (1963):

> Make the faintest possible sound to a boundary condition whether the sound is given birth to as a sound or not. At the performance, instruments, human bodies, electronic apparatus or anything else may be used.

Simple as it seems I have used this latter score with students who experience its richness as an opening to questions about making, listening, spatial awareness, collective presence and the nature of music itself. Did the experience of collective improvisation lead directly to that piece I asked Shiomi or was she already thinking in this way when she began playing with Group Ongaku?

'At that time I was always thinking about sounds and music. To perceive and recognize what sound is, I thought, we should make it the faintest possible to the boundary condition, whether we can hear it or not. It is also true that by the intensive practice of Group Ongaku I got tired of big sounds.'

With hindsight we can see that a desire to find more inclusive and democratic forms of musical practice would be answered by verbal scores of this kind. They have the potential to challenge aesthetic and perceptual orthodoxies at a profound level yet their simplicity allows participation from anybody who is prepared to apply themselves to an interpretation. What we also know is that the quest to find a music capable of articulating and propagating an ideology became a series of frontiers. Once a new frontier of *engagement* had been reached, those in the past were denounced.

In London The Scratch Orchestra devised and interpreted such scores in a more-or-less collective setting. In a balanced essay about the Scratch Orchestra's indebtedness to the visual arts, Michael Parsons wrote:

> A Fluxus-like interest in everyday activities, redefined and transposed into the context of performance, was much in evidence. A glance through *Scratch Music* and *Nature Study Notes* [edited Cornelius Cardew, 1969] reveals many examples of such activities: standing, sitting, walking, running, jumping, smoking, washing, shaving, haircutting, eating, drinking, sweeping, ball-bouncing, stone-throwing, measuring, counting, inventing and playing games of various kinds – the list could be extended ad infinitum. All these and more were liable to occur in performance.

This element of contingency and pragmatism is exemplified by Michael Parsons in *Improvisation Rite* (1969, *Nature Study Notes*):

> The time available is divided by the number of people taking part.
> Each person then plays for a fraction of the total time. He can split it up any way he wishes.

Attractive and effective as they are, these scores failed to cast out the triadic hierarchy. Instead, they proved highly amenable to curation within the art historical narrative generated by museums. In general – though Mieko Shiomi's 'events' are an exception – they compacted revolutionary strategies for collective improvisation into beautiful objects, highly susceptible to recreation as acts of nostalgia for the golden age of the avant-garde.

Unscrewing the inscrutable

Why must we bear such things in the age of Pollock?
YASUNAO TONE

If there can be abstract painting, why not abstract music?
JOE HARRIOTT

6 June 1961, the Dover Street premises of the Institute of Contemporary Art in London, an evening called Project for Noise in which critic and curator Lawrence Alloway introduced a film by John Latham and a discussion of his work. In the previous year at the ICA, 6 December, Brion Gysin had collaborated with BBC technicians on a work for experimental vision and electronic sound. On 15 November 1960, as part of the Michael Horovitz Live New Departures series, Cornelius Cardew and John Tilbury performed new music (Tilbury has no memory of which pieces though it may have been Cardew's *February Papers*, Cage, Morton Feldman or Christian Wolff); Peter Brown (later a lyricist for Cream) and Horovitz performed jazz poems with Alan Cohen, Bruce Turner, Dudley Moore and Ronnie Scott; William Burroughs, Adrian Mitchell and Gregory Corso read from their own texts. Headlining the evening, if there could be said to be a headliner of such a thrillingly disparate crew, was the Joe Harriott Quintet.

Horovitz is quoted as saying something to the effect that Burroughs visibly warmed to Harriott's playing. Burroughs and warmth being words only rarely found in close proximity, it may be that Joe Harriott's decision to play an entirely free form set with his Quintet came as some relief from the more conventional jazz heard that night, particularly for a writer who was describing sounds from the future long before musicians were creating them.

Harriott was a complex, difficult character; difficult in his dealings with other people but also difficult to assess and evaluate within conventional musicology. Born in Kingston, Jamaica, in 1928, he learnt clarinet in the orphanage to which he was consigned shortly before his tenth birthday. The Alpha Boys' Band, as it was known, gave a solid education to young men who might otherwise have fallen into criminality. A long list of Jamaica's most distinguished musicians, including trombonists Don Drummond and Rico Rodriguez, saxophonists Tommy McCook, 'Deadly' Headley Bennett and Eddie 'Tan Tan' Thornton, flautist Harold McNair and drummer Leroy 'Horsemouth' Wallace, also graduated from the orphanage band's strict tuition, meaning that two distinct new styles of music – reggae and free improvisation – have claims to origination in this one benevolent institution.

During his first trip to London with the Ozzie da Costa band in the early summer of 1951, Harriott immediately showed up on the radar of local musicians. By August he was sitting in at Oxford Street's Feldman Club (soon to become the 100 Club); shortly after that he was working. This was hardly surprising. Playing alto saxophone in the style of Charlie Parker, he was fast, fluent, technically brilliant, passionate, imperious. In a scene permanently on one knee to the gods of America his sudden appearance bears comparison with the arrival of Jimi Hendrix in London in 1967, a genius figure who loaned otherness and legitimacy to musicians who hardly dared to believe in themselves.

By 1958 his musical ideas were outrunning those of his contemporaries. 'Trumpeter Shake Keane knew as early as 1958 that Harriott was thinking his way towards something revolutionary,' writes Harriott biographer Alan Robertson. According to Keane:

> We used to talk quite a lot – if Joe could be said to talk – before I joined the quintet. We used … to try to 'unscrew the inscrutable'. That is, we used to deal in all kind of metaphysical aspects of all kinds of occult situations and whatnot. Well anyway, in the middle of this,

we sometimes used to speculate on what would happen if you played jazz without chords.

There was also a car journey from London to Frankfurt described by Coleridge Goode in his autobiography:

> He said he thought it could be possible to play without those pre-determined harmonies and, in fact, without any preconceptions at all about what was to be played and how. The idea would be to rely on complete spontaneity from all the musicians: to let the group's free interaction create harmonies and musical relationships between the instruments that had not been planned in advance.

Free form (Again)

Two years after these unscrewings of the inscrutable, the Joe Harriott Quintet recorded *Free Form*. As is often the case when music moves into unknown territory the band lost members resistant to the new direction but gained others who were open to adventure: Joe Harriott played alto saxophone; Shake Keane, a poet, musician and radio broadcaster originally from St. Vincent, played trumpet and flugelhorn; bassist Coleridge Goode was a Kingston, Jamaica-born engineering graduate and amateur classical player; Pat Smythe, an ex-Oxford and Edinburgh law graduate turned pianist; and there was Phil Seamen, a drummer who was passionate about African music (he introduced a young Ginger Baker to recordings of African drumming). Listen, for example, to Seaman's solo towards the end of 'Coda', Harriott's crying tone reminiscent of Ornette Coleman for a few bars, the music drifting, subsiding, then Seaman taking over the silence with a solo passage, mostly tom toms, a precursor of the polyrhythmic, drum-based, 'static' time of Milford Graves.

As with other examples of early free improvisation, we listen with the wrong ears, unable to comprehend their contemporary impact, only able to hear through the filter of subsequent innovations. Even Coleridge Goode, the most moderate and musically fastidious of avant-gardists, wrote: 'When I listen now to the records we made, I find it hard to understand why there was quite so much controversy. Time changes things. It's a matter of getting your ears used to different combinations of sounds.' Joe Harriott's convictions were ahead of their time – he rejected the orderly queue of solos obligatory in jazz after bebop, the even-numbered choruses, the anchoring matrix of the chords; yet he also refused to make a traumatic break from the tradition. With historical distance, these sessions could be mistaken for the kind of jazz played as background music for a television programme in the black-and-white era, but conservative critics of the day gave them harsh treatment. As musician/critic Benny Green wrote after Harriott's group supported the Dave Brubeck Quartet in 1961: 'It is hard to believe that a jazz musician accomplished as he cannot perceive the difference between free form and no form at all.'

Inevitably, *Free Form* is compared with the earliest Ornette Coleman recording. There were superficial similarities in the angular, buoyant themes for alto and trumpet, some pushing at the edges of instruments through timbre or pitch, but Harriott was a more conventional alto saxophonist than Ornette Coleman. There was no doubting his technical facility or intonation, whereas Coleman's legitimacy in these areas is still debated by those who refuse to accept deviation from the rules. Ultimately, they were very different. Listen, for example, to the first eight bars of 'Coda', bass and piano chiming together like bells heard over English fields, or to the clipped unison fanfare of reed and brass that opens 'Calypso', a foreshadowing of the declamatory themes characteristic of Albert Ayler.

The significant void

Music is shaped by many environmental conditions, collective movements of thought and theory, political events and cultural shifts, not simply by a lineage of narrow musical influence. In an early interview with Harriott, Valerie Wilmer encountered a man rejecting the role of inarticulate, narrowly focused jazz musician: 'He was quite intellectual. I remember when I went to see him he was talking about Paul Klee, the painter, and Picasso. ... At the time I couldn't understand why he was comparing his music to abstract painting. ... He thought of himself as an artist.' How much input was Harriott given into the original cover artwork of *Free Form*, we might ask? The back cover image – abstract expressionist brushwork in the style of Japanese sumi-e (monochromatic ink) calligraphic painting, somewhat in the style of

Mark Tobey's *Space Ritual* of 1957 or Franz Kline's work of the 1950s – was credited to Ken Deardoff, a highly creative designer of many jazz record covers.

This link to abstract expressionism is frequently assumed to be a natural connection between all post-war arts founded in spontaneous gesture: to 'break' a note's purity or to smash down on a piano keyboard with the forearm interpreted as equivalent to dripping or throwing paint. Jackson Pollock's *White Light* was incorporated into the design of Ornette Coleman's *Free Jazz: A Collective Improvisation by the Ornette Coleman Double Quartet*, recorded in December 1960. As a marker of the spontaneous act its significance runs deeper than a design trend. 'What is clear is that American art and Japanese Zen Buddhism and aesthetics intersected in the 1950s and 1960s,' wrote Ellen Pearlman in *Nothing and Everything*. 'Like a pebble dropped into a still pond of water, the first ripple was small and contained yet radiated out into larger and larger circles.' Though he later denied it, Franz Kline was closely involved with the contemporary Japanese calligraphy movement in the 1950s, whereas Robert Motherwell's large black on white paintings were suggestive of Japanese sumi-e but grew out of techniques of automatism learnt from the Chilean surrealist, Matta Echaurren. Motherwell's dilemma, how to break through self-imposed and external constrictions, was solved by a regime of spontaneous action. As he later recounted, referring to himself in the third person:

> In order to overcome a certain apprehension and self-consciousness often attached to his painting, he undertook an experiment, first purchasing ten packets of Japanese rice paper called 'Dragons and Clouds'. Then there came to him 'in a flash' the following instructions for its use: 'PAINT THE THOUSAND SHEETS WITHOUT INTERRUPTION, WITHOUT A PRIORI TRADITIONAL OR MORAL PREJUDICES OR A POSTERIORI ONE, WITHOUT ICONOGRAPHY, AND ABOVE ALL WITHOUT REVISIONS OR ADDITIONS UPON CRITICAL REFLECTIONS AND JUDGEMENT.'

'Everything is open,' he told himself. 'Don't look back.' Rapidity, spontaneity, actions without remorse made with the speed of thought were common currency among many artists and writers of the period. In certain respects they were inspired by jazz improvisation yet they went further than jazz in the search for new forms.

The company Joe Harriott kept in London was even more radical than the American abstract expressionists. This was, after all, an era of extreme fear, instability, a fervour for change. The threat of nuclear annihilation was intense. In its shadow, loose communities united by their resistance to cold war escalation were precursors of environmental action, pop surrealism, multiculturalism, performance art, anti-psychiatry, collective arts practice and experimental literature, many of them traced, embraced or debased in Jeff Nuttall's saturnalian *Bomb Culture*. The bomb, dark void, linked them all. 'No Thing (no particular thing, no defined thing, no isolated thing, all-inclusive totality, total spirit) is Everything,' wrote Nuttall. 'Everything is Nothing. To live completely you must acknowledge the significant void.'

The three Afro-Caribbean members of the Joe Harriott Quintet – one of them, Shake Keane, later to take up a government position in his home country of St Vincent – would surely have been conscious of the sudden collapse of French, British, Dutch, Portuguese and Spanish empires as the colonial project unravelled. In 1960, the year of *Free Form*, 16 African countries including Nigeria, Mali, Democratic Republic of Congo and Chad gained independence from colonial rule; the same process was far-advanced in Jamaica with full independence only two years away. Long-running colonial wars and insurgencies came to an end that year – the Mau Mau uprising in Kenya and the Malayan Emergency in South east Asia – while the Algerian war of Independence headed towards its inevitable conclusion. As British prime minister Harold Macmillan said in a pragmatic speech to the South African parliament in Cape Town during a tour of sub-Saharan Africa in early 1960: 'The wind of change is blowing through this continent, and whether we like it or not, this growth of national consciousness is a political fact. We must all accept it as a fact, and our national policies must take account of it.' In America, meanwhile, the Democratic candidate, John F. Kennedy was narrowly elected, his endorsement by Martin Luther King Sr. giving hope for an end to racial segregation.

Action imperative

Gustav Metzger was born in Nuremberg in 1926. The son of orthodox Jews, he escaped the Holocaust by being sent from Nazi Germany to England through the Kindertransport rescue mission of 1939. Almost before anybody else, Metzger understood the disastrous environmental and moral impact and implications of industrial capitalism. He was a founder member of the Committee of 100, founded by Bertrand Russell and described in the first pamphlet (designed by Metzger) as 'a movement of non-violent resistance to nuclear war and weapons of mass extermination'. ACTION IMPERATIVE, the pamphlet urged, a call for every person capable of feelings of mercy to do everything possible, 'with a view to awakening our compatriots, and ultimately all mankind, to the need of urgent and drastic changes of policy'.

In his first manifesto of Auto-Destructive Art, drafted in 1959, Metzger listed various attributes of an art designed for industrial societies, predicated on disintegrative processes. The following year he added a handwritten note to the typewritten document: 'The amplified sound of the auto-destructive process can be an integral part of the total conception.' In other words, a marker in the history of noise.

At the *Misfits* evening, held at the ICA on 24 October 1962, Metzger created an auto-destructive construction with amplified sound, paper, metal, glass, acid, nylon, luminous paint, plastic and light reflectors. Another of the 'misfits' was Fluxus artist Robin Page, who performed his *Block Guitar Piece*, in which a guitar was destroyed by kicking it off stage (if there was a stage) and round the block. Metzger was instrumental in bringing together these tendencies, what he came to describe as a form of automatism whereby destructive agency was set in motion in order to create new forms. For a passing moment, Metzger's ideas came to the forefront of pop culture through Pete Townshend of The Who. Metzger was invited to lecture at Ealing College of Art in 1962 by Roy Ascott, a pioneer of telematic art. His talk on that occasion – 'auto-destructive Art, auto-creative art: the struggle for the machine arts of the future' – profoundly affected Townshend, a young art student who had enrolled at Ealing in the previous year. To smash guitars and drum kits, use explosives and lighter fuel on stage, was both to amplify the spectacle of rock music using traditional means reminiscent of the circus and music hall but also to step close to the brink of chaos, as if freedom from the restrictions of song forms, set lists and tonality could only come about by destroying instruments. Glimpses of noise and destruction in old footage of Jeff Beck, The Who, Jimi Hendrix, leave us with fragments, irruptions, momentary breaks in continuity.

One of the outcomes of Metzger's theory of destructive tendencies in post-war art was the Destruction In Art Symposium of 1966, held at the Africa Centre in London's Covent Garden. Participating artists included Yoko Ono, Wolf Vostell, AMM, Juan Hidalgo and John Latham, the last of whom was an artist whose work had undergone dramatic transformation in the 1950s, shifting from flat, frame-bounded abstract paintings to assemblages and book reliefs, often spray painted black with all the fixing materials – plaster, metal gauze, wires and bolts – left plainly visible. 'In retrospect,' wrote John A. Walker, 'Latham's book relief ruins can be seen as delayed mourning-work for the "civilisation" responsible for the horrors of the Second World War, the holocaust and the atomic bombs dropped on Hiroshima and Nagasaki.'

Both Metzger and Latham were prophets of crisis, of eschatology, the Cold War equivalents of Cassandra, whose ears were licked clean by temple snakes. Though this allowed her to hear the future, she was cursed by Apollo; nobody believed her predictions. Metzger's lecture to London's Architectural Association in 1965, given at a time of utopian rhetoric about the future technological revolution, accurately predicted the dystopian consequences of environmental pollution, the psychological pressure of continuous noise and vibration, the anti-heroic trajectory of modern war. 'To survive,' he said, 'capitalism must continue to *expand* production. It is *boom or bust!*' Searching for a way to 'do something' as a reaction against such forces, he developed a form of auto-destructive art that addressed human aggression and cruelty, held up a reflection to social deterioration, produced work that refused permanence and all its associated values. For Metzger, destruction in art was a boycott of sickening society, a self-cancellation.

For Latham, art had reached an end point, demanding new strategies, an explosion of thought and praxis. James Joyce's *Finnegans Wake*, Robert Rauschenberg's white paintings, Ad Reinhardt's so-called black paintings, John Cage's *4' 33"*, all navigated the sea of nothingness. In 1974 I was a signatory (along with Marie Yates) to a letter composed by Latham and published in *The Guardian*, in which he described established categories of art – poet, painter or composer – as unrealistic, outdated, expedient: 'However much it might suit administrators to restore those neat distinctions, it is decades since John Cage and Ad Reinhardt (among many) began to reorientate and rephrase the serious capital A activity as quite a different kind of consideration.'

In 1975 I met Coleridge Goode, relaxing with his wife Gertrude at the Latham's barn in Devon. Thirty years later, at the Lisson Gallery opening of John Latham's exhibition, *God Is Great and Belief Systems As*

Such, I learnt from Latham's eldest son, Noa, that his father had asked Joe Harriott to record a soundtrack to one of Latham's early *Skoob* films, either *Talk* or *Speak*. Hectic torrents of coloured circles (a kind of silent music), these films exemplified Latham's event-structural theories by prioritizing time base over more familiar filmic tropes such as spatial depth, narrative or the nature of the object. Noa Latham's version of the story was that Harriott offered a track but this was rejected as being 'too musical' (other recorded scores were rejected for the same reason – one by dancer and electronic music pioneer Ernest Burke; the other a now legendary 'lost' track by Pink Floyd). 'He told me,' says Noa Latham, 'he was disappointed that the music was composed, not improvised.' In a letter to the British Film Institute, sent in June 1960, Latham wrote about the possibility of adding sound to his films, some noise or sound 'on the lines of remote percussion, time-distorted familiar sounds, non-musical tones, which may be effective in breaking into the context which the film is attempting to evoke'. Not hearing what he needed in the music of others he recorded the noise of a circular saw (Metzger's 'amplified sound of the auto-destructive process').

'John was into sound rather than music,' Barbara Steveni [Latham] tells me. From the beginning of the 1960s, she and her husband John lived in Portland Road, Holland Park, where Joe Harriott would come and play their dilapidated piano. They were part of a network of friends: artists Liz and Pip Piper who were neighbours to Coleridge and Gertrude Goode in Notting Hill, Shake Keane living on the first floor with the Goodes, Liz Piper's brother John R. T. Davies, a fez-wearing musician who specialized in remastering classic jazz recordings and performed with The Temperance Seven, one of the bands of that period specialising in a peculiarly British hybrid of music, dance and fashions of the 1920s, New Orleans jazz and the anarchic, absurdist humour typified by Spike Milligan, the *Goon Show* and its successors (Coleridge Goode narrowly missed the chance to play on the *Goon Show* by resigning from the Ray Ellington Quartet shortly before the group became house band for the Goons). Steveni pulls it back to the bomb, to the ominous, destabilizing presence of nuclear threat and its effect on all independent thinkers in the post-war period. 'We went to a nuclear disarmament sit-down in Trafalgar Square,' she says. 'Then we just left. We decided we'd have to *do* something.' This urgent inarticulate need to react against what felt at the time to be an inexorable march into cataclysm sounds not unlike Joe Harriott, speaking to Valerie Wilmer in 1964 about his experiments outside the jazz matrix. 'I just had to do *something*,' he told her.

Spaces and movement

The personality susceptible to the dream of limitless freedom is a personality also prone, should the dream ever sour, to misanthropy and rage.

JONATHAN FRANZEN, Freedom

Exactly what Harriott took from this radical milieu is impossible to say. Even when or how he joined it is uncertain. Noa Latham thinks 1960 is too early; if he was asked to contribute sound to *Speak*, then 1963 would be the latest.

In November 1961 and May 1962, the Quintet recorded their second album, *Abstract*, followed in 1963 by a final free-form venture, *Movement*. By this time, Phil Seaman's heroin addiction had made his regular participation untenable for all concerned. His replacement was the original drummer for the group – Bobby Orr – sharp enough but markedly less inventive or responsive, heavy on snare and ride cymbal whereas Seamen (cigarette invariably hanging from the corner of his mouth) was always sensitive to the tonal and textural possibilities of all elements of the drum kit. Orr's impeccably logical rhythmic thinking contrasted with Seamen's interjections in unexpected places, pulling back the beat or anticipating it, constantly variegating what he played from within its constancy as if shaping the weather.

Of *Movement*'s nine titles, three are developments from the free-form approach. The most striking of these is 'Spaces', an exercise in listening and silence that advances the approach of 'Shadows' from *Abstract*. Nothing like it existed in jazz; the only possible counterpart in Britain was Cornelius Cardew's first indeterminate work, *Autumn 60*, so perhaps the evening at the ICA in 1960 had an effect. Also tantalizing is the knowledge that Harriott was listening to Anton Webern's music at the time, no doubt fascinated (as John Stevens and Derek Bailey would be fascinated later in the 1960s) with the concentrated economy of pieces such as *Five Pieces for Orchestra Op. 10* (1913), the isolated snare drum rolls and barely voiced cymbals, violin ppp sur la touche, the expressive placement of instrumental colour and pitch relationships within emptiness, single and clustered notes from flute, glockenspiel, trumpet, piano illuming each other's materialization and decay like flowers opening at night only to die with the light. Webern's music is not solely a lesson in economy of means and timbral variations. Each sound is locked in close communion, as if a single idea flows from one hand to the next, fleetingly coming to agreement or discord in a group. Alex Ross describes this as the distribution of material in 'clear, linear patterns' but the improviser is likely to perceive it differently, hearing instead the implicit spatial relationship of each sound, the emergence of group conversation apportioned to many discrete voices; sensations and thoughts answered and developed by other sensations and thoughts, 'search and reflect' as John Stevens would say.

If music is conceptualized as a volume-filling space, then its reverse – an empty well into which drops fall – is a revelatory opening for creative possibilities. 'Intellectuals of fin-de-siècle Vienna were much concerned with the limits of language,' Alex Ross writes,

> with the need for a kind of communicative silence. 'Whereof one cannot speak, thereof one must be silent,' Wittgenstein wrote in his *Tractatus Logico-Philosophicus*, marking a boundary between rational discourse and the world of the soul. Herman Broch ended his novel *The Death of Virgil* with the phrase 'the word beyond speech.' The impulse to go to the brink of nothingness is central to Webern's aesthetic. ... The Joke went around that Webern had introduced the marking *pensato*: Don't play the note, only think it.

Joe Harriott's 'Spaces' begins with cymbals, then a high unison blast from saxophone and trumpet, as if to mark the emptiness of the space to be probed. There are total silences in which slight movements of the musicians in the studio are discernible, sectional divisions, unisons and solo passages that move in steps, a dirge for arco bass, saxophone and trumpet that echoes these ascending steps as if in slow motion, a fragile, scribbled unaccompanied solo by Shake Keane followed by a nine-second silence. As if a shadowing of Bill Evans, piano chords tread softly into this silence to be cut by the harshness of unaccompanied alto. Coleridge Goode's arco solo ends plaintively, punctuated by a ritualistic bass drum from Orr, then the reprise of the dirge ending with a quavering chord, one discordant accent from Smythe and the microscopic sounds of Keane's mouthpiece.

Reality set in. 'But it was impossible to ignore the fact that free form was not a commercial proposition,' writes Coleridge Goode. Harriott fell into depression, a proud loner, drinking hard for consolation. 'His disillusionment was such that he gave up writing new material for the group.' Harriott was not finished with innovative music – he continued to perform with a touring poetry and jazz project led by pianist Michael Garrick (a group whose performance I heard live circa 1965, with poets Nathaniel Tarn, Jeremy Robson and Danny Abse though probably not with Harriott), with John Mayer's Indo-Jazz Fusions group and more orthodox jazz sessions – but a spiral of drinking, declining health and homelessness dragged him down. By 1972 he was diagnosed with both tuberculosis and cancer of the spine. On the second day of 1973 he died, aged forty-four.

The cracking of bones and shells

Southampton, 1972: near immobility and destitution in a home not his own, Christmas approaching, death approaching, Joe Harriott finds his only solace in a copy of the Chinese Book of Changes, the *I Ching*, the same book through which John Cage discovered his version of freedom from personal tastes and habits, the aleatoric strategies that grew out of an epiphany, the sudden realization that all things are related. 'Chance operations allow Cage to dissociate his music from his inner turmoil,' writes Kay Larson in her book on Cage and Zen Buddhism. 'He will generate random numbers and use them to find sounds. How can he (or anyone) judge a sound that has arisen of its own accord? It rises and falls, appears and disappears, and has no ego content whatsoever. A single sound is like a thought: here one minute, gone the next.'

How peculiar for Harriott, this upright Jamaican man otherwise impervious to the lure of hippie culture, to become fixated by an ancient divinatory text, so many of its oracular hexagrams reflecting back to him the circumstances of his dreams of freedom – 'The receptive,' 'Fellowship with men,' 'Approach,' 'Gathering together' – then his sheared-off hopes – 'Difficulty at the beginning,' 'Standstill,' 'Work on what has been spoiled,' 'Retreat,' 'Obstruction,' 'The Abysmal'.

How curious also for Harriott to immerse himself in a belief system in which Taoist formlessness and perpetual transformations lay at the heart of Confucian pragmatism and ethics. 'Let us then take from the hands of the gurus a book fundamental to Chinese civilisation,' writes François Jullien,

> the well-known *Book of Changes* or *Yi-jing* (*I-ching*), and profit from its rigour. It has, in fact, no other object than to train us to be vigilant and to educate our concentration: to teach us to read the gradual and continual inflections at the heart of the slightest situation by following the ways in which it splits up in proportion to how it unfolds – like the splits and cracking detected in bones or shells consigned to the fire in the earliest periods of mantic practices; and to observe the reconfigurations which result from the process each time, as they are absorbed, so discretely conferring a new orientation to be disclosed upon the course of things.

This is not the place to enter fully into Jullien's discussion of the disparities between Western and Chinese ways of thinking, though his description of the I *Ching* as neither a narration, nor a discourse, nor a form of reasoning or teacher of a message or deliverer of meaning but a dispositive, a way of bringing about the settlement of an issue, sits well with the nature of improvisation. Improvisation cannot afford to tie itself down to a single method or message; instead it must stay fixed on the settlement of an issue, the creation of a group music without predetermined form. In *The Great Image Has No Form, or On the Nonobject through Painting*, Jullien quotes an eleventh-century art theorist, Shen Gua: 'The ancient painters painted intentionality and not form.' The fundamental idea of the *I Ching* was said to be resonance, as in the story retold by Joseph Needham, of a Mr Yin who asks a Taoist monk about this resonance: 'Mr Yin then said, "We are told that when the Copper Mountain (Thung Shan) collapsed in the west, the bell Ling Chung responded (ying) by resonance, in the east. Would this be according to the principles of the I Ching?"' The monk laughed and gave no answer.

Intentionality and resonance were emerging as two of the most important principles of free improvisation in the early 1960s: to play with diminishing focus on outer forms; instead, to follow the strengthening currents of the age; to follow not the chords, the notes, the tempo, the tradition, the style, the theme and its recapitulations and inversions; instead to resonate with sounds as they emerged from silence, not to invest it all in resolution and symmetry, 'simply' to follow intentionality in search of resonance between materials, even into coincidence, randomness, disagreement and disorder beyond the frame of performance.

Musique brut

Marx once said that 'the consciousness of the past weighs like a nightmare on the brain of the living,' and it is from that nightmare that the modern apocalyptists want to awake. But the nightmare is part of our condition, part of their material.

FRANK KERMODE, *The Modern Apocalypse*, in *The Sense of an Ending*

Perceived at that time as a crisis of humanity, the Cold War mood was apocalyptic, what literary critic Frank Kermode described in his lectures of 1965 as 'the sense of an ending'. Through music, was it possible to become a new kind of human, to play without conditioning, to forget arduously acquired technique or never master those techniques, to play without knowledge as if comprehending and speaking unfamiliar tongues, to play without instruments, to play as if from another cultural dimension, as if raised by wolves without language, as if a child or monster, as if in the grip of madness?

A middle-class boy born in Le Havre in 1901, artist Jean Dubuffet encountered the writings of Hans Prinzhorn while he was still young.

Prinzhorn studied art history in Vienna and singing in London, then became an assistant at the Heidelberg Psychiatric Clinic after the First World War. Further studies in medicine, psychiatry and narcotics led him into psychotherapeutic practice in Germany where he wrote *Artistry of the Mentally Ill* in 1922 and *Artistry of Convicts* in 1926. In Heidelberg he collected many drawings, paintings and sculptures created by psychiatric patients who were predominantly untrained in the arts. These were made spontaneously rather than as products of therapeutic classes. The majority of Prinzhorn's analyses focus on fully realized visual works, though he also quoted extensively from the writings of selected patients and studied what he termed 'Unobjective, Unordered Scribbles'.

In the case of an institutionalized architectural draughtsman, Joseph Sell, the writings detailed his own pleasure in listening to voices and sounds, hearing within them a language that animated the entire world. He accepted that this world was inert and silent for the majority but interpreted his own privileged access to micro-audial communications as religious enlightenment, using that inner conviction to challenge the medical diagnosis of delusion:

> It is the same with the so-called hearing of voices which the gentlemen physicians also want to represent us as sick. There is after all nothing more interesting than to understand the language of each animal, as well as to hear words in every sound caused by friction, e.g. the rustling of leaves, of springs and streams, the blowing of the wind and storm, the thunder, footsteps on gravel and the floor, the ring of church bells and the melodies of each musical instrument, as well as the movement of the muscles of his own body itself.

As for the scribbles, drawings that amass reflex movements of a pencil into patterns reminiscent of work by Henri Michaux, Cy Twombly or Jean Dubuffet (who was profoundly affected by this material and its implications), Prinzhorn saw them as fundamental acts of existence:

> Even the simplest scribble … is, as a manifestation of expressive gestures, the bearer of psychic components and the whole sphere of psychic life lies as if in perspective behind the most insignificant form element. We can call the impulse for the drawing gesture specifically the expressive need. Beyond that we must speak of an activating impulse which we also consider a basic fact of all life and which we distinguish from the expressive need despite their close relationship.

Dubuffet extrapolated these ideas into a personal practice that came to be known as art brut or raw art, invested in 'values of savagery … instinct, passion, mood, violence, madness'. Without Prinzhorn and Dubuffet the current stature of so-called outsider artists such as Adolf Wölfli and Henry Darger would be unimaginable. As a music lover who often played piano (interpreting Duke Ellington compositions), bagpipes, accordion and harmonium improvisations, it was a logical step for Dubuffet to translate these instinctual, 'savage' gestures of the hand into the sonic realm. *Musique Phénoménal* was recorded by Dubuffet and Asger Jorn between December 1960 and March 1961, then released in that year in an extremely limited edition of four 10-inch records. Photographs show them playing ethnographic and Western instruments: shawm, curved animal horn, thumb piano, nose flute, bassoon, siren, double whistle, hurdy gurdy and a variety of stringed instruments, many of them sourced from musician Alain Vian (Boris Vian's brother), proprietor of a Parisian shop specializing in unusual collectable instruments. Dubuffet had travelled in the Sahara and found his taste for the music of his own culture diminishing accordingly.

'Towards the end of 1960, around Christmas time,' Dubuffet wrote,

> my friend Asger Jorn, the Danish painter, invited me round to improvise music with him. I bought a Grundig TK35 tape recorder to capture the spirit of our get-togethers and the first recording of our recreations, done on 27th December was entitled 'Nez Cassé' (broken nose). Many more were soon to follow as we were both so enthralled by these musical experiments that our improvisation sessions were very frequent over the succeeding months.

Though both of them had some musical facility there was no intention of making something polished. Dubuffet felt the same about being a novice in tape recording, preferring the work of amateur technicians who lack the expertise to make perfect documents, remote from the messiness of daily life.

He also made a distinction between music we make and music we listen to. One was a composite of inner moods and motivations mixed with the everyday ambient sounds that are an involuntary constant of living. The other is music that is created to be heard. The sounds of the latter Dubuffet considered to be beyond natural tendencies: 'It is not human at all and could lead us to hear (or imagine) sounds which would be produced by the elements themselves, independent of human intervention.'

His own preferences were for a music 'not structured according to a particular system but unchanging, almost formless, as though the pieces had no beginning and no end but were simply extracts taken haphazardly from a ceaseless and ever-flowing score'. This is exactly what it sounds like: rather than the world ending with either bang or whimper the apocalypse is frustrated and obstructed with vigour, defiance, frantic activity without any regard for technicalities or refined taste: a banjo, as fast as possible; sliding tones on strings and whistles, scribbled with sharp pencils, scraped hard to find the voices hidden within friction; hands flailing, children making noise but then sensible of when to stop. Dubuffet storms the piano keyboard with the force of a violent sea, Jorn screeches artlessly through double reeds. Drums and gongs are dipped in and out of water. Dubuffet and Jorn had no knowledge of John Cage's *Water Music* or *Water Walk*, no background in modern composition. There are very few echoes of history – the nightmare of the past – only mutual, unselfconscious play under the supervision of the Grundig tape recorder – their aural witness and third (or fourth if Alain Vian joined in) participant.

Asger Jorn was profoundly disturbed by the Nazi occupation of Denmark in the Second World War. A pacifist member of the Communist Party of Denmark, his reaction to an impossible situation was first depression, then involvement with the resistance movement. In the post-war years, a period of disgust with civilized values and their path to barbarism, he co-founded COBRA, a group of Marxist artists committed to spontaneity and total freedom in the making of art. For inspiration they looked to the same sources as Dubuffet: folk and so-called primitive arts, the art of children, animals and the creative power of the unconscious (despite their fascination for the marginalized and stigmatized, the world these men considered to be inspirational still excluded women).

Having befriended Guy Debord, Jorn was involved in the founding of the Situationist International in 1957 and spent many years accumulating images for an archive of Nordic folk art. An artist of unshakeable principle, he also attempted a theory of economics for artists, based on the ideal of a supported elite working for the common good within a socialist society. The tragic paradox of contemporary art is that despite the radical politics of Jorn, his refusal of establishment rewards, and his trenchant analysis of art economics under capitalism, his work became extremely valuable. In 2009 a painting called *Underdeveloped Imbecility* sold for 157,000 euros; others sell for far more. To be a good painter was to invest in a mansion; to record improvised music according to similar principles was to buy a tent.

Despair to hope

Already, by the 1960s free improvisation was splitting into two sharply divergent philosophical positions, both adamant that their methodology was the true path to complete freedom. On the side of preparedness was a conviction that only the highest levels of musical virtuosity made it possible to follow each imaginative flight (the line followed by Lennie

Tristano, Joe Harriott, later Keith Jarrett). From the other side was a belief in deconditioning: forget musicality and training; cleave instead to holy fools and children; splatter, scream, rattle among the everyday (the strategy of Group Ongaku, Dubuffet and Jorn).

For the latter group, the years of training and experience obligatory to jazz was problematic, an impediment to spontaneity. 'Despair To Hope' recorded by trumpeter Don Ellis, was an example of the reason why. Ellis had worked in swing bands including the Glenn Miller Orchestra, then found himself as an adept young trumpet player inside the advanced theoretical school of George Russell. He played alongside Eric Dolphy and Steve Swallow on Russell's *Ezz-thetics* album in 1961, a record notable for many reasons, not least the unorthodox version of Thelonious Monk's 'Round Midnight', prefaced by an introduction which sounds freely improvised: sweeping of the piano strings, the animal cries of the brass lurking in the shadows of studio echo, percussive bass, a vivid image of night creatures out of which rises Eric Dolphy's impassioned alto saxophone solo.

In the same year, Ellis released *New Ideas* under his own name, an album for which he brought together Al Francis on vibraphone, pianist Jaki Byard, Ron Carter on bass and drummer Charlie Persip. 'Despair To Hope' was a free improvisation – free from regular time, chords or head arrangement though not free from trite psychological drama – in which random percussive actions form a backdrop for Ellis to come out of those reverberant shadows. Small objects – coins, maybe, or pellets – are dropped, rattled, shaken close to the microphone. Al Francis uses vibraphone to suspend the mood in its shimmer. A larger object is thrown to the floor. Small finger cymbals are rubbed together. When Ellis stops playing he breathes melodramatically, following that with cartoonish glissandi on trumpet and swanee whistle. The piece ends with a stick rubbed along a ridged surface.

Ellis was an experimental thinker, an innovator with wide interests whose work would become widely known through his big bands later in the 1960s, their compound time signatures and Indian influences (he studied with Harihar Rao, a sitar teacher in the ethnomusicology department at UCLA), and then his score for *The French Connection*. Some background in free improvisation is useful in those settings – the open environment in which to work with sonorities, textures, odd combinations, unorthodox instrumental techniques – but despite or because of his virtuosity Ellis was too prone to lapse into cliché to survive more than a few minutes of free improvisation, too ambitious to dwell for long on such a precarious economic precipice. By 1970 his free phase was but a faint memory. 'Also, we're using a bunch of techniques that are "free",' he told Richard Williams. 'I hate to use that word, because I'm not a fan of free music as it's been developed. What we're doing is using further-out techniques, but it's not a case of getting up and just blowing what you want. … For me it has to make musical sense and have an interesting framework.'

A pulse, a texture, a wash

'I had art school friends back in Torquay and Newton Abbott who introduced me to painters, especially to Jackson Pollock,' Phil Minton tells me. 'We used to think, why doesn't music sound like this? It was a general feeling of where we thought music was going.' In 1959 Minton was working as a labourer in Devon, trying to become a musician. With one of those art school friends, a 'duffel-coated beatnik' painter named Mike Tolliday, he tried playing 'action' trumpet (also wearing a duffel coat with Ban the Bomb badge affixed), finger wiggling as he describes it, singing, rolling around on the floor while Tolliday painted.

Drummer Terry Day, an art student friend of Ian Dury, tells his own story of that period, when an entirely new music seemed tantalizingly within reach. In 1960 he met bass player Terry Holman and pianist Russell Hardy (the three of them later to become founder members of the Continuous Music Ensemble and the People Band). Holman was aware of John Cage, Hardy loved the music of Art Tatum, Day had learnt to improvise by playing drum duets with his brother. They played together at a north London pub, The Starting Gate, though nothing was public. 'The trio went straight into improvising,' he says.

> There was no attempt at tunes, structure or plans of any kind. On my part it went back to my brother's influence and that of Charlie Mingus saying there was no need to state a fixed time signature. We therefore played about with time. I developed a pulse, a texture, a wash, a dialogue form of drumming over which a soloist could ride free from the restrictions of time and metre. We did not attempt to emulate any other musicians, style or genre. In that sense we were free from the restrictions of a pre-set form, thus allowing our improvisation to

take us where it chose (in the manner sometimes of the gestural art of the abstract expressionists) and within that process, arriving at a new form.

35 cents

I tell you who else I'd like to mention – Jimmy Giuffre. I learnt a great deal from Mr Giuffre. The work he did in the trio format with Paul Bley (who's another special one) and Steve Swallow is very important to my evolution.
                    ANTHONY BRAXTON interviewed by Graham Lock, 1985

How can we play at a given rate of speed but without a fixed tempo? That was one of the questions that Giuffre, Bley and Swallow were asking themselves during rehearsals, spending as much time talking as playing. For how long is it possible to improvise without reference to a tonic pitch? According to Steve Swallow the trio would stop in the middle of a piece to question some aspect of what they were doing. The year was 1961. Carla Bley was writing material for them, as was Giuffre, but their questions went beyond any reliance on the script. A drummerless trio afforded more latitude than conventional groups but in their recordings they also exploited the potential of permutations – solo, duo and trio – a practice that was to become standard in free improvisation, particularly after Derek Bailey's Company events made it acceptable to try out every possible combination within a group. They all had some experience of working in the experimental end of jazz – Bley with Ornette Coleman, Swallow with George Russell, Giuffre with Shelly Manne – but Giuffre's success with 'The Train and the River' seduced Verve Records into complacency. Assured of endless bounty, Verve found itself trying to sell a sound that almost nobody was going to buy in 1963. The combination is attractive – clarinet, double bass, piano – all of them sensitive players conscious of the halo of silence that enveloped their sound, all of them deep listeners, responsive to each other, capable of coming together, unafraid to break apart, but the music had few entry points for the uncommitted listener.

    According to Swallow, Verve assigned Creed Taylor (famous for introducing the bossa nova to America and for the CTI fusion sound he promoted in the 1970s) as the producer for the first two albums, *Fusion* and *Thesis*. 'These were done quickly,' he says, 'each in a single session as I recall – and without interference. Creed and the engineer just sat glumly in the control room and pushed the appropriate buttons.' For the third record – *Free Fall* – recorded in three sessions, July, October and November 1962, they were given Teo Macero, a much more adventurous producer who had played in the Jazz Composers Workshop with Mingus in the 1950s. The chief engineer for Columbia Records, Fred Plaut, had engineered some of the biggest records in the label's history, from *Kind of Blue* to *West Side Story*, as well as recording sessions with Stravinsky, Copland, Pablo Casals and Varèse; he had no problem with what they were doing and ensured clarity, definition and balance within the converted church acoustic of Columbia's 30th Street Studio.

The importance of the acoustic is made evident by a live concert recording of the trio from 1961 – bass and piano indistinct, clarinet abrasively prominent. When the structure of a music is clear and familiar then a rough live recording can still be exciting. The auditory cortex of the listener fills in the gaps by a process called the continuity illusion. Whatever information is missing can be 'heard' because of its familiarity. Discerning emergent form in free improvisation is dependent on close listening, active memory, concentrating on each moment, following multiple layers or lines simultaneously, making it difficult to fill in the gaps if the recording is poor.

The Giuffre trio has been described as chamber improvisation, another intimation of the future – the practice of quiet (or relatively quiet), mutually attentive small-group improvisation for intimate spaces has become almost the default position for free improvisation in recent years. Giuffre's groups with Jim Hall and Buddy Clark, Ralph Pena or Bob Brookmeyer drew the listener in to a close space, even at an outdoor festival. 'It really made me aware of texture and listening and reacting,' Jim Hall has said. The trio with Paul Bley and Steve Swallow took a further step. Time was not regulated. The impression of rushing forward from plateau to plateau that intensified the infectious spirit of Ornette Coleman's music was given another direction: to follow any direction until a better one came along, to be still, to stop.

Maybe this was the decisive step in breaking with the past? Now, suddenly, silences punctuated the quiet. The quiet was an unoccupied space. 'Threewe', for example, is formed from the most subtle of hints: the tail of a barely voiced bass note echoed by a soft piano chord, fast scrabbling by Swallow roughening the ground under the agile leaps of

Giuffre's clarinet. Given the tendency for mimesis in improvisation there are points of surprising refusal, a few bars of swing that nobody wants to follow. Already there is the realization that standard continuities close off the flexibility of the music. Each moment is there to be caught. 'Poly-free', Steve Lacy called it some years later; at any moment players can change their point of view. No longer the bridge, the channel, the changes, the head; the pivot of change becomes a hinge, a cut, a fold in response to soft or hard, clear or blurred, rough or smooth, short or held, thin or thick, clipped or sustained, assertive or fugitive – the attributes of materials that can change to infinitude within time.

Primordial call

The faunal afternoon makes more mellow
The snore forlorn
That sounds like Pan's horn
…
Then clear as a clarinet-note, her long hair
Called Pan over the fields – Pan, the forlorn wind
From the Asian or African darkness of trees
To play with her dense, with her tree-dark mind.
EDITH SITWELL, *Cacophony for Clarinet*, 1923

A third intimation of future-free improvisation can be heard in Giuffre's unaccompanied clarinet solos. Contrasted against the group mix of tightly scored passages interspersed with free improvisation, Giuffre's five unaccompanied clarinet solos were completely improvised. 'When I was thirteen,' he wrote for the original album notes, 'I performed my first unaccompanied clarinet solos for night campfire at Camp Crockett, a YMCA boys' camp near Granbury, Texas. Performing unaccompanied, therefore, is very natural to me. A player has the opportunity to stop or go – in any direction, speed or fashion – at will.' The titles reveal something of Giuffre's thinking about what a solo implied: 'Propulsion' – split notes and multiphonics, wide intervals but always movement; 'Ornothoids' – bird-like, the solo voice as flight, high as a curlew's scream then fluttering, bending, floating, climbing; 'Man Alone' – solitude and exposure; 'Primordial Call' – the instrument as calling voice, first cry, or as Dubuffet imagined, a music made not by humans at all but by the elements. Then there is 'Yggdrasill', in Norse mythology the tree that sits at the centre of the world, its branches and roots stretching outwards, upwards, downwards to the heavens, to deep springs and wells.

Expansive thoughts, but the business end was just implosion and ignominy. 'Our longest run of work was a European tour of close to three weeks,' writes Steve Swallow. 'I think the approval we found there caused the music to advance considerably. Shortly after our return to New York, we began a residency in a coffee house on Bleeker Street, playing for whatever money was collected at the door. We disbanded on a night we each made 35 cents.' *Free Fall* was an apposite title in more ways than one – Jimmy Giuffre took ten years to make another album. Free improvisation was both blessing and curse.

7 SOLITARY SUBJECTIVITIES

Invisible ear

Like all bodily orifices, the ear is both entrance and exit, ingress and projection, yet of all those orifices the ear in its visible form, cup anatomical, lacks the dark, seductive power possessed by the others. True, James Joyce in the Sirens section of *Ulysses* unspooled dizzying associative threads through which heightened hearing is aligned with sensuality, the erotic, primal nature: ear becoming shell, seahorn, the hair seaweed, pounding ocean of blood resonating within its chambers of shell, shell-like in their mirroring of caves. Within that cave the tympanum, the drum, is rendered sexual through the ribald humour of Joyce's drinkers caught up in the throb and flow of sound.

Inert, conspicuous, out of sight of its twin, the visible ear is nevertheless vigilant, the ever-waker, the Earwicker of *Finnegans Wake*, the watchman. The question of subjectivity is particularly acute within the domain of listening, sound so elusive both in time and space, always the auditory equivalent of invisible. Aural hallucinations foment within the invisible ear – inverted saxophone tunnelling by circuitous route to wild imaginings within the secret chambers of the body.

The title of John Butcher's solo saxophone record – *Invisible Ear* (2003), for tenor and soprano saxophones, amplified, with feedback and multitracked – lifts a stone, uncovers this peculiarity of listening, embodies its unspeakable world. 'Dark Field', 'Bright Field', the track titles say. 'The Importance of Gossip', 'Cup Anatomical'. This process of inversion, by which the mediumistic act of listening with all its symptoms of gathering, sensing, sharing, enhancement, calibration, invention and imaginative resonation is turned inside out to be projected outward into the world, is the key to John Butcher's more introspective work. He dwells on thresholds, within questionable territories, resting upon actions so small as to tremble on the tense meniscus of control at the edge of becoming lost.

Take 'Swan Style', which begins impossibly high, dirties its own purity, works in a field almost indistinguishable from the body's involuntary sonar of tinnitus, otoacoustic emissions, bone creaks, peristaltic borborygmi, pumped blood and nasal whistling, all of those sounds first identified by the natural philosopher Robert Hooke in 1705. Hooke drew up a speculative checklist for diagnosis through auscultation, described by Tom Rice, in *Hearing and the Hospital*, as 'a futuristic micro-acoustics'. The instrument mediates and amplifies, as if scanning this micro-acoustic chaff and translating its broadcasts.

Instabilities necessary to the expressiveness of the saxophone and its activation, particularly the connection between reed and embouchure, are developed into a spare yet eloquent language. Breath within the cavity of the mouth meets the sharp edge of a thin reed. Spittle accumulates within a tube, collecting into a volitional form whose sound is uncannily similar to that of aquatic plant life. The extraneous is cultivated, coerced, entrained. Padded doors open slowly within the tube, a sliding curve, then close again to ring with the chaotic behaviour of amplified sound mirroring itself.

There is an established tradition of solo improvisation, a kind of public research through which the vulnerability of the instrumentalist is exposed, skills simultaneously diluted by the naked air yet reinforced by being laid bare, as if to say, this is what exists in all its eloquence in isolation. John Butcher is exemplary within this tradition. The nature of his playing, lyrical even in extremis, brings to mind unaccompanied solos by reed players from very different times: 'Picasso', recorded on tenor saxophone by Coleman Hawkins in 1948, 'It Could Happen To You', recorded by Sonny Rollins in 1957, then in 1967 Lee Konitz's brief duet with himself on amplified alto saxophone from part 1 of 'Variations On Alone Together', Jimmy Giuffre's clarinet solos of 1962, Eric Dolphy's bass clarinet solo – 'God Bless the Child' – recorded live in Copenhagen in 1961 and 'Love Me' for alto saxophone, released on the *Conversations* album in 1963.

Where jazz improvisation is a form of dynamic counterpoint, such solos approximate torch-lit lines extended into darkness. They impose and stretch their own limits, within which the line remains identifiably a line. In John Butcher's case, the line is not so much taken for a walk as fuzzed, scuffed, smudged, multiplied or expanded to probe the space through which it cuts.

Is cutting the appropriate analogy? Flight comes closer. As Jimmy Giuffre knew, this is language for the birds. 'The bird's throat shook with song,' wrote J. A. Baker in *The Hill of Summer*, 'as though something inside were struggling to get free. The loud whistling power of the notes seemed unrelated to the constriction that produced them, seemed too pure and rich to have passed through the narrow syrinx of a bird.' Neck of saxophone; neck of swan through which human nature in its fullness is transformed, disguised, revealed. 'Now all speech calls for a response,' Jacques Lacan wrote in 1953, adding, 'there is no speech without a response, even if speech meets only with silence, provided it has an auditor.'

There is no solo. Every sound meets the flaring silence of acoustic space, encounters its own shadow in the higher-pitched resonation of electronic feedback, communes with ensembles of the multiple self, doubles back into its own maker even in the moment of its emergence, cries out to the listener who is performer and the hypothetical listener, the invisible ear which will at some point absorb and decipher the mystery, the arresting physicality, of these concise but strange communications.

The peculiarity of solo free improvisations is that the music is primarily collective. Steve Lacy came up through the hard school. Born on Upper West Side Manhattan to Russian Jewish parents, he took up the difficult straight horn, the soprano, and walked (in the wake of Sidney Bechet) into the arms of legends like Pee Wee Russell and Henry 'Red' Allen, progressing from Dixieland to encounters with two of the most demanding pianists in jazz, Thelonious Monk and Cecil Taylor. Lacy always gave the impression that his definition of 'comfort zone' was somewhere angular, spiked with awkward questions. You had to be suitably prepared to even enter. The group was a place of challenge and learning so a solo could only be justified as an adjunct to group work. 'Yeah, but the way I see it,' he said in *Conversations*,

> solo playing for me is only possible as a contrast to playing with a group. In other words, if you only do solo playing, it's no good. It gets worse and worse after a certain point. Unless you're in tune with other musicians, you will not be in tune with yourself. So you have to go back and forth and change the situation you're in. A solo is interesting

to listen to because it's different. And when it is not different, it loses its interest. Change is what interests me.

Improvised music plays out conflicts between the social and the solitary. Without highly developed individualistic techniques the music would absorb and nullify individual contributions and yet the group bends the individual to its volition just as much as the individual bends the group. Even the wildest, most forceful players must consider their responsibilities, their lack of freedom as human beings, social creatures, political animals. 'Free jazz, I never liked that word because it always gave reasons for a lot of misunderstandings,' Peter Brötzmann says. 'There is not the freedom which many people from the very beginning thought, you can do what you want. Of course you can't, because if you are on stage together you want to build up something *together* … it's always a kind of learning, a way of getting more experience and that's what I like.'

For John Butcher there was a direct link, an oscillation between group playing and the evolution of a solo vocabulary, the beginning of a methodology. Playing with pianist Chris Burn, who worked inside the piano, enforced adaptations to his own technique 'that put a certain emphasis onto colour, onto timbre becoming a very important musical parameter so I had begun working on the multiple sound aspects through that'.

As a postgraduate student he worked in quantum mechanics, looking at theoretical models for quarks for his PhD and working out the implications of a theory called quantum chromodynamics. For a non-physicist it is tempting to glance at QCD theory and make wild suppositions. Could these so-called strong interactions between quarks and gluons be somehow related to improvisation?

He is cautious on the subject:

I've thought about this. I think that working in quite high level physics you're presented with something you don't understand. You have to try and understand it and elements of it can be very counterintuitive. I was drawn to those aspects of music where what you're engaged with is a mystery. Through being engaged with it you're trying to discover more about that mystery and particularly what lies beyond the horizon which you can't even glimpse yet. If you go through the process you hope to see that hidden part of the activity. Those were the similarities for me, basically what you learn by attempting to go deeper and deeper into it.

To use contemporary academic parlance within arts and humanities, this could be classified as practice-based research. He rejects the framework of discipline, which implies careful preparation of the music itself, emphasizing instead the important role of obsession, a driving need to prepare the technical and emotional self for whatever music might reveal itself in any given situation, an obsession so engulfing as to be burdensome.

Loosening spaces

Working in a trio with guitarist John Russell and violinist Phil Durrant at the end of the 1990s added new complications. Material transformations of sound were exposed by the spare sound of the group, its pinpointing of extreme detail and the volatility of its internal dynamics, its unpredictable permutations of a trio into sudden solos or duos. 'If we're talking technically,' he says,

> note pressure changes, overtone structure of a sound or a note, I was trying to find parallels of that on the saxophone to have a sound conglomerate whose overtone structure I could change. Very often in the course of rehearsing or a gig something's happening in the music and you semi-hear in your head what you'd like to do but you don't know how to do it. Some of the time you will remember that when you're at home and start working on it. It doesn't come overnight, it's a series of very, very small discoveries that add up to something over a period. There was a time I got extremely methodical about it – for about a year of looking at all the possible fingering combinations and discovering the overtone spectrum and then finding which ones you could bring out multiple tones in that overtone spectrum. If you do that then you get interference tones between them and all these other different tones kick in. I began categorizing different kinds of connections, some in terms of dominant pitches and some in terms of the degree of mellifluousness or harshness of the sound which then enabled you to have different ways of finding your way around the instrument. That connects in with the conventional playing.

Many of the sounds produced by these techniques are beyond words (though comprehensible through experience of our own bodies and the sonic environment): music of inferences, music flayed down to its bones. A fascination with the minutiae of instrumental and vocal capacities is present in all forms of music, as is the desire in some musicians to say less and less the more they know. I send Butcher a link to Lester Young's 'Flic', recorded in 1957. Death was not so far away; alcohol had done its worst, yet like the controversial late-period Willem de Kooning paintings, articular contraction is not reducible to a symptom of alcoholism, Alzheimer's disease, dementia, syphilis, cannabis addiction or whatever the deleterious condition is seen to be. Young's soloing is oblique in the extreme, much left unsaid in passages that glide around and under the changes.

In response Butcher sends me a link to Billie Holiday singing 'Fine and Mellow', filmed for CBS television in 1958. Young's solo uses nothing other than all it needs, a whole life compressed into tone. The camera dwells on Holiday's profile as she listens, head moving from side to side, a study in loss, rueful of all that tender clarity about to finish for both of them. Soft, sad eyes. Nodding, head shaking, she raises those brushstroke eyebrows high as Young holds back further and further from the bar lines, delayed gratification, waving the beat goodnight.

Butcher also sends me an extract from a 1959 French interview with Young, recorded just over a month before his body gave out: 'In my mind, the way I play, I try not to be a repeater pencil, you dig? I'm always loosening spaces, laying out, or something like that … I'm looking for something soft right now. Like a little puff that the lady put on her pussy when she cleans up, and shit like that. Soft eyes for me … It's got to be sweetness, man, you dig? Sweetness can be funky, filthy, or anything – but which part do you want?'

Stream of consciousness

During a conversation with Derek Bailey in 2003, I raised issues of vulnerability that can show up in improvisation. 'Now I think you're talking about, or thinking about, solo playing,' he said.

> I think that's totally different, it's almost a different category. It's playing, for sure, and certain sides of playing probably show up more

in solo playing than in group playing. And the reverse is certainly true. It's true, it's vulnerable. It's a dicey business and in some way I think it's disgusting. I spend most of my time doing it nowadays. Solo playing can be alright, can be enjoyable, but it's usually for some ulterior motive, I think, stimulated by something. Paul Rutherford used to play these stream of consciousness solos, just dribbling on, and I used to love it. I thought he was a great solo player. It was like one voice, on its own, lonely, trying to find out where the fuck it was going.

This is the strange contradiction of free improvisation, that a collective music should generate so much unaccompanied playing. Just in my own collection I have more than one hundred solo records by, among others, John Butcher, Steve Lacy, Evan Parker, Derek Bailey (many of these), Ami Yoshida, Anthony Braxton, Lol Coxhill, Roscoe Mitchell, John Zorn, Sachiko M, Sonny Sharrock, Paul Lytton, Rhodri Davies, Peter Bröztmann, Han Bennink, Conrad Bauer, Roger Smith, Phil Dadson, Martin Küchen, Angharad Davies, Hans Reichel, Peter Cusack, Mattin, Hugh Davies, Frank Perry, Lee Patterson, Adam Bohman, Paul Burwell, Seymour Wright and, yes, Paul Rutherford, 'trying to find out where the fuck it was going'.

Unaccompanied instrumentals are not at all unusual in folk and traditional musics. Subtract the self-accompanying instruments – piano, organ, guitar – and solos that allow drums and bass some relief from their supportive roles and they show up very rarely in jazz and pre-twentieth-century classical music, though there are obvious exceptions such as J. S. Bach's *Cello Suites*, the *Sonatas and Partitas for solo violin* and Paganini's *Caprices*. Either the large number of solo free improvisation recordings and concerts is symptomatic of prelapsarian nostalgia or it has some deeper function within the life of an improviser.

For Evan Parker, his solo playing grew from imagining a music in dialogue with itself. As a lapsing student of botany in the early 1960s, already drawn towards unified theories, he visited the Daphne wine festival near Athens and heard Greek clarinet and lyra music: 'One thing that was sure was that it was a very overtone rich music. I had the sensation of insects or buzzing. Hearing that layer in the music, not in an absolutely analytical way, but suddenly thinking, ah, this is very important, what's happening up there, on top of the line.' At a sitar concert he heard what he describes as two concerts happening simultaneously, fundamental and overtones: 'Then I thought about the conscious control of all of that.

There are thousands of places where you hear a careful use of overtone control to enhance the musical message or impact. I've gradually become more aware that's a place where your consciousness can be occupied.'

A third contribution to these speculations came from reading a review in *Down Beat* magazine of John Coltrane's version of 'My Favourite Things'. The record was unavailable in the UK at that time for contractual reasons: 'I remember reading the *Downbeat* review where it said, "and its sound at one point is as though Coltrane has broken the saxophone into two separate lines". You know roughly what they're talking about but that, as an idea, was very powerful and must be something to do with the way my solo music has developed.' All of these experiences were clustered within a few years, from the beginning of the 1960s.

The idea was latent until his first solo concerts in 1971; in the ensuing years this musical idea has broadened out to ask bigger questions about human consciousness. How much is it possible to combine analytical, critical distance with the physical and emotional work of producing the sound itself? 'I'm trying to do that for myself,' he says,

> to distance myself from the physical and emotional states involved in playing the music and to have a part of me that hovers over the shoulder and edits. Whether it works or not is another matter. Most of the time it doesn't work because those physical and emotional concomitants of the playing activity are too powerful for the ability to stand outside yourself and think, this has gone on far too long.

Improvisers may rationalize solo playing as the development of a vocabulary but for an audience, the compelling aspect of solos is the abject reality of one individual occupying the performance space, beginning from nothing with the hope of occupying an unspecified time with sufficient imaginative unprepared material to hold their interest.

Both parties – audience and player – are aware that if there is a failure of some kind, whether imaginative or technical, then with no other musicians for shelter the consequent risk of deflation, shame even, is high. Born in 1969, Angharad Davies is a classically trained violinist who first played free improvisation when her brother, harpist Rhodri Davies, arranged a session with cellist Mark Wastell and trumpeter Matt Davies in the Hanwell Community Centre (originally a poor law school attended by Charlie Chaplin). Her only previous contact with improvisation was in the same year, hearing her brother performing with Lawrence D. 'Butch' Morris for the 1997 conduction tour of the UK (conduction was originated by Morris as a means of giving direction to improvising ensembles through gesture). The experience left her in a state of 'confusion and awe … not quite taking in what it all was'.

From listening to romantic music – César Franck and Gabriel Fauré, with Paul Hindemith the furthest reach of her contemporary taste – she jumped into improvisation 'feet first', as she says, and established herself quickly as a significantly different voice. One distinctive aspect of her playing is the use of preparations – objects attached or applied to the violin to modify its sound – but there was no conscious strategy, only last-minute contingency, sitting down to play and being offered some object or device by her brother. Again, this went through a self-conscious research stage, perhaps a hangover from higher education. She lists the types of preparations she was using: 'Bits of polystyrene, little plastic pegs, little paper pegs, springs. And I went through a phase of trying to keep a log of what I put on the violin for every concert but that's gone completely out the window.'

Her description of this documentation as a form of diary or self-anthropology is a reminder of stream-of-consciousness fiction in which the everyday is notated faithfully as if giving substance to an otherwise tenuous life. The problem lay with the variables of improvisation, its venues and their acoustic: one night a preparation set in a particular spot on the violin might transform the sound in startling ways; the next night, nothing. 'I'm just thinking of a most recent solo thing,' she says, laughing at her own folly,

> when I did think, I've got to really sit down and work something out. Let's think of some new sound and of course, you know, I'd turn up and try and recreate it and it just didn't appear. It was awful, terrible, and then I was in a situation thinking, why did I start like this because now I've got to try and come out of it somehow? it's good just to try and have a blank canvas, as much as possible. But having said that, I've been very attached to some sounds and preparations. I don't always manage to be completely empty or free of anything.

Derek Bailey's conclusions in his book, *Improvisation*, settle on three necessary functions for solo playing. The first is to fully develop a language. The second is to maintain individuality and independence. 'Having no group loyalties to offend and having his solo playing as an ultimate resource,' he wrote, 'he can play with other musicians, of whatever persuasion, as often as he wishes without having to enter into a permanent commitment to any stylistic or aesthetic position.' This passage is perhaps more revealing than Bailey intended, a manifesto for rigorous detachment which makes free improvisation sound like the libertinism of a 1960s commune.

The third function is barely sketched out: 'Perhaps above all it could offer a method by which one could work continuously on all aspects of a body of music.' He refers to improvisation as an 'uninterrupted activity', with the suggestion that it can flow between sociality and reclusion. Perhaps this is why the 'loneliness' he heard in Paul Rutherford's playing (and Rutherford's story was as tragic as they come) so affected him. Improvising in groups publically exposes each player's capacity to be inventive and responsive within the collective. You learn a lot from improvising with people: their sweetness, their failings, their ruthlessness, their intelligence and sensitivity, their attitude to power. Intimacy, even a masculine type of intimacy in which nothing is said, nothing is acknowledged, is the foundation.

I am reminded of something said by Annabel Nicolson, a filmmaker and performance artist who was closely involved with free improvisation through her relationship with Paul Burwell. One of the only women in a cluster of male-dominated scenes in the 1970s, she was an acute observer and listener, particularly in the improvised music setting of the London Musicians Collective. 'One of the things that puzzled me,' she wrote in *Resonance* magazine,

> was just how little the musicians, all men at that time, seemed to talk to each other. Often they would meet and with barely a word prepare to play together. There appeared to be very little communication in any recognisable sense. Then somehow out of this apparent absence of communication would come the most wonderful sounds. … I think it must have been a certain social ineptitude or awkwardness rather than any lack of sensitivity, but it was all the more noticeable in a situation where people must have had to be acutely aware of each other to improvise so well together.

At the extremes of intimacy, solo improvisation is a public revelation of how it is to be private, to be alone. To be productively lonely is a betrayal of the group (from the group's perspective); this may be one reason why it was, for Bailey, 'disgusting'. Perversely, some might think (though the sharing of intimate and unspeakable knowledge is fundamental to many forms of music, surely one of its most profound contributions to human existence), the solo invites strangers to contemplate the deeply personal and private space of another. For improvisers, communities of practice are sustained by keeping these two extremes – becoming the group and becoming the self – in balance.

8 TROUBLED SEA OF NOISES AND HOARSE DISPUTES

Giant spiders

'Was it only good for giant spiders?' American composer Larry Austin asked in the 1960s, responding to a question about electronics and improvising. Was electronic music, devoid of history, only capable of weird sounds handtooled for B-movie creature features? But in the realm of practice, new inventions of extraordinary potential were appearing all the time, new ways to subvert and dismantle them, attach them to instruments and everyday objects. Look at photographs of David Tudor at work: wired-up toy piano, accordion, bass drum, piano frame, guitar, in-out metal boxes, hanging objects, milk bottles and transducers, worm farms of heaped and tangled cables. Listen to Sun Ra's extra-terrestrialization of electronic keyboards on 'The Magic City' and 'Voice of Space'. Look at Frederic Rzewski, on his knees, tapping at an amplified metal sheet, scraping and drumming on a piano-shaped sheet of window glass amplified with a contact microphone. Live electronics and tape music were moving fast, as were studio techniques for pop music and ways of thinking about montaging existing sounds with processed sounds. The fixity of electronic music on disc or tape was unlocked; as with acoustic music, sounds could be transformed in real time as an audience observed and listened. The physical gestures could be small, even mysterious, yet these sounds could fill a room with the force of heavy industry, warfare, the ocean.

Inaudible or barely audible sounds within the body could also be amplified to become the basis of improvisations in which the body adapted to its own stimuli in a feedback loop. 'I had a kind of vision one night back in 1966 of making music with brainwaves,' says Richard Teitelbaum,

> and contacted [Robert] Moog who had just invented the synthesizer to ask if I could somehow use it with brainwaves. He said yes, the brainwaves could be used as control signals, and I came back to the States and spent a year working in a brainwave lab in the Psychology Department at Queens College in New York, earning enough to buy a used Moog – one of the first – from Moog. He also built me a very high gain (a million to one) amplifier to get the brainwaves up to Moog levels to use as control signals.

Through electronic devices and amplification, improvisers within post-1965 groups such as AMM, MEV and Music Improvisation Company found a brutally effective solution to the bindweed of musical rules and traditions. There was no well-tempered clavier in Rzewski's window glass, only its icy ghost. At the same time, electronics exposed an unvoiced and inconsistent antagonism between musicians who positioned themselves within a 'natural' milieu – often anti-pop/rock and defiantly acoustic – and those who used electronics as a decisive break with the past. The origins of that faultline became apparent in 1963–4, when free improvisation seemed both daunting yet irresistibly the next step.

In 1963, Larry Austin was one of a group of seven musicians – percussionist Stanley Lunetta and soprano Billie Alexander among them – who came together at the University of California, Davis, to improvise without a composer. They called themselves the New Music Ensemble. 'You simply rehearse every day,' he has said. 'We devoted ourselves entirely to the project; we'd spend sometimes as much as six hours per day together, exhilarated!' Austin had heard the Lukas Foss record and the impression he took from that experiment mixed with other influences of the period: Gunther Schuller's Third Stream theories, the encouragement Darius Milhaud gave him at Mills College, John Cage's music and ideas. Austin's *Improvisations for Orchestra and Jazz Soloists* is a cautionary example of what can happen when these worlds collide: a young Don Ellis can be seen playing trumpet in a filmed version of the piece, introduced and conducted by Leonard Bernstein for the Young People's Concert series broadcast by CBS television in 1964.

This is the conventional autobiographical lineage which Austin then applies to his University of California-funded trip to Rome in the following year, describing himself, more or less, as a missionary: 'In terms of primacy of idea then, I may have brought this influence to Europe.' This message 'spawned other groups like the Musica Elettronica Viva with Frederic Rzewski and Cornelius Cardew's group AMM' he said in 2007, despite abundant evidence to the contrary. In the latter case it did nothing of the sort – AMM was not Cardew's group, nor was it launched from a single idea gifted by an American in the mid-1960s.

In Rome Austin met a number of composers – Franco Evangelisti, Aldo Clementi, Ivan Vandor, Cornelius Cardew, Frederic Rzewski and Alvin Curran among them. Austin played tapes of the New Music Ensemble's California sessions, after which Evangelisti, a charismatic communist who researched experimental electro-acoustics, experienced something of an epiphany – a possibility, as he envisaged it, of resolving the contradictions between his political ideology and the life of contrivance to which a bourgeois composer is doomed. Hence, Gruppo di Improvvisazione Nuova Consonanza was born.

Trombonist/cellist John Heineman was present with Austin, Evangelisti and Clementi at the 1964 meeting, held in a sound studio at the American Academy in Rome. His observations expose the gap between aspirations and actuality. Evangelisti insisted that composing should be jettisoned yet the membership of Nuova Consonanza would be restricted to composers. As Austin has said: 'Being a composer was requisite and more important than "just being a performer," an elitist attitude that Franco conveniently overlooked.' For Heineman, this confidence that only composers could be in charge of the future was rattled by what he calls 'a silent jazz influence'. Ivan Vandor, a tenor saxophonist whose interests extended to ethnomusicology and the writing of a book in 1976, *Bouddhisme Tibetain: Les Traditions Musicales*, had studied with Don Byas in Paris. For Heinemann, Vandor's approach added a playful quality to their music, aligned with an unvoiced collective awareness of the concept of the head arrangements of 1930s–1940s jazz. Evangelisti's high seriousness was also undermined by a comic disposition within the group, close to vulgarity and vernacular. He gives the example of 'Ancora un trio', released on the group's *Improvisationen* record by Deutsche Grammophon's Avant Garde label in 1969. Recorded by himself on trombone, Ennio Morricone on trumpet and Walter Branchi on double bass, this short episode of conversational wit was cartoonish in outer form yet subtle in its dedication to close listening, call and response. Typically, Morricone plays as if speaking in dialect, never a pure note, every sound muted, squeezed or forcibly expelled. Ruminative and agitative, the instruments lunge and arch in gymnastic counterpoint.

For Evangelisti, improvisation was a deathbed scenario, an attempt to breathe life back into the corpse of Western music. Frederic Rzewski, a Harvard and Princeton graduate who had performed in Europe as a professional pianist since 1960, played in the earliest manifestation of the group. 'It's true we had different ideas about "improvisation", he says.

> For Franco it was a way out of his compositional crisis; for me it was simply unexplored territory. I was also very influenced by my association with the Living Theater, and dreamed of something like 'living music', an alternative to the rigid thinking of serialism – something to which Franco remained attached. He knew nothing of free jazz, and was not interested, whereas I became increasingly involved in that scene. I was also very much under the spell of Cage and Tudor, and was therefore drawn to live electronics, something in which Franco had only an intellectual interest.

Evangelisti was a disciple of open form: aleatoric, mobile or temporary processes that attacked the determinism of serialism. Immediacy, the lack of a score and collective decisions seperated improvisation from chance music but improvisation had additional potential as a research field for game theory and cybernetics, what Evangelisti described as the 'action-retroaction system' of a feedback loop – players listening and responding to each other to keep the dynamics of the system continually in flux. Also important was the freedom of each individual to coax and compel new sounds from their instruments. The term used by Evangelisti was 'traumatic' (maniera traumatica gli strumenti), as if to force instruments into technical unorthodoxy was a violent, painful necessity. Heineman credits percussionist Mario Bertoncini, in particular, for sharing his 'extensive use of techniques and inventions related to "inside the piano" and the world of the prepared piano in general,' creating new ideas for pieces and group unity through renewed physical relationships to instruments. The effects of this can be seen in a forty-five-minute film of the group at work in 1967. During a concert at the Gallery of Modern Art in Rome they work as a group at the piano, threading clumps and strands of horsehair through its strings. At other moments Evangelisti empties his bag of traumatic devices for piano (scrubbing brushes, a glass bottle, plastic containers and drum mallets); Bertoncini scrapes the floor with a bamboo tube while Morricone plays only the mouthpiece of his trumpet.

As the core of the group fluctuated during the key years of 1964–72 it attracted colourful characters: Evangelisti's central role has been described as giving a heaviness to the group, somewhat offset by the levity of Heineman and Vandor. The Dutch composer, Roland Kayn, played organ and percussion in the Gallery of Modern Art concert (an approach to electric organ impossible to imagine without the innovations of jazz Hammond organists like Jimmy Smith). Over time Kayn's commitment to cybernetics as a model for composing turned him away from improvised performance and Evangelisti's interpersonal 'action-retroaction'. For the rest of his life he made electronic music pieces based on self-generating systems – like mobiles these were set in motion by the composer who then stepped back from the evolving process to become just another listener. As with improvising, it was also a step back from the role of the composer, both as controller of materials (from sound to human resources) and as a professional with social prestige. Typically for the times, the members of Nuova Consonanza were all men. In the film Ivan Vandor is asked for a statement about the group. He looks at the camera, mischievous, a little apologetic: 'It's a real pity that there are no women playing with us, only men. It's really sad.' What exactly he implies by this is unclear.

1965: Listen to 'Osservatori Osservati', from Ennio Morricone's soundtrack to Sergio Leone's *For a Few Dollars More*, a high scream of strings, groaning brass, single hammered notes from piano and bass guitar and from somewhere in the darkness, barely audible, objects being activated. Though composed by one individual it reconstructs or humourously mimics the process of improvisation – sounds discovered in the moment, their unpredictable combinatory emergence improbable except through the operations of a group mind. Only an improviser could successfully do this.

Morricone joined Nuova Consonanza in that same year. Conservatory trained, he had experience in radio work, jazz bands, pop, chamber and orchestral composing and studio arranging by the time he joined the group in his mid-thirties. Like Aldo Clementi, Cornelius Cardew and Richard Teitelbaum he had studied advanced composition with Goffredo Petrassi, an important teacher in this context because of his eclectic open mind, his search for textural transparency through which the timbral transformations of new instrumental sounds achieved clarity within an ensemble. During the previous summer Sergio Leone's *A Fistful of Dollars* had been shown to unimpressed distributors at a few private screenings, then launched at a single cinema in Florence. After a stuttering start it was given a full premiere in Rome in November 1964; over the next three years, as the film took off globally, there was a realization that Morricone's low-budget simplicity of means, sardonic wit and idiosyncratic ear for combinations of sound had revolutionized film composing. Morricone had an ear for the demotic but was clearly just as comfortable with the most extreme (and extremely diverse) musical activities. In the same year he began his association with Leone, for example, he composed Paul Anka's bestselling single 'Ogni Volta' and released an easy listening record – *Musica sul Velluto* – featuring one of the great contemporary interpreters of avant garde flute music, Severino Gazzeloni (the same flautist honoured, if misspelt, by Eric Dolphy with 'Gazzelloni', on his *Out To Lunch* album), along with *A Fistful of Dollars* whistler Alessandro Alessandroni's vocal group I Cantori Moderni.

Private Sea of Dreams

Morricone's capacity to move fluidly between extremes challenges a stereotypical image of free improvisation as a refuge for zealots and fundamentalists with no connection to other musics. Despite the portentous theoretical aspects of Nuova Consonanza, there were intriguing links between the group's distinctive sound – its 'traumatic abuse' of instruments – and the lurid sonic vocabulary of post-war Italian cinema. Was this 'trauma' a break with the legacy of classical music or the squeak of a descending guillotine, the squealing torment of the rack? Ivan Vandor also scored a spaghetti western – the notoriously violent *Django Kill* – as well as composing for Michelangelo Antonioni's *The Passenger* in 1975, while Egisto Macchi's library and film music – *Capsule in Avarial*, *Richiami Spaziali* and *Nebuleuses* as three examples from an extensive but now highly collectable catalogue – inhabited the chainsaw massacre world of giallo Grand Guignol fictionalized in Peter Strickland's 2012 film, *Berberian Sound Studio*. Morricone even used Nuova Consonanza on occasions for soundtracks such as Elio Petri's *A Quiet Place in the Country* (1969), among other qualities notable for a remarkable opening credits sequence, tortured wood and metal sounds underscoring rapidly sequenced still and moving images, and *Cold Eyes of Fear* (1971), which mixed zero-time improvisation with influences from Lalo Schifren's music for *Bullit* and Miles Davis's *Bitches Brew*. In the spirit of the times – provoking audiences and blurring distinctions between popular, mainstream, marginal and experimental – these seemingly disparate worlds questioned and enhanced each other, at times threatening a truly revolutionary scenario in which the avant-garde might be more pop than pop.

Nuova Consonanza continued in various forms until the late 1980s, losing members, gaining new ones, re-forming, fragmenting and producing curios like *The Feed-Back* by The Group in 1970, a new name for what was essentially another version of Nuova Consonanza with added funky drummer. Some records seemed custom-made for suspense and gore yet they fitted just as neatly into an emerging acid trip genre. Frederic Rzewski played tam tam, Chinese wind bell and piano on one of these, a pitch for the psychedelic market released in 1967 under the name of Il Gruppo, *The Private Sea of Dreams*, subtitled *Improvisational mood music for modern dream extensions*. In 'RKBA', for example, there is no staccato, only legato, the protracted screech of cello, piano interior, cymbals and tam tam edges bleeding into Roland Kayn's discords on organ. There were precedents and parallels among other improvisers and composers – AMM in London, La Monte Young, Marian Zazeela, Tony Conrad and John Cale in New York, Karlheinz Stockhausen's *Mikrophonie I* and the micropolyphony of György Ligeti's *Volumina* and *Atmosphères* – but Nuova Consonanza specialized in a sustained examination of micro-frequencies from the early stages of their existence. For them, the 'traumatic' was a kind of signature sound.

With Franco Evangelisti's death in 1980 the group lost a strong, if problematic, nucleus and driving force. 'Franco was also an oddball,' says Frederic Rzewski,

> 'not always easy to talk to. He thought of himself as an unrecognized genius (which he was), and became suspicious of his friends. In 1964, at a DAAD reception in West Berlin, he introduced me to Dr. Gerhard Steinke, who led the electronic music studio in East Berlin. Together with Elliott Carter we made a visit to the studio. Steinke then invited me to do a piece there, which I did in 1965, *Zoologischer Garten*. Later I wrote an article for the Swiss magazine *Du* describing my work there,

in which I mentioned that Franco had introduced me to Steinke. Franco apparently thought that therefore the CIA was following him.

The problem with all these 'classical' improvising groups at that time, I think, is that they were all driven by composers, most of whom had very limited and sometimes naïve ideas about improvisation, and did not realize they were re-inventing the wheel. MEV and AMM were the only ones which made contact with a larger unspecialized audience; and I suppose there were some ideological factors in play there: we were both interested in playing for ordinary people, and did in fact achieve this to a certain extent, whereas others were content to remain within the circle of 'contemporary music', albeit in peripheral venues. I suppose Stockhausen's group did succeed in reaching audiences in larger numbers, but that was of course a very restrictive form of improvisation, which did not make a significant dent, in my opinion.

The Sound Pool

> Don't wear masks: Rejoice in nakedness. Don't forge ecstasy: Return to zero.
> Don't practice magic: Be automatic; Be nothing.
> Make music with whatever means are available.
> …
> Notation becomes superfluous
> when images are put away.
> Only then will people know what to do without
> having to be told.
>
> **FREDERIC RZEWSKI,** from *Notations*, selected by John Cage

The difference is immediately evident: Nuova Consonanza in black suits, sober ties, white shirts; Musica Elettronica Viva (more commonly known as MEV) not exactly Haight Ashbury but sartorially boho by comparison – sports jackets, raincoat, long scarves, roll-neck sweaters. Young composers loosening up. The city was the same – Rome – and the year was more or less the same but in the 1960s, events moved quickly, from the birth of the cool into mass media maelstrom in six months.

Transformations could be dramatic – James Fox's gangster to hippie in *Performance* was not entirely fanciful.

Improvising groups are described in books such as this as 'pointillist', or they create a 'wall of sound'. That may apply as a useful shorthand for one recording, a year or two within the lifespan of the group, even an aesthetic proclivity, a tendency, but each group could sound radically different according to mood, room acoustics, personnel on any given day, instrumentation, recording engineer and equipment, the disposition of the audience and the temper of the times. Listening to *The Sound Pool* by MEV, recorded in 1969, gives a strong sense of their volatility, close to the noise of a riot, a prison in lockdown or Nicolas Slonimsky's memorable entry in his *Lexicon of Musical Invective*, Ernest Newman's critique for the New York *Evening Post*, 2 March 1925, of *Intégrales* by Edgard Varèse as 'a combination of early morning at the Mott Haven freight yards, feeding time at the zoo and a Sixth Avenue trolley rounding a curve, with an intoxicated woodpecker thrown in for good measure'.

Exorcism

Two experiences that opened Alvin Curran's mind: 'smoking a joint with Cornelius Cardew on the banks of the Tiber River'; Takehisa Kosugi's visit to MEV, during which Kosugi zipped himself and an acoustic guitar into a large leather sports bag, then rolled around on the floor.

Frederic Rzewski's *Spacecraft*, recorded live by MEV in Cologne, 1967, for the Mainstream label's *Live Electronic Music Improvised* LP (a record shared with AMM, one side each) was equally immersive yet more redolent of the eerie music of the Yamabushi, Japanese esoteric Buddhist mountain priests, their horagai conch shells, taiko drums and chants of nothingness. Rzewski envisaged it as a form of surrealist automatism, a portal to the unconscious. One section of the piece recalls Nuova Consonanza's 'traumatic' bowing and scraping of instruments (in certain respects the two groups were not so far apart), while the mournful foghorn ending is a pre-echo of *Maritime Rites*, Alvin Curran's ongoing composition based around foghorns and associated environmental and instrumental sounds. With its febrile energy, reverberant clatter, sonorous long tones and ascent to frenzy *Spacecraft* might be construed as ritualistic but is it legitimate to do so? Anthropologist Victor Turner has written of ritual as 'a transformative performance revealing major classifications, categories and contradictions of cultural processes'. Traditionally, ritual marks those occasions in which 'symbols and values representing the unity and continuity of the total group were celebrated and reanimated' but in Turner's view, this need not limit it to a confirmative role:

> Ritual is not necessarily a bastion of social conservatism; its symbols do not merely condense cherished sociocultural values. Rather, through its liminal processes, it holds the generating source of culture and structure. Hence by definition ritual is associated with social transitions while ceremony is linked with social states. Performances of ritual are distinctive phases in the social process, whereby groups and individuals adjust to internal changes and adapt to their external environment.

Rzewski's description of *Spacecraft* was: 'Form for a music that has no form.' This was not fly me to the moon, though its title was surely an acknowledgement of intense competition between the United States and the Soviet Union to build and test a spacecraft viable for human astronauts. But his spacecraft was about the space in which music takes place, a labyrinth which begins as a prison of existing knowledge: 'Each performer begins by making his own music in his own way. The result is chaos, a great tumult and confusion of sound. ... The object of the music-making is to escape from his labyrinth.' He envisaged one of two consequences: if the music took flight then the space, along with everything and everybody within it, would be transformed; if it failed to lift off then each musician would have the difficult task of reaching out to the others, painstakingly nurturing unity by identifying inner and outer resistance, whether images from the past or automatic responses, breaking down this resistance through violence and silence to bring another state into being: 'What the musicians have to make clear is that this change is not just any change, but a fundamental one: the redemption of the space and of everything in it.'

Rzewski characterized this as an exorcism, an anti-music whose origin was sound as awakening but whose true purpose was to 'cast lines into the tumult to another soul'; not, in other words, to cultivate what novelist William Gaddis called 'prescriptions of superficial alterations in vulgarity' but to scare into being a society that was not based on repression, inequality, militarism and alienation. Conforming to Turner's model of liminal processes, a generative source of culture and structure, groups and individuals adjusting and adapting through ritual, *Spacecraft* was also consistent with a turn to spontaneity and the unconscious in American literature, painting and music. In *The Culture of Spontaneity: Improvisation and the Arts in Postwar America*, Daniel Belgrad identifies a resistance to corporate liberalism and the rise of bureaucratic control. He writes, for example, of poet Charles Olson's conception of the poem as a projectile, a ball or rock thrown at the reader: 'It was percussive, oriented toward sound rather than sight; and it was prospective: exploratory, its fruits uncertain at the outset. … By offering unmediated access to unconscious thought processes, spontaneity provided a vantage point from which to question the culture's authority and created the potential for authentic communications exploring new forms of human relatedness.'

MUSICS Magazine, 1978: Curran describes the disorienting sense of autonomic unity that could develop through this process, almost as if he were recounting the effects of a powerful hallucinogen: 'In the infant days of MEV it was just this feeling of stepping into and outside of time that became almost the sole "raison d'etre" for the music – so powerful was its attraction. So when we would get to those magical moments where the music began playing all by itself, there would follow along with the joy an almost frightful awareness, as one might experience on entering a totally unknown place.'

In conversation with Philip Clark for *The Wire* in 2002, Frederic Rzewski summed up the fruitful legacy of this period, when extreme pressure was exerted on all limitations, all constraints, all received thought: 'All the people involved still look to MEV as a source of ideas and we continue to come together. We were radically – even self-destructively – into free improvisation.' The challenge to authority implicit in this method formed a close fit with the political mood of the times. Speaking in a 1995 panel discussion at Mills College Curran reflected on these connections:

> Like many Americans of my generation, I had an abysmal ignorance of history and social and political ideas. At the time, I am sure I never heard the word 'anarchy,' and I'd just begun to discover the significance of Marxism. Nonetheless I was there in the midst of a tumultuous student revolution, barricades, occupations, riots, tear gas, dogs and dope – this was 1968. Consonant with all of this – considering our basic pacifist position – was our aim to make a spontaneous music which we began to call 'collective,' a timely buzzword that resounded then in almost all activity.

Alvin Curran was born in Providence, Rhode Island, on 13 December 1938. 'My father, Martin Curran, played baseball and spoke Yiddish,' he tells me.

His love was his trombone, and his own lovely tenor voice. My mother, Pearl, played ragtime piano and spoke Yiddish. I followed my father to his theatre gigs, accompanying tap dancers and magicians, and swooned to the absurd Anglo-Hebraic harmonies of the temple chorus where my father was lead tenor.

At five years they made us all – three kids – study the piano, so we could be more, or as 'cultured' as the goyim, the non-Jews, but whatever all that Mozart, Mendelssohn, and Schubert was about, I had never been able to understand until I was about fifty years old. I played gigs with my father's Bar Mitzvah band, when I was about thirteen. Meanwhile, I was freely improvising in the early 1950s with my closest friend and poet, drummer Clark Coolidge. Spitting from high up in his apple tree, we decided the world as we knew it sucked and needed a total overhaul. I went to college, to Brown University, presumably to study medicine, and in the middle of dissecting a sand shark, threw the scalpel down and changed to music.

He studied composition with Ron Nelson at Brown University, then with Elliot Carter at Yale School of Music. Even then, in 1963, his musical language was developing through sources that were either grounded in pragmatism – his work as a society band pianist – or leaning towards the exotic – the composition of a chamber opera based on Zeami's fourteenth-century Noh play, *The Damask Drum*. At Yale, Tom Johnson and Joel Chadabe were his classmates; Richard Teitelbaum was his roommate. 'Twelve-tone theory was a daily purge,' he says, with nothing but Webern, and Berg's *Altenberg Lieder*, and *Violin Concerto*, making any sense. Then Elliot Carter invited him and Chadabe to Berlin, where they met Iannis Xenakis, Yuji Takahashi, Luciano Berio, Louis Andriessen, even the ancient Stravinsky. Electronic music composer Joel Chadabe remembers setting out on a marathon drive with Curran through East Germany, only a few years after the construction of the Berlin Wall, eventually landing up in Italy.

Rome was the city where Curran decided to settle, and there he remains, shuttling between Italy and his post as Milhaud Professor of Composition at Mills College. By 1964 his survival came from playing piano in Via Veneto bars and touring in Africa with classical harmonica player John Sebastian Sr. (father of Lovin' Spoonful founder John Sebastian). Then in spring 1966 he co-founded Musica Elettronica Viva, joining up with a grouping of musicians and composers who typified the way in which music at that time was jumping barbed wire fences, reacting to jazz, pop music, new technologies, visual and performance arts, politics and philosophy, cinema and ordinary events from the environment.

They began by playing compositions – Larry Austin, David Behrman, Giuseppe Chiari, Takehisa Kosugi and others. In parallel with a few other groups at the time, Curran, Rzewski, Richard Teitelbaum, Carol Plantamura, Ivan Vandor, Alan Bryant, John Phetteplace and Steve Lacy began to explore the idea of playing without a safety net. John Cage's impact resounded strongly during the early days of MEV. Rzewski had heard Cage and David Tudor at work in Buffalo, and so MEV followed their practice of amplifying objects, materials, surfaces, events and properties of all kinds with contact microphones fed through cheap mixers, what Curran had described during the *Cage's Influence* discussion as an epiphany, a conviction of the times that they had 'tapped into the sources of the natural musics of "everything"'. But Cage may also have connected the pivotal philosophy of sound, all sound, as music, with Curran's natural propensity to process sonic memory and broad musical experience into a personal, overarching aesthetic.

As Rzewski makes clear, from within the often chaotic experiment of MEV, the *Spacecraft* was a resource, a deep well from which individual members could draw as they moved away from collectivism and developed their own voices as musicians and composers. 'We had some very noble and radical ideas,' Curran writes.

After all we were all privileged intellectuals, who could and needed to break out of our well-mannered, composerly destinies. But discovering then the vast lies and deceptions governing most of the music business and the business of music and life, the increasing exploitation of peoples' musics, the alienation and distortion of tradition old and new, and the basic fear of unfamiliar sonic gesture and unpopular music language, led MEV to a fundamental understanding that anyone could make music and anyone could make music with anyone else. This was revolutionary but did not generally have the consequences we'd imagined. What did have consequences is our precocious and profound understanding that music could be made without any order, rules, score, leaders, producers, authority of any kind, and even without knowing in advance when it would start or end. This too was revolutionary, and today practiced, to lesser or greater degrees, everywhere.

Curran describes MEV as

> the wild pot-smoking 'space-making' ecstatic, anarchist, do-it-yourself American hippies, operating in an entirely different world to Nuova Consonanza, sometimes playing luxurious gigs for European radio and new music festivals but also for freaks and hippie scenes, protests (Parliament Hill In London, opening for the Pink Floyd – we lasted two minutes), prisons and with the Living Theater and [French political activist, poet and artist] Jean Jacques Lebel. MEV was quite another musical animal.

Inevitably, a mission to transform the self, break free from personal music history, reclaim the old performance spaces or make entirely new ones created a state of permanent instability. In a letter written to me in 1979, Curran confirmed this:

> Though very close to the original elitist concepts (musicians only/closed group) and music styles of AMM, MEV at this time was in perpetual crisis and seeking ways to accommodate the occasional friends who'd want to sit in, as well as many so-called non-musicians and eventually the whole assisting public. Naturally these diverse conflicting interests and ideals created much tension – personal and musical – among us but the results were always provocative and never without interest (at least to whoever was there, player or listener).

After Jon Phetteplace, Ivan Vandor and Alan Bryant left the group, the basic line-up was Rzewski, Curran, Teitelbaum, with Steve Lacy, Ivan Coaquette, Patricia Coaquette and Franco Cataldi, 'an Italian '68er who never played music till he picked up an old valve trombone of mine and blew into it'. In an interview conducted by Paul Burwell, Herman Hauge, Steve Beresford and myself in 1977, Steve Lacy spoke of the *Zuppa* phase of MEV as an energizing chaos, an expansion and diversion (in the best sense):

> Well I went through many things where I played other instruments. In fact, in that period where we were with MEV that was a time when I was monkeying around with all kinds of things – objects, different sounds and sources and recorded sounds on tape and a lot of those things are not dead – they come up from time to time. … What you come up with is what you're asked for as far as possible.

I asked him to elaborate. 'I've been struck by the best improvised music as sort of called up,' he replied.

> When I was with MEV we went through a thing where we opened the doors and let everybody play and we made what we called *Soup*, *Zuppa*, and there was really an exploring situation where the only music that was called for by each bungler who played with us. … I mean, a guy would pick up a trumpet and he'd never held one before and he'd make a screech and then you'd have to do something with that screech to make it palatable and to not let things die. Meanwhile, other things were going on in the same room. This went on every night for a while and, well, you would come up with all kinds of things that were called for but you would never dream of playing these things normally. And that was some of the best stuff I ever heard. But just impossible to sustain over a long period of time.

United Patchwork, a double LP released in 1978 lost the Coaquettes and Cataldi but gained multi-instrumentalist Karl Berger and trombonist Garrett List. What it reveals is a changed world. The overwhelming, dishevelled inclusivity of *Spacecraft*, *The Sound Pool* and *Free Soup* had come to the end of a phase, as it inevitably must as idealism ran into realpolitik. What supplanted it was pieces that were undeniably attractive but also more modest in their ambition. They acted as bridges between cathartic events in which furniture was set alight to a less volatile future – the role of the individual composer reasserted. Asked by Hannah Charlton in 1980 if anything had come out of this activity, Rzewski replied: 'Well the same people who were doing these things then, many of them are still active today and the things they're doing today would probably not have been possible had they not gone through this sometimes violent process of personal transformation.'

In their communal, tumultuous nature, inciting not just audience participation but also a disruption of the distinction between performer and audience, all of these MEV events of the 1960s embodied the era's political turmoil – students and workers occupying the streets of Paris, student protests in the United States, Poland, Britain, Germany, Italy, Mexico, Japan and Yugoslavia, anti-Vietnam war protests, the Prague Spring triggering a Soviet invasion of Czechoslovakia, the growth of the Black Panther Party in America, the assassinations of John F. Kennedy, Malcolm X, Robert Kennedy and Martin Luther King Jr: free at last, free at last, with all the losses it entailed and the potentiality it discharged.

'Virtually every university in Italy had experienced some form of student strike or occupation by the end of 1967,' writes David W. Bernstein in his notes to *MEV 40*, a collection of MEV recordings spanning the forty years between 1967 and 2007.

> 'Hippies' from Northern Europe – or capelloni – had, since about 1965, migrated to Rome, presumably because of the warm climate, good food, and wine. By the late 1960s this phenomenon became more and more Italian: thousands of long-haired Italian youth were in evidence in such cities as Rome and Milan. The intense political and social climate in both Europe and in the United States which, in 1968 as a result of assassinations, riots, strikes, and student protests had become increasingly intense, certainly had a profound effect on MEV, inspiring the group to bring its music into the streets and to perform in occupied universities and factories.

To improvise was political: as collective action without text, director or historical continuity it had no legitimacy in the institutions; it could act as a vehicle for the unspeakable; at its most potent it could subsume the individual (performer and audience) into a field of uncertainty, threatening the loss of self and the collapse of societal boundaries, though the limitations of that utopian vision are retrospectively apparent. Little is ever said of or by the women who took part in MEV, though Carol Plantamura's voice can be clearly heard on *Spacecraft*. A utopia that fully acknowledged women as equal creative partners would have to wait.

The air is full of noises

Beneath it all, desire of oblivion runs.

PHILIP LARKIN, *Wants*,
from *The Less Deceived*, 1955

A brief section near the beginning of Michelangelo Antonioni's 1970 film, *Zabriskie Point*: a red pick-up truck is driven past billboards, signs, traffic cops, junk yards, containers; huge billboards show rural farming scenes as fantasy facades behind which lies the brute reality of industrial production on the outskirts of Los Angeles. This dissonance is communicated not by the images themselves but by synthesizer noise spurts that seem to shoot out from the images as invisible poisons; aurally they are nails scraping down a rusty metal sheet, pounding hammers, beaten steel. The scene, and its sound, are an echo of Vittorio Gelmetti's electronic backdrop for the beautifully desolate industrial images that open Antonioni's 1964 film, *Red Desert*; the synthesizer bursts were credited to MEV, though in actuality they were produced mostly by Richard Teitelbaum working with Curran, Rzewski and classical bassist Jeff Levine, who played a saz recently purchased in Turkey. After weeks of editing by Teitelbaum to fit music to picture most of what they recorded was discarded (described by Antonioni as not sounding 'quite "American" enough', according to Teitelbaum), to be replaced by a Jerry Garcia guitar solo.

The collective long-duration improvisations and semi-improvisations that were so prevalent in the 1960s and 1970s embodied the era's conjectural societies and their rites, laboratories for hypothetical forms of commutuality: Ornette Coleman's *Free Jazz*, John Coltrane's *Ascension*, Terry Riley's *In C*, Maki Ishii's *Cho Etsu*, Toshi Ichiyanagi's *Music for Living Process*, Marion Brown's *Afternoon of a Georgia Faun*, Miles Davis's *Bitches Brew*, Roscoe Mitchell's *Sound*, Jimi Hendrix's '1983 ... (a merman I should turn to be'/'Moon, turn the tides ... gently, gently away', Pink Floyd's 'A Saucerful of Secrets', MC5's 'Starship', Sun Ra's *The Magic City*, Human Arts Ensemble's 'Lover's Desire', Baikida E. J. Carroll's 'Orange Fish Tears', Clifford Thornton's 'Ketchaoua' and The Scratch Orchestra performance of Cardew's *The Great Learning*, works whose oceanic ancient-futurism spread outwards in ripples to a wider public during a time of social experimentation and discord.

Noise was in the air. A notorious scene in Antonioni's 1966 film, *Blow Up*: The Yardbird's playing 'The Train Kept A-Rollin' in a London club; Jeff Beck smashes a guitar and throws it into the audience, transforming a passive crowd into a hysterical mob. Extraordinary to think it now, but some of the most successful bands in the history of popular music – notably The Beatles, Rolling Stones and Pink Floyd – dabbled in some aspect of free improvisation, whether as players, listeners or benefactors. Lengthy one (or two)-chord jams, improvised noise freak-outs, guitar feedback, tape montages and out-of-tempo improvised passages were becoming almost obligatory for mid-1960s rock and funk groups with radical tendencies – Love, The Seeds, The Beatles, The Rolling Stones, The Byrds, The Velvet Underground, The Fugs, Funkadelic, The Mothers of Invention, Santana, Chicago, Quicksilver Messenger Service, The Temptations, Red Crayola, Gong, The Grateful Dead, even The Monkees – though the sources of this impulse often lay as much with James Brown, John Lee Hooker and Bo Diddley as they did with John Cage, Karlheinz Stockhausen and John Coltrane.

Under the exotic name of Hapshash and the Coloured Coat, the London-based graphic design duo of Michael English and Nigel Waymouth oversaw a whole LP of improvised psychedelia in 1967 – 'electric mayhem and freeform freakout', as *The Flashback: The Ultimate Psychedelic Music Guide* described it. English studied at Ealing Art College where he underwent the deconditioning trials of Groundcourse, a programme of perceptual dislocation and creative problem solving devised by telematic and cybernetic media art pioneer Roy Ascott with guest lecturers such as Gustav Metzger (the same course that proved so formative for Pete Townshend at Ealing and Brian Eno at Ipswich Art College). Blues harmonica, trance rhythms, hand drums and Indian flutes, disembodied voices, quasi-Tibetan and Hindu chants and random noises: *Hapshash and the Coloured Coat, featuring the Human Host and the Heavy Metal Kids* is quintessential summer of love but in its nocturnal aspect. Though in some respects comparable to MEV and AMM experiments in overwhelming both players and listeners with stimulus overload and assaults on conditioned behaviour, Hapshash and the Coloured Coat were closer to the worlds of William Burroughs, Timothy Leary, R. D. Laing's anti-psychiatry and the Tibetan Book of the Dead.

Drums and bass, their pulsation a writhing root system for dancers, earthed whatever tangential material howled and clattered about on the substrate. As an expedient method of brilliant if none too sophisticated simplicity, this has subsequently become a guiding principle for the outer limits of popular music, whether in leftfield disco, dub reggae and hip-hop, shoegaze, funk or dubstep. In their early days, Sly and the Family Stone would begin sets with a warmup they called the jazz riffs, an eight-minute song of five or six short pieces chained together without much concern for the different keys of each section. Grateful Dead drummer Mickey Hart remembered hearing the group at that time: 'The groove never stopped. You'd come out of it in the morning and you had come out of a ritualistic kind of a setting where the music never stopped. It was kind of a religious experience in a Vegas lounge setting.'

In Germany, krautrock grew out of this formula: rage, ecstasy, streaming consciousness, hippie nonsense, karate keyboards and celestial shortwave all held together by repetition. Members of Can, Amon Duul II, Guru Guru, Neu!, Xhol Caravan, Organisation (later to become Kraftwerk) and Tangerine Dream either collaborated with free improvisers such as Peter Brötzmann, Irène Schweizer and Manfred Schoof or were fully conversant with their work. For a moment it seemed as if rock music would develop in the same direction as electric jazz. Listen, for example, to Organisation playing 'Ruckzuck', filmed in performance at the Essener Pop und Blues Festival in April 1970, Florian Schneider's percussive overblown alto flute moving in territory not dissimilar to the freely improvised 'Wednesday' sections of *Miles Davis At Fillmore*, recorded in June that same year.

The core members of Kraftwerk – Florian Schneider and Ralf Hütter – met through a summer improvisation class at the Akademie Remscheid in Küppelstein; for a short period they played experimental music with bassist Eberhard Kranemann and improvising drummer Paul Lovens (later a member of the Alexander von Schlippenbach Trio with Evan Parker, Globe Unity Orchestra, Lovens/Lytton duo and many other groups). Free jazz, improvised noise, Joseph Beuys actions and home-made electronics collided chaotically in the period between 1968 and 1970, their traces later evident, in the case of Kraftwerk, in a sophisticated grasp of syncopation, a performance art aesthetic and an iconoclastic approach to sculpting electronic sound and building custom instruments. During this emancipatory moment of the late 1960s the two visions of freedom swiftly polarized, even though the object from which they recoiled – the Nazi period and its tortuous aftermath – was identical. At one extreme there was a belief in ecstatic liberation through repetition; on the other an expressionism that rejected all external controls. Through musical collaboration they came to understand their mutual antipathy.

'When Can started I was finished with free jazz,' Jaki Liebezeit told David Stubbs. 'In free jazz there was no future, everything was destroyed. Repetition was not allowed, but for me, repetition was one of the basic elements of music. In free jazz, they said, all tones are equal. That's okay for human beings – all human beings are equal, true, but I don't think the same thing for tones!'

Creation

One of the first groups I heard live in a club, probably early 1966, was a band called The Creation. Based just north of London in Cheshunt, close to where I grew up, they underwent the rebirth typical of bands of the time, adapting their R&B, soul or pop origins to a strange influx of avant garde ideas, exotic drugs and drastically enlivened wardrobe. Under the direction of Shel Talmy, producer for The Who and The Kinks, they played straight-ahead songs for mods, competent enough though lacking The Who's panache and energy. Already a music obsessive, I stood close to the front, maybe a few feet from where singer Kenny Pickett spray painted a strip of white lining paper during 'Painter Man', setting it alight while guitarist Eddie Phillips scraped at his strings with a violin bow. I had felt the same airstream myself, playing guitar in a teenage blues band. One night as we played Bo Diddley's 'Road Runner' during a rehearsal my home-made bottleneck left the riff behind and moved over the neck of the guitar as if possessed. 'What were you doing?' somebody asked, clearly hoping it would never happen again. Exactly what it was I couldn't be sure but I knew it would happen again, probably without the riff or the musicians who questioned why.

On the penultimate day of 1966 (I was then in my last year at school, seventeen years old) I queued early for an all-night concert at the Roundhouse in Chalk Farm, north London. Headlined by Cream, the trio of Ginger Baker, Jack Bruce and Eric Clapton formed in July that year, the event also promised the usual lightshow plus the slightly end-of-era support act of Geno Washington and the Ram Jam Band with their non-stop versions of Rufus Thomas, Sam and Dave and Lee Dorsey tracks. A cavernous, gutted shed designed for railway repair in the nineteenth century, this grimy Pantheon had been leased by the vocally socialist playwright Arnold Wesker in 1964. Envisaged as a cultural hub, the building was named Centre 42, opening in July 1966 with a launch for International Times, the underground newspaper. Gustav Metzger's liquid crystal light show lit up the gloom of its outer curves on that occasion. Once I asked him if he did the same for the Cream concert; he thought not, though documentation (in *Gustav Metzger: History History*) exists suggesting that he and a group of assistants used twelve projectors both for that night and the New Year's Eve concert with The Who, The Move and Pink Floyd.

I was there for Cream, having heard them play at a north London club called Bluesville that September. The thing was to be at the front so I remember standing at the edge of the stage. To my right was a temporary structure like a shed with men standing on the roof to operate a light show. What happened next is unclear to me and I am suspicious of it, only because it was so long ago, my memory is vague and I have told the story many times, no doubt refining it through repetition. What I know is that in the semi-darkness and confusion of that early part of the evening a number of men walked onto the stage and began setting up equipment. One of them wore an Italian-style shortie raincoat so it seemed that they had come in directly from the cold (not that the Roundhouse was warm). The equipment included a drum kit but other objects were non-identifiable. There may have been a cello. A tall man bent over to fettle with some device on the floor. Loud electronic noises were emitted. I can remember no response from the audience, still sparse at that point. Truthfully, the details of what I heard and felt are a locked door to me now; I can remember fragments of equal substance from the performances by Geno Washington and Cream, like stills from a lost film.

After a while the men on stage drifted off into the darkness. Not long after setting up his kit the drummer packed it back up again – a sequence which replays itself as the poignant comedy of a Jacques Tati film (particularly since it was the drummer, if my memory is correct, who was wearing the Monsieur Hulot raincoat). There have been occasions during the retelling of this story when I have said it changed my life. Melodramatic perhaps, or exaggeration; the music itself had less immediate impact on my teenaged self than hearing live sets by Jimi Hendrix, Booker T and the MGs, Otis Redding, Roland Kirk and Freddie King. But it was not the music in itself that mattered but the lingering impression I took away of disorganization, of people working together to make sounds and actions that seemed to have no binding coherence. There were hints of this elsewhere: the presentiment of total disintegration that was always latent in a Jimi Hendrix set; even hearing

Thelonious Monk live at London's Royal Festival Hall in 1966 there were glimmers within of a music not quite vacuum sealed for presentation, a little dance around the piano, and, as Jeff Nuttall wrote in his literary portrait of Lol Coxhill: 'Monk's breaking off in the middle of a chorus of "Well You Needn't" to arise and closely scrutinise the Festival Hall organ while the audience waited in silence clearly anticipates Coxhill's behaviour patterns.' But for all of my escalating enthusiasm in 1966 for the avant-garde of art, music, cinema and literature – whether Ornette Coleman or the Destruction in Art Symposium – AMM was more shocking for having no apparent guiding principle, not even destruction. It simply was and then it was not.

Freedom love and peace

How did I know that the group was AMM? I had read about them in *Vogue* earlier that year, also read in *Jazz Monthly* about Keith Rowe's 'bizarre playing in a sort of anti-jazz style' and the 'Turkish flavour that he injected into his solo' in Peter Russell's preview of *Plymouth Sound*, a Westward Television broadcast by the Mike Westbrook Jazz Band. That was September 1965; as a guitarist on the brink of experiment, I took note. Perhaps they were mentioned on posters but in 1966 this was still a group for insiders. Their first public or semi-public 'plays' (as they called their improvisation sessions in rooms within institutions unaware of their existence) only began in June of the previous year. From my outsider viewpoint they seemed connected to a network of events, venues, musicians and artists that I sought to join: DIAS, the Institute of Contemporary Arts, clubs like UFO and the Electric Garden, the Arts Laboratory in Drury Lane, the Anti-University, the Royal College of Art and the Lisson Gallery in Bell Street. The architect of at least some of this activity was Victor Schonfield. A forward-thinking, erudite jazz listener, Schonfield founded an organization, Music Now, in 1967 to promote new music. 'The position in 1967 was that public money was going to support rubbish,' he told Richard Leigh in 1975, 'and geniuses were getting none whatsoever, and the only way to change this was by forming a charity. Music Now was started with the famous motto: "Get their money", and I wanted to get money for the people I liked.' Included among the people he liked were John Cage and David Tudor, who performed at the Royal Albert Hall in 1972 and Sun Ra (my account of his London performance, promoted by Music Now in 1970 can be found in John Szwed's Sun Ra biography, *Space Is the Place*).

After leaving college Schonfield worked briefly for a rock promoter, on the phone fixing gigs for The Crazy World of Arthur Brown and others too terrible for him to name. Through his 'great mate' John 'Hoppy' Hopkins (a polymath political activist who was at the centre of many underground culture ventures in London – the London Free School, UFO and International Times) he tried to do the same for those few groups to which he was genuinely dedicated: 'I was trying to get free jazz, including AMM, some work in the hippie scene because the hippie scene slogans were all about freedom and love and peace.' Similarly remote in its view of youthful music was a description of the event I witnessed, listed in the *AMM factsheet* of all AMM concerts between June 1965 and October 1970 as 'participation in Round House pop concert'.

Money, fame, Skip James, Howlin' Wolf and Marshall amplifiers notwithstanding, only a porous barrier separated AMM from Cream. Ginger Baker's mentor and guide into African rhythm was Phil Seaman, the drummer who played on Joe Harriott's *Free Form* and inspired the Spontaneous Music Ensemble's John Stevens. Harriott had shared the 1960 Live New Departures bill at the ICA not just with Cornelius Cardew and John Tilbury; poet Pete Brown also performed 'jazz poems' with Ronnie Scott, Bruce Turner and Alan Cohen, experiments in fusing spoken poetry and music that were a precursor to Brown's later role as a lyricist for Cream. As for Jack Bruce, his work with Graham Bond and pianist Mike Taylor in the period prior to Cream can be heard as steps taken to the edge of a dangerous brink, past which penury loomed. As Bruce told Duncan Heining:

> I thought [Mike Taylor] was very forward-looking at the time and very open. I was originally in a trio with Ginger and Graham Bond but Graham was only playing alto sax at that time. So, it was very much along the lines of a sort of Ornette Coleman band really in the sense it was a trio without a piano. We were all trying to find our own music as it were.

There were also free improvisation sessions with drummer Jon Hiseman and trumpeter Henry Lowther in early 1966. At the time, both Lowther and Bruce were in employment with Manfred Mann, playing run-throughs of the hits. On their rare nights off they took a handful of door money bookings (earning roughly two shillings and six pence each in pre-decimal coinage) at the Regency Club. On the border of Stoke Newington and Hackney, this basement jazz club had the reputation of being a venue in which the Kray twins owned an 'interest' (Derek Bailey played a regular gig there in the early 1960s and found the Krays to be as tolerable as any other employer). Appreciative of the irony of playing free improvisation in a gangster's paradise, Lowther recalls there was only one rule: 'Late at night these guys came down there to drink. When they came down we used to have to stop. There'd be ten to twenty of these blokes. It was classic East End stuff.'

Group Sounds Three, as they called themselves when previous members of a quintet (Lyn Dobson, Tony Hymas and Harry Miller among them) dropped out, gradually discarded most of the structuring principles then current in jazz: 'By the time we got to the trio,' says Lowther, 'we used to play without any tunes at all except we did have some idea about what it was we would do. Maybe we'd start off with a rhythm – you'd try to maintain that and go away from it but keep coming back to it, which gives it form. Form is important to me, even when I play improvised music.' Mike Taylor wrote arrangements but before the group could develop further the lure of the rock scene broke it apart. That summer Jack Bruce left Manfred Mann to join Clapton and Baker in Cream, while Hiseman took the drum stool left vacant by Baker in the Graham Bond Organisation. Two years later Hiseman formed Colosseum, like Cream a group whose long-form improvisations pushed pop song and blues structures as far as they could go in a rock context. Listen, for example, to the live recording of Cream's performance at Detroit's Grande Ballroom in 1967, much of it a cloudburst of distorted noise only held together by intense listening and the trio's sense of how much was too much. One of the main differences was the crushing volume. Lowther remembers hearing Cream live and feeling nauseous from bass vibrations coming up through the floor.

Plays

There was a line. Beyond that lay the unknown, where free was synonymous with no pay. Those caught up in this dream of freedom would either retreat, move sideways into something less vertiginous or they would step over. AMM, a group of fluctuating membership, was a gradual coalescence of prevailing and contradictory forces in the early 1960s, their playing bringing to light all the implications, half-spoken thoughts and shadow territory that others chose to ignore. The earliest recorded example of AMM (with the exception of an acetate made in November 1965) is a recording from one of their Royal College of Art 'plays'. Initially held in the RCA music room, these sessions began as the result of an invitation from the Jazz and Blues Society in late 1965 and continued on a weekly basis, moving from room to room – student common room to canteen – television or juke box switched on by students and switched back off by a member of the group. This continued for perhaps two years, accessible only to those from the inner circle and their guests (Paul McCartney, Marianne Faithfull, Alexis Korner, David Izenzon and Ornette Coleman among them). If I listen now to this recording from March 1966 (adding imaginary reverberation and amplification to simulate the different acoustic conditions of the Roundhouse) then it becomes easier to understand why my experience had such a profound and lasting impact.

A 6' 26" excerpt edited by Eddie Prévost (included on the double CD, *Not Necessarily 'English Music'* compiled for *Leonardo Music Journal*) begins with a two-note clarinet fanfare played by bassist Lawrence Sheaff, strained and shrill, answered by a forcibly struck single note from Cornelius Cardew on the piano. These two sounds are allowed to decay in a lengthy silence before a reprise of the clarinet, this time echoed by Lou Gare's tenor saxophone, then answered with violent brevity by Eddie Prévost's percussion and Keith Rowe's electric guitar. Each subsequent silence is intensified by the anticipation of these lancings of an invisible fabric. Heavy with presence, silences assert themselves as more than spaces, pauses or non-events; they are treated as silences within a greater silence, replete emptiness, resistant to action yet compelling action, full of possibility. After a particularly piercing amplified sound from Rowe, a long silence unfolds, held for thirty-five seconds in which near-inaudible 'movements' of instruments – amplifier, cymbal, piano – can be heard as presences rather than volition. Choices are made – Cardew's gauche melodramas at the piano, for example – whose inadvisability is sabotaged and salvaged by responses that in any other musical context would be considered irritatingly perverse: the farmyard squawking of the clarinet, an undertow of speech from Rowe's transistor radio buried under scrapings of various guitar- and drum-shaped objects. Perhaps they are irritatingly perverse in this context also, since they agitate and flurry around the conciliatory foghorn (for those in peril on the sea) of Lou Gare's tenor without ever extending support.

Listening to this recording at such a distance of time, interpreting (perhaps unjustly) the impulses and decisions of the players, only emphasizes its complexity as a work within the musical context of the time. Each step and stumble is committed as a public gesture that cannot be retracted, only redeemed in much the same way that Lennie Tristano would pick up the harmonic errors committed by his fellow players and reconcile them to the flow of the music. This is the equivalent of what Paul F. Berliner has described as a technique common among jazz improvisers: 'Improvisers cannot redeem their unintended phrases or unsuccessful "accidents." Rather they react to them immediately, endeavouring to integrate them smoothly into their performances. Mistakes, in particular, they treat as spontaneous compositional problems requiring immediate musical solutions. The solutions result in what may properly be described as musical saves.' Again, a divergence from the ethos of jazz; there is no evidence of smooth integration. Compare AMM's abrasive physicality to those few examples of free(ish) improvisation recorded in Britain prior to 1966 – 'Spaces' by the Joe Harriott Quintet, for example, or 'Culloden Moor', recorded (under the supervision of Victor Schonfield) in June 1964 by The New Departures Quartet of pianist Stan Tracey, tenor saxophonist Bobby Wellins, bassist Jeff Clyne and drummer Laurie Morgan. Both are urbane, skilful and expressive, daring yet disarmingly attractive, their conception of form firmly rooted in a jazz tradition of atmospheres and tone poems: Duke Ellington, Gil Evans, Miles Davis, Charles Mingus.

AMM, on the other hand, worked according to a radically different aesthetic view, a notion of beauty closer to the scarred, scratched, soiled, splashed surfaces of work by Rauschenberg, Latham, Burri, Dubuffet, Bacon, Antoni Tàpies, Alan Davie, David Smith, Eduardo Paolozzi; the unearthly textures of living and dead matter revealed by the photographs of Wols, Bill Brandt, Kawada Kikuji and Raymond Moore; the hallucinatory grain and light of films such as Satyajit Ray's *Panther Panchali*, Ingmar Bergman's *The Silence* and *Persona*. Closer, also, to what Yve-Alain Bois in *Formless: A User's Guide* called (after Georges Bataille) 'base materialism' – '... the formless matter that base materialism claims for itself resembles nothing, especially not what it should be, refusing to let itself be assimilated to any concept whatever', writing of Rauschenberg's work as 'one big celebration of nondialectical, inarticulable waste' and Dubuffet's compulsive drive towards 'rehabilitating mud'.

Insects slashing at steel doors

When you drum on the bottom sheet with your tensely arched finger it booms hollow, amplified, to your ear pressed against the pillow. Cavity mattress, resonance, reverberation: drum delicate and interesting rhythms made complex by time-interval, due to the irregular cavity, weight disposition, the interstices between the whatnots.

B. S. JOHNSON, *Albert Angelo*, 1964

Even now, in the age of noise as both genre and pollutant, the physicality of AMM's conglomerate sound glowers in its confrontation with the orthodoxies of music. Not only was there an extraordinary amount of noise (in other words, the masking of clear signals); they also used as much, if not more distortion than rock bands of the day – Jimi Hendrix Experience, Cream, Pink Floyd, Soft Machine. Even though AMM played at a far lower decibel volume than such bands (some of their sounds were unamplified; others were amplified through contact microphones), their use of extreme contrast, harsh and relentless long-duration sounds made them subjectively louder, an effect emphasized by their level of volume relative to the small rooms, galleries and halls in which they played. Indicative of a move away from conservatoire decorum, Franco Evangelisti's 'traumatic' approach to the instrument with Nuova Consonanza had evolved through AMM from an intellectual position into a combative tactic, a means to invade silence and the sounds made by others, to disgorge raw, unidentifiable sound from the specialist objects of the instrumentalist.

Seymour Wright has located three accounts of AMM's sonic objects and actions as they were in the spring of 1966. The first, from historian Eric Hobsbawm (writing under the pseudonym of Francis Newton for the *New Statesmen*), identified a sitar, xylophone, metronome, tape recorder, two alarm clocks, a burglar alarm, guitar played with a red plastic spoon, picnic tin and steel ruler as part of their 'kit'. Writing in the *East Village Other*, Barry Miles wrote about Cardew's 'silence, dragged chairs, plucked strings, rubbed glass and drummed piano-frame' while Victor Schonfield, writing in *Town Magazine*, vividly described the way Keith Rowe combined

> the manipulation of amplifier feedback with that of violin bow, steel ruler or drumsticks on the guitar strings, which have often previously

been loosened to sagging point. By such means he acquires the melodic resources of sounds like those made by flocks of birds, dogs, sirens, rain on a tin roof, buzz-saws, bubbling lava, giant insects ripping and slashing at steel doors, or electrified cats and babies.

Some of this drama is audible on 'After Rapidly Circling the Plaza', the tempestuous 'track' that makes up side two of their first record: *AMMMUSIC*, recorded in 1966, released on Elektra Records in 1967. Notably lacking in the silences of the earlier RCA 'play', both sides are characterized by a dense high keening of strings, metal and distortion that is everywhere and nowhere, both pressing against the eardrums and sunk in distant reverberation, a muffled bass drum thudding at the core like artillery from far-off battle. In the year of 'All You Need Is Love', Haight Ashbury flower power and Donovan these were gorse-choked thickets of sound, harsh, unrelenting and strident, uncanny as Japanese gagaku; simultaneously slow and febrile, they unfolded as a ruined landscape evocative of the lesions of post-war, bomb-damaged London. It would be misleading, however, to hear the music purely as a document of bomb culture created by young men whose childhoods were despoiled by wartime. As with MEV, the abnegation of individualistic control gave release to an almost delirious rejection of European music and its axioms: equal temperament, the conceptual division of audible time into bar lines and mathematical values, notation on paper, any system of intervallic relationships, the tuning of instruments to common accord, 'correct' intonation and instrumental technique, not to mention a repertoire which would reflect the compositional truisms that music should have clarity, balance, dynamic contrasts, light and shade, a degree of craftsmanship and some form of developmental narrative or discernable structure. These were all accomplished musicians possessed of their own craftsmanship and with knowledge of their own and other musical worlds. So what were the enabling factors that produced a music seemingly based on renunciation? Was it a degree zero music, or even a very English strategy for embodying in the most extreme form possible an otherwise silent yet profound discontent with existing cultural and social orthodoxies?

Music groups are rarely planned; they 'become formed' through circumstantial connections of proximity, school, job, friendship, an advert placed somewhere, a chance meeting. AMM's formation was little different: Eddie Prévost has described this convergence as being the opposite of a conscious decision for him; Gare and Rowe, more a case of their exclusion, self-willed and otherwise, from existing situations. The origins, simplified and reconstructed, were as follows: in the southwest of England, three painting students at Plymouth College of Art – Keith Rowe, Malcolm Le Grice and Mike Westbrook – came together in 1958 to play mainstream jazz. After a fortuitous conversation with Rowe in a record shop, baritone saxophonist John Surman, still a schoolboy, joined in with workshops run by Westbrook at the local art centre. By the early 1960s they had moved to London. After studying at the Slade School of Art Le Grice was to become a central figure in structural and expanded cinema: 'Then the other big influence for me was jazz improvisation,' he has said, 'particularly Ornette Coleman, Dizzy Gillespie. …' The others formed the core of what was now the Mike Westbrook Band with Henry Lowther, drummer Alan Jackson, bassist Lawrence Sheaff and a tenor saxophonist, Lou Gare. Born in the West Midlands industrial town of Rugby in 1939, Gare moved from band to band, gravitated south to London, took a phone call from a musician offering work in a band with trombone, baritone and tenor horn – 'I thought that would sound rather gloomy – all those deep sounds,' he says – quickly finding himself within the Westbrook line-up playing opposite Jeff Nuttall's band in a pub where the musicians had to be protected from drunks by a barricade of chairs and tables.

Like Rowe, Gare had the sensibilities of a painter. Both he and Lawrence Sheaff maintained parallel lives as art students and musicians, Sheaff at Ealing and Gare at Hammersmith. As the Westbrook band developed in the early 1960s into a force within British jazz the alienation of Gare and Rowe from its aims became apparent. Westbrook's suffusing of Duke Ellington sensibilities with an Albion mythos – William Blake, Salvation Army bands and so on – was interesting but no place for radicals. Both chafed against the restrictions. 'It was all tied up with painting ideas as well,' Gare recalls.

> Jackson Pollock and some of the American painters – apparently random kind of things. I didn't see any reason why you couldn't do that in music. It all seemed to tie together although I think the last gig I ever did with Westbrook's band was in Coventry and it ended up with me on one end of the stage and the rest of the band all down the other end.

Rowe's approach was a more direct trans-sensory passage from visual arts to the imperatives of the jazz bandstand. Initially he would find a magazine image, the packaging from a fruit pie, or a drawing by Paul Klee (in itself, inherently musical) that corresponded at an intuitive level to the score that Westbrook presented to him; one of these images would be pasted onto the opposite page to his part and he would interpret it as a form of notation. But the post-war Americans offered a more dramatic exit from the confinements of moderation. Roy Lichtenstein was given a major exhibition at the Tate Gallery in 1964, showing paintings whose emotionally charged subject matter – love, war, death – was flipped, or double-flipped by Lichtenstein's witty appropriation of comic book and advertising graphics. An explosion could be flattened (just as real-world violence of the time was increasingly flattened by mass mediation), yet the perfect hard edges were marred by the drips of Lichtenstein's painterly technique, the solidity of an image revealed as illusion by the grossly enlarged Ben-Day dots. Robert Rauschenberg's work was shown at the Whitechapel Gallery in London in the same year. To the adventurous but frustrated mind his ideas, along with Lichtenstein's, were easily extrapolated to music: white paintings, black paintings, mouldy wet oil paintings pressed into dirt and gravel, images from magazines and reproductions of Velázquez's *Rokeby Venus* and Rubens's *Venus At Her Toilet* lifted from their pages and transferred by silkscreen process or solvent and friction onto a new substrate. *Broadcast* (1959) could have been a template for AMM's sound: three radios tuned to different stations concealed within a combine painting of fabric, newspaper, printed reproductions and a plastic comb.

Rowe's early style has been described by Mike Westbrook as an emulation of Barney Kessell, a guitarist noted for dexterity of movement between complex percussive harmony and fast melodic lines. From the point of view of an outsider or apostate to the jazz tradition, the problem with such guitarists after Charlie Christian – Kessell, Kenny Burrell, Jim Hall, Tal Farlow, Johnny Smith, Joe Pass, Wes Montgomery, Herb Ellis – by the beginning of the 1960s was their consummate technique and tastefulness (there were far rougher examples to follow – Pat Hare's corroded distortion on James Cotton's 'Cotton Crop Blues', for example, or Link Wray, Bo Diddley, Paul Burlison and Johnny 'Guitar' Watson, but these were unlikely to come to the attention of a British jazz player of the time).

Artists, on the other hand, were dealing in shit, dirt and rust, sharp edges, surfaces that could wound or infect, cheap images, accidents, a physical showdown with materials chosen not because they worked within a tight set of regulations but because they happened to be lying in the gutter: waste, pungent debris, mass-produced objects, rubber tyres or the stuffed Angora goat that Rauschenberg bought from a second-hand furniture store on Seventh Avenue. Elements once controlled in space or time or through niceties of aesthetics now opened up an exploded field of potentiality. As Helen Molesworth has written about Rauschenberg's black paintings (though this is applicable to much of his early work, I would suggest, and inadvertently descriptive of improvisation): 'The paintings enact the body liberated through excretion. They are a narcissistic fantasy of self-birth; they give way to the delirium of the body producing its own knowledge.'

Into the dark

At the beginning of the 1970s I would go to The Place, a London dance studio close to where Dorothy Miller Richardson once lived and wrote, to hear AMM's weekly plays. They had established a new weekly residency there in July 1969. The room was not large, no stage, no special lighting. The group tended to set up across the width of the room, opposite the door. Audiences were small enough to make these occasions feel like the gathering of an estranged family, rather uncomfortable yet deeply affecting. No physical boundary separated musicians and players, yet as Alvin Curran has noted, an implicit and explicit self-containment kept the group apart from their audience. One night a man came to sit in, produced an instrument and crossed this invisible divide between them and us. AMM fell silent, leaving him adrift on a leaky boat. A version of freedom then, though not MEV's free-for-all. The room was invariably dark, illuminated only by evening light from a single window. Evan Parker remembers dance mirrors that doubled the red glow of amplifier lights. Lawrence Sheaff had left or been ousted from the group by this time to become involved with Maharishi Mahesh Yogi's 'transcendental meditation' organization, his place filled by Christopher Hobbs, one of Cardew's young students from the Royal Academy of Music. Cardew paced in his socks. The music had become less torrid, more refined but there were passages that attacked all undefended parts of the body to create internal havoc. I remember Lou Gare with a large sheet of white polystyrene foam, walking it edge-wise along the floor, exploiting its potential as one of the most distressing sonic by-products of the chemical industry.

Gare had the beatnik look and manner of a man out of time, his lugubrious tone and phrasing more reminiscent of Sonny Rollins or Coleman Hawkins than the iron-edged glossolalic African American tenor players emerging in the wake of John Coltrane: Frank Wright, Albert Ayler, Pharoah Sanders and Giuseppi Logan. It should be stressed that none of these latter players could be heard in Britain before the second half of 1965; as their records appeared they were available only from a few jazz specialist shops at a high price. The first *Melody Maker* review of Albert Ayler's ESP release, *Bells*, complained about the high price of forty-five shillings and six pence for a single-sided record. The music was fairly well received though journalists were fearful of praising the king's new clothes. 'Is the New Wave just a passing fad?' asked a *Melody Maker* headline in January 1966. 'Their preoccupation seems entirely with producing sounds and evoking moods rather than producing melodic lines,' answered Bob Dawbarn. 'Theirs is the ultimate in self-expression with no apparent attempt to communicate with an audience.' In January of the same year a more sympathetic critic – Bob Houston – showed reserved enthusiasm for Ayler's *Spirits*: 'Ayler's direct assault on the emotions will shock anyone not familiar with his work, but personally I find that familiarity with his initially unattractive tenor playing provides great satisfaction.'

This was the free jazz context in Britain, barely a rumour and regarded with deep ambivalence. As Keith Rowe became increasingly marginalized or self-excluded within the increasingly tight arrangements of Westbrook's repertoire, Gare sought opportunities to play with less constraint, less queuing up for a solo behind John Surman and Mike Osborne. The weekly music paper, *Melody Maker*, had been employment notice board of choice for jazz musicians for many decades. Edwin 'Eddie' Prévost, a Bermondsey-based drummer who had worked an apprenticeship in marching bands, trad jazz and skiffle groups, formed a modern jazz group in the style of Art Blakey's Jazz Messengers – no-nonsense East Coast swinging hard bop – and so advertised for a tenor saxophonist, no doubt hoping for a British Hank Mobley or Wayne Shorter.

There are no clear breaks in the history between one style of music or another, no sudden changes in activity, personnel or musical approach. Rowe, Prévost, Gare, Westbrook, a bass player named Mal Hawley, Henry Lowther occasionally, would gather at Westbrook's flat in early 1965 to play informally. As Seymour Wright surmises: 'This activity was socially overlapping, but practically distinct from Westbrook's group. It is quite possible that these plays were in part an attempt to work through, perhaps even a hopeful compromise with, the emerging tensions between freedom and form in the larger group.'

What is certain is that the playing became progressively less dependant on tunes, head arrangements or durational conventions. One piece might last for two hours, so linking the emergent practice of free improvisation with one of its ancestors – the after-hours jam sessions of New York clubs like Minton's Playhouse. A tension between polarities – music as clandestine experiment at one extreme; an ignominiously functional, even vulgar branch of the entertainment industry at the other – was particularly acute for the growing pains of free improvisation. Music is predominantly a social activity however and so musicians have the instinct to find an audience, whatever their aversion to putting on a show. The informal group found itself moving its private activities to the marginally more public Royal College of Art and so a messy transition ensued in which the core of Gare, Prévost, Rowe and Scheaff became the group known as AMM.

Cornelius Cardew joined in January 1966. On the lookout for musicians who could interpret *Treatise*, his graphic indeterminate score of 1963–7, he was introduced to Keith Rowe by Alan Cohen. A contemporary of Cardew and Richard Rodney Bennett at the Royal Academy of Music, Cohen was a versatile musician and jazz arranger who had attended summer schools with Nono and Maderna – such broad interests led to his recurrent appearance as a go-between in the AMM story. According to John Tilbury, a performance by himself, Cardew, Rowe, John Surman and others was organized at the ICA by Mark Boyle (an artist who later became known for collaborating with Joan Hills on light shows for Soft Machine). Rowe subsequently invited Cardew to the RCA plays. In his biography of Cardew, Tilbury quotes Eddie Prévost: 'I think it had been a lifelong ambition of his to play in a jazz band and we were the next best thing.' Tilbury continues:

> This jocular remark may have been nearer the truth than Prévost realised at the time; for years Cardew had collected jazz records and had taken vicarious pleasure in listening to jazz. For apart from some Jimmy Yancey transcriptions at Live New Departures events in the early sixties, and the occasional private indulgence behind closed doors, Cardew always fought shy, for whatever reason, of the jazz performance area.

Self-deprecation aside, not only was it unnecessary for Cardew to have the encyclopaedic knowledge and fluency of the jazz musician – changes, chops, turnarounds, the song book and so on – to be capable of playing with these improvisers; there was also the possibility of anonymity. The group had no leaders, no soloists, no manifested hierarchy. Nobody was tied to a particular instrument unless they wished to be and there were signs, a continuation from the later Westbrook period, of resistance to the extreme specialization of virtuosity. Picasso's dismemberment of the guitar's solid, familiar form in his constructions of 1912 can be construed as a coded missive to musicians, of how far they might go in deconstructing the prosthesis of the instrument. Likewise the transformation of a piano into tuned percussion by the preparation techniques devised by Henry Cowell and John Cage. Photographs taken in Sound Techniques studio for the Elektra record show Rowe's guitar laid flat on a table, played with a violin bow. The interior of the piano is littered with objects. Lou Gare recalls a phase of playing saxophone like a shofar during this period, depressing all the keys and overblowing. He also remembers Eddie Prévost laying out his drums in different parts of the room, then having to rush from one to the other as if negotiating a new map of the world.

By early 1966 they had collectively decided on a name – the cryptic three letters of AMM – but even that had no connotations, no discernible connection to a style of music. Decisions were being made, unconsciously or otherwise: to play without special lighting, or any lighting, to set up the instruments informally without regard for those orthodoxies of spatial status that still prevailed in jazz groups, rock bands and orchestras (important people at the front; functionaries behind). All of these refusals of the past contributed to a profound structural break: the paradox of a music almost without personality or identity yet instantly identifiable; a music that subsumed individuals into the group yet allowed each one of them as much freedom as they were able or willing to take.

Robert Rauschenberg's *Erased De Kooning Drawing* of 1953 was one of the precursors of a strategy of cancellation and self-cancellation. In Rauschenberg's mind, to methodically erase a drawing willingly given by Willem de Kooning for this purpose was a poetic act that connected drawing with the emptiness of his white paintings (the same white paintings whose 'gathering in' of light and shadows into their emptiness acted as the catalyst for Cage's formulation of a composition to frame and interrogate silence, *4' 33"*). Through the elimination of something important, using similar gestures to the making of the original work, new possibilities were created, a collaborative work that echoed and pre-echoed surrealist games such as The Exquisite Corpse and the procedural exchanges between Oulipians, the literary workshop founded in 1960 by, among others, Raymond Queneau.

For the editors of *Collectivism After Modernism* – Blake Stimson and Gregory Sholette – art after the Second World War abandoned the collectivist spirit of modernism that led Kazimir Malevich to say that collectivism was the path to 'world-man' or Piet Mondrian to react against 'everything individual in man'. 'While there were plenty of group exhibitions, ersatz and real professional organisations, international conferences and journals, and other developments in the 1950s and 1960s that helped to make the likes of abstract expressionism, happenings, Fluxus, pop art, minimalism, conceptual art, and others over into art-historical categories,' they write, 'none of these brought the question of collective voices to the fore in the same way, none sought first and foremost to generate a voice that declared its group affiliation, its collectivization, as the measure of its autonomy.' But their account only makes sense if art activity is reterritorialized and prioritized as a primarily visual medium defined by galleries, museums and dealers. Only by ignoring the tendency towards intensive hybridity in post-war arts, through which disparate art practices sought common objects, shared ideals and a trans-sensory blurring of their essential character, is it possible to overlook the collective tendency in improvised music.

Driven by necessity, ideology and the structural implications of the music, post-war improvisers turned towards collectivism, rather than away from it, a shift observable in musician-led organizations such as Sun Ra's Arkestra (with its communal living/rehearsal house and El Saturn record label, all based in Philadelphia), the Jazz Composer's Guild in New York City, the AACM in Chicago, the Musician's Coop in the UK, then later the London Musicians Collective and collectives in Bristol, Manchester and other cities. Independent record labels founded on more or less collective principles were also launched by and for specific communities of musicians – Instant Composer's Pool (ICP) in the Netherlands, Incus in London and Free Music Production (FMP) in Germany – again followed in the 1970s by many labels including BVHAAST (Willem Breuker), Po Torch (Paul Lytton and Paul Lovens), Parachute, Metalanguage, Trans Museq (La Donna Smith and Davey Williams), Matchless, Emanem, Bead Records and the collectively edited and produced UK magazine *Musics*. All of this activity was to some extent pragmatic – if nobody else within the music world was sufficiently motivated to support the music through traditional channels then the musicians must do it themselves – but it was also profoundly embedded within the edgeless interrelationship of work and life. Each collective, label or publication presented an identity to the world, each identity an articulation of specific conditions pertaining to aesthetics, place and history: to be a black musician in Chicago, to be a German in Berlin after the Nazis, to be an outsider not only to the worlds of jazz and 'classical' music but to the art world, the academy and all form of centralized media.

This activism – making concerts, producing records, building a discourse – was a form of social bonding, a political and philosophical response to the state of the world but more precisely an argument against the narrow range of class-bound art and entertainment milieus in which musicians were expected to perform, the restrictive capitalist model of record production and, to compound these problems, indifference or hostility from media outlets. The music was resistant also: an embodiment of intimacy without concordance, work of perpetual transitions, ephemeral, seemingly without beginning or end. Being neither one clear thing or the other it bore the taint of impurity, unforgivably close to life itself.

Cloud of unknowing

Packaged inside the box of AMM's *The Crypt: 12 June'68* (released in a variety of versions, edited and unedited, but I am thinking of the double LP released in a box by Matchless in 1981), was a paper insert giving the names of the musicians, short texts by Cardew and Gare and an extract from Chuang-Tzu's Taoist text, *The Realm of Nothing Whatever*, a part of the seven inner chapters that can be reliably ascribed to this person – Chuang-Tzu, Chuang Chou, Kwang-tse, Zhuangzi and various other romanizations – who may or may not have actually existed in China in the late fourth century BC. The parable concerns a tree – Ailantus Glandulosa or fetid tree (translated as stinktree by Thomas Merton; tree-of-heaven by A. C. Graham) with twisted branches, a divided trunk and toxic leaves. Chuang-Tzu tells the owner of this apparently worthless, noxious tree to plant it in the realm of Nothing Whatever, in the wilderness, where he can enjoy it for itself: 'There you might saunter idly by its side, or in the enjoyment of untroubled ease sleep and dream beneath it. Neither bill nor axe would shorten its existence; there would be nothing to injure it. What is there in its uselessness to cause you distress?'

What can be deduced from the story, whose key tenets – 'in the realm of nothing whatever' and 'what is there in uselessness to cause you distress' – were revived as track titles for the CD issue of *AMMMUSIC 1966* in 1989? Was this form of improvisation so rebarbative to a wider public, so lacking in use value that it caused its makers to despair? Sinologist and translator Angus Graham describes the theme of this section of the inner chapters – 'Going rambling without a destination' as the original compilers of *Chuang-tzu* called it – as 'soaring above the restricted viewpoints of the worldly'. With self-determination and the abandonment of music's recognized structuring principles came an inevitable separation from normative society and its scope of understanding, an alienation from popular tastes (if such a complex phenomenon can be summed up in two words) whose irresolvability would eventually break AMM apart. This is a story to be examined in a subsequent volume to this book. But in the early days of the group, as it became publically known, a counter narrative was essential for survival, optimism, self-belief, the will to continue. Although AMM's reputation grew steadily, the response from establishment critics was supercilious, dismissive, totally aloof from the serious intent of the music. Take Felix Aprahamian, writing with tightly compressed class-contempt in the *Sunday Times* in 1971:

> A total non-event was AMM Music's desultory doodling by some slouching half-lit figures in the [Queen Elizabeth Hall] on Thursday before an even sparser audience. Most of it consisted of endless microtonal inflections and percussive accretions to a held organ-chord – B flat major, second inversion – a chord with which, as Sir Jack Westrup recently declared in similar circumstances, I am not unfamiliar. After an hour, I fled next door to the sanity of the 'Eroica' by the RPO under Dorati, ashamed that at times I have been bored by a surfeit of Beethoven: never have these strains sounded more blessed.

Adding to this estrangement from the traditionalists of musicology and classical music, their music's intensity and its ancillary activities of regular discussion sessions and explorations of many different philosophical paths – reinforced its excavatory and anonymising nature. Darkness was significant. Sounds emerged ambiguously, the identity of their makers unclear. Rooms, particularly the music room at the London School of Economics, where they played from May to September in 1966, were small and dark. The solo and accompaniment model disappeared. 'You couldn't tell what you were playing,' says Lou Gare. 'You'd hear the sounds and you didn't know which were your sounds until you actually stopped. You'd think you were doing something, you'd stop and that would carry on and you'd suddenly realize it was somebody else making that noise. I suppose it's got much more of a physical impact in the dark – you're sort of inside the sound.' This immersiveness led to heightened listening, shadowed by the implication of silence:

> You'd have this fantastic noise going on and out of it you'd get all these subtle vibrations and sound, you know, subtle sounds which you could probably only feel. You almost felt it rather than heard it and then it would end up quite often with a long silence or nothing – something very slight going on for quite a long time in the dark and you'd end up feeling quite elated.

Darkness and volume fused, provoking a robust form of dialogical communication, adversarial and attritional at times, only obliquely responsive and rarely directly mimetic or convergent. The 1960s utopia of freedom, love and peace that Victor Schonfield had hoped to exploit in his informal role as a manager was a different world. 'It was quite a hard scene to play in,' says Gare,

> because there was no quarter given. If the others were playing too loud and they couldn't hear you that was just tough. You'd have to sit there until it got quiet again, doing what you were doing or doing something that could be heard. It got louder and louder – it got incredibly loud for quite a long period. You'd end up with your ears ringing for a couple of days.

For Gare, contradictions were built into the music. The enveloping atmosphere created an invisible safety zone yet within that zone there were tensions:

> The main thing was you always felt as though you were invulnerable in a strange way. As long as you kept playing the music nothing harmful would happen – probably a total illusion. I think it was quite violent

music at times. We used to talk quite a lot about silence, the self and inner silence but actually, when it came to it, the music could be quite violent and unpleasant but that seemed to be necessary to break through somehow to the silence sort of reality.

'Silence sort of reality' suggests a silence more comprehensive, more subtle, than mere absence of sound; silence as an originating and perpetual condition through which all sound, including unvoiced, sensed and imagined sound, emerges, persists and decomposes. This hard struggle to attain silence, to fight for it by fighting against it from within a group of wilful individuals who have chosen not to take the easier route to silence (to compose it for obedient performers) underlines a significant difference between free improvisation and indeterminacy. A common assumption is that AMM merged John Cage's indeterminacy with African American free jazz. Eddie Prévost laughs at the idea that Cage's ideas shaped the group from its inception:

> No, not really. A nice little story to amplify that … fairly early on I know we were interviewed by [Barry] Miles. He was obviously talking to everybody but at this point I was talking to him alone and he said, was the music influenced by John Cage? I said, well that's a drummer I've never heard play. I didn't know who John Cage was from Adam. I thought he was a drummer. Very naïve of course.

Cornelius Cardew's role as both charismatic emissary of such avant-garde ideas and Trojan horse, 'infiltrating the bourgeois notion of "natural" superiority and leadership', is examined by John Tilbury in his biography of Cardew: 'The necessarily antithetical relation of the "individual" to the "collective" is one of the principle canons of bourgeois ideology, and the disparagement of collectivity, especially in Art, was for AMM, at that time, intimidating.' Cardew seemed at once to soothe and inflame these insecurities. But despite the complexities of the relationship there is no question that Cardew's entry into the group energized them, imparted confidence and contributed new ideas. As with Gare, Rowe and Sheaff, there was some background in art training – in 1961 Cardew studied typography at the London School of Printing and Graphic Arts. Unsurprisingly, given his family background as the son of a notable potter, he was influenced by artists such as Jasper Johns. He also had first-hand experience of Stockhausen, Cage and Tudor, La Monte Young and the improvising scene in Rome. Tangible consequences came out of these connections – the use of contact mics to amplify surfaces and resonating bodies, for example, and portable radios with their found sound from the aether – but also an influx of philosophical reflections and propositions to ameliorate some of the problems caused by performances of such radically new music.

'I think Cornelius influenced me quite a lot,' says Gare.

> I remember once we played somewhere and someone threw some rubbish at us and a tomato or something splattered on the gong. I remember for ever afterwards there was this tomato stain all down the gong and he never cleaned it off. I think there was this idea that you didn't have to worry about things that happened, they were just sort of events and you could either try and erase it or you just accept it as part of what was going on. We played at some quite odd things where people would throw coins at us or they'd rush up and try and stop you playing or things like that.

Takes a trip

As the monochrome anarchic anger of post-war bomb culture elided into a more youthfully glamorous psychedelic scene in 1966–8, AMM found themselves precariously aligned to this fashionable world, if only from performances at clubs such as UFO, All Saints Hall, Middle Earth and the Trip at the Marquee, recording for Elektra (otherwise home to Love, The Doors and Tim Buckley), transient attention from rock aristocracy and the kind of dizzy write-ups they engendered in the underground bible that was *International Times*. 'You see, clearly the sound shines within,' wrote composer Michael Chant (soon to become one of the more politically active members of the Scratch Orchestra). 'Surrender your body, this work of time. What does it prove? Simply the eternal proof. If you are good, if you have time, it is light, if you arrive.' AMM's response was largely bemusement but brief alliances were formed, exemplars of ways in which the extreme avant-garde can seep outward into homeopathic versions of itself.

Syd Barrett's biographer, Rob Chapman, hears the influence of AMM's 'Later During a Flaming Riviera Sunset' in both title and where-the-wild-things-are intro to Pink Floyd's 'Flaming', recorded for *The Piper*

At the Gates of Dawn. Influence may be too directional a word but Barrett is reputed to have attended the recording of *AMMMUSIC* at Sound Techniques in June 1966 and was clearly affected by witnessing Keith Rowe's guitar techniques during the gigs on which both Pink Floyd and AMM performed. Footage of Pink Floyd shot (also at Sound Techniques) by filmmaker Peter Whitehead shows Barrett playing guitar laid flat on his thighs, applying objects to the strings, playing glissandi with a steel slide and at one point beating the strings with his fists. My clearest memory of Pink Floyd live during this period comes from their closing set at the 14 Hour Technicolour Dream, held in north London's Alexandra Palace in April 1967. Dawn was breaking and the noise from the stage was superficially (take away the uninspiring drumming) close to AMM live. The difference was in its partial nature, its lack of total conviction, one inspired yet damaged acolyte already on his way out of a band destined for bigger things.

Common ancestors were shared between musicians who might over time fall into roles so antipathetic as to be irreconcilable: rock casualty, rock legend, multimillionaire, political activist, avant-garde survivor. Another tantalizing example is John Cale, whose time as a student at Goldsmiths College in southeast London brought him into contact with Cornelius Cardew. On 6 July 1963, both Cardew and Cale were involved in the organization of the Little Festival of New Music. Two concerts held at Goldsmiths on the same day featured work by Cardew, John Cage, George Maciunas, Nam June Paik, La Monte Young and others, performed by a large group including Maciunas, Robin Page, Cale and Cardew. Shortly afterwards, Cale would leave London on a Leonard Bernstein scholarship for study at the Berkshire Music Center, Tanglewood, Massachusetts, then from there to New York City, to collaborations with La Monte Young and Tony Conrad and to the formation of the Velvet Underground with Lou Reed. In their most outré recordings – 'Loop', produced by Cale under the name Velvet Underground for Aspen magazine in 1966, for example, or the 'traumatic' strings and feedback that characterized 'European Son' and 'I Heard Her Call My Name' – their music trembled and howled on the edge of disintegration – again, not so far from the sound of AMM at that time.

'Trying to find a role in classical music that had anything to do with the outside world was certainly not clear in my mind,' John Cale has said, 'and I was using improvisation as a way of finding footing in my own personality.' This was also true for AMM, but collective improvisation also acted as an agent of destabilization. 'The strict egalitarian nature of AMM's structure meant that one's individual ego had to always be expanding to encompass the whole group,' Lawrence Sheaff told Rob Chapman.

> I think this posed a continuing challenge to the members, all of whom were strong personalities. But in performance, whenever that unity was fully actualised as a living flow, it was invincible. Nothing could deny the authority of that wall of sound. When I saw some individual members beginning to lay some claim to certain territories of sound, it signalled on a deeper level that it might be time to move on.

'Everything came out much more explicitly in the Scratch Orchestra – the mysticism, the morality, the politics,' Cornelius Cardew said in 1980, a year before being knocked down and killed by a hit-and-run driver. 'The struggle in AMM never developed to fighting it out.' Yet this struggle was enacted within and embodied by the cloud of unknowing that was AMM's ensemble sound, certainly from the Royal College of Art 'plays' of 1966 to the Crypt concert of 1968 (the Christian allusion here is deliberate; there are analogies between the spiritual guidance of this anonymous fourteenth-century text, its 'cloud of forgetting', for example, and Taoist ideas threaded through AMM's work). Is it exaggeration to claim that absorption into this cloud was a form of immersive deconditioning, from within which some form of grounding would become imperative to personal and artistic survival? Perhaps, but the intervention from within – Keith Rowe's turn to Mao Zedong Thought – was followed by Cardew but opposed by Prévost and Gare. As the solidity of AMM cracked open, the latter pair adapted to this painful break with a form of duo playing more closely related to their first collaboration in hard bop. 'There's a distinct possibility that what I would do in my life was to produce AMM music,' Keith Rowe has said. Later events were to prove him only partially right but this powerful sense of quest, undertaken no matter what the cost, is applicable not only to AMM but to all the improvisation groups of this era.

9 COLLECTIVE OBJECTIVITIES

FIGURE 4.1 Drawing of Angharad Davies and Lina Lapelyte by Calum Storrie.

Not tethered to a single mind

Near-darkness. Two violinists – Angharad Davies and Lina Lapelyte – stand back to back. Slowly, they circle as they play, like the enwrapping of a climber plant ascending its host. A single light illuminates one sliver of hair. The sound is thin, unstable, trembling, like a squeaky gate (just as the detractors say). They hum and sing strange intervals; violins cease. Their rotation reverses direction. Horse hair strokes steel; widdershins turning sheds a faint trail of intangible friction debris in its wake. This sound disguises itself as breath whistling through teeth, breeze disturbing the crust of a sand dune, two caterpillars eating the entangled leaves on which they teeter. I think of François Jullien writing of what he calls 'the subtle', a term to confront the dualism of concrete and intangible:

> There are various angles from which the subtle becomes accessible to experience. In aesthetics, for example, there is the exquisite flavour of the barely perceptible, whether in sound or image, in the transitional stage between silence and sonority in music or between emptiness and fullness in painting, when the sonic or pictorial realisation is barely evident or on the point of vanishing. Whether just barely outlined or already beginning to fade the subtle ceases to impose the brute opacity of its presence and can no longer be confined. Diffuse, vivid and insinuating, it continues to emanate indefinitely.

Two months later Shelley Hirsch was in London for a short stop and we talked again of stream of consciousness, her speech by way of illustration of the process and its importance to her singing suddenly branching into organic, unpredictable storylines, talking suddenly about an essay she had come across at the beginning of her life as a singer: Virginia Woolf's *Street Haunting: a London adventure*. Woolf sets out to buy a pencil, the excuse to immerse herself into human life, its grotesques, the passing snatches of its exchanges, glimpsed scenes, overheard chatter, press and movement within the atmospheres of the city.

I told her I knew the essay well. I have a copy in *The Death of the Moth*, collected essays published by the Hogarth Press in 1942, tattered now, barely retaining its book jacket illustrated by Vanessa Bell, sister to Virginia Woolf. Her drawing for the front is of entangled trees and grasses, many black pen lines pulling and curling in vertical movement, little differentiation made between figure and ground.

Woolf urges walking as an opening of the senses but this movement goes beyond the physical, through streets and over river into the meanders of her own mind. Nothing in life repeats. 'The sights we see and the sounds we hear now have none of the quality of the past,' she wrote (and this was in 1930); 'nor have we any share in the serenity of the person who, six months ago, stood precisely where we stand now.' She experienced all of these bodies as a potential dissolution of the self:

> Into each of these lives one could penetrate a little way, far enough to give oneself the illusion that one is not tethered to a single mind, but can put on briefly for a few minutes the bodies and minds of others. One could become a washerwoman, a publican, a street singer. And what greater delight and wonder can there be to leave the straight lines of personality and deviate into those footpaths that lead beneath brambles and thick tree trunks into the heart of the forest where live those wild beasts, our fellow men?

After the conversation, we walked over the road to Cafe Oto's project space to hear a septet of string players: Jennifer Allum, Bruno Guastalla, Guillaume Viltard, Hannah Marshall, Tim Fairhall, Angharad Davies, Ute Kanngiesser. They present themselves in a horseshoe shape in that order, from left to right, taking half the interior of the building. The other half is occupied by a small audience, largely improvising musicians – myself, Shelley Hirsch, Steve Beresford, Eddie Prévost, Marjolaine Charbin, John Chantler, Daichi Yoshikawa – a mirror septet of silent players.

I listen closely for a while, studying the sandbagged air-raid shelter ambience of the Project Space. Then as Viltard squeezes a second bridge between the fingerboard and strings of his double bass I open my notebook. Sometimes to write is to listen closer, if only because each moment of listening and observation demands a fitting language, a mark, but also suggests its own digressions. Angharad Davies flicks the strings of her violin and I think of school, bullying 1950s style, a bigger boy flicking his victim hard to the head with an audible pop. From outside we can hear a loud Jamaican voice. Periodically trains pass, their metal rush wadding the room. A constant motion of small cries, whistle tones, dark notes and silver wisps flits through acoustic space like invisible birds. I am struck by the sight of so much grained brown wood – two violins, three cellos, two double basses – and how the swirling grain is a static echo of those physical movements from which musical form is developed. Sliding, striking, flicking, muting, bounding, abrading, tapping, snapping, drawing and pulling. The angularity of an arm moving according to its nature as a hinge. The spring of horsehair held in tension.

There is also doing nothing: looking up at the corrugated plastic skylight or down at the floor. Ideas move as if contagions. Bass sneezes;

cello catches a cold. There are shouts outside. Many years ago these would have been bothersome. Now the music absorbs whatever enters its domain. Then a sudden cessation during which quieter voices can be heard from the street; a long pause, intensity trembles in the air until released by a subtle shift of body language. The heart of the music falls silent once more, covered as it must be by the brambles and thick tree trunks of ordinary living.

10 IMAGINARY BIRDS SAID TO LIVE IN PARADISE

Writing and its thin monophonic slime trail, can it rise up to the flighted mingling of voices, all different species, the temporal layers, the uncertain centre and boundaries of group music?

Some glimpse of that.

Threaded through his evocation of group music there is shame, a rebuke to the self and all humankind within James Agee's account from *Let Us Now Praise Famous Men*, an Alabama July day of 1936 spent in the company of a white landowner and his sharecropping tenants, the men among them summoned to sing, 'to demonstrate what nigger music is like' for Agee and Walker Evans ('though we had done all we felt we were able to spare them and ourselves this summons').

Too much howling was the response of the landowner but Agee, hearing sped plants, hammers and coldchisels and his own self-reproach requested another song:

> Their heads and their glances collected toward a common centre, and restored, and they sang us another, a slow one this time; I had a feeling, through their silence before entering it, that it was their favourite and their particular pride; the tenor lifted out his voice alone in a long plorative line that hung like fire on heaven, or whistle's echo, sinking, sunken, along descents of a modality I had not heard before, and sank along the arms and breast of the bass as might a body sunken from a cross; and the baritone lifted a long black line of comment; and they ran in a long slow motion and convolution of rolling as at the bottom of a stormy sea, voice meeting voice as ships in dream, retreated, met once more, much woven, digressions and returns of time, quite tuneless, the bass, over and over, approaching, drooping, the same

declivity, the baritone taking over, a sort of metacenter, murmuring along monotones between major and minor, nor in any determinable key, the tenor winding upward like a horn, a wire, the flight of a bird, almost into full declamation, then failing it, silencing; at length enlarging, the others lifting, now, alone, lone, and largely, questioning, alone and not sustained, in the middle of space, stopped; and now resumed, sunken upon the bosom of the bass, the head declined; both muted, droned; the baritone makes his comment, unresolved, that is a question, all on one note; and they are quiet, and do not look at us, nor at anything.

This weird nightmare

New York City, 1960: Charles Mingus revisits his noirish ballad, 'Weird Nightmare', first recorded with singer Claude Trenier in Los Angeles, 1946, then recorded through subsequent years under other names: 'Pipe Dream' (by Lady Will Carr with Baron Mingus and his Octet), 'Smooch', with Miles Davis, Mingus on piano (a smouldering version of the tune under this name was recorded by Steve Lacy and Mal Waldron) and 'Vassarlean', with Eric Dolphy playing bass clarinet.

The title permits otherwise forbidden music to rise up and fall away, just as nightmares remain vivid in the mind with the shock of waking, then pass into dissolving memory. For thirty seconds the drummer-less group improvises freely, Mingus deliberately buzzing the bass on two notes, pianist Paul Bley hammering at a single key as he damps strings inside the piano, flautists Eric Dolphy and Yusef Lateef and trumpeter Ted Curson skittering in shadows. Then a sudden break, brutal as a cinematic edit; as if opening her eyes, vocalist Lorraine Cousins sings of love, loss and the Hollywood Freud unconscious: 'Weird nightmare, you haunt my every dream … take away the grief you've caused.'

Bird of paradise

Amsterdam, April 1964, shortly after a performance by the Charles Mingus sextet at Amsterdam's Concertgebouw: Eric Dolphy, thirty-five years old, a multi-instrumentalist whose unique approach to reeds and flute sparked like fireworks, illuminating new approaches to timbre, intervallic relationships and the sound of an ensemble, was interviewed by Michiel de Ruyter for Dutch radio. The melancholy reality was that America was no place for jazz innovators; like Albert Ayler, Don Cherry and all the other African American jazz musicians who had drifted through Copenhagen, Paris, Amsterdam, Stockholm, Dolphy observed what seemed to be, correctly or not, a more open society and decided to stay for a while. For the interview, De Ruyter probes with simple questions, hinting at something deeper: when will you step out of the sideman role, how will you find a group that allows you more freedom? I think you like to be in a group where you are as free as possible, he suggests. 'Yes, I would like to, for a while,' Dolphy equivocates, arguing for broad experience, 'because when you think about it, when you hear music after it's over, after it's over, it's gone in the air, you can never capture it again, so it's pure creation.'

An edit of that poignant quote has become famous for being included as a short, poignant addendum to *Last Date*, a record made in Hilversum with drummer Han Bennink, pianist Misha Mengelberg and bassist Jacques Schols on June 2 of that year. Before the month was out, shortly after his thirty-sixth birthday, Dolphy died in Berlin. Music, life, transience. Whatever his potential or the paths he might have taken, an undiagnosed diabetic condition closed them off. And if the edit of the quote misdirects us to think that Dolphy conceived of music as an essentially tragic art there is ample evidence to underline his more optimistic meaning: music is a respiratory motion – created in the moment of action then fading away – and through that common bond of presence and absence all sounds are connected. We know that he transcribed bird song. 'At home (in California) I used to play,' he told *Down Beat* magazine in 1962, 'and the birds always used to whistle with me. I would stop what I was working on and play with the birds. … Birds have notes in between our notes – you try to imitate something they do and, like, maybe it's between F and F-sharp, and you'll have to go up or come down on the pitch.' We also know that he studied and played Indian music, had a deep interest in ethnomusicology, that his reference points were extremely wide. In notes for *Other Aspects*, a posthumous release of pieces from Dolphy's personal tapes, flautist James Newton writes about Dolphy's studies of world folk music, the piece for flute, tablas and tamboura – *Improvisations and Tukras* – he recorded in 1960 for dancer Drid Williams and his hunger to build upon the learning he already possessed: 'Eric also had conversations with Ravi Shankar about some of the organisational devices of North Indian music. In certain sections of *Jim Crow*, one can think of some of the spatial implications of Gagaku court ceremonial music.'

Though I can hear in the latter part of 'Jim Crow' some trace of Japanese gagaku, its aerial melodic lines, glacial tempo and sudden percussive markers, I also hear an attempt to inject the instrumental fluidity and dynamism of jazz into the austere world mapped by Anton Webern in his pieces for soprano voice and ensemble. Similarly, Dolphy's two flute solos, both titled 'Inner Flight', are experiments in amalgamating jazz phrasing, expressive tone and free-flowing lines with the tightly 'graphic' abstraction of Varèse's *Density 21.5*. If inner flight suggests Dolphy's liberated self, producing works that would have destabilized the defining of him exclusively as a black jazz musician, 'Jim Crow' is a title that refuses to be ignored, weird nightmare evocation of racial segregation laws still in force in the American south at the date of these recordings and, within the context of music, a barrier to any musician who would wish to work both within and beyond the confinement of musical territories demarcated by race, class and types of education. He could be the sideman, a cipher for so-called Negro music in the realm of white jazz, but could he be the composer? Perhaps this is why Europe appeared alluring, though such a belief was dependent on amnesia in the case of a composer whose music he loved – Arnold Schoenberg, Jewish and 'musically degenerate' (Entartete Musik, as it was called) – driven from Europe to America in 1934 by the Nazi Party's rise to power.

How tempting to contemplate what might have been, had Dolphy not died so tragically young, had he instead returned to Amsterdam to work again at exploratory leisure with the co-founders of the Instant Composers Pool, Bennink and Mengelberg (as alto saxophonist John Tchicai was to do in 1968). According to Dolphy biographer Vladimir Simosko (who seems to think Mengelberg, Bennink and Schols are Scandinavian, rather than Dutch), Dolphy did in fact write to Mengelberg, discussing future plans for a reunion. Dolphy had the background and talent to thrive in any contemporary setting. 'I keep hearing something else beyond what I've done,' he once said. 'There's always been something else to strive for. The more possibilities of new things I hear, it's like I'll never stop finding sounds I hadn't thought existed until just now.' He played on Ornette Coleman's *Free Jazz* in 1960, toured with the John Coltrane Quintet, performed Gunther Schuller's (frankly awful) *Journey Into Jazz* with Richard Davis, Don Ellis and the New York Philharmonic for Leonard

Bernstein's televised *Young People's Concerts* series in 1964, contributed to Schuller's self-conscious but nonetheless engaging hybrid of modern jazz, free playing and Alban Berg – the *Jazz Abstractions* project – alongside Jim Hall, Scott LaFaro and Bill Evans, and recorded with some of the most advanced jazz talents of his time, including Booker Little, Andrew Hill, Abbey Lincoln, Mal Waldron and George Russell.

But listen to 'Alone Together', Dolphy's bass clarinet duet with bassist Richard Davis, from the *Conversations* LP of 1963. One of three duets recorded in a week of New York sessions, this was strikingly different. The language of empathy, its silences, its free movement (though essentially tonal), most of all a sensitive dwelling on the richness of sounds in close combination and as markings cast into empty space, anticipates a type of improvisation that is indebted to jazz yet not confined by its frame. Again, the title is significant, a Broadway show tune: 'we can weather the great unknown, if we're alone together …' whose melody recurs as revelatory object within multiphonics, breath expulsions, abrupt explosive runs, unanticipated convergences and twists born of close listening between two alone-together entities. The song was a standard recorded by many others – Miles Davis arranged by Mingus, for example, and Steve Lacy on his first record as a leader. In this setting it acts as ghost presence, absent and present, a new balancing of song's melodic and lyrical functions with oblique instrumental contextualization. Implicit within this one piece were two options: one was to forget the song book entirely, the path of free improvisation (but not free jazz, which invariably retained ties to theme and variation); the other was to find greater parity between song and accompaniment.

Five years later, Richard Davis found himself in an unlikely position of informally appointed session leader for recordings by an ascendant but not yet world-famous singer named Van Morrison. Forced by Morrison's recalcitrance or shyness, whichever it was, to lead a group of stellar musicians (including Connie Kay from the Modern Jazz Quartet, and percussionist/vibraphonist Warren Smith, who had played with Mingus and Dolphy) through the songs of *Astral Weeks*, Davis shifted orthodoxy by a few degrees. Instead of directly supporting the singer he glided through pauses and gaps, nudging and dragging at the metre, constructing his own melodies from the epicentre of a constantly shifting field. Listen to 'Beside You', almost free rhythm, weaving in and out of the chords, or to the ending of 'Slim Slow Slider', double bass, soprano saxophone, slapping on the body of the guitar, a moment of free improvisation at the end of the record, as if to say, this is only a beginning (and surely knowing it was concurrently an end, a flash of potential with little commercial future).

Contrapuntal noise

> Some Afro-Cuban followers of Osanyin [Yoruban spirit of herbalistic medicine] say that one of his ears is of monstrous size but hears absolutely nothing, while the other ear is diminutive but picks up the noise of butterflies in flight.
> **ROBERT FARRIS THOMPSON,** *Flash of the Spirit*

If I ask students for analogies of improvisation, sooner or later somebody will make the comparison with conversation. Dwell on this truism for a while and it rings false. Simultaneous 'speech' is the norm in music, so babble is more apposite. Babel is even better. Nor is it common for one person to soliloquize over a Greek chorus of supporting speech, to radically adjust the timbre of their voice from moment to moment, to join others in reciting identical words in unison, or to be continually mimicking and shadowing, though all these things can happen, particularly when drink is involved or unbalanced power relations. To complicate this further, these are narrow ethnocentric judgements. Dwell on *them* and they also become suspect. There are cultural differences to the accepted forms of conversation, just as there are circumstances in all cultures – formal, ceremonial, ritual and in high emotion – through which conversation becomes a form of music. In his study of conversation in an Antiguan village, Karl Reisman – anthropologist and devotee of *Finnegans Wake* – made explicit connections between the 'hubbub of ordinary speech' and a musically contrapuntal 'noise'.

He wrote, for example, of ambivalent attitudes to noise in Elizabethan England, 'noise' variously denoting a band of musicians, an 'agreeable or melodious sound' and a quarrel. In Antigua, to make noise was a means of assertion through which three 'channel functions' (who is speaking, when they speak, who is spoken to, who hears them, etc.) – boasting, cursing and argument – work as conventions in the making of what Reisman calls a 'contrapuntal noise'. Every voice has its own tune to maintain as voices sing independently and simultaneously. Reisman frames this distinctive, expressive musicality against cultural contexts in which a strikingly different contrapuntalism is (or was, in the early 1970s when his research was underway) highly valued – the conversational silences of certain Native American peoples, Sami people in northern Sweden and among small informal groups in Denmark. 'We have looked at some conventions about silence and transitions,' he wrote.

> By contrast Antiguan conventions appear, on the surface, almost anarchic. Fundamentally there is no regular requirement for two or more voices not to be going at the same time. The start of a new voice is not in itself a signal for the voice speaking either to stop or to institute a process which will decide who is to have the floor.

So Dolphy and Davis exemplify a particular style of conversation, their hypersensitive listening and coiling responsiveness interspersed by articulate outbursts of reverse vocalese, bass clarinet bursting from restraint like an assertive speaker whose voice spontaneously rises up in flaring passion. They are exemplars of the deep humanistic values of jazz, traceable back to social structures, audible as egalitarian sonic relationships in many forms of African music. But assaults on the specific terms of conversation as a political, social and cultural medium opened unbridgeable rifts in the 1960s landscape. In the field of twentieth-century music outside America, jazz afforded an expressive outlet for largely working-class men and women who aspired to the freedom and humanity of a predominantly African American art form. What would it mean when the forms taken by jazz, even free jazz, lost their primacy for players who no longer felt invested in the traditions and future of jazz?

'Black musicians had invented a new kind of music – jazz,' Keith Rowe has said, 'and we wanted to do that, but we were skinny white European kids, young men, and what did that mean? We wanted to make a form of music which had never existed ever before in the history of music.' The self-disparagement is revealing. Perhaps Rowe senses the awkwardness of this position; cutting away from jazz (even trad jazz still thriving in the early 1960s) and its African American ancestry is as problematic for him as it is for this book, seeking as it does to define the undefinable: an improvised music that separates itself (but only partially and not in every case) from the history of jazz, even while indebted to, preoccupied by and enfolded in its ongoing presence.

How to put an end to being just another derivative British jazz musician? Rowe confronted this need for a more personal music by a simple physical movement, laying the guitar flat on a table – 'the transformation of a utilitarian object into an art object,' as he put it. He was far from being the first to discover that horizontal amplified guitar strings have their own distinctive potential for unusual sounds – listen, for an example, to the 1950s recordings of steel guitar players Buddy Merrill and Speedy West – but in his case the break was a symbolic turn: music as performance becoming sound as philosophy. 'I thought about this for years,' he has said,

> and, in a flash I found the solution. Look at the American school of painting, which was very provincial in the 1800s: they really wanted to do something original but didn't know how. The clue was to get rid of European painting but how could they? Jackson Pollock did it – he just abandoned the technique. How could I abandon the technique? Lay the guitar flat!

Like Rowe, Pollock was not the pioneer of a radical change, simply the most influential within his milieu. Those Asian artists who practised the 'splashing and smearing ink' technique for centuries were working on silk or paper laid flat. For Pollock in 1946, working on *The Blue Unconscious*, it was initially expedient – a solution to the problem of a canvas too large to stand vertically in the small upstairs bedroom of the house he shared with Lee Krasner. By degrees a more profound relationship to the unfolding process evolved, partially influenced by his encounter with Navajo sandpainting demonstrated at MOMA in 1941. That summer, for example, he made a series of paintings using this technique – *Sounds In the Grass* – as if walking through a three-dimensional trans-sensory field in which marks could be heard. 'Painting parts of the image from all four sides, he discovered, *automatically* fragmented the overall image as seen from any one side,' wrote the authors of *Jackson Pollock: An American Saga*. 'Finally, he discovered a strange new satisfaction in working on a canvas placed on the floor, in walking around it, standing over it, and bending down beside it. Something about this new way of working satisfied a deep, inarticulate need, a need that, once aroused, would begin to seek fuller, more direct gratification.'

As escapology from a career of imitating Jim Hall, Rowe's laying of the guitar on its back worked perfectly. Like a clock repairer's workbench or a factory worker's production line, everything was more accessible, more gestural; objects could be placed on the strings or attached to them. No more scalar runs, chords, arpeggios. Less easy to escape was the living ancestor in the attic: jazz. As Rowe is well aware, the historical discourse has been poisoned by what trombonist George Lewis calls the Eurological perspective, an insidious denigration of jazz improvisation by academic musicologists and experimental godfathers alike. Lewis recognizes the rewarding complications of a transcultural approach in free improvisation. To give one example: two South African percussionists – Louis Moholo-Moholo and Thebe Lipere – improvising with Derek Bailey, a guitarist from Yorkshire who had long since abandoned any explicit reference to jazz. But Lewis also identifies significant differences in the perspectives of Eurological and Afrological improvisation. 'One important aspect of Afrological improvisation,' he writes,

> is the notion of the importance of personal narrative, of 'telling your own story.' … Part of telling your own story is developing your own 'sound.' An Afrological notion of an improviser's 'sound' may be seen as analogous to the Eurological concept of compositional 'style,' especially in a musically semiotic sense. Moreover, for an improviser working in Afrological forms, 'sound,' sensibility, personality, and intelligence cannot be separated from an improviser's phenomenal (as distinct from formal) definition of music. Notions of personhood are transmitted via sounds, and sounds become signs for deeper levels of meaning beyond pitches and intervals.

Silence is already perfect

And it is not really talking, or meaning, but another and profounder kind of communication, a rhythm to be completed by answer and made whole by silence.

JAMES AGEE, *Let Us Now Praise Famous Men*

The perfect illustration of Lewis's theory is *Sound* by the Roscoe Mitchell Sextet, a three-track album recorded in Chicago, August 1966. Born in Chicago in 1940, Mitchell grew up within a church-going family. He learnt to play clarinet, then saxophone, baritone and alto, in a high-school band, then joined the army in 1958. According to George Lewis's comprehensive study of the AACM, *A Power Stronger Than Itself*, Mitchell was posted to Heidelberg in Germany where a student jazz cellar called Cave 54 hosted jam sessions for Europeans like Karl

Berger and Albert Mangelsdorf alongside visiting Americans. Hard bop was the lingua franca but many of these musicians were on the edge of something more enmeshed in the precarious times. It was in post-war Europe's landscape of ruin and reconstruction that Mitchell first heard Albert Ayler. The experience was powerful, a glimpsed vision of the future. Discharged from the army and back in Chicago he improvised with Jack DeJohnette in long informal sessions described by DeJohnette as stream of consciousness. Like a lot of other musicians at the time he knew there was another 'there' there, but how to get to it? Then in 1963 he met pianist and composer Muhal Richard Abrams at a gathering of the Experimental Band, a rehearsal band convened at the C&C Lounge to exchange knowledge, talk, try fresh ideas as a way of augmenting or displacing existing models: commercial music's compromises and the competitive aggression of jam sessions. 'Moreover, competition-based models of music-making tended to relegate collectivity and solidarity among musicians to the background,' Lewis writes, 'at a time when more collaborative notions of the relationship of community to individuality were being pursued in many segments of the African American community.'

This collective tendency among African American musicians in Chicago was instituted formally by their founding of the Association for the Advancement of Creative Musicians (AACM) in 1965. Released on Bob Koester's independent jazz and blues label, Delmark, *Sound* was the first record to reveal the AACM approach to the rest of the world. The title track, in particular, was unlike any other improvised music of its time. The piece begins with percussionist Alvin Fielder, a wash of cymbals struck with mallets, then the stately theme fading softly away into the sound of bells, a can half-filled with water, recorder blown gently, artlessly. What follows is somewhere between passionate conversation, orderly collective reasoning and ring shout, the ecstatic, antiphonal West African rite of counterclockwise circling and shuffling that survived through slavery in America into the twentieth century and contributed to the evolution of jazz. Folklorist Harold Courlander spoke about it as a clearly defined circle that might give way to an amorphous crowd moving around a single point. 'At the high point of the excitement, such exclamations as "Oh Lord!" and "Yes, Lord!" turn into nonsense sounds and cries; seemingly wild emotional responses, they nevertheless are related to the music as a whole, and no notation which omits them can give a fair picture of what is heard,' he wrote. Pianist James P. Johnson heard ring shouts when he was a young boy, growing up in Brunswick, New Jersey in 1900: 'They danced around in a shuffle and then they would shove a man or a woman out into the centre and clap hands.' This would go on through the night, Johnson gradually falling asleep in the dark at the top of the stairs. 'In 1818 a group of white Quaker students observed a Negro camp meeting,' wrote Lawrence W. Levine in *Black Culture and Black Consciousness*.

> They watched in fascination and bewilderment as the black worshippers moved slowly around and around in a circle chanting:
> We're traveling to Immanuel's land
> Glory! Halle-lu-jah
>
> Occasionally the dancers paused to blow a tin horn. The meaning of the ceremony gradually dawned upon one of the white youths: he was watching 'Joshua's chosen men marching around the walls of Jericho, blowing the rams' horns and shouting, until the walls fell.'

As if called upon to flatten Jericho single-handed, trumpeter Lester Bowie takes the first solo, stepping quietly into silence with bent cries and low gurgles, plaintive as an animal in distress, evoking the ghosts of Rex Stewart, Bubber Miley and Cat Anderson with pachydermous blasts. As Duke Ellington once said, introducing Cat Anderson, 'This is the tipping and whispering.' This is how it goes, tipping and whispering, each soloist – Bowie, Maurice McIntyre on tenor saxophone, Lester Lashley on trombone, Roscoe Mitchell on alto saxophone – shadowed either by Malachi Favors on bass or Fielder's cymbals. The form of the music grows organically as a procession through silence. Conventions of jazz are observed – theme, solos and counterpoint, theme – but transfigured into a music of shifting edges. A person is called forward to speak out boldly, with wit and vigour, at length, each one supported and echoed by what became known as the little instruments – harmonica, sleigh bells, siren – or just one part of the conventional supportive instruments, cymbals but not the whole kit. Aside from the striking transparency this gives to the piece, it produces two major effects: to change perspective within the ensemble to give a dramatic sense of dynamic range and spatial relations; also to allow soloists to go deep into the micro-audial range of their instruments, the sounds of mouth and mouthpiece, percussive pads, friction of metal and strings. Individual sounds may be intimately physical and expressive but they stay within the bounds of restraint. Within the orthodoxies of free jazz, such expressivity would be the spark to light a raging fire. Here, the group keeps cool and disciplined. With the exception of one heated passage for saxophone, cymbals, bass and cello, 'Sound' maintains a balance between austerity, humour and physicality.

'What amazes me about music is how several different people can have a different description of the same piece of music,' Roscoe Mitchell tells me when I send him some of these thoughts.

> To me music is fifty percent sound and fifty percent silence. Silence is already perfect so, as musicians, when we make a sound we have to make sure that sound carries the same power as the silence around it. Each instrument does start out on its own and then proceeds to create a sound sculpture that fits the constraints of the sound environment created by the compositional framework. The cymbals are a part of the compositional structure and the sustained sound created by the cymbals manifests a sound environment that induces each musician to create an improvisation based on sound instead of notes following notes to create a melody.

He gently chastises me for using the word 'free': 'I don't know if I agree with you on the term "free improvisation" as I've always worked very hard on my music and have never looked at it as just getting up there and doing whatever I want.' The method through which *Sound* evolved upheld this approach. 'What I remember about this recording session,' he says,

> is that we rehearsed daily for a month and a half leading up to the recording date. This gave everyone a chance to internalize the music. One thing I enjoyed about being in Chicago at this time is that so many musicians in the Association for the Advancement of Creative Musicians had their own individual approach to their music. The structure of the AACM itself inspired me and taught me to embrace the whole world of music.

I ask him about their approach to time. Other than the theme, initiator and closer of the piece, repetition has been eliminated and so the theme takes on a ceremonial significance, like a solemn marker delineating a sacred space, not dotting a line but closing a circle. There is no pulse – the music expands and contracts in the flux of conversational time – and yet the playing constantly *recalls* time, timing and pulse, particularly when two instruments are playing together. 'I like the fact that there are so many ways of using time that do not require the use of tempo,' he says. 'Implied time can give a feeling of being grounded while allowing the opportunity for a different orientation for the placement of musical ideas where one is not required to be in any specific place or any specific time.'

Time's presence on the record was multi-layered. 'Sound' was originally recorded in two versions. In excess of twenty-six minutes, the preferred take from 10 August was considered too long for one side of vinyl. Another version was recorded on 26 August, then a composite was edited together from the two. This was an intense time in the civil rights struggle. On 25 August, American Nazi Party leader George Lincoln Rockwell (originator of the term 'white power') was shot dead by one of his own excommunicated followers. In June of that year James Meredith, the first African American student to confront the colour bar at the University of Mississippi, was ambushed and shot by a white gunman on the second day of his March Against Fear. Also in June there were three days of rioting in Chicago after police shot a young man during the Puerto Rican Parade. In July a race riot broke out on Chicago's West Side, followed by violent racial attacks on 5 August when Dr Martin Luther King led a protest against discriminatory and exploitative housing policies through an all-white neighbourhood.

Asked by Valerie Wilmer about the Black Panther party in 1970, Mitchell's response was non-commital: 'Well, the Panthers did their thing in a completely different way to how music is done.' Music was a model for evolving identity and dialogical social cooperation, a 'peaceful revolution' as Wilmer put it; as such it was the AACM's positive rejoinder to the violence, hatred and segregation of the time. As a musical revolution it was conceived in the spirit of discipline, learning and tradition. Asked by Wilmer about multi-instrumentalism and the use of seemingly unorthodox 'little instruments', he emphasized their history within jazz: ' "If you look at the pictures of the old bands you'd see each cat would have a whole lot of reed instruments there and the same would go for the drummers," he said, recalling what Sunny Murray once said of the Ellington drummer Sonny Greer: "He had everything from a squeeze horn to a hair-comb".'

You stepped out of a dream

They had no conversation properly speaking. They made use of the spoken word in much the same way as the guard of a train makes use of his flags, or of his lantern.

SAMUEL BECKETT, *Malone Dies*

A room in Amsterdam, early in 1967. John Stevens wakes from sleep and sees a visual score fully formed. He draws it out, shapes and colours. Stevens played drums, cornet, used his voice, but he studied, like others in this story, at Ealing College of Art. Junior Art School they used to call it, a training for children who planned to go further in fine arts, trades or crafts, and by 1955, at the age of seventeen, he was working, albeit reluctantly, in a design studio. So drawing out his vision on paper was not a problem but to realize it as music he had to return to England. Amsterdam was awash with drugs, heroin to acid. Step on stage to improvise and somebody you'd never seen before, off his head on some drug cocktail, would step up with you and scream through a saxophone. That was their idea of freedom. Stevens and his Austrian wife Anne temporarily left Britain in 1966. Copenhagen's Café Montmartre was the place to be, the club where Eric Dolphy, Cecil Taylor, Archie Shepp, Don Cherry and Albert Ayler appeared as emissaries of the new thing, but with no work permit in Denmark and the prospect of gigs with John Tchicai and Jeanne Lee in Holland they left Denmark at the end of December. After six weeks in Amsterdam they returned to London where a pool of young musicians – Trevor Watts, Derek Bailey, Evan Parker, Kenny Wheeler, Dave Holland, Barry Guy and Paul Rutherford among them – gathered to create an unknown entity called free music.

'He's still completely underrated, is John,' Derek Bailey told me in 1992, 'because nobody realises he invented a group music and that's very rare. I found mostly everything he did interesting. I don't think he ever realised how good he was, John. I don't think he ever recognised how special he was at organising musicians.'

Bailey used to wonder why Stevens didn't pursue total improvisation with more commitment, or why he failed to make more of an impact outside Britain. 'When he was really totally involved he did take a lot of shit,' he said.

I think he was quite sensitive. It seemed to bother him. We did a broadcast once for *Jazz Club* on the BBC and we did a suite of his which was called *Seeing Sounds and Hearing Colours*. [Presenter] Humphrey Lyttleton came up and said, 'Can we have a little chat about this?' and John talked seriously to him about it. Then during the broadcast, Lyttleton says, 'Now the Spontaneous Music Ensemble,' leaving a pause for sniggers, 'will perform a piece which John Stevens tells me is called *Seeing Sounds and Hearing Colours*. Personally I think it was something he ate.' This was the fucking announcement.

Poor jokes aside, a recording of this transmission reveals that his announcements also praised the musicians for their seriousness. Lyttelton, the old Etonian, if socialist, voice of the establishment whose 'Bad Penny Blues' sparked an image of jazz in many young minds (Evan Parker among them), said more than he knew. This oneiric, synaesthetic composition that came to Stevens fully formed reacted against an indigestible professionalism of dried-up conversations, music dessicated to little more than just another job within a spirit-crushing system. Stevens would sit in his back garden, looking at the willow tree and the grass, and imagine how much closer to nature people could be if music were pure interaction rather than statements. These were exactly the kind of thoughts that made him the object of mockery throughout his life.

He had also been listening to *Spiritual Unity*, Albert Ayler's 1964 trio record released on Bernard Stollman's ESP-Disk label, in particular the interaction between bassist Gary Peacock and drummer Sunny Murray. A percussionist friend with a BBC orchestra had visited New York, returning with gifts: a pre-release copy of *Spiritual Unity*, silkscreen cover, and a copy of the New York Art Quartet of Tchicai, trombonist Roswell Rudd, bassist Lewis Worrell and drummer Milford Graves, with a recitation by Imamu Amiri Baraka. But it was the mystery of what was happening on *Spiritual Unity* that really excited him, slow delicacy and lightning shimmer in which the pulse was both unearthly slow and insectivorously fast, slithering between deep bass heartnotes and featherlight cymbal flicker. As for Ayler, there was nobody like him. Listen to the early recordings he made in Finland in 1962 with the Herbert Katz Quintet, picking his way respectfully through evergreens like 'Summertime' and 'On Green Dolphin Street', then erupting out of jazz good taste into a phoenix being, the elasticity of his phrasing and the depth of his tone overpowering, as if a smartly dressed man sheds his clothes in full public view to suddenly transform into a dazzling bird of paradise. What would happen to individuals in a society, Stevens dreamt, if all musicians could play with that degree of freedom? Evan Parker had joined him in Copenhagen where they heard Ayler play live. In a car journey to the gig, Stevens asked if a play was possible. Ayler replied with a question: can you do this? His fingers clicked very slowly, one, two, one, two, like the implicitly slow two-beat Peacock uses to work in and around Ayler's slippery, rising and tumbling unpredictability. 'We almost got to jam,' says Parker, 'but they took him to an upstairs room and he never came down.'

Sounds of blood and breath

For a young person reading post-war literature in 1967 and the questions it asked of desperate or distant freedoms, novels like *Malone Dies* by Samuel Becket, *The Bell Jar* by Sylvia Plath, B. S. Johnson's *Trawl*, *Cain's Book* by Alexander Trocchi, *I Hear Voices* by Paul Ableman, Doris Lessing's *The Golden Notebook*, James Baldwin's *Another Country* and Alain Robbe-Grillet's *Jealousy*, the notion of the self in the world was an alienated, unreliable, unravelling voice locked in dark labyrinths, soul 'turning in its cage as in a lantern' in Beckett's indelible phrase, either transfixed by surfaces or rambling through depths and broken time. 'All my senses are trained full on me, me,' Beckett wrote. 'Dark and silent and stale, I am no prey for them. I am far from the sounds of blood and breath, immured.' The prevailing mood was fixed on the impossibility of communication but Harold Pinter, a playwright commonly assumed to epitomize this impasse, disagreed: 'I think that we communicate only too well, in our silence, in what is unsaid, and that what takes place is a continual evasion, desperate rearguard attempts to keep ourselves to ourselves. Communication is too alarming. To enter into somebody else's life is too frightening.'

Recognizing this interior conversation with the self, an inheritance from stream of consciousness and surrealist automatism, as a symptom of the age, the dilemma for improvisers was how to turn it to collective authorship, to enter the lives of others through group music undirected by any single individual. 'If somebody says literature I say Beckett,' John Stevens told Victor Schonfield in 1992. 'If somebody says theatre I say Beckett, if somebody says poetry I say Beckett, if somebody says humour I say Beckett. But finding Anton Webern was like that for me, discovering Beckett. I'd landed on my feet with an area of music I wasn't sure I'd be able to have a full inroad into. All this stuff, in relationship to freedom was all potentially experienced within what jazz offered, which basically was freedom, freedom of expression, freedom in terms of improvisation. I suppose that had some sort of effect on what I started to feel was possible.'

Coming as it did out of the night, *Seeing Sounds and Hearing Colours* seemed to offer an answer to the question of how to work through to this elusive freedom. As a suite – introduction and three movements – the piece was transmitted on the *Jazz Club* slot of a BBC Light Programme format called *The Jazz Scene*, on March twenty-sixth, 1967. Soon to become BBC Radio 2, the Light Programme was the popular mainstream voice of radio, previously a natural home to jazz as deracinated music for romancing and dancing. Displaced by rock, soul and pop and increasingly stigmatized as esoteric and intellectual, jazz was shunted to the highbrow Third Programme. As Benjamin Piekut points out, the institutional view was convoluted in its prejudices: '… the English experimentalists could not move out of history – historical patterns were always getting repeated, in funding structures, criticism, labor rules, "expert" judgement, and in the legacies of racial discourse. For example, the constant relegation of the improvisers' creative practice to second-tier status by institutions like the Musicians' Union and the Arts Council demonstrates, in the words of George E. Lewis, "the degree to which even European free jazz musicians, with few or no African Americans around, still experience the reception of their art through the modalities of race." '

So it was that Lyttelton warned listeners of their imminent displeasure, pleading that their complaints should not be addressed to him personally. The suite had been recorded once already in March, in a session engineered by Eddie Kramer at Olympic Sound Studios. Kramer studied classical piano at the South African College of Music (it was Kramer who introduced Stevens to South African exiles the Blue Notes – Dudu Pukwana, Mongezi Feza, Johnny Dyani, Louis Moholo and Chris McGregor). Once in London he worked himself up from tea boy to one of the leading studio engineers of the 1960s, famous for recording Led Zeppelin, The Rolling Stones, The Beatles and *Are You Experienced*, *Axis: Bold As Love*, *Electric Ladyland* and *Band of Gypsies* by Jimi Hendrix, along with a number of the posthumously released albums. The first Hendrix records were made at Olympic in Barnes. According to John McDermott: 'As fellow Olympic engineer Terry Brown recalls Kramer would get most of the "weird" assignments that would come into the studio, and his love of sound and experimentation, regardless of the musical style, made him the obvious choice to work with the "raggedy" group [the Jimi Hendrix Experience] Chas Chandler was bringing to record.'

The Spontaneous Music Ensemble, as Stevens named the group in September 1965, was one such supposedly weird assignment. Working in various studios between 1966 and 1968 (before relocating to New York in April 1968 to work on *Electric Ladyland*), Kramer recorded a succession of SME- and John Stevens-related projects: *Challenge*, the group's first album, *Withdrawal* (soundtrack for a film later destroyed), versions of Krzysztof Komeda compositions for Roman Polanski's film *Cul-de-Sac* (never used), the Peter Lemer Quintet, the Jeff Clyne-Ian Carr *Springboard* album, *Seeing Sounds and Hearing Colours*, the unissued 'Willow Trio' sessions, *Familie*, *Karyobin*, and a thus-far unissued double trio with two drummers, Stevens and Rashied Ali, two saxophones, Parker and Watts, and two bassists, Peter Kowald and Dave Holland.

Elegant music

They dance with nimble, graceful jumps, accompanying their steps by swinging and striking their tiny bronze timpani with both hands. The sound of these dō-byōshi is weird, extremely high-pitched and whirring; it is supposed to imitate the song of the Karyobinga, the Buddhist propitious bird Kalavinka, who by his incredibly sweet and ethereal song reveals the 'Three Truths' of sufferance, Nirvana and transcendence of this world.
                        A History of Japanese Music, **ETA HARICH-SCHNEIDER**

Ancient as it is, Japanese gagaku epitomises the hybridity of music, the allure of its transcultural portability. William P. Malm describes it as perhaps the oldest extant orchestral art music in the world: 'Through all the viccissitudes of Japanese imperial history a hard core of gagaku music tradition has managed to survive. The net result is that one can hear today music that is over a thousand years old played in a style which is apparently close to the original.' Yet for all the identification of gagaku as a national imperial treasure, its originary form coalesced out of prototypes from all over Asia, imported along with Buddhism and other fashionable new ideas in the third, fifth, seventh and eighth centuries from Manchuria, China, the kingdoms of Korea, India and South east Asia. *Karyōbin*, for example, was said to have been introduced to

Japan in 736 by Bodhisena, the Baramon Sojo or Brahman Abbot from India. A standard gagaku orchestra of winds, strings and percussion was established in the ninth century, gradually filtering out the identifiable character of these foreign strains, enduring neglect, reconstruction and the taint of nationalism to become as venerable as the great Buddhas of Kamakura and Nara.

John Stevens had heard whispers about gagaku; instinct told him that this would be an important listening experience, but how to hear it in the days when such recordings were almost impossible to find? In 1965 he took a job at Boosey and Hawkes, music publisher and manufacturer of musical instruments. His compatriots from the RAF – Trevor Watts and Paul Rutherford – also worked in the shop, so it was a congenial way of surviving while Stevens focused on what he described as his 'burning desire to be involved in a free form of music'. One lunchtime, Steeleye Span violinist Peter Knight, then working upstairs in the record department, played him a short track of gagaku included on one of the Folkways collections, *Music of the World's People*. 'It was almost more phenomenal than I thought it would be,' Stevens told Victor Schonfield. 'It was almost like Albert Ayler, it was so beautiful. I managed to find a full LP of this music and one of the tracks on there was called *Karyōbin are the imaginary birds said to live in paradise*. I was listening to this music and it was moving so slowly and elegantly and all the overlapping dissonances with the instruments that they're using – I don't like the word dissonance but microtones or whatever you want to call it. I just loved it. I thought, wouldn't it be amazing if we could be in an environment that moves so slowly like that?'

Being time, music has the capacity to radically alter our perception of time. For improvisers experimenting with long duration, beatless, zero-time music, the effects were transformative and so they were drawn to precedents. In 1980 I asked Eddie Prévost if gagaku had affected AMM in a similar way. 'I think it would be dishonest to say there wasn't any influence,' he replied,

> but it was largely deriving from initial recognition. ... Whether the intention was the same is something else obviously but the effect on us of some parts of that music and certainly a lot of Buddhist chanting as well seemed to us to be the same as some of the effects we felt when we were playing so in that sense it was encouraging. It made us feel that that kind of music making was timeless.

For Stevens, frustrated by linearity, it added a vital piece to the puzzle. If he could bring together what he heard in the syncopated interaction between Ayler, Peacock and Murray, the field of tonal colours and seemingly centripetal movement of Webern's *Five Pieces for Orchestra* and the slowness and overlapping microtones of gagaku, then a genuinely new interactive music might be possible, one in which there were no hierarchies. There is no such thing as a linear music; all music exists in complex time and in relation to factors such as environmental reverberation, timbral densities and combinatory sounds. But the structure of gagaku, part of its appeal to neophyte listeners, lay in its transparency: the wind instruments – hichiriki oboe, transverse flutes and sho mouth organ – playing eerie, attenuated melodies and chord clouds sounding like the out-breath of mythical creatures; clipped arpeggios or single notes echoing contrapuntally from one stringed instrument to the other; percussion instruments – drums and a small muted bronze gong – functioning as colotomic markers. Colotomic structure was a term given by Dutch ethnomusicologist Jaap Kunst to Javanese gamelan as a way to describe its 'nested cycles' whereby the divisions of any given measure are marked by gongs of different sizes, the largest of them marking both the beginning and end of a repeating cycle. Perhaps influenced by Indian tala patterns, gagaku is structured similarly, the slow beat (somewhere around an irregular, gradually quickening forty-three beats per minute, in the case of *Karyōbin* as played on the Lyrichord record Stevens heard) and its finer divisions no doubt immediately audible to a drummer who understood instantly when Albert Ayler clicked his fingers slowly and asked, 'Can you play this?'

Interactive ritual

These were musics that spread laterally, creeping through infinitude rather than pressing forward to resolution. Self-confessedly no bookworm Stevens was obliged to apply his intuitions and hypotheses through practice. On a passing whim he considered booking downtime at Olympic with Eddie Kramer to record a basic track with Derek Bailey. They would play sparse single sounds on the percussion instruments in the studio, then bring in other musicians to overdub on top. Why Bailey? Perhaps because Bailey had been obsessed (to use his own word) by Webern, listening almost daily to a tape of the complete works, developing as he did so the kind of fragmentary ideas for a new guitar language heard on the 1966–7 home recordings: *Pieces For Guitar*. This studio-based project was soon abandoned, probably because the vision of music that Stevens was nurturing aspired to freedom not as experimental aesthetics but at a deep social level: 'It wasn't so much wanting to juxtapose various different instruments together,' as he told Schonfield, 'it was finding people who would want to take part in that particular interactive ritual.' Those few pieces realized and recorded in this formative SME period were comparable in their soundworld to a piece like *Le Marteau sans Maître* by Pierre Boulez, an image of glittering exotic birds in perpetual flight, yet the methodologies were antithetical, one almost fanatical in the hidden complexities of its mathematical organization, the other searching for similar effects with little or no direct instruction.

For Stevens, person came first; instrument second; player first; composer second. Then there was freedom in the body. These thoughts on time, recorded plays and conversations with collaborators like Watts and Bailey were guiding him to a music in which the basic elements were radically simplified down to two: click and sustain. These principles became fundamental in two fields of activity. One was the highly specialized research-in-performance of minimal click-based pieces called (among other titles) 'Flower', 'Open Flower' and 'Face To Face' played both in public and in intensive rehearsal by Stevens and Trevor Watts in 1972–3; the second field was a development that became known as *Search and Reflect*. These were improvisation workshop exercises ('springboards to liberation', singer Maggie Nicols has called them) collected together over time, eventually used as a programme of learning in his role as director of Community Music in the 1980s. First John Tchicai, then many others subsequently, have described SME music as 'pointillist', just as (following Evan Parker's lead) they have described AMM's music as 'laminar'. Parker offers another formulation for these tendencies: 'independent coexistence versus interconnected coexistence'. Pointillism versus laminar may be helpful as an entry point, guiding listeners past initial unfamiliarity to a recognition of structural methodologies, but such terminology quickly hardens into a prescriptive limitation. Both are misleading, anyway. John Stevens knew art history, knew that pointillism and divisionism were techniques founded in optics, designed to create the illusion of luminosity within a unified field of complex colour. Historically speaking (and also misleadingly), pointillism was equated with Klangfarbenmelodie, the sound–colour–melody of Schoenberg and

Webern, but close attention to SME reveals a balance (just as in gagaku, Webern or AMM) of mark and line, quick and slow, cut and prolong.

In 1971, Paul Burwell and I took part in the first improvisation workshops led every Monday afternoon by John Stevens at Ealing College of Higher Education. An Ealing student, Chris Turner, was the catalyst for the workshops and these were facilitated (and joined, on piano) by his composition tutor, the senior lecturer in music, Christopher Small. Turner, a harmonica player, attended a series of jazz workshops organized by the London County Council. 'I remember I was coming from rock,' he says, 'and I walked into a room of people improvising madly. It seemed like a lot of fun.' Stevens was one of the tutors. Turner was so impressed – he describes Stevens as 'my main mentor, particularly in the listening thing' – that he took Chris Small to an SME concert. Stevens talked persuasively about his aims in workshops and so the Ealing gatherings became his first opportunity to impliment the method on a regular basis.

One afternoon, Burwell brought along a child's wooden rattle. Stevens objected because the indeterminate nature of the sound was not a direct consequence of volition. For Stevens, action and sound should match. It was an example of his purism, both enlightening and irritating to us at the time but consistent with his overarching convictions of how music should function for self and society. As he told Victor Schonfield, almost as a confession: 'I felt that if that could be an ongoing thing that could be achieved, where we agreed to function in that sort of way, and if people received it positively, in some way I felt the world would have improved. But it's like a certain type of naive idealism. I used to think, well I don't want SME to get any gigs but if we got gigs it might mean people were doing it for the wrong reason, but as it happened nobody wanted us anyway. But that's how personally I felt. The passion for that, and the intensity of me, turned it into my group because more and more my concept was taking over and I was trying to, not goad, but attract these people into a certain thing that I felt very strongly about. That's not to say that the people weren't on that sort of track anyway, but not to the same degree I was.'

Disappointment haunts these words. In September 1994, two years later, Stevens died from a heart attack at his home in Ealing. As he might have known (and sometimes later resented), the musicians who passed through the Spontaneous Music Ensemble in its early days were too strong, too gifted (Stevens included) to give themselves up to a music so pure that it existed only within the bubble of its own integrity, nor were they willing to accede to the whims of a leader prone to messianic tendencies. Only a religious community or monastic order would stay together under such conditions. I asked Evan Parker and Barry Guy if they could remember anything about instructions or a score for *Seeing Sounds & Hearing Colours*. Neither could, and as Barry Guy implies, ideas had already coalesced by the time they were presented to the full group:

> There might just have been one single sheet of manuscript paper with some ideas and pitches, but I'm really not sure. Perhaps Trevor Watts might recall more details since he was writing material for the SME at the time. There were a lot of conceptual ideas – almost workshop-like in their presentation without always recourse to the documented format, so there may have been nothing concrete, only our brains.

Critical consequences were mixed: intrigued by the ideals but hardly propitious for the advancement of personal careers. In his review of *Karyobin* in *Melody Maker*, Bob Houston wrote:

> Ego is completely absent from the nameless selections which make up this set. In that respect, Stevens has achieved his aim. The relationships within his group are all-important, but it makes for music which is interesting at a very subdued and personal level. Everybody seems to be whispering musical intimacies to each other, canvassing opinion and reactions from among the various instruments rather than attempting to communicate to us outside.

From knowing these musicians at the other end of their careers, hindsight clarifies the startlingly original nature of their individual contributions, held back insofar as they immersed themselves into the group in order to learn a new way to interrelate. Listen, for example, to the contributions of Trevor Watts throughout *Withdrawal* and *Seeing Sounds Hearing Colours*, playing alto and soprano saxophone, oboe, flute, vibraphone and glockenspiel with extraordinary confidence and inventiveness, given the unprecedented nature of the music. 'At the time,' says Watts,

> and in spite of all John's talk about freedom, I felt that he was more interested in control. So most of the music was played within a fairly strict idea of what freedom was. I found the challenges it gave me were

something to try to overcome. How to express myself within a fairly tight concept that had certain expectations. Of course, in the long term, this kind of involvement gives you as many problems as it solves in other ways. That's why I got disenchanted, for a while, with that way of playing. Once I discovered musicians outside of the improv scene I started to feel curiously more liberated, and as I've said before in various interviews I found the African musicians I played with had a much freer, more open concept to playing music than many of the improv players who had quite stilted ideas of what is allowed and what is not. Maybe John found more freedom in what I perceived as restrictions, and that's fair enough for him. I found more freedom elsewhere, but it was a stage I have no regrets about going through as I learnt a lot in other ways.

Lost John made a pair of shoes

John Stevens was born in 1940 in Brentford, west London. His parents were bookmakers, father taking illegal bets in the pub, mother at home on the phone. There were police raids and when the business sank his mother took a job in a legitimate betting shop. As a sideline his father boxed, gave dancing exhibitions and had a tap dancing act as an 'eccentric' specialist who could tap while feigning drunkenness. There were visits to the Chiswick Empire to see variety acts like dirty Max Miller, otherworldly Tommy Cooper, the male impersonator Ella Shields, even the static nude tableaux of the time, Stevens banished to the bar; with his mother there were musicals at the cinema, the rattling feet of Gene Kelly, Dan Dailey, Donald O'Connor, Fred Astaire and Ginger Rogers.

At the age of thirteen or fourteen he joined a skiffle group called the Muleskinners, guitar and tea chest bass with Stevens scratching away with sweeping brushes on the lid of the rag-filled Smith's Crisps tin in which his mother kept her boot polish. 'Lost John made a pair of shoes' was in their repertoire, a Kentucky folk song popularized by Papa Charlie Jackson in the 1920s. Skiffle is more important than we allow, rough music with a junkyard aesthetic. As a British craze of the 1950s, an offshoot of the trad jazz scene dithering between folk, blues, country string bands and emergent rock 'n' roll it was home-made music far from home, steeped in barely fathomable Americana and an ancestry of strange improvising bands from medicine shows and vaudeville, Memphis street groups playing kazoo, jug, washboard, stovepipe, harmonica, bricolage banjo and other technologies on the frontiers of organology. Music made from sticks; the great depression swept it all away. Watch film, for example, of Whistler and his Jug Band play 'Foldin' Bed', three jug players in vulgar counterpoint, huffing and hooting like a walrus chorus. It was music of chronic privation but the scrappy passion ported easily to Britain's post-war destitution and desires. The Beatles, Mick Jagger, Van Morrison and Jimmy Page began here, but so did a number of improvisers, Stevens and Barry Guy among them. 'Lonnie Donegan was a big hero,' Evan Parker tells me. 'There was a degree of possession in Lonnie Donegan's approach to things, he was a driven kind of energised presence.'

Theatre of the absurd

After the theatre of war came the theatre of the absurd. 'In the Theatre of the Absurd,' Martin Esslin wrote, 'the audience is confronted with actions that lack apparent motivation, characters that are in constant flux, and often happenings that are clearly outside the realm of rational experience. Here, too, the audience can ask, "What is going to happen next?" But then anything may happen next.'

If, as Esslin maintained, the Theatre of the Absurd – Beckett, Jean Genet, Eugène Ionesco, Arthur Adamov, Harold Pinter – faced up to a post-war world in which god and morality were immolated in the inferno, then post-war comedy danced in the flames. Taking two examples: *The Running Jumping and Standing Still Film*, a collaborative short film made in 1959 by Peter Sellers and Spike Milligan of *The Goon Show*, American filmmaker Richard Lester, comic actor Mario Fabrizi and artist Bruce Lacey. Most of the action, absurdist and mildly satirical, takes place in fields. At one point a character in the distance plays discordant violin, cycles some way to a music stand to turn the page of his score, cycles back to his starting point where he reads the notation through a telescope, playing more discordant violin over the modern jazz soundtrack. In another scene a character produces a record from his overcoat, lays it down on the 'turntable' of a tree stump, produces a gramophone horn and tone arm, then runs in circles around the tree to the sound of a music hall song playing at the wrong speed. In 1962 Lacey also featured in *The Preservation Man*, Ken Russell's short film for BBC television's *Monitor* arts programme, at one point playing 'Show Me the Way To Go Home' on a penny farthing bicycle amplified through a valve amp and gramophone horn, plucking the strings of the small wheel, striking violently at the large wheel with an animal bone. No experimentally minded guitarist seeing this at the time could be immune to the implications.

For a second example, look at Spike Milligan's 'Dustbin Dance', filmed for Milligan's live broadcast television series, *Son of Fred*, directed by Lester in 1958: Milligan and Sellers stand in dustbins, both wearing what appear to be liturgical vestments or asylum nightwear. A trumpeter and trombonist (members of The Alberts) dressed in cardboard blast out a ragged theme, halfway between trad jazz and free jazz, Sellers loosely following on piano, Milligan singing: 'Oh when your friends forsake you and you can't find romance, jump into a dustbin and dance.' Between the words, Milligan and Sellers dance themselves and their dustbins in a clattering circle. Mercifully, the humour evades explanation, being simply four men (two of them notorious for their struggles with psychiatric disorders) reacting to non-specific lunacy with lunacy, a long echo of dada's cardboard outfits, ersatz jazz and shouted nonsense, ancestral to a strain of barbed futility that included Monty Python, John Lennon, Gilbert and George, The Kipper Kids and Reeves and Mortimer.

Films like Sidney Lumet's *The Hill* (1967) approached the same issue through a traumatic scenario in which hypermasculine brutality and empty discipline propagated violence and madness but it was the comedy that made a bigger impression. Seeing *The Running Jumping and Standing Still Film* was almost obligatory for British artists, art students and would-be rebels throughout the 1960s (The Beatles were so impressed that they hired Lester to direct *A Hard Day's Night* and *Help!*) but its consequences are impossible to calculate. Permissions tacitly given – to make noise, for example, or to make a record player from a tree – were absorbed unconsciously through laughter, bemusement or irritation; few musicians would cite such non-musical sources as influences yet they created a climate in which it was easier to play instruments in the wrong way, emit unorthodox sounds and create music with household objects, radios, old electrical parts and rubbish.

Comedian Eric Sykes once claimed that the best way to generate good comedians was to reintroduce National Service, under-occupied young people forced against their will to make the best of discipline and farce. This was the ambience which John Stevens voluntarily joined. Having made the decision to be a full-time jazz musician, the only way to fulfil any part of that dream was to join the Royal Airforce. In 1958 he signed up for five years in order to study at the RAF school of music in Uxbridge and play in the military band. Trevor Watts and Paul Rutherford had made the same decision, as had saxophonist/flautist Bob Downes, another jazz musician whose Open Music Trio experimented with free playing in the 1960s. 'I had some Marty Paich arrangements from the *Down Beat*,' Watts recalls, 'and I remember getting together with John. His enthusiasm was immense, but his technical abilities didn't match. He played so loud it sounded like he was falling down the stairs with the kit.'

Not long after meeting in these unlikely circumstances they were posted to Germany. A strong jazz scene based around bandleader Kurt Edelhagen, along with the lack of restrictions on visiting American players meant there were many opportunities to hear or play with experienced musicians. 'Military Band practice was about one hour per day,' says Trevor Watts.

> After that we could use the band room for individual practice or do anything else you wanted to, and particularly as John, Paul and I were in Germany and based in Cologne we could hang out late. We had a cellar bar we could play in and Derek Humble and occasionally Jimmy Deuchar would come down and play with us. There also was a regular gig at a place called Kintops Saloon where visiting American artists would play with a local rhythm section. But what it did for us was bring out our naturally rebellious nature. We had to be like that as we had to kick against the constant idea of discipline. We were known as the jazzers and our love for all the latest trends that were coming out in that music, be it Coltrane or Dolphy or whoever, influenced the way we wanted to play and led to our own experimentation.

Stevens recounted an occasion in the band room, rehearsing the *1812 Overture*. All of the drummers were set up on a rostrum. Stevens, playing tubular bells, spotted a passage in the score calling for ad-lib. 'Where it said adlib I thought they actually wanted us to create war,' he told Schonfield.

> When it gets there we'll just go for it. So I've got this hammer and Larry's got his snare drum, and there's the bass drum and we're all going – I'm going – Pow! – hitting these tubular bells, they're swinging and clanging. … Suddenly I looked down and the whole band has stopped and they're all looking up like this, with *shock* on their faces

and the guy conducting went absolutely bananas, screaming at us. So it's like freedom in a way. That is like a search for freedom and we should be free.

Absurdity beget absurdity. 'When we were on parade with the band,' says Watts,

> it was sheer chaos at times as you marched up and down the parade ground. You noticed it particularly when we had to do a move where the band turns in on itself and you march through the ranks of the band. It was there that you'd hear people jamming away, playing any old thing, John Stevens playing a bit of jazz drumming or the piccolo busking away. It's amazing how the piece of music, which could be the *Radetsky March* or any number of tunes like that, sounded anything like it should. But that was a way of getting back at authority. We did it in every little way we could, and I think that shaped our approach to the music.

Hothouse

Out of the armed forces and back in London, Stevens was persuaded into a group called The Don Riddell Four, standing, singing, playing the drums, a bit of comedy and the demands of a generic showbiz for which he was unsuited. It seems he played drums on a 1964 novelty called 'We Love You Beatles' by The Carefrees, maybe on a cover version of 'Girl Of My Best Friend', all of which drove him further into the arms of the jazz scene, clubs like the Mandrake, then the holy grail, Ronnie Scott's, and musicians such as Tubby Hayes and Phil Seaman. With pianist Pete Lemer and one of three different bass players he started playing the type of music exemplified by Andrew Hill, Paul Bley and the Bill Evans Trio, progressive, interactive but still acceptable to the kind of modern jazz fan who liked to drink and talk through priceless music (for evidence of this, listen to the chattering throughout *Bill Evans: The Complete Live at the Village Vanguard 1961*). A chance reunion with Trevor Watts and Paul Rutherford in 1963 intensified their mutual frustration. For all of them, acceptance within the London jazz scene was an obstacle to experimentation, though Watts and Rutherford had gone further in this direction than Stevens. As Stevens told Ian Carr:

I needed a group involvement which I didn't have on the professional jazz scene. There were occasions when you would have that, when people were just getting together for the sheer joy of playing together. But I found it less and less in the actual gigs, and more and more in the afternoon rehearsals and the things I was doing in my spare time.

The answer came with the Little Theatre Club. A jewel of a venue, the Theatre Club was housed in the crow's nest of a building in Garrick Yard, the gloomiest of courtyards secreted away from tourists and theatregoers choking St Martins Lane and Monmouth Street. All drummers, double bass players and amplified guitarists hated the climb up those stairs, particularly during the 1970s when drum kits were expanding to include exotic gongs, scrap metal, giant drums, scaffolding frames and electronics. Right by the entrance was a bar the size of a cupboard, curtained off from a few rows of raked seats that focused on the floor area that served as the stage. In my experience it was quite possible to find yourself playing in painted theatre sets of flimsy doors and opaque windows. None of those disadvantages mattered because the room's pindrop acoustics and dark velvet atmosphere nurtured intimate, exploratory music.

Jean Pritchard, who ran the club, allowed Stevens to organize gigs on six nights a week. The opening night – January third 1966 – featured Trevor Watts with his own quintet, with Rutherford on trombone, Jeff Clyne and John Ryan on basses and Stevens on drums, the Mike Taylor Quartet, Pete Lemer with Clyne and Stevens and later in the evening, Graham Bond on alto saxophone and Les Carter on flute. A contemporary review – *jazz in a garret* by jazz critic Barry McRae – praised the Watts quintet for its 'stimulating, free form jazz', chided the Taylor and Lemer groups for their shortcomings and welcomed the club's inclusive approach. Economically it was madness, musicians earning less than their travel costs, but the sense of being both in the centre of the action and at a lofty remove from its compromises accelerated the music's evolution. Two important factors converged. The progressing thought behind the Spontaneous Music Ensemble, with the Little Theatre Club as its public workshop space cultivated a hothouse environment for those players drawn into its ethos: Watts, Stevens, Rutherford, Barry Guy, Dave Holland, Maggie Nicols, Johnny Dyani, Kenny Wheeler, Derek Bailey, Evan Parker and others. The intention was to build a community of like-minded players; in effect, this vision was as much an apprentice system for individualistic virtuoso musicians in search of a platform, either because they were advanced players like Watts, on the edge of a breakthrough; young and inexperienced, like Maggie Nicols and Evan Parker; or highly experienced but breaking into the London scene, like Derek Bailey.

Jazz was the common link. For Evan Parker there was an important transition, giving up skiffle by selling his Lead Belly records to Twickenham art student Ian McLagan (later to join the Small Faces) and converting to modern jazz. At the age of fourteen he bought a cheap saxophone, becoming an aspirant to the soft floating style of altoist Paul Desmond. Then the impact of John Coltrane hit him, first from records, then the concert with Eric Dolphy during Coltrane's 1961 UK visit. 'Because my father worked for BOAC for so many years I could fly for nothing,' he says.

> I went to New York in 1962 [aged eighteen] and '63 in the summer for about two weeks each time, saved up, did holiday jobs in dodgy factories and stuff where I'm lucky I've still got all my limbs and then went to New York. Spent all the money on records. Never left Manhattan. I knew Sam Goody's [record store] and saw Eric Dolphy at Birdland, saw Cecil Taylor, Jimmy Lyons, Sunny Murray before they came to Café Montmartre the first time. I saw Steve Lacy and Roswell Rudd with the *School Days* band [Roswell Rudd, Henry Grimes and Dennis Charles]. Steve said we'll play any tune by Thelonious Monk. I requested 'Four in One', he said yes, we can play that. Played 'Four in One' for me. There were about six people in the audience.

Although some of this music was familiar to him from records, the realization that the music had moved on significantly was 'a shock and a liberation'. To be in the same space as Eric Dolphy and hear the acoustic sound of his saxophone was, he recalls, 'amazing. … Dolphy was on fire.' After the Cecil Taylor gig, he and a friend stayed to meet Taylor, Lyons and Murray:

> I guess the audience was ten including us at the most and then afterwards we just hung around and they all were very friendly. Jimmy Lyons obviously had a home to go to whereas the other two were like – that was their home, you know, the after hours hang in the jazz club, that was their life, which Cecil has continued to do at the highest of levels for the rest of his life, but they were super friendly and super keen to talk about stuff, just anything, not only the music but also life and politics and the situation.

At university in Birmingham he studied botany, only to be ejected after the second year for knowing less about the subject than when he started. 'Don't forget that at this time behaviourism was the god of psychology,' he says, 'terrifying thought, but there were all kinds of equivalent thinkings in all the sciences. … The climate of opinion in science was absolutely the polar opposite of what I'm interested in. I'm very interested in a etiology and unified theory, the relationship between the disciplines, not separate subjects but one subject.'

The orthodox method of understanding musical development is to trace a lineage of musical ancestry, a chain of influence, but what becomes clear is that these musicians agglomerated many diverse life experiences in the process of inventing their own form of group improvisation. For Parker this was a philosophy of instrumental practice and group communication informed by the sciences; for Watts, growing up in the manufacturing powerhouse of Halifax with no defined sense of what his future might be, it was the freedom of expression he heard in 78rpm records by Nellie Lutcher, Fats Waller, Duke Ellington and Ernie Henry, brought back from Canada and the United States by his father in the 1920s and 1930s; from Stevens it was his father's tap dancing and boxing, the American musicals he saw at the cinema with his mother and then a totally unexpected (for somebody of his class and education) encounter with Webern and Japanese gagaku; for Rutherford it was, as Richard Williams put it in the *Guardian* obituary written after Rutherford's death in 2007 – 'leftwing views and a teasing wit from his father, a former soldier who worked at the Woolwich Arsenal … [and] an older brother's enthusiasm for Charlie Parker', all of which came together in a search to integrate musicking (to borrow Christopher Small's neologism) with Rutherford's political convictions as a lifelong communist.

Open music

To some degree shaped by his participation in the John Stevens improvisation workshops of 1971–2, Small's descriptive verb – musicking – shifts the emphasis of musicology, or simply thinking about music, from music as object to music as event. Music becomes participatory, active, a listening practice, a physical engagement with music through dancing, preparation for music, even the practical facilitation of music. Musicking is only partly a continuum of concerts, practice and rehearsal. Other activities break into professionalism: a profound listening experience, something imagined, a conversation, an apparently unrelated task.

In the summer of 1965, the Coltrane-influenced group of friends with whom Parker played was invited by a Royal College of Art student, Gavin Owen, to record music for his short science fiction film entitled *TV - Future World Channel*. Only the bass player – Walter Haffenden – and Parker were interested in taking up this challenge. In among the electronic bleeps and deteriorated audio quality of Owen's prophetic media dystopia there are brief fragments of duets Parker recorded with Haffenden. Parker had owned a tenor saxophone for just two and a half years but the harrying urgency and physicality that qualified him for brutal records like Peter Brötzmann's *Machine Gun* three years later was already apparent. 'That was what they call a Schlüsselerlebnis in German, a key experience,' he says of the film music,

> because we were trying to make this music set in the future. What would music sound like in those days? With the band we were trying to play basically as much like the Coltrane Quartet as we could, that was our idea of how you played the music but we couldn't do that for this futuristic music. We had to do something else so we probably did quite a lot of squeaking and scrapings and all kinds of rattlings and what later became part of ...' His words tail off. The language of improvised music, I suggest.

Less problematic to leave the ellipsis, perhaps, since what is implied – an unnameable fascination with sounds from the edges and bowels of the instrument, altered, muted, violently forced, deflected, plumbed within interiors, flicked at, scratched at almost absent-mindedly, allowing spit and air and half-controlled gestures to interpose themselves within the orthodoxies of proper technique – returns more easily to Michel de Certeau's 'legends and phantoms whose audible citations continue to haunt everyday life', the tradition of the body that is heard but not seen, the sounds that escape writing: 'resonances produced by the body when it is touched, like "moans" and sounds of love, cries breaking open the text that they make proliferate around them, enunciative gaps in a syntagmatic organisation of statements'.

Cinema was once a laboratory for this kind of musical futurology: the otherworldly modernist-Hawaiian-electronic hybrid of Toshirō Mayazumi's music for Kenji Mizoguchi's *Akasen Chitai* in 1956, Bebe and

Louis Barron's electronic score for *Forbidden Planet* in the same year, the industrial drones of Michelangelo Antonioni's *Red Desert* in 1964, even the jittering, tapping electric guitar of 'Audio Bongo' from the *Dr. No* soundtrack of 1962. In attendance at the Royal College of Art diploma show of 1966 for a screening of Owen's completed film project, Parker was introduced to John Stevens by Alfreda Benge. Artist, songwriter and partner to Robert Wyatt, Benge was serving behind the bar at Ronnie Scott's at the time; she had seen Owen's film, heard the music and introduced Parker to John Stevens. 'John was there to see [painter] Geoff Rigden's work because he was tight with him,' says Parker, 'and then we met. John said, oh, I'm starting a club, you'll have to come down, sit in, and that was the key moment then, that was my introduction.' After hearing a BBC broadcast organized by Stevens in the previous year, Parker desperately wanted to join the circle. Gradually he found his way into the workings of the Spontaneous Music Ensemble, negotiating what he calls a 'gnomic approach to control':

> John was interested in controlling other people but part of that would be in order that you would have an experience that would take you to the next place. … Conceptually I think it was probably beyond where he could even articulate verbally. He did try very hard to articulate some of the things but I think that there were things where he could only provoke responses.

By summer 1967 they had grown close, playing without head arrangements in an approach they were more likely to call 'open' rather than 'free'. SME was reduced to a trio of Stevens, Watts and Parker as other musicians followed their own paths. Then Stevens, tactless and somewhat ruthless in putting the progress of the music before loyalties or personal feelings, alienated Trevor Watts by asking him to play more like Parker. After the first set at Ronnie Scott's Old Place, Watts packed up his saxophone and walked out, leaving Parker and Stevens to function as a duo until fences could be mended. 'Perhaps because of my limitations,' Parker speculates, 'maybe there were Svengali-like possibilities that he saw – that I could be a more willing participant in his experiments or something, I'm not sure.'

Bookings were taken wherever there was an opening: at the fringes of psychedelia in UFO, playing opposite Pink Floyd and Soft Machine, and in the Greek Street basement of Les Cousins folk club, playing a season opposite the blues duo of Alexis Korner and Victor Brox with the four of them playing together at the end of each evening. They also played in trios with bassists Barre Phillips, Dave Holland and Peter Kowald (apostles aspiring to the heights of the Albert Ayler Trio's *Spiritual Unity*) and with David Bowie's mentor, dancer Lindsey Kemp, an association curtailed by a performance with Kemp at Les Cousins in which the dance element climaxed in a knife attack on a shop mannequin. 'There were red ribbons inside,' says Parker,

> anyway it was pretty graphic but it left a hell of a lot of mess on the floor of Les Cousins and [owner] Mr. Matheou said, tell those boys they've got to find somewhere else to play, so then we went back to the – well we didn't stop doing the Little Theatre Club, it was an extra gig every week. We were doing things at the Old Place too with different people but all within a tight little radius … the psycho-geography, or whatever Iain Sinclair calls it, of free music locations.

Their music at that time was founded in the core values of this dialogical, non-hierarchical, close-listening style of improvisation. Stevens played extremely quietly, sometimes at the threshold of audibility, developing a new kit to retain the transparency of click and sustain. Each element of this drum kit – small cymbals, Chinese drums and temple block, tuneable single-headed tamboures without bells and a children's double-headed bass drum – was evolved to go beyond the fulfilment of specific functions in rhythmic music, becoming instead a melodic/temporal instrument. Concepts such as interval, chord or melody transmuted into a world of relationships determined by listening, silence and the properties of materials, wood, skin, metal, rather than harmonic rules. The music fluttered, light and restless, open, quick as eyelids or scattering dust yet exhaling and inhaling slowly in convulsive episodes. Time, experienced through listening, seems to me now both splintered into showering fragments and static; to borrow the words of François Jullien: 'the concepts of transition and duration, the phenomenology of the moment and of seasonal existence, as opposed to a notion of time delineated by "a beginning" and "an end"'.

Small music

As Trevor Watts has suggested, in conversation with Julian Cowley: 'One thing you have to understand about the SME "small music" is that John was trying to make us fit into his drumming patterns. I think that trying to sound like stick patterns, or play rhythmically in the gaps, was the beginning of Evan Parker's staccato style and Derek Bailey's more pointillistic side.' The importance of this, to some degree its irony, was that individualistic technical styles and 'handwriting', so personal as to be instantly identifiable with their originator and resistant to imitation, grew as organic developments from a collectivist ethos, albeit one driven by a charismatic individual. Though not explicit or even intended, the political inference was clear, particularly after Warsaw Pact troops crushed the Prague Spring in 1968: it was possible, within small communities, to develop a collective, dialogical practice that embraced rather than suppressed dissent, idiosyncrasy and independence, simultaneously nurturing an altruistic responsibility for the integrity and coherence of the group.

A sound world was created, too refined perhaps to sustain an entire life's work yet sufficiently robust to give birth to a succession of groups adhering to its central tenets of intimacy, fluent emulation and reflection, fervour so quick as to seem tranquil, close group listening, transparency and modesty of scale: the 1971–2 SME quartet of Stevens, Watts, bass player Ron Herman and singer/guitarist Julie Tippetts; a 1971 session of Stevens, Watts, Wheeler, Bailey and Holland released by Tangent as *So, What Do You Think*?; the minimalist duos performed by Stevens and Watts (and in trio with Derek Bailey) in the early 1970s; recorded duos with Bailey (*Playing*, 1993) and Evan Parker (*The Longest Night*, 1977, and *Corner To Corner*, 1993); and then the metamorphosing group formed in 1976, beginning as a quartet of Stevens, cellist Colin Wood, violinist Nigel Coombes and guitarist Roger Smith and continuing through varying line-ups until the death of Stevens in 1994. Insect music is how bassist Kent Carter described it, as if a flowerpot were overturned to reveal myriad tiny creatures scurrying to some relentless synchronized yet unknown purpose in the dark mud beneath. I prefer to think of it as the glittering interweaving flight of birds of a feather, if not in paradise, in some cloistered parallel domain.

Marvellous abandon

'Who shall unravel the mystery of an artist's nature and character? And who shall explain the profound instinctual fusion of discipline and license on which it rests?'

THOMAS MANN, *Death in Venice*

The *Melody Maker and Rhythm*, 12 July 1947: a photograph of Alan Davie in the company of musicians; already dressed like a beatnik, bearded, a wave of long hair, upright posture with tenor saxophone. Davie was born in Grangemouth, Scotland, in 1920, died in 2014. His latter-day reputation came to rest on paintings – riotous works of saturated colour, visceral gestural markings and indeterminate symbols, teeming sexual, occult shapes and lines, creatures of the imagination. A furiously energetic polymath who played modern jazz, organized army bands during the war, made jewellery, wrote poetry and improvised on a multitude of instruments, he was fascinated by psychic automatism, dreams and James Joyce's stream-of-consciousness writing, by cave painting, so-called primitive art and by the image of Japanese zen portrayed in Eugen Herrigel's influential book, *Zen In the Art of Archery*; in 1960 Davie described the role of the artist as alchemist and 'arch-priest of the new spiritualism'. Like Eric Dolphy, he was sensitive to the transience of sounds in the act of listening, the ephemerality of improvisation. In a documentary – *Alan Paints For a Film* – Davie improvises at the piano, stops, laughs: 'It's an amazing machine, this. It's so clean. Paint is so messy.' He waves his hands wildly, as if paint is flying through the air. Then he lifts his arms. 'The trouble is it all goes into space. Then we've lost it.' The core of Davie's work was intuition, digging down into the self, a disgorgement of unconscious material released by the act of making. 'They are not pictures of anything,' he wrote, 'but experience itself, caught in terms of paint.'

After the Second World War he took up the life of a professional jazz musician with Edinburgh bands such as the Tommy Sampson Orchestra and the Cam Robbie Band, drawn by 'the joys of spontaneous improvisation, the losing of the ME, and the active audience participation, the fire of the heart and belly, and the marvellous abandon'. As Michael Horovitz wrote in a 1963 monograph, this was doomed to fail, not least because of the bandleader's 'commercial insistence that they must be "accurate, consistent and polished at all times"'. Davie was not about to swap one army for another. So many of these players – Albert Ayler, Roscoe Mitchell, Anthony Braxton, Eric Dolphy, Stevens, Watts, Rutherford, Lol Coxhill, Tony Oxley and Derek Bailey – served in the armed forces. Whatever they learnt as musicians from military bands, their subsequent devotion to various versions of musical freedom and freedom of living stood in stark contrast to the discipline forced upon them. In extreme cases (and perhaps Davie was one of them) the army reacted upon existent sensitivities to catalyse a traumatic initiatory passage. AACM reeds player Joseph Jarman experienced something close to a shamanic crisis. Once discharged in 1958 he wandered around the United States, ending at his aunt's house in Arizona. In George Lewis's book he is quoted as saying: 'I couldn't talk during this period; I was mute. I went to the Milwaukee Institute of Technology. They got me to be able to talk again, and I haven't shut my mouth since.'

Intuitive actions and improvisation were to some degree interchangeable, so Davie was drawn to improvised music and released a number of LPs through his gallery, Gimpel Fils: a quietly delicate duo with percussionist Frank Perry, *Suite for Prepared Piano and Mini Drums*, recorded in Davie's Hertford studio in 1971, and a duo with Tony Oxley recorded in Hertford and Cornwall in 1974–5, with Davie playing six instruments and ring modulator (a record best enjoyed by those enamoured of the sound of a ring modulator).

'Davie jibbed at the explicit marking of time,' wrote Horovitz, 'from which he was gladly delivered in jazz music and in the mode of painting he gradually evolved.' But Davie's bebop playing of the 1940s and his free improvisation, whenever that transition took place, were different, though there were signs of a free improviser's thinking very early, a focus on sounds layered on sounds, as if in his mind, like Henri Michaux, he was improvising all the time. 'But perhaps most was the sounds,' he wrote in 1963,

> the clicking and clashing the bone clappering the stick and saucepan drum and soon the magic of the grass whistle in the meadow with the crickets creak and the bees buzz and soon the pennyflute and soon the harmonica and soon the fascination of the ting tang ivory and ebony hammer joys on the piano strings and soon the dreams of guitars and mandolins harps ocarinas oboes clarinets organs violins piccolo horn trumpet trombone saxophone double-bass alto tenor and musical saw. What a magical manipulation of noise vibration buzz bell and wave with tongue lips fingers feet body and soul.

Red planet

Engaged as they were in a public social activity – serial confrontations with audiences, dark interiors, fellow players and convoluted geography, committed to the maintaining of instruments and technique, successions of dates, places and times and their poor remunerations – even the idealists and dreamers who pioneered free improvisation tended to cultivate a defensive dose of scepticism, a residue of pragmatism kept sacrosanct from hard realities of a career in which economic returns bore no relation to the needs of life. Alan Davie's unabashed talk of alchemy and marvellous abandon was not common currency in such circles. Even so, one improviser – drummer Tony Oxley – has said this: 'I think two of the most influential people for me have been Derek Bailey and Alan Davie.'

Born in Sheffield in 1938, Oxley played piano and learnt drums but then studied music theory and played orchestral percussion in the regimental band of the Black Watch, performing popular classics by the predictables: Beethoven, Haydn, Dvorak et al. Tours took him to Germany and America where he heard Horace Silver, Art Blakey, the big bands of Ellington and Kenton. 'Having been in classical music you can't ignore what you've been exposed to,' he told Hannah Charlton in 1981.

> You're led eventually to the development of classical music which leads you to twelve-tone music. Once you've become aware of the development of classical music and move from the diatonic system of harmony to the twelve-tone system it becomes quite interesting. And of course it also becomes interesting from the point of where jazz fits in the history of musical activity. Once you're aware of classical music in that period – we're talking about the twenties and before – it puts it in perspective and consequently you are aware of percussion as more to do with sound and the rhythm aspect of it. American jazz uses a certain language – to me that didn't seem adequate for what I wanted to do or produce or play, because of my experience in a language that was a lot older.

Oxley's frustration with what he perceived as the restricted role of the drummer in jazz was symptomatic of a general shift towards equality among the instruments. Working at Ronnie Scott's Club as a member of the house band Oxley encountered some visiting Americans who wanted nothing more from the drummer than timekeeping. There were exceptions – Bill Evans, Charlie Mariano and Johnny Griffin – who were more adventurous. 'Rhythm doesn't have to be repetitious,' he told Charlton, citing the example of *Ionisation* by Edgard Varèse. As for musicians who treated the drummer as a metronome: 'If they can't keep time for themselves they shouldn't be there.'

Through a sequence of fortuitous events Oxley found himself working in the same band with two compatible souls, Derek Bailey and a bass playing philosophy undergraduate – Gavin Bryars – whose studies were taking second place to the life of a professional musician. As Bailey told me in 1984:

> I worked with Tony and Gavin in 1963. Tony and I were doing a job in Chesterfield. I'd been working in Bournemouth with Winifred Atwell. I came back to start this job. Musically and socially there's so many factors in this. My father was dying at the same time. Being in Chesterfield allowed me to live at home with my mother and father. My first marriage had broken up. I did two weeks for this guy and during that time I met Tony and Gavin who did a dep [deputised] for a couple of nights. Then I came back and did a booking for a Latin American band in this club. The guy had wanted me to stay in Chesterfield. I was living in Putney – this guy rang. I thought I'd go back up there. But the one necessary factor was the kind of atmosphere I'd found in this band, things I didn't know about. Also we actually started a jazz club at the same time. So I went back up there, I stayed in Sheffield.

Over time the relationship of the trio deepened. 'It was probably the most significant period of my life,' says Oxley. At the suggestion of Gavin Bryars, their group was named after an obscure English composer active in the early twentieth century: Joseph Holbrooke. An Edgar Allan Poe enthusiast who experimented with what we would now call mixed-media – projecting lantern slides and film onto screens while the orchestra performed, Holbrooke shared some characteristics in common with the group for whom his name was usurped. He had worked as an accompanist to music hall singer Marie Lloyd, conducted for a touring pantomime and composed in a bewildering variety of styles, ranging from light music, operas and 1920s 'jazz' to the reluctant avant-gardism of *Four Futurist Dances*; moreover, he was known to be cantankerous, talkative, belligerent and subject to a volume of critical abuse in proportion to the prolific nature of his output.

Developing a personal music over a period of three years from 1963 to 1966, particularly in regular sessions at a Sheffield pub named The Grapes, the Joseph Holbrooke trio moved through a number of phases.

At the beginning they worked within the orthodoxies of British modern jazz of that period, founded in the Bill Evans Trio and John Coltrane's music subsequent to *Giant Steps*; inevitably, given the predelictions of Coltrane and Miles Davis at the time there was a modal phase, followed by experiments in disrupting the pulse, non-causal harmony inspired by Webern and ideas learnt from John Cage. Inverting the cliched model of free improvisation as a perpetual opening out into boundless creativity, their method was free from, rather than free form. As Oxley says, 'You're always clear what you don't want. ... We were very lucky – for three of us to be in the same place at the same time, particularly in a provincial city. ... We very soon found that we had similar ideas about what we didn't want.'

I asked Gavin Bryars about these strands of experimentalism, their significance for the group, and Bailey's lifelong work of exploring intervals rather than developing a facility for fast runs. 'I don't know whether it's any more than a coincidence that what you call "jazz experimentalism" appears around the same time, early to mid-sixties, as post-Cage experimentalism, late sixties into early seventies,' he answered.

> There were, of course, some people who overlapped such as Cornelius [Cardew] playing with AMM. Derek subsequently disliked any allusion to jazz in reference to his own work. But it is true that the kinds of jazz we related to in Joseph Holbrooke grew out of the Bill Evans 1959–61 Trio, especially the Village Vanguard sessions [Paul Motian on drums, Scott LaFaro on bass], and I would see Bill Evans having strong connections with Lennie Tristano. You probably know too, in fact, that the three of us accompanied Lee Konitz on a tour in 1966. There was not a great deal of interest in Chico Hamilton although certain things in Gabor Szabo's sound could be close to Derek at times. He got very interested in close intervals – I can still see his hand making the awkward stretch to voice minor ninth chords – and this was something in Bill Evans's left hand voicings. But he was also interested in Webern, especially the *Piano Variations* and this affected the way he approached things melodically, and, by extension, harmonically, once you put those melodic intervals into vertical alignment.

Such developments may have been indigestible to jazz lovers reluctant to accept their implications but for listeners prepared to go deeper they enriched the music. Bassist Chuck Israels, Scott LaFaro's replacement in the Bill Evans Trio after LaFaro's accidental death, had this to say about a sixteen-measure chorus played by Evans in his 1959 version of 'When I Fall in Love':

> Bill thinks it's one of the most disjointed things he's ever recorded, but I think it's a masterpiece of modern musical construction. The rhythmic freedom on that, the uses of little Webern-like snatches, made me realize the connection between *that* music and jazz. When you talk about it like that it sounds so academic, but it sounded so natural when Bill played it.

In his book, *Improvisation*, Bailey wrote:

> These were some of the means by which we reacted against the commitedness of the inherited improvising language, its nostalgia, and looked for fresher, less worn material with which to work. By this time most of the music was collectively improvised and solos were unaccompanied. Such accompaniment as happened was a sort of occasional commentary from the other instruments.

How closely the trio's music would have matched the reputation they have accrued from a section in *Improvisation*, and from the unquestioning panegyric of Ben Watson's biography of Bailey is impossible to say. Only one recording has been released from the period when they were active, a rehearsal tape made in Gavin Bryars's front room in 1965. The tune they work out and play over the course of ten and a half minutes is 'Miles' Mode', an interesting choice, given the group's interest in Webern and twelve-tone composition. Although credited to John Coltrane from its first release on the *Coltrane* album of 1962, there are theories that the composition was in fact Eric Dolphy's 'Red Planet' (recordings exist of Dolphy playing the piece both with Coltrane's group and with Herbie Hancock and the University of Illinois Big Band). Since the angular main theme is palindromic – a twelve-tone row and its retrograde – it seems to fall more naturally into the purview of Dolphy and his passion for Schoenberg's music. This mystery may never be resolved but its significance for Joseph Holbrooke was as a bridge between two barely compatible languages (or three, if indeterminacy and instrumental iconoclasm were factored in via Bryars and his enthusiasm for John Cage).

Audacious by comparison with conventional British jazz groups of the time, their approach was hardly revolutionary for anybody cognizant with American music of the previous five years or 'Spaces' and 'Movement' by the Joe Harriott Quintet (more radical developments in Japan would take some years to become known and contemporaneous experiments in Europe would remain underground until 1966). Yet even though their music was recognizably jazz, albeit an egghead strain, the advances to come are evident: unpredictable pauses lurk as traps laid for fixed expectations, silent openings for other surprises, brief passages in which Bailey scrubs at his strings or dwells on one spot in Gabor Szabo's jazz-raga style (probably the closest Bailey ever came to flower power). A passing moment of high arco bass from Bryars injects the timbre of a sorrowing voice into an emotional disposition that feels otherwise suppressed (this is a rehearsal, so hardly likely to catch fire). The tune is discarded almost completely in the central section though Oxley's hustling drums only relent twice – momentarily when he rubs a drum stick against the skin of the snare drum, then silenced for a bass solo. Clearly they were on the edge of something, arguably a threshold over which others had already passed. Contrast them, for example, with the barely contained intensity of 'Vigil', John Coltrane's 1965 duet with Elvin Jones, or recordings from the same year by the New York Art Quartet and Albert Ayler, and even further back, George Russell's 'Chromatic Universe', recorded in 1959 and occupying a similar territory of analytical playing disrupted by less codified passages.

Nihilismus

The New York Art Quartet make an interesting comparison, given Oxley's hostility to the time-keeping role of jazz drumming. Originally a quartet of John Tchicai on alto saxophone, Roswell Rudd on trombone, Lewis Worrell followed by Reggie Workman on bass and Milford Graves on drums, they formed in the summer of 1964. In 1962 Tchicai and Rudd were members of two related groups – the New York Contemporary Five with Archie Shepp and Bill Dixon's group with Shepp and drummer Dennis Charles.

Two years later, July 1964, they played together with Albert Ayler, Don Cherry, Gary Peacock and Sonny Murray on *New York Eye and Ear Control*. Recorded as a soundtrack for Canadian artist/musician Michael

Snow's first major film and released by ESP-Disk, the session was free from any obvious thematic material or compositional devices. Except for a brief overture, essentially a duet of Don Cherry and Gary Peacock, the flow of the music was guided primarily by listening and response. Snow had been deeply affected, derailed even in his ambitions to become a New York gallery artist, by his first encounter with these musicians though he questioned their ties to the orthodoxies of jazz. In an interview from 1999, he spoke about the unusual 'structurelessness' of this specific record:

> They all used to play 'heads', you know, a tune of some kind, and then a solo, and then 'head' again, and I found myself disagreeing with that. When I had them come to the studio to record the soundtrack, I was careful to tell them that I didn't want any themes, but as much as possible ensemble playing. They accepted and they performed this way, but in my opinion, this is one reason why the music is so great. I mean, they're great, fantastic musicians, but they were stuck in that business of the statement of theme, alternating with solos.

The clash here is between the detachment of a 'structuralist' (if the maker of *Wavelength*, a turning point in the development of structural cinema, can be described as such) and musicians more concerned with the immediacy and detail of playing – a striking example of the productive tensions inherent in the emergence of free improvisation. In its ebbs and flows, an organic evolution by way of mimesis and brusque exchanges, the record stands as an extant template for collective improvisation in which the energy of the music either thrives or founders on the stamina and zeal of the musicians.

A prototype version of the New York Art Quartet rehearsed in Snow's loft space. This was where Graves first heard them. In 1964 they took part in the October Revolution in Jazz, a festival initiated by Bill Dixon. 'With his festival,' wrote Ekkehard Jost in *Free Jazz*, 'Bill Dixon was able to show, first of all, that there was an enormous pool of musicians in New York who deserved a hearing, and second, that there was a (predominantly young) public which was just as fed up with ossified musical norms – and with the commercial hustle of established jazz clubs too – as were the musicians themselves.' The signature sound of *New York Art Quartet & Imamu Amiri Baraka* and *Mohawk*, their first albums – deliberately ragged, bleary themes tumbling out in spasms, notes tailing away as if lost to daydream, the music so open that total collapse seems perpetually imminent, held aloft by the extraordinarily inventive energy of Rudd counterbalancing Tchicai's hypnotic incantations – was quite unlike the music of their peers. 'Dry romances' was the apt description given to the group by John Litweiler in his book, *The Freedom Principle: Jazz After 1958*, and there are traces of extended jazz ballads in their slower pieces. 'Rosmosis', 'Everything Happens To Me' (a nod to Monk), 'Quintus T.' and 'Sweet V.' follow in the slipstream of previous dry romances – Cecil's Taylor's solo of retardations and encroaching silences on 'African Violets', recorded in 1958, and Ornette Coleman's 1960 deconstructions and dismemberments of ballad form, 'Embraceable You' and 'Beauty Is a Rare Thing' – whereby the slowness of the ballad, once parched of romance, melancholy or existential despondency, enabled discontinuous movement outside the interlocking grids of metre and harmony.

But in the case of the New York Art Quartet it makes little sense to speak of slow or fast. Their drummer, Milford Graves, operated in a time zone where such terms shed their assumed meaning. 'I work with speed a lot,' Graves told Paul Burwell in 1981, 'not to show I've got fast chops, but to get from one thing to another. If you hear something of mine it sounds slower than it would look, because I'm doing five things to get one sound.' This temporal contradiction can be heard in all of Graves's work of this period, records such as Albert Ayler's *Love Cry*, Sonny Sharrock's *Black Woman*, The Giuseppi Logan Quartet, Paul Bley's *Barrage*, his Yale University concert with Don Pullen and in its clearest manifestation, *Milford Graves Percussion Ensemble with Sunny Morgan*, released on ESP-Disk in 1965. On the eve of this breakthrough Graves could be heard playing drums and timbales alongside pianist Chick Corea on Montego Joe's *¡arriba! con montego joe* LP from 1964; even in this context, Latin jazz bordering on exotica, his sound was distinctive.

Each track on the Milford Graves percussion album for ESP-Disk was titled with a numbered variant of the word 'nothing'. Listen to 'Nothing 11 – 10', overlaid rhythms stepping as if masks on stilts: high-tuned drums, shaken bells, shakers that move as the hand moves, incantatory vocalizations barely audible behind the night forest of sound, deep drums, a deeper drum – the ground and its deeps. Rather than rushing forward in an imagined line of unfolding time, stasis and perpetual movement oscillate in circles of shingled layers, a centripetal spiralling inward to the centre of nothingness: deep drum, gong, silence. Pan-Africanist, herbalist, acupuncturist, martial artist, healer and teacher, Graves had developed a conception of this music that went beyond jazz and the ching-a-ding of the ride cymbal. 'There's an ethnic problem involved because of slavery,' he told Valerie Wilmer, 'and coming up through the New Orleans period. People completely lost their identity and so what drummers have been playing up to now has little to do with their African make-up. This has been a problem of all the musicians in America – they're playing with a Western vision.'

Some of this new approach came about through technical innovation, some of it through research into the human body. Borrowing from Indian and Nigerian drummers Graves applied tuning paste to some of his drum heads; he also took the front and bottom heads off the drums for a bigger sound. 'It was the difference between talking with your hand over your mouth or not,' he told Burwell. 'I relate the drum skin to a body of water,' he said, describing the vibrational effects of tuning a drum to a low pitch, then hitting it close to the bright screen of a cathode ray tube. 'As a musician, you are schooling yourself to deal with some of the most sensitive things in the universe: emotion, frequency, life, the vital force … we're involved with one of the most subtle things in life. Sound – that's it!'

I just play man

Live and invent. I have tried. I must have tried. Invent. It is not the word. Neither is live. No matter. I have tried.

SAMUEL BECKETT, *Malone Dies*

As John Stevens recounted the story to Victor Schonfield, he was in Chesterfield with the Don Riddell Four, met Tony Oxley for the first time, invited him to his flat to listen to records when Oxley was in London. Can I bring a friend? asked Oxley. That friend was Derek Bailey, who claims that Stevens was staying with Ginger Baker when they met. It seems strange that Bailey, having moved to London in 1961, moved away again, moved back in 1966, was not already a part of London's emergent improvising scene but his hands were full, back and forth to gigs in the north, regular plays with Oxley and Bryars in Sheffield, the complicated family life and ongoing vicissitudes of a trade that appears, in retrospect and in print, more colourful than it did on the shop floor, playing fussy arrangements of light music, waiting for the machine gun jokes of a comedian like Bob Monkhouse to abate, keeping half an eye on the bandleader as barely remembered stars of the variety era ran through their turns.

'I've always felt there was more to music than a string of gigs,' Derek Bailey told me in 1994. Years later we attempted to talk about actual playing, as if discussing the wearing of a garment rather than its cut, fabric, designer, colour, size, buttons, zips, frills, fringes, function, wardrobe life, price, popularity, cultural and political significance. I asked him, how is it possible to have a conversation about playing? 'I wish I knew,' he replied, adding,

> I've thought about that quite a bit. 'I just play, man' – I think that was a philosophical statement, whether they knew it or not. It was a whole philosophy in a nutshell, especially for the very early jazz players, like the New Orleans guys. I don't know to what degree drugs were involved, but some guys, they used to call them playing fools when they couldn't stop them playing. Mind you, they used to be expected to play for hours on end anyway, but some guy would take off on the clarinet or something and eventually they'd all have to jump on him to get him to shut up. That kind of thing is where the playing takes over but then you would have the stimulus of other people, which is where you're likely to discover the stimulus.

This account is reminiscent of Arctic hysteria or the fifteenth-century European epidemic of tarantism, described by I. M. Lewis in *Ecstatic Religion*: 'In times of privation and misery, the most abused members of society felt themselves seized by an irresistible urge to dance wildly until they reached a state of trance and collapsed exhausted. … The frenetic dancing would last for hours at a stretch, the dancers shouting and screaming furiously, and often foaming at the mouth.' It also seems not so far from Alan Davie's conception of the artist as an inspirational channel for what he called 'direct experience'; in this case, it was music flowing, rather than paint. 'I have to say, in the dim and distant,' Bailey said,

> when I used to work in the musical trenches, as I sometimes describe it, you would meet people like that. I might even have been one. I used to play, as near as possible, twenty-four hours a day, like maybe thirteen, fourteen hours a day. Work in the afternoon, in a dancehall, after that in a jazz club, and then either do a morning gig, because in that period you could always do a morning gig. If anybody wanted music they had to have musicians. So I played at, like, the opening of furniture stores, things like that. If there wasn't a morning thing, then

practice, and practice in between sets. I wasn't alone in being obsessed with playing like that, and it was all playing. It wasn't practicing reading or something.

As Bailey admitted, avoidance was implicit in this total commitment to the instrument, avoidance of 'civilian' life, responsibilities he encapsulated in the act of washing up, which is to say domesticity, home life, relationships outside what was then the largely masculine world of music. 'If you're not in a situation where some action is forced on you,' he told me in 2004, 'where the house is burning down or something and you have a choice, if you're a player that seems to be the thing you would choose to do, it's your preferred activity.' A tactile bond, body to body, is formed with the personified instrument, devotional object and devourer of time, complex and fraught with other touchings, holdings, intimacies. Over time the body is shaped against and by the instrument, as if merging. 'But there are different ways of relating to the instrument, aren't there?' he asked. 'I'm a very traditional relater to the instrument. Unless I hold it in a certain way I can't play it.' Despite his thorough reconstruction of guitar language, Bailey considered himself to be a conventional musician. His holding of the guitar had been formed over time, determined in the first instance by the priorities of post-war entertainment in which the relationship of performer to audience remained deferentially in service, a doffed cap, downstairs to the upstairs. Sometimes in later years he might wander through the musical events in which he found himself, a tall and somewhat bemused anthropologist equipped only with an acoustic guitar for technical support, but his customary pose was seated, feet planted solidly, leaning forward very slightly, head bowed in order to study his left hand with deep concentration. The meeting place of fingers, strings and wood was where the music happened; not in the mind, or any mystical or theoretical place, but in the action of the moment.

 How painful it must have been then, to lose this communicative fluency, through which the body rides its own volition, sparking and engaging with others in their moments, moving through unknown intervallic relationships and fractional timbral adjustments. 'Sometimes there's nowhere to put your feet,' Bailey said to me during the same conversation, discussing a compulsion to play with groups in which unfamiliarity predominated. 'It's like walking across ice floes and it might just disappear and you have to react much quicker, even if the music's slow. Maybe that's something to do with playing.'

Playing was Bailey's blood, food and air. When he was diagnosed with carpal tunnel syndrome, a painfully disabling disorder of the hand and wrist, he recorded his struggle to discover a new physical relationship to the guitar. Unable to hold a plectrum, he was forced to play with his thumb. Others would have kept this faltering process behind the closed door of the practice room, but a forensic sense of autobiography in Bailey's playing had shifted over time from purely sonic content to the anti-drama of a figure on the stage: the whole person caught in a spotlight of its own devising. Like Samuel Beckett's *Krapp's Last Tape*, there was the feeling of memory, recording, performative speaking and writing all conflating under the pitiless gaze of age itself.

We become complicit in this during the first track of Bailey's CD release, *Carpal Tunnel*, released in 2005 by John Zorn. Bailey begins to play in much the same way as on many previous solo records, yet a faltering imprecision is immediately apparent, and breathtaking, as if the sure virtuosity, invention and rightness of the previous forty years has gained sudden clarity and deeper meaning through reflection in a clouded mirror. As he plays, he speaks a letter to a person, thanking her many times for some unknown compliment and explaining the reduced nature of his playing ability. The track is a private letter, perhaps destined never to reach its target yet certain to be heard by many unknown listeners on the way; at the same time it exposes in public the corrosive nature of the disability and its effect on Bailey's traditional relationship to the instrument. There are echoes of other players forced by drive or circumstances to begin again after serious illness – Sun Ra in a wheelchair, Roland Kirk half-paralysed after a stroke, or Billie Holiday who continued to sing after her voice was shot to pieces by addiction. To add further poignancy, the problems of playing were rooted in a far more serious source. Unknown to Bailey, he was suffering the first effects of motor neurone disease. At the age of seventy-five he died on Christmas Day, 2005, at home in London, from complications arising from this illness.

On this and other recordings of what Bailey called 'chats', there was little artifice. His voice was conversational, if mildly self-conscious, negotiating the guitar in a rudimentary fashion: no fancy counterpoint or dramatic pauses. Co-founder of Incus Records in 1970 with Evan Parker and Tony Oxley, a landmark label in the history of UK independent record production, Bailey experimented with many channels for publishing: one-off reel-to-reel tapes in the early 1970s; VHS video tapes that he claimed nobody wanted but released them anyway; CD-Rs with a simple cover and a felt tip scrawl on the disk. *Chats* is one of the latter, a sequence of open letters to Eugene Chadbourne, Henry Kaiser, Fred Frith, Steve Beresford and others. The way he described this in the first track, 'Explanation', is that he was interested to discover if he could do two things at once. Actually, he does three things at once: talks, plays and takes the piss. Bailey could be acerbic, confrontational, sarcastic, recklessly abrasive and outright rude, famously so. I asked Steve Beresford, one of the victims of *Chats*, for his opinion of this side of Bailey. 'What it reminded me of,' he said,

> was an episode of *The Larry Sanders Show*. There was an old guy who insulted people. Everybody goes up to him and says, please insult me, and he says, go away, I'm too busy. Derek's insults might have had a grain of truth in them but you couldn't be hurt by them. At least I'm in his consciousness. He was showbiz, deconstructing show business, and for anybody to be so obsessed with deconstructing show business they have to have come out of show business.

Handling an instrument

When I interviewed him for the mid-1980s Channel 4 television series, *Chasing Rainbows*, Bailey discussed his time in the Bob Sharples Band with *Opportunity Knocks*, a long-running British television talent show. Among the acts he accompanied was a body builder who in 1964 twitched and rippled his muscles in time to an insufferably buoyant instrumental called 'Wheels – Cha Cha'. All of this so-called amateur talent was professional, the audience vote was rigged and the unctuous sincerity of the host – Hughie Green – was a mask donned for transmission to disguise an otherwise foul-mouthed Lothario. 'Wow, that was revealing,' Bailey said. 'It was a totally professional show. I liked the way they hoodwinked the public.' Off-camera (Green was still alive at that time), he revealed that Green, the family entertainer, used to describe the famous Clapometer purported to register audience applause as the Wankerphone or Pox Detector. Much of Bailey's scepticism, or cynicism, about the sacred cows of entertainment – the communion of audience and performers, for example – was formed in the days when he played in variety shows and television with stars such as Shirley Bassey and Russ Conway. 'Even now,' he said, 'I don't want to believe that the worse it is, the better they like it, but there's an awful lot of evidence pointing that way.'

'I made a living as an arranger and a transcriber but it's always been additional,' he said.

> Pre-rock 'n' roll you could be asked to do virtually anything on guitar. I've worked on, for instance, religious programmes on the radio and I've played for strippers. I worked with a symphony orchestra very briefly and I've played solo so the social scope of it – it was a case of doing whatever to make a living. I've always been a player. If I was handling an instrument there was already one end achieved.

Working for the BBC in Manchester he accompanied a clergyman for a programme called *The Act of Worship*: 'I think it was a fifteen minute broadcast and he liked to sing little songs he'd written himself. They were kind of folk songs in that particularly unappealing English folk tradition. He used to teach me the songs and I used to play them.'

At Granada TV he played inserts for a current affairs programme, featuring politicians of the day – Richard Crossman and Quintin Hogg – talking to students. He also played in a sextet on BBC radio's long-running comedy series, *I'm Sorry I'll Read That Again*, featuring a cast including John Cleese, Bill Oddie and Jo Kendal:

> Bill Oddie, at some point in one of the shows wanted some free music. Now he must have been one of the only guys there who knew what he was talking about. He asked for this thing and the pianist objected, he says, we're not playing that shit, and Bill Oddie says, why, can't you play it? Now Oddie, I think, because he collected records he followed things that were going on. We were playing at the Little Theatre then but both Kenny [Wheeler] and I were in that band. [The pianist] knew that Oddie was talking about something viz a viz me and Kenny that he didn't know about so we did play a bit.

In a letter written to me in 1996, two pages finely balanced between compassion and wit encompass the difficulties of my personal circumstances at the time, health problems that had kept him out of airports for a year, the tap dancing of Savion Glover and Will Gaines ('... but they both talk about Tap as something you listen to'), his antipathy to holidays and then this paragraph:

Is it a period (mine) thing that makes me think that one part of popular music which is ignored, anathema in fact, is that North American white stuff (beyond the pale, perhaps; ah, sorry) associated with big bands, stuff that was popular in the late 30s and 1940s? Some of the instrumental stuff was hugely popular (strange TRUMPET PLAYERS were, like, stars) and singers like Dinah Shore, Peggy Lee (when young), June Christy and male equivalents whose names I can't remember. Maybe Sinatra mopped up all the residual tolerance for that kind of stuff. I know some people still listen to it – some radio stations in the US play nothing else – but it has no *credibility*. I can't imagine Greil whatsisname mentioning them, for instance. I think I'd better keep quiet about this.

A 1930 birthdate meant that Bailey was close to a generation older than most of his Joseph Holbrooke and Little Theatre Club colleagues, only Kenny Wheeler the same vintage. What this meant in practice was that his formative musical references were not modern jazz or rock 'n' roll but swing. In contrast to Oxley's dogged modernism and Bryars's post-Cage experimentalism, Bailey developed a personal guitar language by applying the circumstances of daily playing to a unique marrying of Webern's serialism with the harmonic innovations of pre-bop guitarists such as Alan Reuss, George Van Eps, Freddie Green, Oscar Moore and Charlie Christian. With the exception of Christian they were predominantly rhythm players. Listen, for example, to Van Eps play 'Dancing In the Dark', near smothering the melody in the complexity of chordal soloing, or to 'The Elder', Freddie Green's rare solo – again, all chords – with the Count Basie Band. Trading with the band's urbane smoothness and heavyweight punch, Green's acoustic guitar operates like a crafty lightweight, deceptively frail and fibrous in its human scale; for thirty-two bars the music zooms in on the materiality of an instrument in possession (through its player) of its own oblique, insouciant strength.

In the late 1930s Green played a high-action Epiphone Emperor guitar. In 2001 Bailey and his partner Karen Brookman travelled to New York to buy a similar acoustic archtop guitar. The instrument chosen was an Epiphone Emperor Regent, not entirely suitable for playing the solo ballads and standards recorded for Zorn's Tzadik label, as Bailey admitted, but nevertheless a talismanic connection with those ancestral figures who had shaped one phase of his musical life. But Bailey was equally committed to amplified electric, its potential for distortion, bite and sustain, the drama of its dynamic range and its capacity to fight back against tough opposition. Though extremely varied in its timbres, his home tone was far closer to the thick, pugnacious sound of Charlie Christian than the dampened politesse of the post-war guitarists. Celebrated as one of the first to play electric guitar, Christian's brief life was cut short by tuberculosis at the age of twenty-five. Though famous for feature solos such as 'Solo Flight' and 'Flying Home' with the Benny Goodman Orchestra, Christian was also recorded in 1941, playing bebop in an after-hours jam session at Minton's Playhouse in Harlem, endlessly flowing choruses streaming from his guitar in convoluted trails that in the daring of their interval leaps anticipated both Eric Dolphy and Derek Bailey. Not that any of these guitarists were necessarily direct influences but the art of rhythmic playing was a more holistic way to think about the potential of the guitar. Rather than developing a music out of chromatic scales, Bailey worked quickly across and along the fretboard and onto the body of the instrument, making chord shapes and clusters that were rarely conventional chords, never settling in a place that could be identified as a key, a tonal centre or a recognizable harmonic transition. Knocks, ticks, scumbled runs, dry chiselling at the strings, choked harmonics, gnarled cut notes which in their bluntness burst in a cloudy aura of ringing resonance, a microtonal wavering hanging over a void of silence, close to.

Unlike most guitarists with ambition, Bailey enjoyed playing rhythm, particularly as accompaniment to a singer. When British casinos were legalized in 1961 by the Betting and Gaming Act, American mafiosi moved in:

> I played with a woman called Damita Jo. She was owned by the mafia. . . . They took over a lot of nightclubs and they took over this one I was working in. There was a band already there and they augmented it up to about fourteen and they brought this rhythm section and singer over to open it. They brought [heavyweight boxer] Joe Louis to front the gambling rooms. He just used to walk around and meet anybody who wanted to meet him. Very nice guy, it was kind of ridiculous. But she was a great singer. I'd never heard of her before or since. She only worked in Las Vegas. She was a kind of Dinah Washington type singer but she had a fucking amazing voice, rough, shouting voice. I played with The Supremes for a week. I was playing second guitar because they brought a guitar player. I thought they were very good. So you were caught up with it for a few nights and then they've gone.

I thought it was alright, actually. It's better than screwing car handles on doors. I've always had that attitude.

'If I'd carried on being a commercial musician', said Bailey, 'I'd have been made redundant by now.' At one point his ideal job was to take the place of guitarist Oscar Moore in the Nat King Cole Trio, but since that chair was filled admirably by Moore, then usurped by string orchestras, making a living was the only serious option. During the *Chasing Rainbows* interview, he described this period as 'wanting to be a black jazz man in south Yorkshire … hopeless, from an employment point of view'. To complicate George Lewis's binary of Afrological and Eurological improvisation, Bailey's aversion to jazz was a reaction based not so much on the music itself but the rigid formalism that followed each innovatory period and the fantasy of aspiring to live the jazz life in all its clichéd mimesis of a remote culture. What struck him as being absurd became even more so as African American musicians like Milford Graves and Joseph Jarman increasingly positioned jazz within the ideology of Afrocentrism. What hope for a Sheffield man who wore cardigans? Perhaps there was some degree of self-loathing in this, or simply unflinching self-knowledge. Nevertheless, he was happy to play with musicians from the jazz tradition – Anthony Braxton, Tony Williams, Cecil Taylor, Steve Lacy, Lee Konitz and, in the 1980s, a trio with Milford Graves and butoh dancer Min Tanaka – if they weren't intent on playing jazz.

Dance hall

The alternative to this Oscar Moore dream was working in provincial dance halls, where, as he said,

> the criminal classes were well represented – they attended almost religiously. … The dance hall in a provincial town was the hub of many things, the centre of crime, prostitution, whatever passed for youth culture, the idea of these penguins flitting around dancing was nothing to do with it. They were outcasts. They were hated and everybody hated them and they hated the musicians. The music was never right for them anyway. They'd rather be in some little room dancing to Victor Sylvester records. The dancers were usually people

who were there to rub up against each other or to leap around in corners and they were always under attack from this tiny minority of swoopers and lingerers who were dressed up.

Within the covert, shadowy nature of this environment in which many things passed unnoticed there were opportunities to feel an unprecedented freedom, more free perhaps than the improvising situation – a duo with Han Bennink, for example – in which there were known unknowns, both for players and audience.

In 1992, he related a conversation with Karen Brookman's brother. 'I was telling him,' said Bailey,

> what I'd really like is to carry on doing exactly what I like doing, and for it to be useful. It wasn't to play some useful music, but to play something that somebody would find useful. One of the things I used to like about working in the dance halls, in the small groups, where you had total freedom really as regards what you played within what you knew what to play. I didn't want to play free in those days but I wanted to play some stuff. Largely it would be jazz related things but it wasn't only jazz. It would be all kinds of funny stuff. People used to make tunes up on the spot in that game. You're working in a quartet, you go on at three o' clock and you've got forty-five minutes to play, and there's nobody in the dance hall at all. You've got to play for that forty-five minutes, so depending on the management and your knowledge of the situation, you can play anything at all. When jazz waltzes came in, in the 1950s [after Max Roach's *Jazz in 3/4 Time*, released in 1957], we used to play jazz waltzes for forty-five minutes just to get used to it. There was a type of playing that went on that I was totally into. Retrospectively, I think it was a perfect situation because whatever we did was musical wallpaper. We couldn't even offend the dancers because they never expected anything from us. If the big band had done it they'd immediately complain. The dancers went for a cup of tea when we were on. You could do anything that you liked, but you were useful.

Bailey also talked about the exercise of writing tunes on the bandstand, one player inventing an introduction and verse, another inventing a middle-eight, another inventing a chorus, audience oblivious to what was going on and each member of the band having to remember what the others came up with. This was a pragmatic game, necessitated by having to play for long durations and maintain interest in the job, but also an intellectual and competitive pleasure, a pride in musicianship. Clearly, there was also a nascent methodology which later evolved in Joseph Holbrooke. In his notes for the Tzadik release of *Joseph Holbrooke Trio: The Moat Studio Recordings*, recorded in 1998, Bryars wrote about the rehearsal ideas examined by the group, including a device of playing modally but allowing a soloist to take as many choruses as they wished.

Bailey dismissed most theories that affixed the origins of free improvised music to any one group or individual player, but he could be persuaded to discuss certain musics that contributed to its emergence. One major strand – the ecstatic expressionism of free jazz – seemed to interest him very little. Although capable of holding his own in the most musically violent company, he was wary of music being used as an emotional gusher, an expression of power and endurance. He would sometimes talk about the underrated pianist Herbie Nichols. Compared in their day to Webern or to Bartok's *Mikrokosmos*, compositions of the mid-1950s by Nichols – 'Cro-Magnon Nights', '2300 Skidoo' or 'Love, Gloom, Cash, Love' – were more like obsessive, witty, maddening puzzles than the default romanticism of the piano trio. Nichols spoke about his love for old and unrespectable upright pianos, whose muted strings, faded woodwork and uneven innards would give up fast and resonant overtones, each note shooting back at the pianist like a bass drum. 'In such a situation,' he wrote, 'as soon as I find that I am not financially liable, I let myself go and use any kind of unorthodox touch needed to dig out the strange "sounds" which are in the instrument.'

For the notes written for *Pieces For Guitar*, recorded in 1966–7, released by John Zorn in 2002, Bailey revealed his obsession with Webern during the mid-1960s: 'The library close to where I was living had the recordings made by Robert Craft of Webern's compositions,' he wrote. 'Not an enormous corpus. I copied them onto a single reel of tape and played it almost daily.' Hearing Webern's *Variations for piano, Op. 27*, the tension of its intervals and silences, is like an eerie pre-echo of Bailey solo recordings such as *New Sights, Old Sounds*, produced by Aquirax Aida in 1978, *Incus Taps*, the rare 1973 recordings reissued by Organ of Corti, or the exquisitely muted *Lot 74*, released as Incus 12 in 1974. On the other hand, as Chuck Israels said of Bill Evans, 'it sounded so natural'; Bailey's additions were a burred, blunt aggression on *Incus Taps*, quickness and a floating aura of feedback on *Lot 74*, layered complexity and a profound sense of intimacy in relation to place on *New Sights, Old Sounds*.

Whatever their differences, silence is central to these recordings, a reminder that in studying the works of Cage during the Joseph Holbrooke period, Gavin Bryars had encountered Cage's book, *Silence*, and begun to play with lower and lower volume. 'The music started from silence,' said Tony Oxley, interviewed for Bailey's book, *Improvisation*: 'It didn't start from the rhythm section "getting it on". It started from what we accept as silence.' This silence was to become the backdrop for improvisation, a silence of unoccupied rooms and empty chairs, ideal for a music in its formative stages to discover itself. 'I used to play to nobody at the Little Theatre Club,' said Bailey.

> It was the only place I could play. I was trying out some things like some electric stuff and maybe stereo and stuff. Anyway, when you've carted an amplifier up four flights of stairs you're not going to not play, right? There were a number of reasons why I started playing solo and part of it was to work out some kind of music. One of the reasons I got into regular solo playing was through John Stevens, because when the SME imploded to a duo he used to say to me, why don't you play solo opposite? That was kind of an interesting period. Initially with Evan and later with Trevor. Again, that was provoked from some outside source, although I was already, as you know, hauling everything up there to play solo to nobody. So it was good to be playing to two musicians who were waiting to play.

This was amusing to both of us, since I remember hearing Bailey play his solo electric set-up at the Little Theatre Club on the same night as the minimalist duo of Stevens and Watts (I still have the poster, April fourteenth, probably 1973). He played with that familiar stance, one foot on a volume pedal, the other on a Fuzz Face pedal, used judiciously to add thicker volume and some dirt to otherwise clean sound. The volume pedal was crucial in the early days. It allowed him to play electric guitar as if it were breath controlled: volume lifted from silence to a roar, a low growl or a mysterious floating up of uncanny weather, a rising up in the iridescent colours of a bird of paradise opening its wings. Almost full on allowed him to play percussively while foot flat down at full volume generated subtle feedback sustain, as if giving voice to the intimate relationship between player, instrument and amplifier.

Bailey's working world gradually collapsed. Dance halls and variety theatres metamorphosed into rock venues or bingo halls as the Beatles/Rolling Stones took hold. 'To play the guitar and not sing suddenly put you in an extinct species category,' he said. Singing was off the menu so there was a sideways move into what he described as 'the murder real ball-aching jobs' of pit work in theatres and studio sessions, the latter hateful for being a wasp's nest of players who considered enthusiasm for music to be a sign of unreliability. For a year he worked in the pit at the Prince of Wales Theatre in London's Leicester Square, a musical called *Sweet Charity*. When he finished he would walk to the Little Theatre Club, still in evening dress, and play.

'I never played the same thing twice,' he said.

You can play the same thing but you're not playing the same thing. You look in all the cracks for whatever interest. I used to play a [Fender] Telecaster. One of the things you can do on a guitar like that is play – not only can the guy in the next room not hear you, the guy sitting next to you can't hear you. I used to play all the time in the pit, it was a good place for practicing, and all I had to do was get the volume up by the time it was my turn to play. Some variation, although it was frowned upon, was not catastrophic.

Over time the person who moved between these two drastically different worlds could no longer disguise his transformation: 'One of the things that changed was that there was no longer much of a connection between the music I wanted to play – I couldn't get away with it. It was no longer ignorable. It couldn't be disguised as something else, in the way that jazz will fit into a nightclub.' In one instance the manager of the Cabaret Club in Manchester, a jazz fan, rejoiced when Bailey joined the band: at last I'll have something to listen to. After six months he wanted Bailey to leave: I don't know what's happening to you but I don't want to listen to that shit all night. 'I wasn't plinking and plonking,' Bailey said, but nevertheless, the difference was palpable.

But what was detectable as a warning signal to the subconscious mind, like a burglar alarm silently ringing in a distant police station, invariably failed to translate into discernment for the floating subtleties of improvisation. Reconciled rather than pessimistic, this was Bailey's summation of the distance between music with some sort of fixed structure and music without:

> Ears that aren't concerned quite closely with music don't hear anything. What they hear is an outline or something, like an aural gesture which if it's clear enough can be accepted. If it's clear and familiar enough the ear will take it in. Otherwise it bounces off the ear leaving a pain. The organ that's used doesn't respond to it. It's like it's not fit enough. Maybe that's what music is essentially – a familiar, clear gesture repeated over and over again. Everything else, like the stuff we're doing, is something else. I don't mind accepting that. The idea that gradually what we do would become more acceptable as people get used to it, I don't believe that.

11 POSTSCRIPT: THE BALLAD OF JOHN AND YOKO

Yoko Ono's *voice piece for soprano*, written in autumn 1961, is also open music, a kind of freedom opening to spontaneity, an improvisation, even in its silence. A soprano singer screams against the wind, against a wall, then against the sky. Speaking of silence, Ono's *Soundtape of the Snow Falling at Dawn* recorded in three locations was sold by her in 1965 at 25 US cents per inch. How many inches were sold is unknown. On a mind map of the promiscuous connectivity that was the 1960s, Yoko Ono occupies a linking node between La Monte Young (The Velvet Underground), Toshi Ichiyanagi, John Cage, Richard Maxfield, Nam June Paik, the Lathams (Joe Harriott), The Beatles, Ornette Coleman and the Spontaneous Music Ensemble. They were connections that would not endure except in the long echo of their consequences for thought, action and belief but for a few seasons they created a strange magic.

A photograph by Valerie Wilmer shows four figures on a stage: alto saxophonist John Tchicai stage right, ramrod stiff, the alto looking tiny against his imposing height; singing into a microphone centre-stage is Yoko Ono, her hair merging with the black floor-length dress she wears; behind her, John Stevens with his small drum kit, playing cymbals with sticks; to his left, cross-legged on the floor, his back to the audience and almost under the piano, is John Lennon, dressed in denim, holding a guitar up to a Fender amplifier to generate feedback. One notable aspect of the scene is that Tchicai and Stevens both wear sensible woollen sweaters, mindful of the March chill. Not difficult then to assess in a glance who is part of a wider world of fashion, image and celebrity and who is not.

The event was called Natural Music: International Avant Garde Concert Workshop, held at Lady Mitchell Hall, Cambridge, Sunday 2 March 1969, at 2.45 pm. The poster promised a large number of musicians: Willem Breuker from Holland, John *[sic]* Dyani, Mongezi Feza, Louis Moholo and Chris McGregor from the Blue Notes, John McLaughlin, John Stevens, John Tchicai, Yoko Ono, Barre Phillips, Trevor Watts and Peter Lemer. A handwritten appendage to the list says: + John Lennon. Just over a year before, on the 29th of February, Yoko Ono had performed at the Royal Albert Hall with Ornette Coleman, David Izenson, Charlie Haden and Ed Blackwell. A photograph shows them rehearsing in a bare-brick room, Ono leaning against a wall, head thrown back and eyes closed, Coleman playing trumpet. An extract from their playing was released on Yoko Ono/Plastic Ono Band. No contribution is audible from Blackwell until Ono screams repeatedly, at which point the music heats up as if suddenly charged with power.

Listening to the confidence with which Ono leads the session and Coleman's willingness to work closely with what she is doing I am reminded of something he said to me in an interview in 1995. I asked him why he invited Fakir Musafar to perform ritual body piercings at a notorious concert in San Francisco the previous year, an event that provoked protests and walk-outs from a well-heeled audience. 'That concert, for me,' he responded,

> was really heading towards civilisation. The civilisation I grew up in was a caste civilisation. The civilisation that I hope to see exist one day is where every person, regardless of their race, creed or colour, or their ability, or their knowledge, or their sexual preference, will find a way to be an individual and make a contribution to each other's relationship. That, I think, will raise the consciousness of why human beings exist to relate to each other.

As a question, I suggested an interpretation of his elusive concept of harmolodics: a method that allows harmonious, independent improvising yet creates an expressive environment in which one player's contribution will not obscure any of the others. Gracious to a fault, Coleman seized upon my definition with enthusiasm. Exceptional among his peers, his understanding of musical freedom proposed a music beyond personality, instruments, virtuosity, genre, style, even personal taste. Almost a music beyond music.

Weird and fragmented

Knowing that guitarist Fred Frith (a Cambridge University student of English literature at the time) was present in the audience for the Cambridge concert I asked him for his impressions of the event: 'The original poster for the event is framed above our dining room table so I see it every day,' he replied.

> Anthony Barnett the promoter was a friend of mine and Tim Hodgkinson's then landlady Janet Downs, so the address where you could get tickets in advance was actually where I used to live, by one of those odd or not so odd coincidences. Given this fact it's hardly likely I could possibly have avoided going to the show. At the time I knew little or nothing about the British free jazz scene. Henry Cow was emerging from being a blues band into broaching experimental waters, but more coming from exposure to Cage and Cardew and Frank Zappa than from jazz, though we were knowledgeable about Ornette, Mingus, Miles, Coltrane. I was a big fan of McLaughlin's first LP, and he was on the poster, and it was obviously THE event.
>
> That's the preamble. What actually happened is kinda blurry but first it became clear that the poster was more of a wish list than a reality. McLaughlin wasn't there and it wasn't exactly clear who was. But I doubt if I'd remember anyway at this point (Breuker? Don't recall seeing him, for example). But John and Yoko sure were, and they got right to it, with Yoko basically wailing and screaming accompanied by a cross-legged Lennon sitting and holding his guitar in front of the amp and letting it feedback continuously. I had never heard anything remotely like it before and was mesmerized. And at some point, maybe after twenty minutes or so but it seemed a lot longer at the time (many in the audience were distinctly restless), a group of musicians kind of ambled on stage and started playing along. That first core group consisted of Barre Phillips, John Stevens, John Tchicai and maybe Trevor Watts, but in the latter case I don't really remember.
>
> They were playing without microphones so they immediately sounded far away, but it felt slightly aggressive, as if they were saying 'enough of this, let's get down to some real music.' Shortly afterwards John and Yoko stopped playing and left the stage. My friend Andy Powell and I then went backstage hoping to meet them (Lady Mitchell Hall is more

of a lecture hall then a theatre so everything was very easily accessible and there was, unbelievably, no security.) Back stage there was a lot of tension, with Lennon feeling like he and Yoko had been disrespected by people who didn't understand what they were trying to do and who had rudely commandeered the stage. I have no idea to this day whether or not this was actually the case, but it was sufficiently fraught that we abandoned any hope of having a conversation and left. This take on it has been erased from all official reports that I have seen, since it now reads like it was some kind of avant-garde love fest. It wasn't. It was a weird, fragmented, tense and chaotic event that left much of the public bemused, like all the best happenings!

My subsequent experience of the concert was undoubtedly coloured by what I had witnessed. The free jazzers were playing away and it wasn't doing anything for me, so in the end I left. Because of it I remained disinterested in British free music for a long time afterwards. I had already purchased Barre's first solo record [Barre Phillips, *Unaccompanied Barre*, 1968] which blew me away and gave me the idea of wanting to do for the guitar what he did for the bass. But hearing these players together for the first time actually pushed me away from this scene rather than towards it. The only concert I ever saw at the Little Theatre Club was Derek [Bailey], two years later in 1971, after Lol [Coxhill] told me to check him out. I was the only person in the audience and this became an enduring friendship. But it was very much the exception.

Postscript to a postscript

On 18 February 1968, the Spontaneous Music Ensemble were recording *Karyobin* at Olympic Sound Studios with Eddie Kramer. There was a ring on the doorbell, a sound that broke through onto the tape because of faulty circuitry in the studio electrics. The visitor, her request for entry still audible on the record, was Yoko Ono. Shortly after there were two performances at the Drury Lane Arts Lab by the SME of Stevens, Bailey, Parker and Ono; this was the link between Stevens and Ono.

A recording of 'Cambridge 1969' was released on *Unfinished Music No. 2: Life With the Lions*, by John Lennon/Yoko Ono in 1969. This is only an extract, just over twenty-six minutes, the first fifteen or so just Ono and Lennon before the bass drum becomes audible, followed by a wash of cymbals, then at twenty minutes, like a lone pìobair battling a gandiegow in the Scottish highlands, Tchicai's crying alto struggles to rise over coruscating droning from Lennon's guitar. The wall of sound's subsidence leaves double bass audible, maybe piano and another saxophone player – Trevor Watts – keening under Tchaicai's customary repetition of short phrases. Intensity collapses into indecision and anti-climax.

But what takes place in the first fifteen minutes is extraordinary: two agonized cries wreathed in a statement that is free in the sense of being free of music (no slight is intended here). In *Grapefruit*, Ono described her music as more of a practice (gyo) than a music. Did she mean practice, I wonder, in the way that Derek Bailey would use the word, or practice in the more contemporary sense of a way of making artwork? In other contexts her singing can grow tiresome through its impervious, impossibly narrow obduracy. Possessed here by a frankness and raw pain, it speaks directly to the guitar's howlinground unstable flux, blaring thickness and screeching hysteria. The aesthetic quality of Japanese butoh, dance of darkness and trauma, is invoked, renouncing refinement or fixity. Stark sudden silences (of the guitar) and erratic movements of pitch speak of all the biographical details we now know: the cries of a mother who has lost her child; the son abandoned by his mother. An eerie anticipation of Lennon's discovery the following year of Arthur Janov's book, *The Primal Scream*, this duet also carries buried within it the principles of the Destruction In Art Symposium (Ono was the only woman invited to that event), alongside the grinding rockabilly distortion of Paul Burlison's lead guitar with the Johnny Burnette Trio.

Beginning sympathetically, even predictably, the entry of acoustic instruments into this tight world dilutes its power, just as their power is nullified by the screams and feedback. Phrases of pitched notes sound heretical; even the instruments sound old-fashioned, just for being instruments. An aesthetic mismatch is played out, a sign that assumptions about improvisation and freedom may seem to move along a similar path yet prove to be incompatible.

Ono rejected collectivism in art, again in *Grapefruit*, along with any single direction. If there was a lesson to be learnt, it was a painful one, necessitating a rethink for the end of the 1960s. Many freedoms swirled within the dream of freedom – the challenge was to find ways for them to coexist.

12 RAIN FALLING DOWN ON OLD GODS

You won't hear it nicely. If it hurts you be glad of it. As near as you will ever get, you are inside the music; not only inside it, you are it; your body is no longer your shape and substance, it is the shape and substance of the music.

JAMES AGEE, Let Us Now Praise Famous Men

Shock, transition, time

Yoko Ono's WOOD PIECE, autumn 1963, from *Grapefruit*, making sounds by hitting a piece of wood, using different angles, hitting different parts of the wood.

Then in Wuppertal, Germany, 11 March 1963, Joseph Beuys walked into the gallery carrying a sledgehammer, took a swing at Nam June Paik's prepared piano and smashed it to pieces before anybody could stop him or, worse, document the event – a crime in such circles. Hapless unprepared prepared piano, defiled altar, music sacrifice and coffin, but Beuys had pianos on his mind, notably an unrealized Earth Piano from the previous year, *Das Erdklavier*, pianos cut out of the earth, sculpted from earth, buried in earth.

The exhibition was *Exposition of Music. Electronic Television*, held at architect Rolf Jährling's Galerie Parnass. The original proposition for Paik to present an evening concert had expanded as his ideas rapidly evolved, moving away from music to focus on rooms themselves. He began to conceive of television as an art medium. In his exhibition notes the influence of a painter named Karl Otto Götz was acknowledged. During the war Götz conducted experiments with ground-based radar, at one point regretting the fact that it was impossible to control or fix Brownian tubes. This word – fix – fixed itself in Paik's consciousness. 'Yes – then it must be the most fitting means to deal with indeterminism,' he wrote, '(today the central problem in ethics and aesthetics, perhaps also in physics and the economy).' Electronic music felt fixed and deterministic for Paik, both in compositional methods and its medium of repeatable reproduction, magnetic tape. How was it possible to break open the fixity of a medium like broadcast television, upset the traditional fixed role of the audience or disrupt time's one-way flow (towards death) in traditional music? 'The freedom must have more than two ways,' he wrote, 'directions, vectors, possibilities, of time.' For an exhibition never realized – *Symphony for 20 Rooms* – Paik had ideas for five rooms of audience participation, in which people could push stones, metal and wood around the room, jump around or fight on a metal floor plate fitted with contact microphones, play prepared pianos, whistles, toys and a gramophone with records.

The Wuppertal exhibition grew complicated, a sprawling labyrinth of television sets, old pianos, turntables, sound pieces of various kinds, press reports on the death of Marilyn Monroe, a shop-window mannequin in a bath, mirror foil strips blown by a hot-air fan, an American flag soaked in menstrual blood (in 1963 American involvement in the Vietnam War was escalating, while the Korean War was only ten years in the past), a tape recorder connected to a television, transistor radios hanging from a coat hanger above a chair and in the garden, *zen for wind*, rattles, clappers, a tin, a key, wooden doll, a metal bolt, a sandal and other objects hanging on strings to be played by the wind. At the entrance was a cow's head, taken away by police after a few days because it contravened a law that cadavers must be buried three metres underground. For Paik the cow's head was a reference to the shamanism he had experienced in Korea as a child:

> Korean shamans wear that big head. All day they drink and eat. They put it on their heads. Little women wear tall heads. They become very excited, they dance, they get high, you know. There was that strange experience I had. Every October my mother organised a shaman festival. That was very good. That was pretty grotesque and interesting. And I thought that when people come to my concert, to see my objects, they must have a different state of mind.

Installing all these elements entailed prodigious labour, so three local artists – Manfred Montwé, Tomas Schmidt and Peter Brötzmann – were drafted in to assist Paik, participate and provide daily maintenance. The young Brötzmann, a painter already playing jazz saxophone, is seen in photographs taken during the exhibition opening, demonstrating a piece called *Random Access* – strips of audio tape fixed to a wall 'like the map of a city', playable by disconnected tape heads connected to a tape recorder by extension leads. Chaos ensued during the opening because many objects, including small musical instruments, were laid on the staircase for visitors to investigate. Brötzmann is photographed sitting on the stairs blowing small whistles held in his right hand, a double-reed aerophone with large gourd resonator in his left. 'The staircase must have been very popular as a focal point for communication,' writes Susanne Neuburger,

> where the juxtaposition of highly diverse objects provided the greatest contradiction to the notion of a bourgeois household. One critic even compared it to a 'department store after a bomb attack.' It must also have been very loud, with one press report complaining of 'squeaking sounds that get on your nerves' and 'whining tapes and tirelessly rotating records.' The visitors seem to have accepted the challenge to make use of the instruments, showing a lively interest on the first day at least.

A photograph taken by Brötzmann shows a toy piano prepared exquisitely with tea strainer, tube studded with nails and other indefinable objects. The upright pianos were particularly beautiful in their preparation, guts eviscerated, bricolaged with underwear, shoe, a clock, photographs, string, a bell, nails, toys, bags, the keys connected by electrical contacts to other devices such as sirens, heaters, tape recorders and lighting effects – the instrument unbound. Joseph Beuys arrived about an hour after the opening, no doubt timing his entrance for the maximum crush of visitors: 'Beuys had a big hammer in his hand,' said Manfred Montwé in 2008.

> It was a chopper, with one sharp edge and the other blunt. He came into the hall, stood right in front of the piano, swung the axe, and struck it really hard. He had this incredible commitment and intensity, just as I witnessed him during the twenty-four-hour happening in 1965 [a Fluxus happening at the same gallery]. He attacked it with all his might! It was like an explosion, and the whole room suddenly

fell silent. Completely silent. It was so quick; in a few minutes it was all over.

Most accounts of Peter Brötzmann's life and work as an improvising musician and painter skip quickly, too quickly, past this early collaboration with Nam June Paik and the provocation by Beuys. '[Nam June Paik] opened up another world for me,' Brötzmann says in a book of conversations with photographer Gérard Rouy. But still, I want to know more about that world, the small instruments on the stairs, his feelings about Beuys taking freedom to the limit. After all, this was no juvenile gesture. 'Provocation for Beuys', one of his disciples has written, 'should embody a thrust of energy such that the subconscious could open itself to new experience, such that indifference could be transformed into interest.'

In freedom, how free are you permitted to be?

Overlap/transition

This civil strife of factional and ideological freedoms battling opposing versions of themselves would be the most compelling extra-musical narrative of subsequent years. How free can you be? Where are the boundaries and limits of free improvisation? How can improvisation define itself? How can it function within society and act upon society? How can it renew itself over half a century to continue to be improvisation without falling into routine, cliché and style? These are questions to which I will return in the second volume of this book, beginning with an account of German musicians such as Peter Brötzmann, Peter Kowald, Paul Lovens, Alexander von Schlippenbach and the activities of the FMP label, the Dutch scene based around Han Bennink, Misha Mengelberg, Willem Breuker and Instant Composers Pool, The Continuous Music Ensemble/People Band/Amazing Band, the Blue Notes from South Africa, Irène Schweizer and Pierre Favre from Switzerland, the Taj Mahal Travellers and Masayuki Takayanagi from Japan, the continuing evolution of the Spontaneous Music Ensemble in London (plus those groups that evolved from it, such as Amalgam and Music Improvisation Company), the convolutions of AMM and the central importance of individual players such as Evan Parker and Anthony Braxton, both of them developing a singularity of approach that encompassed an entire world view.

The Baden-Baden Free Jazz Meetings organized by Joachim-Ernst Berendt from 1966 onwards brought together musicians like Don Cherry, John Stevens, Evan Parker, Peter Brötzmann, Irène Schweizer, Dave Holland, Paul Rutherford, Trevor Watts, Norma Winstone, Johnny Dyani, Irene Aebi and Steve Lacy. They helped to establish internationalism at the centre of the music's development, with transnational groups such as Brötzmann, Bennink and Fred van Hove becoming the norm. At the same time an uneasy relationship to jazz, free jazz in particular, was complicated by new factors, particularly an influx of so-called second-generation players (myself included) who had little or no background in jazz. Volume two, then, will backtrack somewhat, tracing the evolution of scenes in Germany, Holland, Belgium, France and Switzerland, along with the British groups of the 1960s I have not fully covered in this first volume, and then the gradual shift from first principles as musicians from extremely diverse backgrounds gravitated towards free playing to change its perception of itself.

The story of the 1970s is one of collective organization and actions running in parallel with independent record labels – an international scene that had its followers in mainstream media but with the exception of rock/improvisation groups like Henry Cow and the exception of all exceptions, Lol Coxhill, operated at the furthest margins of the music industry. Although each organization, whether the Instant Composers Pool in Holland or the London Musicians Collective in the UK, functioned according to their own beliefs there was a feeling of common aims. Certain key records – *Machine Gun* by the Peter Brötzmann Octet, for example – made a lasting impact as a benchmark of the fiercest imaginable energy, yet the politics of the time also gave rise to highly significant groups like the Feminist Improvising Group and Derek Bailey's Company, arguably at the opposite end of the spectrum to *Machine Gun* in every respect yet at the same time still indebted to its remorseless disdain for compromise.

What followed from the early 1970s to the present was as much a question of survival as anything else, improvised music persisting, self-organizing, networking and mutating its way through precarity and public neglect to become a recognized, even respected, activity connecting up electronic and electro-acoustic music, cracked lo-fi and laptop, noise and minimalism, turntablism, experimental composition, performance art, field recording, reductionism, live coding and pretty much anything else in sound and listening that makes a poor fit with the prevailing orthodoxies of music. The increasing ease with which musicians could travel and communicate after the 1990s meant that uncompromising players were no longer locked within small scenes, so their global influence grew out of all proportion to the hard realities of indifference back home. Japanese musicians such as Otomo Yoshihide, Sachiko M, Taku Sugimoto and Toshimaru Nakamura became well known as performers and collaborators outside the onkyo scene of Tokyo, to some extent following the example of the 1970s generation of American players – John Zorn, Eugene Chadbourne, LaDonna Smith, Henry Kaiser, George Lewis and others – who travelled frequently to Europe. Now it is possible to visit Singapore, Beijing, Moscow, Seoul, Taipei or Rio de Janeiro and hear local versions of improvised music that have evolved in their own fashion. The music is descended from its ancestral pioneers (often by the thinnest line) yet at the same time has a character that is particular to its own time and place. The idea that improvisation can be defined in some way by country, city or even those specific spaces in which it finds a temporary home, still pertains, particularly in relation to radically new tactics of so-called reductionism developed by musicians in Berlin, Vienna, Tokyo and London during the 1990s. But as with the transnational groups of the 1960s and 1970s, the musicians operate in an oscillating localism/globalism, accepting unstable identity in pursuit of a less easily articulated dream, inchoate intimations of a way to be and to live as yet undefined.

Acknowledgements

This book would not have been possible without the conversations, interviews and answers to questions so generously given by the following:
Jennifer Allum, Steve Beresford, Derek Bailey, Giorgio Battistelli, Gavin Bryars, John Butcher, Cornelius Cardew, Andrea Centazzo, Marjolaine Charbin, Mike Cooper, Ornette Coleman, Alvin Curran, Martin Davidson, Drew Daniel, Angharad Davies, Terry Day, Max Eastley, Fred Frith, Lou Gare, John Godfrey, Barry Guy, Sylvia Hallett, Raymond Salvatore Harmon, Shelley Hirsch, Linda Hirst, Philip Jeck, Lee Konitz, Steve Lacy, Noa Latham, Adam Linson, Takuro Mizuta Lippit, Henry Lowther, Sachiko M, Phil Minton, Roscoe Mitchell, Pauline Oliveros, Evan Parker, Daniel Pennie, Eddie Prèvost, Keith Rowe, Frederic Rzewski, Christoph Rothmeier, Mieko Shiomi, Victor Schonfield, Irène Schweizer, Barbara Steveni, Anne Stevens, Richard Teitelbaum, John Tilbury, Chris Turner, Yasunao Tone, Matthew Waters, Trevor Watts, Seymour Wright.

In 2010, when I was trying to figure out a way into this book, I was thrown a lifeline by Sound & Music, specifically John Kieffer, awarding me invaluable support for a set of interviews which broke through the wall of resistance the subject was presenting. I am also grateful to London College of Communication's research community – the most inspiring group of sound specialists one could ever hope to be a part of, unfailingly generous with emotional and intellectual support. At a fragile moment when I felt inadequate to the task of even getting started Steve Beresford gave me the kind of encouragement I really needed and then, years later, read through the section on the Spontaneous Music Ensemble and gave invaluable feedback. Thanks are also warmly extended to the following: Hannah Charlton, who very generously allowed me to transcribe and use her interview tapes from the 1980s; Seymour Wright, who allowed me access to his hugely informative PhD on AMM and was also open and expansive with ideas and information; Paul Wilson at the British Library, who gave detailed help with the section on John Stevens; my editor at Bloomsbury, Ally Jane Grossan, who showed incredible patience with my prevarications and delays; Geoff Winston, Calum Storrie and Ross Lambert for allowing me to use their drawings; Gérard Rouy and Roberto Masotti, both great photographers and tireless documenters of this music, who selected photographs for me. It's no reflection on their abilities that I decided, after much deliberation, against including photographs for this volume of the work.

I am indebted to the many improvising musicians with whom I have collaborated over the years but in particular to the two people who got me into this thing at the beginning of the 1970s – Paul Burwell and John Stevens – sadly, neither of whom is alive to read this book, and also to friends and colleagues who have supported me with a word or an ear through the long process of making it happen, particularly Andrew Brenner, Rie Nakajima, Elaine Mitchener, Lawrence English and Daniela Cascella. My PhD students have been gracefully tolerant of my absences and have patiently listened to my monologues on improvisation, for which I hope to reward them with more attentive supervision in the future. Many of my more recent ideas about improvisation have been worked out with those students from BA Sound Art & Design and MA Sound Art at London College of Communication who have taken my annual improvisation classes since 2005. It's quite possible that I've learnt more from them than they have from me.

NOTES

Numbers in right-hand column denote pages in the volume.

1 (only begin) A descent

Richard Williams, *Melody Maker*, 21 November 1970, p. 32.	5
Polly Devlin, *Spotlight – Music: AMM*, *Vogue*, May 1966, p. 17.	5
Edwin Prévost, *Minute Particulars*, Copula, 2004, p. 4.	5
Takuro Mizuta Lippit, email communication to the author, 12 November 2013.	6
Philip Jeck, email communication to the author, 17 July 2014.	7
Sachiko M, email communication with the author, 18 June 2014.	7
Edgar Allen Poe, *A Descent Into the Maelstrom*, Poe Tales of Mystery and Imagination, J. M. Dent, 1959, pp. 243–58.	9
William Faulkner, *The Sound and the Fury*, Vintage, 1995, p. 17.	11
Vladimir Nabakov, *Speak, Memory: An Autobiography Revisited*, Penguin Books, 2000, p. 17.	12
John Zorn (ed.), *Arcana III: Musicians on Music*, Hips Road, 2008, p. 138.	13
Vladimir Jankélévitch, *Music and the Ineffable*, translated by Caroline Abbate, Princeton University Press, pp. 78–9.	14
Derek Bailey, personal letter to author, undated.	14
Artemy Troitsky, liner note to *Sainkho Namchylak: Out of Tuva*, Cramworld CD, 1993.	16
Michel de Certeau, *The Practice of Everyday Life*, University of California Press, 1988, p. 163.	17
Stephen Nachmanovitch, *Free Play: Improvisation In Life and Art*, Jeremy P. Tarcher/Penguin, 1990, p. 9.	17
Luciano Berio, *Two Interviews*, with Rossana Dalmonte and Bálint András Varga, Marion Boyars, 2009, pp. 84–5.	18
Simon Critchley, interviewed by Dan Fox (*A Kind of Faith*), *Frieze*, Issue 135, November to December 2010, p. 96.	19
Linda Hirst and David Wright, *Alternative Voices: Contemporary Vocal Techniques*, in John Potter (ed.), *The Cambridge Companion to Singing*, Cambridge University Press, 2000, p. 193.	20
Linda Hirst, email communication to the author, 12 June 2014.	20

Bruce Christian Bennett, *Notes on Luciano Berio's Thema (Omaggio a Joyce) (1958) and Visage (1961)*, published at: http://brucechristianbennett.com/SFSU/MUS504/readings/Notes_on_Berio.pdf [accessed 16 June 2014]. 20
Eric Hobsbawm, *Pop Goes the Artist: Our Exploding Culture* (1964), published in *Fractured Times*, Abacus, 2014, p. 270. 20–1
Jacques Derrida, unpublished interview, 1982, available at https://www.youtube.com/watch?v=xT106qB65-A [accessed 12 June 2014]. 21
Victor Schonfield, liner notes to *Karyobin*, The Spontaneous Music Ensemble, Island Records, 1968 (reissued on CD by Chronoscope, 1993). 21
Peter Rivière, *Tribes Without Chiefs*, *The Listener*, London, September 1972, p. 366. 23
Jo Freeman, *The Tyranny of Structurelessness*, available at: http://www.jofreeman.com/joreen/tyranny.htm [accessed 12 June 2014], 1970. 24–5
Richard Sennett, *Together: The Rituals, Pleasures and Politics of Cooperation*, Penguin Books, 2013, pp. 19–20. 25
Ibid., p. 274. 25
David Toop, *Haunted Weather*, Serpent's Tail, 2004, p. 240. 26
George E. Lewis, *A Power Stronger Than Itself*, University of Chicago Press, 2009, p. 99. 27
Tim Ingold and Elizabeth Hallam (eds), *Creativity and Cultural Improvisation*, Berg, 2007, p. 7. 28
Derek Bailey, *Improvisation: Its Nature and Practice In Music*, Moorland Publishing, 1980, p. 3. 29
Roger Sutherland, *New Perspectives In Music*, Sun Tavern Fields, 1994, p. 204. 30
Mike Heffley, *Northern Sun, Southern Moon*, Yale University Press, 2005, p. 3. 30
Roger T. Dean (with Hazel Smith), *New Structures in Jazz and Improvised Music Since 1960*, Open University Press, 1992, p. 177. 30
Richard Sennett, op cit., pp. 57–9. 31

2 Free bodies

Patrick Wilcken, *Claude Lévi-Strauss: The Poet in the Laboratory*, Bloomsbury, 2010, pp. 122–3. 33
Aimé Césaire, *Solar Throat Slashed: The Unexpurgated 1948 edition*, translated and edited by A. James Arnold and Clayton Eshleman, Wesleyan University Press, 2011, p. 47. 34
Mark Polizzotti, *Revolution of the Mind: The Life of André Breton*, Black Widow Press, 2009, p. 187. 35
Franklin Rosement, *André Breton and the First Principles of Surrealism*, Pluto Press, 1978, p. 21. 35

Jacques Derrida and Ornette Coleman, *The Other's Language*, accessed at http://www.alansondheim.org/ornette.pdf [accessed 20 June 2014], p. 322.   35

Carmen Blacker, *The Catalpa Bow: A Study of Shamanistic Practices in Japan*, George Allen & Unwin, 1975, p. 133.   36

Austin Osman Spare, *The Book Of Pleasure (Self-Love): The Psychology of Ecstasy*, private printing, 1913 (reprinted edition, undated, p. 55).   36

Alex Owen, *The Place of Enchantment: British Occultism and the Culture of the Modern*, The University of Chicago Press, 2004, p. 257.   36

Martin Clark and Mark Osterfield, *The Dark Monarch: Magic and Modernity in British Art* (curated by Michael Bracewell, Martin Clark and Alun Rowlands), Tate St Ives, 2009, p. i.   36

Jane Austen, *Emma*, Wordsworth Classics, 1994, p. 278.   37

Gary Peters, *The Philosophy of Improvisation*, The University of Chicago Press, 2009, pp. 42–3.   37

Daniel B. Smith, *Muses, Madmen, and Prophets: Hearing Voices and the Borders of Sanity*, Penguin Books, 2007, pp. 44–5.   38

Michel de Certeau, op cit., p. 162. [quoting Marguerite Duras, Nathalie Granger, 1973, and the interview by Benoît Jacquot, in *Art Press*, October 1973].   38

Ami Yoshida, interviewed by Yoshio Otani (translated by Cathy Fishman), *Improvised Music from Japan from 2002-2003*, IMJ-301 (launch issue), p. E–6.   38–9

William James, *The Stream of Consciousness*, Psychology, Chapter XI, Cleveland & New York [psychclassics.yorku.ca/James/Jimmy11.htm, accessed 7 July 2014].   39

David Toop, *Haunted Weather*, op cit., p. 19.   40

Dorothy Miller Richardson, *The Tunnel*, Forgotten Books, 2012, pp. 13–14.   41

Phil Minton, interview with the author, 22 July 2014   43–4

Ross Simonini, *Black Water*, Frieze, Issue 163, 2014.   44

Georges Bataille, *Formless*, in *Visions of Excess: Selected Writings, 1927-1939*, University of Minnesota Press, 1985, p. 31.   45

Michel Leiris, *Spittle*, in *Encyclopedia Acephalica*, edited by Robert Lebel and Isabelle Waldberg, translated by Iain White, Atlas Press, 1995, p. 80.   45–6

John Gray, *Heresies: Against Progress and Other Illusions*, Granta Books, 2004, p. 174.   46–7

Timothy Day, *A Century of Recorded Music: Listening To Musical History*, London, 2000, p. 11.   47

Jed Rasula, *The Cambridge Companion to Jazz*, edited by Mervyn Cooke and David Horn, Cambridge University Press, 2003, pp. 59–60.   47

Jacob Smith, *Vocal Tracks: Performance and Sound Media*, University of California Press, 2008, p. 135.   48

Reid Badger, *A Life In Ragtime: A Biography of James Reese Europe*, Oxford University Press, 1995, pp. 182 and 195.   48–9

Deborah Lewer, *Performance and the Anti-Revue*, in *Hannah Hoch*, Prestel/Whitechapel Gallery, 2014, p. 31.	49
Gennifer Weisenfeld, *Mavo: Japanese Artists And the Japanese Avant Garde, 1905-1931*, University of California Press, 2002, p. 234.	50
Ibid., p. 95.	50
Ibid., p. 235.	50
Toru Takemitsu, *A Single Sound*, in *Confronting Silence*, Fallen Leaf Press, 1995, p. 51.	52
Bruno Bartolozzi, *New Sounds for Woodwind*, translated and edited by Reginald Smith Brindle, London, 1967.	52
Albert Glinsky, *Theremin: Ether Music & Espionage*, Urbana and Chicago, 2000, p. 158.	53
Antonin Artaud, *The Theatre of Cruelty: First Manifesto* (1932), *Antonin Artaud, Collected Works, volume 4*, Calder & Boyars, 1974, p. 73.	53–4
Douglas Kahn, *Noise, Water, Meat: A History of Sound In The Arts*, London: The MIT Press, 1999, p. 87.	54
Bettina L. Knapp, *Antonin Artaud, Man Of Vision*, Swallow Press, 1980, pp. 160–1.	56
Alan S. Weiss, *Breathless: Sound Recording, Disembodiment and The Transformation of Lyrical Nostalgia*, Wesleyan University Press, 2002, pp. 129–30.	57
Felicitas D. Goodman, *Speaking In Tongues*, The University of Chicago Press, 1972, p. 152.	58
Ibid., p. 71.	58
Jean Marcel, *The History Of Surrealist Painting*, Weidenfield & Nicholson, 1960, p. 126.	58
Robert Desnos, in *Surrealist Games*, edited by Mel Gooding, Redstone Press, 1991, p. 19.	58
John Cage (with Joan Retallack), *Musicage: Cage Muses On Words, Art, Music*, Wesleyan University Press of New England, 1996, p. 270.	58–9
Ibid., p. 274.	59
Ibid., pp. 270–1.	59
Cole Gagne and Tracy Caras, *Soundpieces: Interviews with American Composers*, Scarecrow Press, 1982, p. 78.	59
Sabine M. Feisst, *John Cage and Improvisation*, in Gabriel Solis and Bruno Nettl (eds), *Musical Improvisation: Art, Education, and Society*, University of Illinois Press, 2009, p. 48.	60
David W. Bernstein and Christopher Hatch (eds), *Writings Through John Cage's Music, Poetry, + Art*, The University of Chicago Press, 2001, pp. 177–9.	60–1
John Cage (with Joan Retallack), op cit., p. 127.	61
James Lincoln Collier, *Louis Armstrong*, Pan Books, 1985, p. 100.	63
Valerie Wilmer, *As Serious As Your Life*, Quartet Books, 1977, p. 106.	66
Viv Broughton, *Black Gospel*, Blandford Press, 1985, p. 7.	66

3 Collective subjectivities 1

Enrique Villa-Matas, *Bartleby & Co*, translated by Jonathan Dunne, Vintage, 2005, p. 26. — 69

4 Overture to dawn

Isaiah Berlin, *Two Concepts of Liberty*, 1958. — 81
Martin Luther King, *I Have a Dream* speech, Washington DC, 28 August 1963. — 81
W. E. B. Du Bois, *The Souls of Black Folk*, Dover Publications, 1994, p. 24. — 81
James Joyce, *Finnegans Wake*, Faber and Faber, 1975, p. 378. — 82
Zhang Hongxing, *Masterpieces of Chinese Painting 700-1900*, Victoria and Albert Museum, 2013, p. 37. — 82–3
François Jullien, *The Great Image Has No Form, or On the Nonobject through Painting*, translated by Jane Marie Todd, The University of Chicago Press, 2009, p. 22. — 83
James Lincoln Collier, op cit., pp. 61–2. — 84
Barry Ulanov, *A History of Jazz In America*, The Jazz Book Club, 1959, p. 226. — 85
Frank R. Rossiter, *Charles Ives and His America*, Victor Gollancz Ltd, 1976, p. 51. — 85
Michael Dregni, *Django: The Life and Music of a Gypsy Legend*, Oxford University Press, 2004, pp. 127–9. — 86
Ibid., p. 28. — 86
Evan Parker, interview by Philip Clark, *The Wire*, Issue 279 (May 2007), p. 36. — 87
Nina Parish, *Henri Michaux: Experimentation With Signs*, Rodopi B.V., 2007, p. 287. — 87–8
Henri Michaux, *Darkness Moves*, selected and translated by David Ball, University of California Press, 1994, pp. 325–7. — 88
Henri Michaux, *Spaced, Displaced/Déplacements Dégagements*, translated by David and Helen Constantine, Bloodaxe, 1992, pp. 69–71. — 88
Henri Michaux, *Untitled Passages*, The Drawing Center, New York/Merrell, 2000, pp. 110–211. — 88–9
Ornette Coleman, liner notes, The Ornette Coleman Quartet, *This Is Our Music*, Atlantic Records, 1961. — 89
Barry Unlanov, op cit., p. 239. — 90
Frank Kofsky, *Black Nationalism and the Revolution In Music*, Pathfinder Press, 1970, p. 145. — 90
D. W. Winnicott, *Playing and Reality*, Routledge Classics, 2005, p. 129. — 91
Ibid., p. 70. — 91
Ibid., p. 64. — 91

Alun Morgan, liner notes, Erroll Garner, *Overture To Dawn (The Apartment Sessions, Vol. 1)*, Charly Records, 1995. 92
Matt Endahl, *A Shot In the Dark*, http://mattendahl.blogspot.co.uk/2012/07/free-improvisation-series-erroll-garner.html, 2012 [accessed 18 July 2014]. 93
Boris Vian, *Round About Close To Midnight: The Jazz Writings of Boris Vian*, translated by Mike Zwerin, Quartet Books, 1988, p. 143. 93
John F. Szwed, *Space Is the Place: The Lives and Times of Sun Ra*, Pantheon Books, 1997, p. 73. 94
Matt Endahl, *A Shot In the Dark*, http://mattendahl.blogspot.co.uk/search/label/Stuff%20Smith 95
http://mattendahl.blogspot.co.uk/2013/07/free-improvisation-series-robert-crum.html, 2013 [accessed 23 July.2014]. 98
Pierre Schaeffer, *In Search of a Concrete Music*, translated by Christine North and John Dack, University of California Press, 2012, pp. 3–22. 99–100
Eunmi Shim, *Lennie Tristano: His Life In Music*, The University of Michigan, 2007, pp. 28–9. 101
Miles Davis with Quincy Troupe, *Miles Davis: The Autobiography*, Picador, 1990, p. 137. 103
Warne Marsh interviewed for NRK (Norwegian Broadcasting Corporation) documentary, 1983. 104
Eunmi Shin, op cit., p. 54. 104
Ibid., p. 87. 104
Lennie Tristano interview, NRK, op cit. 104–5
Warne Marsh interview, NRK, op cit. 105
Edgar Allen Poe, *The Fall of the House of Usher*, *Poe's Tales of Mystery and Imagination*, J. M. Dent, 1959, p. 135. 105
Lee Konitz, interview with the author, London, 14 May 1987. 106–8
Ben Watson, *Derek Bailey and the Story of Free Improvisation*, Verso, 2004, pp. 92–3. 109
Lee Konitz interview, op cit. 110
Robert Gordon, *Jazz West Coast*, Quartet Books, 1986, p. 93. 115
Thomas de Hartmann, *Our Life with Mr. Gurdjieff*, Penguin Books, 1964, p. 92. 110
Ibid., p. 123. 111
G. J. Blom, *Gurdjieff: Harmonic Development, The Complete Harmonium Recordings 1948-1949*, Basta Audio-Visuals, 2004, p. 21. 111
Ibid., pp. 57–8. 111
Vincent Buranelli, *The Wizard from Vienna: Franz Anton Mesmer and the Origins of Hypnosis*, Peter Owen, London, 1975, pp. 125–6. 112
Alvin Curran, interview with the author, 27 July 2014. 112–13
Andy Hamilton, *Giacinto Scelsi*, *The Wire*, 314, April 2010, p. 46. 114
Giorgio Battistelli, interview with the author, 19 September 2014. 114
Jordan R. Young, *Spike Jones and his City Slickers*, Disharmony Books, 1984, p. 66. 115

Brian Priestley, *Mingus: A Critical Biography*, Quartet books, 1982,
  p. 29. — 118
Ibid., p. 59. — 119
Charles Mingus, liner note to *Jazz Composers Workshop No. 2*,
  Savoy, 1956. — 119
Buddy Collette quoted in Robert Gordon, op cit., pp. 135–6. — 120
Fred Katz interview, The Idelsohn Digital Archive, http://digitalarchive.
  idelsohnsociety.com/videos/fred-katz/ [archived 1 August 2014]. — 120
Lewis MacAdams, *Birth of the Cool: Beat, Bebop, and the American
  Avant-Garde*, The Free Press, p. 192. — 121
Robert Gordon, ibid., pp. 95–6. — 122
Paul Bley interviewed by Bill Smith, 16 August 2008, http://
  vancouverjazz.com/bsmith/2008/08/paul-bley.html [accessed
  19 July 2014]. — 122–3
John Godfrey interview with the author, 1 August 2014. — 123
Pauline Oliveros interviewed by Miya Masaoka, http://www.
  miyamasaoka.com/interdisciplinary/writing/sfbg_pauline_
  oliveros.html [accessed 31 July 2014]. — 123
Pauline Oliveros, interview with the author, 6 January 1995. — 124
Pauline Oliveros interviewed by Cory Arcangel. Bomb 107,
  Spring 2009. — 124
Pauline Oliveros, interview with the author, 12 August 2012. — 124–5
Robert Carl, *Terry Riley's In C*, Oxford University Press, 2009,
  pp. 17–18. — 125
Bruno Nettl, *Nettl's Elephant: On the History of Ethnomusicology*,
  University of Illinois Press, 2010, p. 143. — 125
La Monte Young interviewed by Richard Kostelanetz in 1966,
  published in La Monte Young, Marian Zazeela, *Selected Writings*,
  Heiner Friedrich, 1969, unpaginated. — 126
Pauline Oliveros, op cit. interview with the author, 12 August 2012. — 126–7
Lukas Foss, liner notes to *Studies In Improvisation*, Lukas Foss and the
  Improvisation Chamber Ensemble, RCA Victor, 1961. — 127–8

5 Collective subjectivities 2

Richard Sennett, op cit., p. 101. — 129
David Toop, letter to Derek Bailey, 27 February 2003. — 129–30
Derek Bailey, letter to David Toop, undated, February 2003. — 130
Gary Peters, op cit., pp. 44–6. — 130
Ibid., pp. 42–3. — 131
Steve Beresford, *Musics*, No. 16, February 1978, p. 15. — 133
John Butcher, interview with the author, 17 January 2011. — 134
Fred Frith, Raymond Salvatore Harmon, Daniel Pennie, Drew Daniel,
  Andrea Centazzo, Sylvia Hallett, Mike Cooper, Facebook,
  1–6 August, 2014. — 134–7

6 Into the hot

Yan Jun, *I Was Stupid In the Year of the Snake*, Wire online, March 2014.   139
Gutai translation from Rie Nakajima and Aki Onda, email communication, 9 August 2014 to 12 August 2014.   139
Ming Tiampo, *Gutai; Decentering Modernism*, University of Chicago Press, 2011, p. 30.   139
Ibid., p. 49.   139
Thomas R. H. Havens, *Radicals and Realists in the Japanese Nonverbal Arts*, University of Hawai'i Press, 2006, p. 21.   140
Fujiko Shiraga, *Gutai*, no. 4, 1 July 1956, p. 25, quoted in *Atsuko Tanaka: The Art of Connecting*, Ikon Gallery Birmingham, Espai d'art contemporani de Castello, Museum of Contemporary Art Tokyo, 2011, p. 42.   140
Yasunao Tone, quoted in Thomas R. H. Havens, ibid., p. 137.   141-1
John Lely and James Saunders, *Word Events: Perspectives On Verbal Notation*, Continuum, 2012, p. 234.   141
William A. Marotti, *Sounding the Everyday: The Music Group and Yasunao Tone's Early Work*, published in *Yasunao Tone: Noise Media Language*, Errant Bodies Press: Critical Ear Series, Vol. 4, 2007, p. 28.   141
Yasunao Tone, interview with the author, 2 September 2012.   141-2
Yasunao Tone, *Improvisation as Automatism*, 20thCentury Dance, No. 5, 1960, pp. 15-16.   142
Mieko Shiomi, interview with the author, 10 August 2012.   143
Yasunao Tone, interviewed by Miki Kaneda, *Post: Notes On Modern & Contemporary Art Around the Globe*, Research At Moma, http://post.at.moma.org/content_items/178-the-john-cage-shock-is-a-fiction-interview-with-tone-yasunao-1 [accessed 1 February 2015].   143
Yasunao Tone, interviews with the author, 3 and 4 September 2012.   144-6
Doryun Chung, *Tokyo 1955-1970: A New Avant-Garde*, published in *Tokyo 1955-1970: A New Avant-Garde*, The Museum of Modern Art, New York, 2012, p. 72.   145
Mieko Shiomi, op cit.   147
Michael Parsons, *The Scratch Orchestra and Visual Arts*, Leonardo Music Journal, edited by Nicolas Collins, The MIT Press, Vol. 11, 2001, p. 7.   147
Yasunao Tone, quoted in William A. Marotti, op cit., p. 22.   148
Joe Harriott, quoted in uncredited liner note to *Free Form*, Joe Harriott Quintet, Jazzland, 1960.   148
ICA: Institute of Contemporary Arts, 1946-1968, Institute of Contemporary Arts, London, 2014, p. 189.   148
John Tilbury, email communication with the author, 18 August 2014.   148
Anthony Horovitz, quoted in Alan Robertson, *Joe Harriott: Fire In His Soul*, Northway Publications, 2003, p. 109.   149

Shake Keane, quoted in Alan Robertson, ibid, p. 58. 149–50
Coleridge Goode and Roger Cotterrell, *Blue Lines: A Life In Jazz*,
  Northway Publications, 2002, p. 128. 150
Ibid., p. 154. 150–1
Benny Green, quoted in Alan Robertson, op cit., p. 83. 151
Valerie Wilmer, quoted in Alan Robertson, op cit., p. 75. 151
Ellen Pearlman, *Nothing and Everything: The Influence of Buddhism on
  the American Avant-Garde*, 1942-1962, Evolver Editions, 2012, p. 97. 152
Robert Motherwell, quoted in Mary Ann Caws, *Robert Motherwell: With
  Pen and Brush*, Reaktion Books, 2003, pp. 90–1. 152
Jeff Nuttall, *Bomb Culture*, Paladin, 1970, p. 149. 153
Lawrence James, *The Rise and Fall of the British Empire*, Abacus,
  1994, p. 616. 153
Gustav Metzger, *History History*, Generali Foundation, Vienna/Hatje
  Cantz, 2005, p. 101. 154
John A. Walker, *John Latham: The Incidental Person – His Art and Ideas*,
  Middlesex University Press, 1995, p. 38. 155
Noa Latham, email communication with the author, 16 August 2014. 156
Mark Webber, notes to *John Latham Films: 1960 to 1971*, DVD, Lux, 2010. 156
Barbara Steveni, interview with the author, 14 May 2010. 156
Jonathan Franzen, *Freedom*, Fourth Estate, 2010, p. 445. 157
Alex Ross, *The Rest Is Noise*, Fourth Estate, 2008, p. 63. 158
Coleridge Goode, op cit., p. 160. 159
Kay Larson, *Where the Heart Beats: John Cage, Zen Buddhism, and the
  Inner Life of Artists*, Penguin Books, 2013, p. 175. 159
François Jullien, *The Silent Transformations*, translated by Krzysztof
  Fijalkowski and Michael Richardson, Seagull Books, 2011, pp. 70–1. 160
François Jullien, *The Great Image Has No Form, or On the Nonobject
  through Painting*, op cit., p. 218. 160
Joseph Needham, *Science & Civilisation In China, Volume II: History of
  Scientific Thought*, Cambridge University Press, 1956, p. 304. 160
Frank Kermode, *The Sense of an Ending*, Oxford University Press, 2000,
  p. 121. 161
Joseph Sell, quoted in Hans Prinzhorn, *Artistry of the Mentally Ill*,
  translated by Eric von Brockdorff, Springer-Verlag, 1972, p. 205. 162
Ibid., p. 42. 162
Jean Dubuffet, UbuWeb, http://www.ubu.com/sound/dubuffet.html. 163
Don Ellis interviewed by Richard Williams, *Melody Maker*, 24 October
  1970, p. 26. 166
Phil Minton, interview with the author, op cit. 166
Terry Day, interview with the author, 24 January 2014. 166–7
Anthony Braxton interview in *Forces In Motion: Anthony Braxton and
  the Meta-Reality of Creative Music*, Graham Lock, Quartet Books,
  1988, p. 69. 167
Steve Swallow, liner note to Jimmy Giuffre, *Free Fall*, CD release, 1998. 168

Jim Hall, Jazz Conversations with Jim Hall, Larry Applebaum, Library of Congress, https://www.youtube.com/watch?v=HCOIDcm8BLg [accessed 22 August 2014]. 168
Steve Lacy interviewed by Isabelle Galloni d'Istria, *Futurities*, published in *Steve Lacy: Conversations*, edited by Jason Weiss, Duke University Press, 2006, p. 112. 169
Edith Sitwell, *Collected Poems*, Duckworth Overlook, 2006, p. 39. 169
Jimmy Giuffre, original liner note to *Free Fall*, Columbia Records, 1963. 169
Steve Swallow, op cit. 170

7 Solitary subjectivities

Tom Rice, *Hearing and the Hospital*, Sean Kingston Publishing, 2013, p. 58. 172
J. A. Baker, *The Hill of Summer*, Collins, 1969, p. 52. 173
Jacques Lacan, *Écrits: A selection*, translation by Bruce Fink, W. W. Norton & Company, 1999, pp. 40–1. 173
Steve Lacy, *In Search of the Way* – interview with Jason Weiss, in *Conversations*, op cit., p. 99. 173–4
Peter Brötzmann interview, *Free The Jazz*, KVB, 2014, https://www.youtube.com/watch?v=KHlshNgkmOE [accessed 23 August 2014]. 174
John Butcher, interview with the author, 17 January 2011. 174–5
Lester Young, interviewed by François Positif, 1959, in *You Just Fight For Your Life: Lester Young*, Frank Büchmann-Møller, Praeger, 1990, p. 218. 176
Derek Bailey, interview with the author, February 2003. 176–7
Evan Parker, interview with the author, April 2001. 177–8
Evan Parker, interview with the author, 23 February 2012. 178
Angharad Davies, interview with the author, 20 January 2011. 179
Derek Bailey, *Improvisation: Its Nature and Practice In Music*, op cit., p. 132. 179–80
Annabel Nicolson, *Resonance Magazine*, vol. 8, no. 2/vol. 9, no. 1 (double issue), 2000, p. 17. 180

8 Troubled sea of noises and hoarse disputes

'A troubled sea of noises and hoarse disputes' is originally from John Milton but taken here from Geoffrey Hill's *Scenes From Comus*, Penguin Books, 2005, p. 9. 183
Larry Austin, *Forum: Improvisation, Source: Perspectives of New Music*, Vol. 21, No. 1 & 2, Autumn 1982 – Summer 1983, p. 27. 183
Richard Teitelbaum, interview with the author, 14 September 2014. 184

Larry Austin, *Improvisations for Orchestra and Jazz Soloists*, https://www.youtube.com/watch?v=nQx5Oixx44g [accessed 28 August 2014]. 184

Larry Austin on Source: music of the avant garde, interview by Douglas Kahn, 2007, *Source: Music of the Avant-Garde, 1966-1973*, edited by Larry Austin and Douglas Kahn, University of California Press, 2011, p. 1. 185

John Heinemann, *Personal footnote, Azzione: Gruppo di Improvvisazione Nuova Consonanza 1967-69*, die Schachtel, 2006, p. 67. 185

Frederic Rzewski, interview with the author, 17 January 2014. 186

Franco Evangelisti, *From the Temporary form to the Gruppo di Improvvisazione*, die Schactel, op cit., p. 57. 186

John Heineman, die Schactel, op cit., p. 67. 186

Nuova Consonanza: Komponisten improvisieren im Kollectiv, eine film von Theo Gallehr, Norddeutscher Rundfunk, 1967. 186

Frederic Rzewski, interview with the author, 14 January 2014. 189–90

Rzewski is referring to Stockhausen's *Aus Den Sieben Tagen*, From the Seven Days, a brush with free improvisation devised in 1968 and described by the composer as intuitive music. 190

Frederic Rzewski, in *Notations* by John Cage, Something Else Press, 1969, unpaginated. 190

Nicolas Slonimsky, *Lexicon of Musical Invective*, University of Washington, 1965, p. 214. 191

Victor Turner, *The Anthropology of Performance*, PAJ Publications, 1988, pp. 157–8. 192

Frederic Rzewski, *Spacecraft, The Source*, edited by Larry Austin, Issue no. 3, published in *Source: Music of the Avant-Grade, 1966-1973*, op cit., pp. 130–3. 192

William Gaddis, *The Recognitions*, Atlantic Books, 2003, p. 285. 192

Daniel Belgrad, *The Culture of Spontaneity: Improvisation and the Arts in Postwar America*, University of Chicago Press, 1998, p. 29. 193

Curran, Alvin, *Cage's Influence, Writings Through John Cage's Music, Poetry, + Art*, edited by David W. Bernstein and Christopher Hatch, The University of Chicago Press, 2001, pp. 177–9. 193

Curran, Alvin, *Multiple Reflections On MUSICS 15, MUSICS*, London, UK, Issue no. 16, February 1978, p. 8. 193

Rzewski, Fredric, *Manufacturing Dissent*, interview by Philip Clark, *The Wire*, London, issue 220, June 2002, p. 32. 193

Chadabe, Joel, personal conversation with the author, 21 June 2004. 194

Curran, Alvin, interview with the author, 10–12 July 2004. 194

Alvin Curran, interview with the author, 9 January 2014. 195–6

Alvin Curran, personal letter to the author, 31 July 1979. 196

Steve Lacy, interviewed by David Toop, Paul Burwell, Steve Beresford and Herman Hauge, *Musics*, no. 12, May 1977, London, pp. 4–5. 197

Frederic Rzewski interviewed by Hannah Charlton (from transcript), 13 October 1980. 197–8

David W. Bernstein, notes to Musica Elettronica Viva, *MEV 40*, New World Records, 2008, p. 14. 198

Richard Teitelbaum, interview with the author, op cit.	199
Vernon Joynson, *The Flashback: The Ultimate Psychedelic Music Guide*, Borderline Productions, 1988, p. 144.	200
Mickey Hart quoted in Joe Selvin, *Sly and the Family Stone: An Oral History*, Avon Books, 1998, p. 41.	201
Jaki Liebezeit interviewed by David Stubbs in *Future Days: Krautrock and the Building of Modern Germany*, Faber & Faber, 2014, p. 117.	202
Sabine Breitwieser, *Gustav Metzger: History History*, Generali Foundation, Vienna, 2005, p. 141.	203
Jeff Nuttall, *The Bald Soprano: A Portrait of Lol Coxhill*, Tak Tak Tak, 1989, p. 14.	204
Peter Russell, *Plymouth Sound: Mike Westbrook Jazz Band*, Jazz Monthly, September, 1965, UK, p. 17.	204
Victor Schonfield interviewed by Richard Leigh, *MUSICS*, London, UK, issue no. 5, December 1975/January 1976, p. 4.	204
Victor Schonfield interviewed by David Toop and Hannah Charlton (unpublished), 23 October 1980.	205
Jack Bruce interviewed by Duncan Heining (2007), in Heining, *Trad Dads, Dirty Boppers and Free Fusioneers: British Jazz, 1960-1975*, Sheffield, 2012, p. 209.	205
Henry Lowther interview with the author, 1 October 2014.	206
Paul F. Berliner, *Thinking In Jazz: The Infinite Art of Improvisation*, The University of Chicago Press, 1994, p. 210.	208
Yve-Alain Bois, *Base Materialism*, in Yve-Alain Bois and Rosalind E. Krauss, *Formless: A User's Guide*, Zone Books, 1997, pp. 53, 59.	208
B. S. Johnson, *Albert Angelo*, published in *B. S. Johnson Omnibus*, Picador, 2004, p. 102.	209
Seymour Wright, *The Group Learning of an Original Creative Practice: 1960s Emergent – AMM*, unpublished PhD thesis, 2013, pp. 100–1.	209
Lou Gare, interviewed by David Toop and Hannah Charlton (unpublished), 3 November 1980.	211
Malcolm Le Grice interview, *Malcolm Le Grice: Film and Video Artist*, Luxonline vodcast, www.luxonline.org.uk, 2008.	211
Helen Molesworth, *Before Bed*, published in *Robert Rauschenberg*, edited by Branden W. Joseph, October Files 4, The MIT Press, 2002, p. 83.	213
Evan Parker, interview with the author, 9 February 2011 to 10 February 2011.	213
Is the New Wave just a passing fad?, Bob Dawbarn, *Melody Maker*, 22 January 1966, p. 6.	214
Jazz history from a Danish club, Bob Houston, *Melody Maker*, 1 January 1966, p. 10.	214
Lou Gare, op cit.	214
Seymour Wright, op cit., p. 69.	214–15
Alan Cohen interviewed in *Melody Maker* by Christopher Bird, 9 January 1971, p. 14.	215

John Tilbury, *Cornelius Cardew (1936-1981): A Life Unfinished*, Copula, 2008, p. 283.   215

Blake Stimson and Gregory Sholette, *Collectivism After Modernism: The Art of Social Imagination After 1945*, University of Minnesota Press, 2007, p. xi.   217

A. C. Graham, *Chuang-Tzu: The Inner Chapters*, Hackett Publishing Company Inc., 2001, p. 43.   219

Felix Aprahamian, *The Sunday Times* (The Arts/Television/Music), London, 13 June 1971, p. 30.   219

Lou Gare, op cit.   220–1

Eddie Prévost, interviewed by David Toop and Hannah Charlton (unpublished), 24 October 1980.   221

John Tilbury, op cit., p. 292.   221

Michael Chant, AMM, *International Times*, London, 31 May to 13 June 1968.   222

John Cale interview, https://www.youtube.com/watch?v=ySKrgnVXDNs [accessed 20 January 2015].   223

Lawrence Sheaff, interviewed by Rob Chapman for *Syd Barrett: A Very Irregular Head*, Faber and Faber, 2010, p. 167.   224

Cornelius Cardew, interviewed by David Toop and Hannah Charlton (unpublished), 12 November 1980.   224

Keith Rowe, interviewed by David Toop and Hannah Charlton (unpublished), 19 November 1980.   224

9 Collective objectivities

François Jullien, *Vital Nourishment: Departing from Happiness*, translated by Arthur Goldhammer, Zone Books, 2007, p. 25.   226

Virginia Woolf, *Street Haunting: A London Adventure* (1930), published in *The Death of the Moth*, The Hogarth Press, 1942, pp. 27–8.   226–7

10 Imaginary birds said to live in paradise

James Agee, *Let Us Now Praise Famous Men*, Picador Classics, 1988, pp. 29–30.   229–30

Eric Dolphy interviewed by Michiel de Ruyter, 10 April 1964, transcript at http://adale.org/Discographies/deRuyter.html [accessed 21 January 2015].   231

Eric Dolphy interviewed by Don DeMichael for *Down Beat* (12 April 1962), quoted in *Eric Dolphy: A Musical Biography & Discography*, by Vladimir Simosko and Barry Tepperman, Da Capo Press, 1996, p. 13.   231

James Newton, sleevenotes to Eric Dolphy, *Other Aspects*, Blue Note LP,
original release 1987. 231–2
Eric Dolphy quoted by Robert Levin, sleeve notes to *Eric Dolphy In Europe
Vol 1*, Stateside LP, 1964. 232
Robert Farris Thompson, *Flash of the Spirit*, Vintage Books, 1984, p. 43. 234
Karl Reisman, *Contrapuntal Conversations In An Antiguan Village*,
published in *Explorations In the Ethnography of Speaking*, edited by
Richard Bauman and Joel Sherzer, Cambridge University Press, 1974,
pp. 110–13. 235
Keith Rowe, interviewed for *Amplified Gesture: An Introduction to Free
Improvisation, Practitioners and Their Philosophy*, a film by
Phil Hopkins, UK, 2009. 235
Keith Rowe, *Rainforest Crunch*, The Wire, Issue 216, February
2002, p. 25. 235–6
Keith Rowe, interviewed by Dan Warburton, *The Wire*, Issue 206,
April 2001, p. 37. 236
Steven Naifeh and Gregory White Smith, *Jackson Pollock: An American
Saga*, Barrie and Jenkins, 1989, p. 521. 236
James Agee, op cit., p. 71. 237
George E. Lewis, *Improvised Music after 1950: Afrological and
Eurological Perspectives*, Black Music Research Journal, Vol. 22,
Centre for Black Music Research, Columbia College Chicago and
University of Illinois Press, p. 241. 237
George E. Lewis, *A Power Stronger Than Itself*, op cit., p. 61. 237
Harold Courlander, *Negro Folk Music*, Columbia University Press,
Jazz Book Club edition, 1966, pp. 194–5. 238
James P. Johnson quoted in *Jazz Dance*, Marshall and Jean Stearns,
Schirmer Books, 1979, p. 31. 239
Lawrence W. Levine, *Black Culture and Black Consciousness*, Oxford
University Press, 1977, pp. 37–8. 239
Roscoe Mitchell, interviewed by the author, 30 January 2015. 240–1
Roscoe Mitchell interviewed by Valerie Wilmer, *Melody Maker*, 11 April
1970, p. 8. 241
Samuel Beckett, *Malone Dies*, Penguin Books, 1977, p. 17. 242
John Stevens interviewed by Victor Schonfield, British Library Sound
Archive, recorded by Paul Wilson, 1992. 242
Anne Stevens, interviewed by the author, 9 February 2015. 242
Evan Parker interviewed by the author, op cit. 244
Samuel Beckett, op cit., p. 14. 244
Harold Pinter, speech made at the National Student Drama festival in
Bristol, 1962. 244
Benjamen Piekut, *Indeterminacy, Free Improvisation and the Mixed
Avant-Garde: Experimental Music in London, 1965-1975*, Journal of
the American Musicological Society, Vol. 67, No. 3, Fall 2014, p. 809,
quoting George E. Lewis review of *Northern Sun, Southern Moon* by
Mike Heffley, *Current Musicology* no. 78, Fall, 2004, p. 84. 245

John McDermott with Eddie Kramer, *Hendrix: Setting the Record Straight*, Warner Books, 1992, pp. 65–6. 245–6
Eta Harich-Schneider, *A History of Japanese Music*, Oxford University Press, 1973, p. 171. 246
William P. Malm, *Japanese Music and Musical Instruments*, Charles E. Tuttle Company, 1974, p. 77. 246
John Stevens interviewed by Victor Schonfield, op cit., 1992. 247
Eddie Prévost interviewed by the author, op cit., 1980. 247
Jaap Kunst, *Music In Java*, Martinus Nijhoff, 1949, pp. 299–306. 248
Maggie Nicols, in *Search & Reflect: A Music Workshop Handbook*, Rockschool, 2007. 249
Evan Parker, op cit. 249
Chris Turner, interviewed by the author, 5 April 2015. 250
Barry Guy, interviewed by the author, 24 February 2015. 251
Bob Houston, review of *Karyobin* by the Spontaneous Music Ensemble, *Melody Maker*, 1968. 251
Trevor Watts, interviewed by the author, 9 August 2012. 251–2
Evan Parker, op cit. 253
Martin Esslin, *The Theatre of the Absurd*, Pelican Books, 1968, p. 406. 253
Trevor Watts, op cit. 255
John Stevens, op cit. 255–6
Ian Carr, *Music Outside*, Northway Publications, 2008, p. 52. 257
Evan Parker, op cit. 258–9
Trevor Watts, op cit. 259
Richard Williams, obituaries: Paul Rutherford, *The Guardian*, 10 August 2007, p. 29. 259
Christopher Small, *Musicking*, Wesleyan University Press, 1998, p. 9. 259
Evan Parker, op cit. 260
Michel de Certeau, op cit., p. 163. 260
François Jullien, *Vital Nourishment: Departing From Happiness*, Zone Books, 2007, p. 7. 262
John Stevens response to reader's enquiry about his drum kit, *Any Questions*, *Melody Maker*, p. 42, 6 November 1971. 262
Julian Cowley, *Spontaneous Combustion*, The Wire, Issue 224, October 2002, p. 32. 262–3
Thomas Mann, *Death In Venice*, Vintage Classics, 1998, p. 240. 263
Alan Davie, quoted in *Alan Davie*, edited by Alan Bowness, Lund Humphries, 1967. 264
Alan Davie in *Alan Paints For a Film*, directed by Fabrice Grange, Cinquième Lune Productions, 2009. 264
George Lewis, *A Power Stronger Than Itself*, op cit., p. 66. 265
Alan Davie, Michael Horovitz, Methuen, 1963, unpaginated. 265
Alan Davie, from *I Confess*, exhibition catalogue: *Visione Colore*, Palazzo Grassi, Venice, July to October 1963. 265
Tony Oxley, interviewed by Hannah Charlton, London, 19 August 1981. 266

Derek Bailey, interviewed by the author on five occasions between
   April 1984 and February 2003. 267–86
Gavin Bryars, interviewed by the author, 2005. 268
Derek Bailey, *Improvisation: Its Nature and Practice In Music*, op cit.,
   p. 105. 269
Chuck Israels, quoted in sleevenotes by Conrad Silvert for Bill Evans,
   Spring Leaves, Milestone LP, 1976. 269
Michael Snow interviewed by Athina Rachel Tsangari (17 September
   1999), *The Austin Chronicle*, http://www.austinchronicle.com/
   screens/1999-09-17/73924/ [accessed 13 April 2015]. 271
Ekkehard Jost, *Free Jazz*, Da Capo Press, 1994, p. 85. 271
John Litweiler, *The Freedom Principle: Jazz After 1958*, Da Capo Press,
   1984, p. 137. 272
Milford Graves interviewed by Paul Burwell, *Bäbi Music, Collusion*,
   London, issue 1, summer 1981, p. 33. 272
Milford Graves interviewed by Valerie Wilmer, *As Serious As Your Life*,
   Quartet Books, 1977, p. 167. 273
Milford Graves, *Collusion*, op cit., pp. 32–3. 273
Samuel Beckett, *Malone Dies*, op cit., p. 25. 273
I. M. Lewis, *Ecstatic Religion: An Anthropological Study of Spirit Possession
   and Shamanism*, Penguin Books, 1971, pp. 41–2. 274
Steve Beresford, interview with the author, 2005. 277
Derek Bailey, letter to the author, 5 February 1996. 278–9
Herbie Nichols, quoted in the sleevenotes to Herbie Nichols Trio,
   Complete Studio Master Takes, Lonehill Jazz CD, 2005. 283
Derek Bailey, notes for *Pieces for Guitar*, Tzadik, 2002. 283

11 Postscript: The ballad of John and Yoko

Yoko Ono, *Grapefruit*, Simon & Schuster, 1964, unpaginated. 287
Ornette Coleman, interview with the author, 13 September 1995. 288
Fred Frith, interview with the author, 15 March 2015. 289–90
Evan Parker, interview with the author, 26 March 2015. 290

12 Rain falling down on old Gods

James Agee, op cit., p. 16. 293
Yoko Ono, *Grapefruit*, op cit., unpaginated. 293
Nam June Paik, *Exposition of Music Electronic Television Revisited*,
   Verlag der Buchhandlung Walther König, Köln, 2009, p. 71. 293
Nam June Paik, ibid., pp. 83–4. 294

Ibid., p. 35.	295
Ibid., p. 99.	295–6
Peter Brötzmann, *We Thought We Could Change the World: Brötzmann Conversations with Gérard Rouy*, Wolke Verlag, 2014, p. 24.	296
Lucrazia De Domizio Durini, *The Felt Hat: Joseph Beuys, A Life Told*, Charta, 1977, p. 26.	296

DISCOGRAPHY

I question the point of including a discography in a twenty-first century book, given the fact that many of these recordings are currently available online for either reference listening, purchase or illicit downloading. Online realities can change very quickly, however, so whatever is easily available now through one channel or another may be ring-fenced or have vanished by the time of publication. As for record shops, they could collapse entirely or be flourishing in twelve months' time – I have no idea. Added to that, my decision to split the book into two standalone volumes will make each respective listing somewhat unbalanced and partial if consulted separately. The selection for this volume is quite odd as it reflects an account mostly dedicated to the period before improvised music labels really got started. Whatever, odd is not such a bad thing if it seduces somebody into listening to Coleman Hawkins play 'Picasso'. A lot of people enjoy lists of records and I assume readers are smart enough to sort all of this out for themselves, so – a list rather than a discography, not comprehensive or even particularly rational. As ever, records are listed in a mix of formats and labels reflecting my collection as much as anything else, alphabetical according to first name or name of group.

Alan Kaprow, *How To Make a Happening*, Mass Art Inc., 1966.
Alan Davie/Frank Perry, *Suite for Prepared Piano and Mini Drums*, ADMW Records, 1971.
The Alan Davie Music Workshop, *The Tony Oxley Alan Davie Duo*, ADMW Records, 1974.
Albert Ayler, *Spirits*, Debut, 1964.
Albert Ayler Trio, *Spiritual Unity*, ESP, 1964.
Albert Ayler, *Spirits Rejoice*, ESP, 1965.
Albert Ayler, *Bells*, ESP, 1965.
Albert Ayler, Don Cherry, John Tchicai, Roswell Rudd, Gary Peacock and Sonny Murray, *New York Eye and Ear Control*, ESP-Disk, 1966.
Ami Yoshida, *Tiger Thrush*, Improvised Music from Japan, 2003.
AMM, *AMMMUSIC*, Elektra, 1967.
AMM, *The Crypt – 12 June '68*, Matchless Recordings, 1981.

AMM, *AMMUSIC 1966*, Matchless/ReR, 1989.
AMM & MEV, *Live Electronic Music Improvised*, Mainstream, 1970.
Baby Dodds, *Talking And Drum Solos*, Folkways 1959.
Bill Evans, *The Complete Live at the Village Vanguard 1961*, Riverside, 2003.
The Cecil Taylor Quartet, *Looking Ahead!*, Contemporary Records, 1959.
Charles Ives, *Ives Plays Ives: The Complete Recordings of Charles Ives at the Piano (1933-1943)*, New World Records, 2006.
Charles Mingus/John LaPorta, *Jazzical Moods*, Period Records, 1995.
The Chico Hamilton Quintet, *Spectacular!*, Pacific Jazz Records, 1962.
Christian Marclay, *Records*, alp, 1997.
Coleman Hawkins, *Bouncing With Bean*, Le Chante du Monde, 2005.
Derek Bailey, *Lot 74 Solo Improvisations*, Incus, 1974.
Derek Bailey, *Incus Taps*, Organ of Corti, 1996.
Derek Bailey, *Ballads*, Tzadik, 2002.
Derek Bailey, *Pieces for Guitar*, Tzadik, 2002.
Derek Bailey, *Carpal Tunnel*, Tzadik, 2005.
Derek Bailey and Han Bennink, *Selections from Live Performances at Verity's Place*, Incus, 1972.
DJ Sniff, *ep*, psi records, 2010.
Duke Ellington, *The Blanton-Webster Band*, Bluebird RCA, 1986.
Edgard Varèse, *Density 21.5, Ecuatorial*, from *The Complete Works*, Decca, 1998.
Ennio Morricone, *A Quiet Place In the Country*, The Omni Recording Corporation, 2014.
Eric Dolphy, *Last Date*, Fontana, 1964.
Eric Dolphy, *Other Aspects*, Blue Note, 1987.
Eric Dolphy, *Conversations*, Jazz World, 1998.
Errol Garner, *Overture To Dawn (The Apartment Sessions, vol. 1)*, Charly, 1995.
Evan Parker, *Saxophone Solos*, Incus, 1976.
Evan Parker, *Monoceros*, Incus, 1978.
Evan Parker and Keith Rowe, *Dark Rags*, Potlatch, 2000.
Gagaku: The Imperial Court Music of Japan, Lyrichord, 1964.
The George Russell Sextet, *Ezz-thetics*, Riverside, 1961.
Group Ongaku, Hear Sound Art Library, 1996.
Gruppo di Improvisazione Nuova Consonanza, *Azioni 1967-69*, die Schachtel, 2006.
Gruppo Nuova Consonanza, *Improvisationen*, Deutsche Grammophon, 1969.
Gurdjieff, *Improvisations*, Basta, 2004.
Han Bennink, *Solo*, ICP, 1972.
Hapshash and the Coloured Coat, *Featuring the Human Host and the Heavy Metal Kids*, Drop Out, 1967/1988.
Henry Cowell, *The Banshee*, from *Piano Music*, Folkways, 1963.
Herbie Nichols Trio, *Complete Studio Master Takes*, Lonehill Jazz, 2005.
Jazz Composers Workshop/Charles Mingus, Nippon Columbia, 1992.
Jimmy Giuffre, *Free Fall*, Columbia/Legacy, 1998.
The Jimmy Giuffre 3 & 4, *New York Concerts*, Elemental Music, 2014.
The Joe Harriott Quintet, *Abstract*, Redial, 1998.

The Joe Harriott Quintet, *Free Form*, Gottdiscs, 2007.
The Joe Harriott Quintet, *High Spirits/Movement*, Vocalion, 2012.
John Butcher, *Invisible Ear*, Weight of Wax, 2003.
John Lennon/Yoko Ono, *Unfinished Music No. 2 – Life With the Lions*, Vack, undated reissue.
Joseph Holbrooke, *Joseph Holbrooke'65*, Incus, 1999.
Lee Konitz, *The Lee Konitz Duets*, Milestone, 1967.
Lennie Tristano, *Abstraction & Improvisation*, FiveFour/Cherry Red Records, 2007.
Lucas Foss, *Studies In Improvisation*, RCA Victor, 1961.
MEV, *United Patchwork*, Horo Records, 1978.
Milford Graves Percussion Ensemble With Sunny Morgan, ESP-Disk, 1965.
Musica Elettronica Viva, *The Sound Pool*, BYG Records, 1970.
Musica Elettronica Viva, *MEV 40*, New World Records, 2008.
Nam June Paik, *Works 1958-1979*, Sub Rosa, 2001.
The New Departures Quartet, Hothouse Records, undated reissue.
The New York Art Quartet, *Mohawk*, Fontana, 1965.
New York Art Quartet and Imamu Amiri Baraka, ESP-Disk, 1964.
Nigel Coombes and Steve Beresford, *White String's Attached: Improvised Violin and Piano Duets*, Bead, 1980 (reissued on Emanem CD, 2014).
Olivier Messiaen, *Oraison*, on *OHM: The Early Gurus of Electronic Music*, Ellipsis Arts, 2000.
Ornette Coleman, *Beauty Is a Rare Thing: The Complete Atlantic Recordings*, Rhino/Atlantic, 1993.
Percy Grainger, *Free Music No. 1* and *Beatless Music, Spellbound: Original Music for Theremin*, Mode, 2008.
Peter Brötzmann, *Solo*, FMP, 1976.
The Roscoe Mitchell Sextet, *Sound*, Delmark, 1966.
Sainkho M., *Out of Tuva*, Crammed Discs, 1993.
Sachiko M., *Sine Wave Solo*, Amoebic, 1999.
Sauter Finegan Orchestra, *New Directions In Music*, Bluebird/BMG, 1989.
Severino Gazzelloni, *20th century Music for Flute*, CBS Classics, 1970.
Shelley Manne, '*The Three*' and '*The Two*', Contemporary, undated reissue.
Shelley Hirsch/David Weinstein, *Haiku Lingo*, Review Records, 1989.
Shelley Manne, *2-3-4*, Impulse/GRP, 1994.
Spontaneous Music Ensemble, *Karyobin*, Island Records, 1968.
Spontaneous Music Ensemble, *Withdrawal (1966-7)*, Emanem, 1997.
Spontaneous Music Ensemble, John Stevens and Evan Parker, *Summer 1967*, Emanem, 1999.
Steve Lacy, *Solo (1972)*, Emanem, 1974.
Stuff Smith and Robert Crum, *The Complete 1944 Rozenkrantz Apartment Transcriptions*, AB Fable, 2002.
Teddy Charles, *New Directions*, Prestige, 1999.
Terry Day, *Interruptions*, Emanem, 2006.
Trevor Watts, John Stevens, Ian Carr and Jeff Clyne, *Springboard*, Polydor, 1966.
Various artists, *Not Necessarily 'English Music'*, Leonardo Music Journal CD Series Volume 11, 2001.

INDEX

AACM   27, 217, 237–8, 240, 265
Abramović, Marina   59
Abrams, Muhal Richard   238
Aebi, Irene   297
Agee, James   229, 237, 293
Alberts, The   254
Ali, Rashied   246
Allum, Jennifer   70–1, 74, 80, 227
Alterations   131
Amalgam   296
AMM   5, 155, 184–5, 189–91, 196, 205–13, 215–16, 218–24, 247, 249, 296
Anderson, Cat   239
Antonioni, Michelangelo   188, 199, 261
Aragon, Louis   143
Armstrong, Louis   62, 84, 89
Artaud, Antonin   53, 56–7
Ascott, Roy   154, 200
Atwell, Winifred   267
Austen, Jane   37, 39
Austin, Larry   183–5, 195
Ayler, Albert   30, 34, 62, 64, 66, 151, 214, 231, 238, 242–3, 247–8, 264, 270, 272
Ayler, Donald   62, 89

Bailey, Derek   5, 12, 14–15, 22, 24, 29, 106, 109–10, 129–30, 157, 167, 176–7, 179–81, 206, 237, 242, 248–9, 257–9, 263–4, 266, 273–86, 290–1
Baker, Ginger   150, 202, 273
Baker, J. A.   173
Ball, Hugo   49

Baraka, Imamu Amiri   243, 271
Barbara, Joan La   44
Barrett, Syd   222–3
Barron, Bebe and Louis   261
Bartolozzi, Bruno   52
Bashō, Matsuo   83
Basie, Count   63, 279
Bataille, Georges   45, 208
Battistelli, Giorgio   114
Bauer, Billy   101–3
Beatles, The   200, 245, 253–4, 285, 287
Bechet, Sidney   46, 62, 87, 90, 173
Beck, Jeff   154, 200
Beck, Julian   121
Beckett, Samuel   130, 242, 244, 253, 273, 276
Beisen, Kubota   82
Benge, Alfreda   261
Bennink, Han   5, 12, 24, 62, 177, 231–2, 282, 296
Benny, Jack   45
Berberian, Cathy   20
Berendt, Ernst-Joachim   297
Beresford, Steve   15, 43, 71, 80, 97–8, 131–3, 196, 227, 277
Berg, Alban   233
Berger, Karl   197, 238
Bergman, Ingmar   208
Berio, Luciano   18, 29, 194
Berlin, Isaiah   81
Bernstein, Leonard   127, 184, 223, 232
Bertoncini, Mario   186
Best, Denzil   101
Beuys, Joseph   201, 293, 295–6

Blackwell, Ed   64, 89, 288
Blakey, Art   214, 266
Bland, Bobby 'Blue'   64
Bley, Carla   167
Bley, Paul   122, 167–8, 230, 256, 272
Bohman, Adam   177
Bois, Yves-Alain   208
Bond, Graham   205, 257
Bostic, Earl   64
Boulez, Pierre   100, 126, 249
Bowie, Lester   239
Branchi, Walter   185
Brandt, Bill   208
Braxton, Anthony   167, 177, 264, 281, 296
Brecht, George   143
Breton, André   33–5, 40, 46, 143
Breuker, Willem   217, 288–9, 296
Brookman, Karen   279, 282
Brown, Marion   199
Brötzmann, Peter   5, 174, 177, 201, 260, 295–7
Brown, Earle   126
Brown, James   64, 200
Brown, Pete   205
Brownlee, Archie   65
Brox, Victor   261
Brubeck, Dave   99, 151
Bruce, Jack   202, 206
Bryars, Gavin   109, 267–70, 273, 279, 283–4
Burke, Ernest   156
Burlison, Paul   212, 291
Burn, Chris   174
Burroughs, William   148–9, 200
Burwell, Paul   132–3, 177, 180, 196, 250, 272–3
Butcher, John   134, 171–4, 176–7
Byas, Don   92, 109, 185
Byrds, The   121, 200

Cage, John   19, 58–61, 126, 133, 140–1, 148, 155–9, 164, 166, 186, 190, 195, 200, 204, 216, 221, 223, 268–9, 284, 287, 289

Cale, John   189, 223
Can   201–2
Cardew, Cornelius   30, 147–8, 157, 185, 187, 191, 199, 205, 207, 213, 215–16, 218, 221–4, 268, 289
Carr, Ian   246, 256
Carroll, Baikida E. J.   199
Cassavetes, John   117
Centazzo, Andrea   132, 136–7
Certeau, Michel de   38, 260
Césaire, Aimé   33–4
Chadabe, Joel   194
Chadbourne, Eugene   135, 277, 298
Chant, Michael   222
Charbin, Marjolaine   70, 72, 78, 227
Charles, Dennis   258, 270
Charles, Teddy   52, 116
Charlton, Hannah   197, 266
Cheeks, Julius   64, 66
Cherry, Don   63, 89, 231, 242, 270–1, 297
Chicago   200
Christian, Charlie   212, 279–80
Chuang-Tzu   218–19
Clarke, Harry   9
Clementi, Aldo   185, 187
Clyne, Jeff   208, 246, 257
Cohen, Alan   148, 205, 215
Cole, Nat King   281
Coleman, Ornette   30, 34–5, 63–4, 89, 108, 115, 150–1, 167–8, 199, 204–5, 207, 211, 232, 272, 287–8
Collette, Buddy   118, 120
Collier, James Lincoln   63, 84
Coltrane, John   30, 34, 64, 87, 178, 199, 214, 232, 255, 259–60, 268–70
Company   106, 109, 167, 297
Conrad, Joseph   12
Conrad, Tony   189, 223
Coolidge, Clark   194
Coombes, Nigel   97, 263
Cooper, Mike   132, 137
Courlander, Harold   238

Cousins, Lorraine   230
Cowell, Henry   54, 61, 216
Coxhill, Lol   137, 177, 204, 264, 290, 297
Crazy World of Arthur Brown, The   205
Cream   202–3, 205–6, 209
Creation, The   202
Critchley, Simon   19
Crum, Robert   94–8
Curran, Alvin   60–1, 112, 114, 185, 191, 193–6, 199, 213
Curson, Ted   230
Cusack, Peter   131, 177

Daniel, Drew   136
Davie, Alan   30, 208, 264–6, 274
Davies, Angharad   177–9, 225, 227
Davies, Hugh   177
Davies, John R. T.   156
Davies, Rhodri   177–8
Davies, Matt   178
Davis, Eddie 'Lockjaw'   63–4
Davis, Miles   22, 87, 103, 106, 118, 128, 189, 199, 201, 208, 230, 233, 268
Davis, Richard   232–3, 235
Day, Terry   131, 133, 166
Dean, Mal   12, 23
Dean, Roger   30
Deardoff, Ken   152
Debord, Guy   164
Debussy, Claude   14, 47, 52, 90, 92–3
DeJohnette, Jack   238
de Kooning, Willem   176, 216
Deren, Maya   125
Derrida, Jacques   21, 35, 37
Desmond, Paul   99, 109, 258
Desnos, Robert   46, 58
Diddley, Bo   200, 202, 212
Dixon, Bill   270–1
DJ Olive   40
DJ Sniff (Takuro Mizuta Lippit)   6
Dodds, Baby   61–2
Doesberg, Theo and Nelly   50

Dolphy, Eric   116, 119, 165, 172, 188, 230–3, 235, 242, 255, 259, 264, 269, 280
Donegan, Lonnie   253
Downes, Bob   255
Du Bois, W. E. B.   81
Dubuffet, Jean   161–5, 208
Duchamp, Marcel   96, 107
Durrant, Phil   175
Dury, Ian   64, 166
Dyani, Johnny   245, 257, 288, 297

Eldridge, Roy   89–90
Ellington, Duke   44, 92, 107–8, 145, 162, 208, 211, 239, 241, 259, 266
Ellis, Don   122, 165–6, 184, 232
Endahl, Matt   93, 95
Eps, George Van   279
Ernst, Max   46, 84
Esslin, Martin   253
Europe, James Reese   48–9
Evangelisti, Franco   30, 185–7, 189, 209
Evans, Bill   158, 233, 256, 266, 268–9, 283
Evans, Gil   103, 116, 118, 208
Extended Organ   2

Faithfull, Marianne   207
Falkenstein, Claire   124–5
Faulkner, William   11, 34
Favre, Pierre   296
Feisst, Sabine   60
Feldman, Morton   116, 148
Feminist Improvising Group   297
Feza, Mongezi   89, 245, 288
Fielder, Alvin   238–9
Fishkin, Arnold   101–3
Five Blind Boys   65
Foregger, Nikolai   47
Foss, Lukas   127
Franzen, Jonathan   157
Freeman, Jo (Joreen)   23–5
Freud, Sigmund   34–5, 101–2
Frith, Fred   135–6, 277, 289–90

Fugs, The   200
Funkadelic   200

Gaddis, William   192
Gal, Sharon   43–4
Gare, Lou   207–8, 210–11, 213–16, 218, 220–2, 224
Garner, Errol   91–3, 96, 98
Garrick, Michael   159
Gazzeloni, Severino   188
Gelmetti, Vittorio   199
Giles, Mike   136
Giuffre, Jimmy   115–16, 167–70, 172–3
Globe Unity Orchestra   201
Godfrey, John   123
Gong   200
Goode, Coleridge   86, 150, 155, 158–9
Goode, Gertrude   155–6
Goodman, Felicitas D.   57–8
Gordon, Robert   115, 122
Götz, Carl Otto   293–4
Graettinger, Bob   116
Graham, A. C.   218–19
Grainger, Percy   30, 54–5, 61, 65, 76, 90
Grateful Dead, The   200
Graves, Milford   30, 62, 150, 243, 270, 272, 281
Gray, John   46
Green, Freddie   279
Green, Hughie   277
Greene, Gene   48
Greer, Sonny   241
Griffin, Johnny   64, 266
Grimes, Henry   66, 258
Group Ongaku   143–7, 165
Group Sounds Three   206
Gruppo di Improvvisazione Nuova Consonanza   185, 187–91, 196, 209
Gurdjieff, George   110–12, 114
Guy, Barry   242, 251, 253, 257
Gysin, Brion   148

Haden, Charlie   64, 288
Hadi, Shafi   117
Haines, Paul   26
Hall, Jim   120, 168, 233, 236
Hallam, Elizabeth   28
Hallett, Sylvia   137
Hamilton, Chico   116, 119–22, 268
Hancock, Herbie   269
Hapshash and the Coloured Coat   200
Hardy, Russell   166
Hare, Pat   212
Harich-Schneider, Eta   246
Harland, Philip   125
Harmon, Ray Salvatore   135
Harrington, Curtis   125
Harriott, Joe   86, 145, 148, 150–1, 153, 156–9, 165, 205, 208, 270, 287
Hart, Charlie   133
Hart, Clyde   90
Hartmann, Thomas de   110–11
Hauge, Herman   196
Hawkins, Coleman   89, 109, 172, 214
Heffley, Mike   30
Heineman, John   185–7
Hendrix, Jimi   22, 149, 154, 199, 209, 245–6
Hennings, Mary   49
Henry Cow   289, 297
Herman, Ron   263
Hiseman, Jon   205–6
Hijikata, Tatsumi   50
Hirsch, Shelley   39–40, 226–7
Hirst, Linda   20
Hobbs, Christopher   213
Hobsbawm, Eric   20, 209
Hoch, Hannah   49, 90
Hodeir, André   122
Holbrooke, Joseph (composer)   267
Holiday, Billie   176, 276
Holland, Dave   22, 242, 246, 257, 262–3, 297
Holman, Terry   166

Hooke, Robert   172
Hopkins, John 'Hoppy'   205
Hove, Fred Van   5, 96, 297
Horovitz, Michael   148–9, 264–5
Huelsenbeck, Richard   49
Human Arts Ensemble   199
Hunter, Tommy 'Bugs'   94

Ichiyanagi, Toshi   145, 199, 287
Improvisation Chamber
    Ensemble   127
Ingold, Tim   28
Ishii, Maki   199
Isou, Jean-Isidore   125
Israels, Chuck   269, 283
Ito, Teiji   125
Ives, Charles   30, 46, 85–6, 90
Izenson, David   207, 288

Jackson, Willis 'Gator Tail'   64
James, MR   45
James, William   39, 303
Janco, Marcel   47
Jankélévitch, Vladimir   14
Janov, Arthur   291
Jarman, Joseph   265, 281
Jazz Composers Workshop   52, 116,
    122, 168
Jeck, Philip   8
Jenkins, Leroy   97
Jeter, Claude   65–6
Jo, Damita   280
Johns, Jasper   221
Johnson, Blind Willie   62
Johnson, B. S.   209, 244
Johnson, James P.   238–9
Johnson, Vernard   62
Jones, Elvin   106, 270
Jones, Spike   115–16
Jordan, Louis   11, 22
Jorn, Asger   162–5
Joseph Holbrooke (group)   109,
    267–70, 279, 283
Joyce, James   34, 39, 82, 84, 155,
    171, 264

Joyce, Lucia   51
Jullien, François   83, 160, 226, 262

Kaiser, Henry   277, 298
Kandinsky, Wassily   17, 110
Kanngiesser, Ute   71, 227
Kaprow, Alan   27–8, 39
Katz, Fred   120
Kay, Connie   233
Kayn, Roland   187
Keane, Shake   149–50, 153, 156, 158
Kemp, Lindsey   262
Kennedy, John F.   153, 198
Kenton, Stan   266
Kermode, Frank   161
Kerouac, Jack   30
Kessell, Barney   212
Kim, Jin Hi   15
King, Martin Luther   81, 153,
    198, 241
Kirk, Roland   203, 276
Klee, Paul   151, 212
Kline, Franz   144, 152
Knight, Peter   247
Ko, Ishikawa   15
Kofsky, Frank   90
Konitz, Lee   101–3, 106–10, 172,
    268, 281
Korner, Alexis   207, 261
Kosugi, Takehisa   141–3, 146,
    191, 195
Kowald, Peter   141, 246, 262, 296
Kraftwerk   201
Kramer, Eddie   22, 245–6, 248, 290
Kunst, Jaap   248

Lacan, Jacques   173
Lacy, Steve   141, 169, 173, 195–7,
    230, 233, 258, 281
Lacey, Bruce   253
LaFaro, Scott   233, 268–9
Lambert, Ross   69, 71
Lapelyte, Lina   225
Larkin, Philip   199
Latham, John   11, 148, 155, 208, 287

Latham, Noa   156–7
Lateef, Yusef   230
Léandre, Joëlle   114
Lear, Edward   124
Led Zeppelin   245
Lee, Jeanne   242
Lee, Okkyung   10–11
Le Grice, Malcolm   211
Leiris, Michel   45
Lemer, Peter   246, 256–7, 288
Lennon, John   254, 287–91
Leone, Sergio   187–8
Lester, Richard   253–4
Lévi-Strauss, Claude   33, 46
Lewis, George   27, 237–8, 245, 298
Lewis, I. M.   274
Lichtenstein, Roy   212
Liebezeit, Jaki   202
Liebling, A. J.   89
Ligeti, György   189
Lincoln, Abbey   233
Linson, Adam   70, 72, 74, 76–9
Lipere, Thebe   15, 237
Little, Booker   233
Living Theatre   121, 186
Logan, Giuseppi   64, 214, 272
Louis, Joe   280
Love   121, 200
Lowther, Henry   205–6, 211, 214
Lubin, Numar   87
Lytton, Paul   177, 201, 217
Lovens, Paul   201, 217, 296
Lyons, Jimmy   258
Lyttleton, Humphrey   243, 245

M, Sachiko   7–8, 177, 298
Macchi, Egisto   188
Macero, Teo   52, 118, 168
Maciunas, George   223
Mac Low, Jackson   121
Macmillan, Harold   153
Malevich, Kasimir   217
Malina, Dorothy   121
Malm, William P.   246
Mangelsdorf, Albert   238

Mann, Thomas   263
Manne, Shelley   115, 122, 167
Marclay, Christian   10–11, 13
Mariano, Charlie   266
Marinetti, F. T.   46, 55
Marsh, Warne   101–2, 104–5
Martenot, Maurice   53
Marx, Karl   161
Marx, Chico   94–5
Marx, Groucho   117
Marx, Harpo   95
Masaoka, Miya   15, 123
Masson, André   34, 46–7
Matmos   136
Matsudaira, Yoritsune   140
Mayazumi, Toshirō   260
Mayer, John   159
MC5   199
McCarthy, Paul   2–3
McCartney, Paul   207
McGregor, Chris   245, 288
McLaughlin, John   288–9
McNeely, Big Jay   62, 64
Mehring, Walter   47–8
Mengelberg, Misha   96, 231–2, 296
Merrill, Buddy   236
Merton, Thomas   217
Mesmer, Franz Anton   112
Messiaen, Olivier   54, 56
Metzger, Gustav   153–5, 200, 203
MEV (Musica Elettronica Viva)
   60–1, 184, 190–1, 193,
   195–200, 210, 213
Michaux, Henri   87–9, 162
Miles, Barry   209, 221
Miley, Bubber   67, 239
Miller, Mark   136
Milligan, Spike   156, 253–4
Mingus, Charles   22, 52, 116–19,
   122, 166, 168, 208, 230, 233
Minton, Phil   39, 43–5, 166
Mitchell, Roscoe   177, 199,
   238–41, 264
Mitchener, Elaine   43–4
Mizoguchi, Kenji   260

Moholo-Moholo, Louis   80, 237, 245, 288
Mondrian, Piet   217
Monk, Thelonious   90, 92, 145, 165, 173, 204, 258
Monkees, The   200
Monkhouse, Bob   273
Montaigne, Michel de   25–6
Moog, Robert   184
Moore, Judy   101
Moore, Oscar   279, 281
Moore, Raymond   208
Morgan, Laurie   208
Morricone, Ennio   185–8
Morris, Lawrence D 'Butch'   179
Morrison, Van   233, 253
Morgan, Sunny   62, 272
Mothers of Invention, The   11, 121, 200
Motherwell, Robert   152
Mulligan, Gerry   99, 103, 118
Murakami, Saburō   139–40
Murayama, Tomoyoshi   50
Murray, Sunny   30, 66, 241, 243, 248, 258, 270
Musafar, Fakir   288
Music Improvisation Company   184, 296

Nabakov, Vladimir   12
Nakamura, Toshimaru   298
Namchylak, Sainkho   15–16
Nance, Ray   107–8
Nanton, Joe 'Tricky Sam'   44, 67
Nao, Deguchi   36
Needham, Joseph   160
New Departures Quartet   208
New Music Ensemble   184
New Phonic Art   18
New York Art Quartet, The   270–2
Newton, James   231
Nichols, Herbie   283
Nicols, Maggie   39, 131, 249, 257–8
Nicolson, Annabel   180
Niebergall, Buschi   5

Nilsen, Fredrik   2
Nuttall, Jeff   153, 204, 211

Oddie, Bill   278
Ohno, Kazuo   50
Oliver, King   63
Oliveros, Pauline   30, 123–8
Olsen, Charles   193
Ono, Yoko   143, 287–91, 293
Organisation   201
Orr, Bobby   157–8
Owen, Gavin   260
Owen, Robert   31
Oxley, Tony   109, 264–8, 270, 273, 276, 279, 284

Page, Robin   154, 223
Paik, Nam Jun   223, 287, 293–6
Panassié, Hughes   86
Parker, Charlie   22, 109, 149, 259
Parker, Evan   22, 26, 87, 137, 177, 201, 213, 242–4, 246, 249, 251, 253, 257–63, 276, 296–7
Parsons, Michael   147–8
Paulekas, Vito   121
Payne, Davey   133
Peacock, Gary   243, 248, 270–1
People Band, The   133, 166, 296
Perry, Frank   265
Peters, Gary   37, 130–1
Petrassi, Goffredo   187
Phillips, Barre   109–10, 262, 288–90
Picasso, Pablo   151, 216
Piekut, Benjamin   245
Pennie, Daniel   136
Pilcher, Barry Edgar   133
Pink Floyd   5, 156, 196, 199, 200, 203, 222–3, 261
Pinkney, St. Clair   64
Pinter, Harold   244, 253
Plaut, Fred   168
Plantamura, Carol   195, 198
Poe, Edgar Allan   8–9, 100, 104–5, 267
Pollock, Jackson   139, 144, 148, 152, 166, 211, 236

Potts, Joe   2
Presley, Elvis   99
Prévost, Eddie   5, 207, 210, 221, 224, 227, 247
Prinzhorn, Hans   161
Pritchard, Jean   257
Proust, Marcel   39
Pukwana, Dudu   245
Pyne, Joanna   137

Quicksilver Messenger Service   200

Ra, Sun   34, 62, 94, 183, 199, 204, 217, 276
Rauschenberg, Robert   155, 212–13, 216
Ray, Satyajit   208
Recchion, Tom   2
Red Crayola   200
Reich, Wilhelm   101–2
Reinhardt, Ad   155
Reinhardt, Django   85–6, 90
Reisman, Karl   234–5
Retallack, Joan   58–9, 61
Richard, Little   62
Richardson, Dorothy Miller   41, 213
Riley, Howard   98
Riley, Terry   124–6, 128, 199
Rivière, Peter   23
Roach, Max   282
Rogers, Shorty   115
Rolling Stones, The   200, 245, 285
Rollins, Sonny   172, 214
Rosemont, Franklin   35
Rosenkrantz, Timme   92–4, 97
Roussel, Raymond   58
Rouy, Gérard   296
Rowe, Keith   5, 26, 204, 207, 209–12, 214–16, 221–4, 235–7
Rudd, Roswell   243, 258, 270, 272
Rush, Loren   124–5
Russell, George   106, 116, 165, 167, 270
Russell, John   175
Russell, Ken   253
Russolo, Luigi   50

Rutherford, Paul   177, 180, 242, 247, 255–7, 259, 264
Rzewski, Frederick   30, 183–6, 189, 190–3, 195, 199

Sanders, Pharoah   64, 214
Santana   200
Sauter-Finegan Orchestra   116
Scelsi, Giacinto   112–14
Schaeffer, Pierre   99–100, 105, 145
Schlippenbach, Alexander von   96, 98, 201
Schneider, Florian   201
Schoenberg, Arnold   17, 47, 99, 143, 232, 249, 269
Schols, Jacques   231–2
Schonfield, Victor   21, 204–5, 208–9, 220, 244, 247, 249–50, 273
Schoof, Manfred   201
Schuller, Gunter   110, 184, 232
Schweizer, Irène   98, 201, 296–7
Schwitters, Kurt   47, 51
Scratch Orchestra   147, 199, 222
Seaman, Phil   150, 157, 205, 256
Seeds, The   200
Sell, Joseph   161–2
Sellers, Peter   253–4
Sennett, Richard   25, 31, 129
Shankar, Ravi   231
Sharrock, Sonny   272
Sheaff, Lawrence   207, 211, 213, 221, 224
Shepp, Archie   242, 270
Shiomi, Mieko   141–3, 146–8
Shiraga, Fujiko   140
Shiraga, Kazuo   139–40
Shorter, Wayne   87, 214
Shûko, Mizuno   141–3
Sissle, Noble   49
Sitwell, Edith   169
Slonimsky, Nicolas   191
Sly and the Family Stone   201
Small, Christopher   250, 259
Smith, Daniel B.   37
Smith, LaDonna   217, 298
Smith, Roger   177, 263

Smith, Stuff   92–8
Smythe, Pat   150, 158
Snow, Michael   271
Soft Machine   209, 261
Soupault, Philippe   46
Spare, Austin Osman   36
Spontaneous Music Ensemble
   (SME)   21, 205, 243, 246,
   249–51, 257, 261–4, 287,
   290, 296
Stalling, Carl   96
Steveni, Barbara   156
Stevens, John   14, 21, 27, 157, 205,
   242–52, 273, 284, 287–90, 297
Stewart, Rex   44, 67, 89, 239
Stockhausen, Karlheinz   30, 126,
   142, 189–90, 200, 221, 311
Strickland, Napolean   62
Strickland, Peter   188
Sugimoto, Taku   298
Supremes, The   280
Surman, John   211, 214–15
Sutherland, Roger   30
Suzuki, Akio   141
Swallow, Steve   165, 167–8, 170
Swan Silvertones   64–5
Szabo, Gabor   119, 268, 270
Szwed, John F.   94, 205

Taj Mahal Travellers   141, 296
Takamizawa, Michinao   50, 90
Takayanagi, Masayuki   296
Takemitsu, Toru   52, 140, 142, 145
Tanaka, Atsuko   140
Tanaka, Min   281
Tati, Jacques   132, 203
Tatum, Art   84–5, 92–3, 103, 166
Taylor, Cecil   30, 34, 62, 98, 108,
   145, 173, 242, 258, 272, 281
Taylor, Mike   205, 257
Tchicai, John   242–3, 249, 270, 272,
   287–91
Teitelbaum, Richard   109, 184, 187,
   195–6, 199
Temptations, The   200
Theremin, Leon   53

Thompson, Lucky   92, 118
Thompson, Robert Farris   234
Thornton, Clifford   199
Tiampo, Ming   139
Tilbury, John   148, 205, 215, 221
Tippett, Keith   98
Tippetts, Julie   263
Tobey, Mark   61, 152
Tone, Yasunao   140–6
Tornadoes, The   113
Tosatti, Vieri   113
Townshend, Pete   154, 200
Tracey, Stan   208
Tristano, Lennie   99–106, 108, 116,
   165, 208, 268
Tudor, David   116, 141, 183, 186,
   195, 204, 221
Turner, Chris   250
Turner, Othar   62
Turner, Victor   191–2
Twombly, Cy   162

Uitti, Frances-Marie   114
Ulanov, Barry   85, 90, 96, 101–3

Vandor, Ivan   185, 187–8, 195–6
Varèse, Edgard   52–4, 61, 191,
   232, 266
Velvet Underground   128, 200,
   223, 287
Vian, Alain   163
Vian, Boris   93, 163
Vila-Matas, Enrique   69
Viltard, Guillaume   227

Waldron, Mal   118, 230, 233
Wall, Max   45
Waller, Fats   39, 91, 145, 259
Wang Mo   82–3
Wastell, Mark   178
Watts, Trevor   242, 246–7, 249,
   251–2, 255–9, 262–4, 284,
   288–91, 297
Watson, Ben   109, 269
Webern, Anton   128, 157–8, 244,
   248–9, 268–9, 283

Weiss, Alan S.   57
Wellins, Bobby   208
West, Speedy   236
Westbrook, Mike   204, 211–12, 214, 216
Wheeler, Kenny   22, 242, 257, 263, 278
Whistler and his Jug Band   253
Whitehead, Peter   223
Who, The   154, 202–3
Williams, Cootie   67
Williams, Davey   217
Williams, Drid   231
Williams, Mary Lou   92
Williams, Richard   5, 166, 259
Williams, Tony   281
Wilmer, Valerie   66, 157, 241, 273, 287
Winnicott, D. W.   91
Winston, Geoff   71, 78
Winstone, Norma   297
Wols   208
Wolfe, Christian   148
Wolpe, Stefan   116
Wood, Colin   263
Wood, Leona   125

Woolf, Virginia   34, 39, 226–7
Wray, Link   212
Wright, Frank   64, 214
Wright, Seymour   177, 209, 214
Wyatt, Robert   261

X, Malcolm   198
Xiao-Fen, Min   15

Yagi, Michiyo   15
Yancey, Jimmy   84, 215
Yan Jun   139
Yardbirds, The   200
Yates, Marie   155
Yoshida, Ami   38–9
Yoshihide, Otomo   298
Young, La Monte   126, 128, 189, 221, 223, 287
Young, Lester   106, 176

Zazeela, Marian   189
Zhang Zao   83
Zappa, Frank   11, 289
Zorn, John   13, 177, 276, 279, 283, 298